Leisure Education Program Planning:
A Systematic Approach

Second Edition

Leisure Education Program Planning:
A Systematic Approach

Second Edition

John Dattilo, Ph.D.
University of Georgia

Venture Publishing, Inc.
State College, PA

Production Manager: Richard Yocum
Manuscript Editing: Richard Yocum, Michele L. Barbin, and Diane K. Bierly
Cover Design and Illustration: ©1999 Sandra Sikorski, Sikorski Design

Bal du Moulin de la Galette, Montmartre
Renoir Auguste (1841-1919)
Orsay
©Photo RMN - J. G. Berizzi

Printing and Binding: Jostens Printing and Publishing

Library of Congress Catalogue Card Number 99-62854
ISBN 1-892132-05-2

For

Anne, David, and Steven

"Life is wonderful."

Table of Contents

Acknowledgements

I wish to thank my dear friend and colleague, William Murphy, who co-authored the first edition of this book with me. Throughout my academic career he has provided me with more support than I could have ever imagined. Appreciation is extended to the many students and colleagues across the country who have contributed to drafts of this book. I wish to thank Linda Caldwell and Gail Hoge for their valuable input associated with revising a leisure education course syllabus, which subsequently resulted in positive changes to the book targeted for this course. Appreciation is also extended to Ellen Broach, Mary Ann Devine, Gisele Gaudet, Diane Groff, Richard Williams, and Robin Yaffe who, at different times, helped me teach the courses that utilized earlier drafts of this text and provided me with specific information to improve the book. In addition, I wish to thank Katie Bemisderfer and, again, Richard Williams who used their experiences in teaching community leisure education courses to help me revise each of the specific leisure education programs contained in the Appendices of this book. In addition, Yeunjoo Lee contributed information on prompting strategies, Dave Loy helped create the initial figures in the text, and Brenda Arnold and Lynne Cory patiently edited and typed drafts of the book before it was sent to Venture Publishing; I thank you. My appreciation is extended to Richard Yocum and the entire Venture staff for their contributions in making this book a polished product. I would also like to thank my friend and colleague Douglas Kleiber, for his review of the text and for creating a work environment conducive for me to write yet another edition of this book. Finally, I wish to thank Anne, David, and Steven, my primary sources of leisure, for the love, joy, and laughter they bring to my life which continues to give me the energy to complete projects such as this book.

Preface

By looking at the outside of this book it becomes obvious that it has changed a great deal from the first edition. Since its publication in 1991, we have used this book to help teach many undergraduate and graduate courses devoted to leisure education. Each time these courses were taught we thought of ways the book could be improved to better meet the needs of students in the class. Other instructors of leisure education courses, graduate assistants, and students enrolled in courses on leisure education provided valuable feedback for ways in which the book might be improved. At conferences I have had the opportunity to meet professionals who were using the book to help them structure services. They, too, provided constructive input on ways in which the book could be improved.

In this preface the major components of the book are outlined and a description of how they have evolved from the first edition is presented.

First and foremost, recent information has been incorporated into this book since the printing of the first edition. Since material on and relevant to leisure education continues to be written, it seems critical that such material be reflected in the most recent edition of this book.

The most significant change to this book is noted by the expansion of the initial section of the book, from six to ten chapters. Because the first edition was so lengthy, to accommodate the expansion of this section, the section that previously contained information on leisure education programs devoted to specific recreation activities has been removed. The six specific leisure education programs contained in the first edition of this book (i.e., swimming, walking, gardening, bowling, volleyball, and softball) have been revised and, along with four additional specific programs (i.e., camping, canoeing, cooking, and painting), will be available in the book titled *Leisure Education Specific Programs* to be published by Venture Publishing, Inc.

As with the first edition, the book begins with an introductory chapter which provides basic information about leisure, leisure education, and this book. This chapter has been expanded to include information on the rationale for leisure education.

When we taught the courses on leisure education we found ourselves presenting information beyond the scope of the text to help provide students with an understanding of leisure behavior. Therefore, Chapters 2 and 3 are new and were developed to address the foundations of leisure education and the potential of leisure education. Chapter 2 includes information to answer three questions: (a) How does society influence leisure attitudes? (b) What motivates people to participate? and (c) What prevents people from experiencing leisure? In the third chapter three questions are addressed: (a) How can constraints to leisure be managed? (b) How can leisure experiences be facilitated? and (c) How can leisure education promote leisure?

With the continued publication of literature on or related to leisure education, the chapter in the first edition of the book devoted to reviewing the literature has been replaced with two chapters. Chapter 4 presents literature on (a) models for leisure education, (b) leisure education curricula and program manuals, and (c) general recommendations to consider when developing leisure education programs. The fifth chapter is restricted to presenting research studies examining the impact of a variety of leisure education programs.

The information presented in Chapters 6-9 focusing on the content and process of leisure education programs as well as ways to teach and adapt leisure education programs has been updated, revised and expanded. Although the chapters have changed, the material presented is similar to the information contained in the first edition. Since culture dramatically influences leisure participation, Chapter 10 is a new chapter included in this edition which presents multicultural considerations for developing and implementing leisure education programs.

The next section of the book contains leisure education programs associated with six leisure education components identified in the text— appreciate leisure, be aware of self in leisure, be self-determined in leisure, interact socially during leisure, use resources facilitating leisure, and make decisions about leisure. On numerous occasions over the past several years we have field tested and systematically evaluated various components of these six leisure education programs. Based on our experiences, revisions have been made to each of the programs contained in the Appendices that are designed to improve the clarity and flow of the programs.

As mentioned previously, not only is the content substantially different from the first edition but also the book looks very different. Over the past several years I have tried to use a variety of graphics in class and at conferences and workshops to best illustrate the ideas presented in writing; therefore, all the figures have been changed in an attempt to improve readers' comprehension of the material.

Hopefully, readers will find the book to be informative. For those readers familiar with the first edition of the book, I hope you are pleased with the way this second edition of the book contributes to the body of literature on leisure education.

—J. D.

Chapter 1
An Introduction

Leisure is not free time;
it is freedom's time.
-Charles Sylvester

Introduction

The purpose of this book is to provide the reader with information needed
to develop a comprehensive leisure education program regardless of the
people being served or the place in which the services are delivered. Considering the following words of Csikszentmihalyi (1997) may help the
reader appreciate the importance of leisure education for all people:

> The popular assumption is that no skills are involved in enjoying
> free time, and that anybody can do it. Yet the evidence suggests the
> opposite: free time is more difficult to enjoy than work. Having
> leisure at one's disposal does not improve the quality of life unless
> one knows how to use it effectively, and it is by no means some-
> thing one learns automatically. . . . All of this evidence points to the
> fact that the average person is ill equipped to be idle. (p. 65)

The introduction to this book contains an explanation of the main concepts used in this book and information covered in the remaining chapters.
To accomplish these goals, the following questions are addressed:

(a) What is leisure?
(b) What is leisure education?
(c) Why leisure education?
(d) Why this book? and
(e) What is in this book?

What Is Leisure?

Risisky, Caldwell and Fors (1997) suggested that to understand leisure education, an understanding of leisure is helpful. In addition, one of the fundamental tasks of leisure education is to help people clearly define what leisure

means to them. Through leisure education people develop an understanding of themselves and leisure (Bullock & Mahon, 1997). Although in the past there has been some debate and discussion over the definition of leisure and the associated terms of recreation and free time, there does appear to be some consensus regarding their meanings among consumers, practitioners, researchers, and theorists. This section attempts to clarify these concepts.

About Recreation

Typically, recreation has been defined as an activity, such as swimming, table games, and dance, in which people engage primarily for enjoyment and satisfaction. The notion of recreation is related directly to the activity and is dependent on the feelings and experiences of individual participants.

Although the activities in which people engage vary widely, generally the term "recreation" refers to some form of organized activity intended for social ends (Kelly, 1990). Recreation is intended to be beneficial for a society and is organized and supported with the expectation of such benefits. People may participate in recreation activities and experience enjoyment and satisfaction. However, it is possible that people may participate in recreation activities in which they encounter failure, rejection, and feelings of helplessness. Therefore, in spite of its common usage, defining leisure as an activity is problematic (Russell, 1996).

A Problem With Free Time

"Free time" is a phrase that is generally used today to describe unobligated time; that is, time not spent in daily tasks associated with subsistence or self-maintenance. Free time occurs when people are not obligated to perform specified tasks; thus, it is discretionary and can be used according to one's judgment or choice. Many people make choices relative to the use of their free time that result in enjoyable and satisfying experiences. Other people may be in circumstances where the opportunity for choice is lacking for a variety of reasons. For instance, individuals may not have an array of options from which to choose, or they may not have the ability to make choices. As a result, some individuals' free time may be associated with boredom, anxiety, and despair. According to Russell (1996, p. 33), "some people perceive free time as an empty space that, if left unfilled, becomes something negative." Therefore, Csikszentmihalyi (1997, p. 112) noted that "one person might enjoy free time and the other be bored when there is nothing to do."

Several authors (e.g., Cooper, 1989; Hunnicutt, 1988; Kelly, 1996; Teeters, 1991) stated that leisure conceptualized as free time relies on a limited definition of leisure and is problematic. These authors claimed that leisure as a portion of time has minimized the importance of leisure as an opportunity for fulfillment. For example, Hunnicutt (1988) reported that the definition of leisure as time has resulted in leisure being void of meaning and being viewed as work rather than being viewed as essential for progress. Therefore, leisure when defined as free time has been associated with idleness. This is an example of how the definition of leisure as a portion of time has influenced a devaluation of the concept of leisure.

The Freedom of Leisure

Although the definition of leisure may include elements of recreation and free time, conceptualizing this term entirely within these perspectives appears to be too limiting. Kelly (1990) stated, "neither time nor activity provides a clear quantitative definition of leisure" (p. 20). For example, Argyle (1996) included both free time and activity in his definition of leisure, but emphasized that what motivated people to participate in an activity was the most critical aspect of something being considered to be leisure. Argyle defined leisure as:

> . . . those activities which people do in their free time, because they want to, for their own sake, for fun, entertainment, self-improvement, or for goals of their choosing, but not for material gain. (p. 3)

Many people believe the term "leisure" should emphasize the importance of a person's perception that he or she is free to choose to participate in meaningful, enjoyable, and satisfying experiences. Csikszentmihalyi (1997, p. 17) concluded that "while what we do day in and day out has a lot to do with what kind of life we have, how we experience what we do is even more important."

The word "leisure" is derived from the Latin word *licere* which means "to be free" (Welton, 1979) and, according to Prager (1998, p. 150), "freedom is being able to do what will bring you happiness." Freedom as it applies to leisure has been discussed by many writers as the "freedom to be" (Godbey, 1985; Kelly, 1987). "Leisure experiences provide the opportunity for maintaining personal autonomy, self-definition, and choice often absent from other aspects of life" (Russell, 1996, p. 342). Through freedom of choice, a person experiences self-determination (Dattilo & Kleiber, 1993) and without choice and self-determination leisure does not exist (Haygood, Kew, & Braham, 1989). Sylvester (1985) suggested that freedom has two different meanings depending on if the freedom is "from" or the freedom is "to." Mannell and Kleiber (1997) explained that "freedom from" refers to the absence of duress, coercion, and interference while "freedom to" involves willful choice and action on the part of the individual.

Although self-determination is the power to act as a causal agent, Samdahl (1986) reminded us that freedom is inherently limited. Social norms limit freedom, and, thus, limit self-expression. Samdahl (1986) emphasized that authentic and true self-expression results in people experiencing the freedom that is central to leisure. Part of the essence of leisure is that the individual is engaged in an activity for its own sake (Cooper, 1989). Therefore, Kelly (1996) defined leisure "as an activity chosen in relative freedom for its qualities of satisfaction" (p. 3).

According to Mannell, Zuzanek, and Larson (1988), leisure is best understood from the subjective perspective of the participant; therefore, perceived freedom and intrinsic motivation are key components of leisure. Self-expression and intrinsic motivation are closely linked to leisure with self-expression implying that individuals can live aspects of their life in which intrinsic desires are satisfied. If people engage in only instrumental activity, or drudgery, in which they are not intrinsically motivated to participate, they will encounter difficulty in expressing themselves.

Pieper (1963) stated that leisure is a state of mind, of being, and a spiritual attitude. Pieper implied that to pursue the essence of oneself is to "leisure." Simply to participate in an activity is not "leisureing," unless individuals are engaged in expressing and enhancing their spirit (Neulinger, 1974). Although Mannell and Kleiber (1997, p. 107) recognized that "the most central and commonly agreed upon set of attributes" of leisure is associated with freedom, freedom of choice, self-determination, or lack of constraint, they also identified the following attributes that have been proposed: (a) intrinsic motivation, (b) self-expression, (c) relaxation, (d) enjoyment, pleasure or affect, (e) escape, (f) spontaneity, (g) timelessness, (h) fantasy and creativity, (i) adventure and exploration, and (j) lack of evaluation. Figure 1.1 is designed to summarize quickly the material presented in this section.

What is Leisure Education?

Although leisure education has been defined in various ways, often the phrase "leisure education" is used to describe a developmental process designed to enhance an individual's understanding of himself or herself, leisure, the relationship of leisure to his or her lifestyle, and the relationship of leisure to society in general (Aguilar, 1986; Mundy & Odum, 1979). More specifically, Johnson, Bullock and Ashton-Schaeffer (1997) described leisure education as a "process of teaching various recreation and leisure related skills, attitudes, and values" (p. 31). Leitner, Leitner and Associates (1996) stated that leisure education is simply a process designed to facilitate maximal leisure well-being. In a paper highlighting the Charter of Leisure

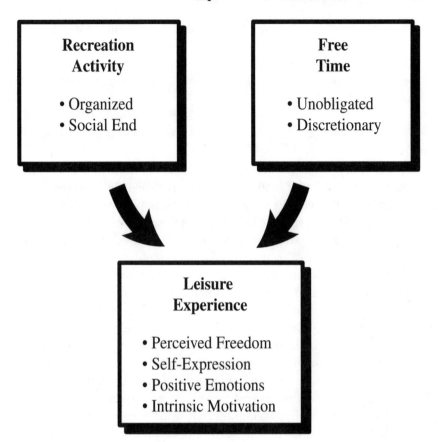

Fig. 1.1

Education by the World Leisure and Recreation Association, Sivan (1997) described leisure education as:

> . . . a directed, methodological, structured process, recognizing the individual's right to leisure and the wise use of it, whose objective is to impart and foster desirable patterns of leisure behavior (p. 42).

Leisure education is a complex process in that leisure and education are closely and irrevocably intertwined (Kelly, 1996). Brightbill and Mobily (1977) proclaimed that leisure leads to education, and education back to leisure. Through education, individuals learn and prepare for expressions of leisure, and in leisure they use education to teach themselves further about leisure's relative freedom and self-determination (Kelly, 1990). According to Bullock and Mahon (1997), leisure education must encourage self-determination if service providers intend to meet the needs of their participants. Bullock and Mahon (p. 38) concluded that:

Leisure education is an individualized and contextualized educational process through which a person develops an understanding of self and leisure and identifies and learns the cluster of skills necessary to participate in freely chosen activities that lead to an optimally satisfying life.

Ultimately, the goal of the leisure education process is to "enhance the quality of a person's life through leisure" (Chinn & Joswiak, 1981, p. 5). More specifically, the goal of leisure education is to develop leisure skills that enhance the quality of individuals' daily lives (Heyne & Schleien, 1996). Askins (1997) concluded that learning how to incorporate leisure into a person's lifestyle is more than learning the skill needed to play a sport, tend a garden, or paint a picture—it involves developing leisure values, an understanding of the benefits of leisure, problem-solving skills, assertiveness, and learning about leisure resources in the community.

According to Kleiber (1981), the premise for leisure education may include a recognition that free time is often misused and that leisure may be the best context for self-actualization. If leisure service providers are interested in promoting individuals' self-actualization, Howe (1989) suggested that they provide leisure education. Through leisure education, leisure service professionals can foster the development of self-directed, freely chosen, healthy, intrinsically motivated, and pleasurable leisure participation patterns. "The concept of education for leisure aims at exposing all people to the possibilities that leisure may hold for them to live creatively and give expression to the wide assortment of their capabilities" (Bucher, Shiver, & Bucher, 1984, p. 290).

Why Leisure Education?
(An Historical Perspective)

Although leisure and leisure education have become recent concerns of leisure service providers, previously they were the domain of the philosopher. Leisure ideas have been traced to the Greek philosophers Aristotle and Plato, and the Roman philosopher Seneca (Welton, 1979). According to Argyle (1996), these philosophers believed that:

The main purpose of life was the proper use of leisure, by self-development through education and contemplation, the pursuit of virtue through knowledge, and the practice of music, philosophy, ritual and athletics. (p. 14)

Welton stated that philosophically, leisure was discussed as a method of personal growth and social advancement in Athens, Greece, during the fifth century B.C. Welton (1979) stated that this period was considered the "Golden Age," a period recognized for its various intellectual advances. Thus, the Greek term for leisure *schole* has since evolved into words such as "school" and "scholar" (Welton, 1979). In his writings *On Politics,* Aristotle wrote:

> The real test then of a people's education is not so much the way they work or fight, but the way they use their leisure. To show excellent qualities in action and war but in times of peace and leisure to be no better than slaves is to miss the happiness that is the end of human living. Hence the importance in schools of subjects like music, which is studied solely with a view of leisure spent in intellectual activity and makes the heart of men glad.

Cooper (1989) stated that Plato, in his *New Republic,* identified leisure as activity and the basis of learning and autonomy. Pieper (1963) stated that Aristotle discussed the occurrence of leisure through contemplation to be the foundation for cultural development and necessary for reasoning and growth. Goodale (1991) added that Aristotle expressed leisure as the most complete pleasure because it necessitates use of the divine element in humans. However, according to Goodale, Aristotle considered leisure possible for only those who did not need to work. Although Pieper (1963) agreed with Aristotle to the extent that he described leisure as contrary to the ideal of the everyday worker, Goodale and Cooper reported that our society is work-oriented. Specifically, Goodale (1991) insisted that if "leisure is to be a possibility for us, then it must infuse our work."

Around 1350 A.D., philosophers described leisure as providing the necessary balance for mind and body. Mundy and Odum (1979) emphasized that during the Renaissance, education for life became synonymous with "Education for Leisure." The Renaissance was a time of great activity in painting, music, literature, and science (Argyle, 1996). However, with the Reformation in the 1500s came the birth of the "Protestant Work Ethic." The work ethic was reflected in Colonial America, where work for survival took center stage. The Protestant work ethic was a primary force that emphasized the image of leisure as time. This view of leisure as time when not earned through hard work was associated with idleness and sin (Mundy & Odum, 1979). As a result, leisure was viewed as unimportant, and much of leisure was thought to be wicked (Argyle, 1996).

According to Teeters (1991), the Industrial Revolution, which began in the 1800s, reinforced the notion of leisure as time. During this time, "work was now very sharply distinguished from leisure, though there was little time or energy for leisure, apart from recovering from work and its frustrations" (Argyle, 1996, p. 20). Teeters (1991) viewed the initiation of "Clock Time" associated with industrialization as reducing self-actualizing work to labor as workers began to sell their time rather than their skills, crafts, and work. According to Teeters, the selling of time resulted in loss of personal meaning and enjoyment and reinforced the divisiveness of work and leisure which contributed to a devaluation of the possibilities of leisure experience in any activity.

In the 1920s, the Gospel of Consumption, led by Henry Ford, was established on the premise that if the need for traditional products were being met, then new needs could be discovered and marketed (Hunnicutt, 1988). Hunnicutt described how Ford and his colleagues saw leisure as the perfect time to pursue goods consumption which led to "Merchandised Leisure." Sports, amusement parks, resort hotels, and excursions were promoted. According to Hunnicutt (1988), this effort was so successful that work was soon perceived as necessary for a leisure income. Hunnicutt cited documents that showed how educators (formerly the teachers of leisure) were encouraged by the government and through grants from business to teach preparation for work rather than leisure. In addition, Hunnicutt reported that scientists and engineers (once supporters of technology to increase leisure), now viewed their role to be creators of work.

Today, rather than work for leisure as people did in the late 1800s and early 1900s, people now work to satisfy endless material wants (Hunnicutt, 1988). This contention has been emphasized by Schor (1992) who found that people are not experiencing leisure in work because it is not of value in and of itself. Work is pursued to purchase consumer goods, which Schor described as a work-and-spend lifestyle. In a work-and-spend lifestyle people work hard to buy goods, and the more they spend, the more they must work.

According to Schor (1992), commercialization of free time has resulted in many people devaluing leisure and being bored. Lippmann (1930) predicted that the temptations of luxury and mass production of pleasure would destroy the individual's ability to exercise free will. Lippmann stated that "pleasure as created by others had become an antidote to boredom, and the dosage had to grow even larger to prevent further boredom" (p. 212). More recently, Rybezynski (1991) contended that feeling unfulfilled in leisure is a result of a dependency on external pleasures and an inability to find pleasure within oneself. When discussing "commercial leisure," Hunnicutt (1988) agreed that it ". . . may be less satisfying and hence less desirable as it becomes less active, creative, personal, and connected to others" (p. 312).

Cooper (1989) concluded that leisure is important for having a balanced life. Iso-Ahola (1994) added that quality of life is reduced for individuals who are not being challenged through leisure. Succumbing to the powerful forces of marketing external pleasure (Hunnicutt, 1988), less self-actualizing work (Teeters, 1991), and the limited view of leisure as free time (Cooper, 1989; Goodale, 1991) has resulted in people seeing limited value in leisure. Aristotle considered leisure the aim of life. That aim, according to Hunnicutt (1988), has been abandoned. In presenting the World Leisure and Recreation Association's Charter for Leisure Education, Sivan (1997) concluded that:

The main goals of leisure education in the community are empowerment, accessibility, life-long learning, social participation, diminishing constraints, inclusivity, civic and moral responsibility, and preservation. (p. 43)

The information in this section of the chapter was provided to identify factors that have influenced the way people think about and have treated leisure. A time line of the material is depicted in Figure 1.2. In summarizing the history of leisure, Argyle (1996) stated that:

Leisure has shown extraordinary variations from one historical period to another, in the amount of leisure people had, what they did with it, and what they believed they should do. (p. 31)

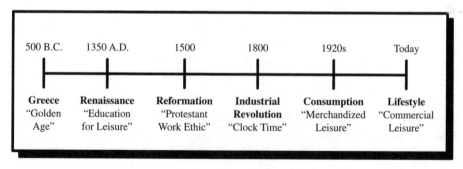

500 B.C.	1350 A.D.	1500	1800	1920s	Today
Greece "Golden Age"	**Renaissance** "Education for Leisure"	**Reformation** "Protestant Work Ethic"	**Industrial Revolution** "Clock Time"	**Consumption** "Merchandized Leisure"	**Lifestyle** "Commercial Leisure"

Fig. 1.2

Perhaps if professionals develop an awareness of the actions occurring throughout history, an understanding of the influence that decisions made throughout history have had on society's attitudes, and a sensitivity to perceptions of leisure over time they will be better able to understand the potential and need for leisure education.

Why Leisure Education?
(A Health and Economic Perspective)

The characteristics associated with leisure have been shown to contribute to improved health (Wankel, 1993). While these characteristics of leisure are beneficial in themselves, their presence contributes to improved health and provides support for the need to develop and implement education programs. Askins (1997) reported that there is a distinct relationship between leisure patterns and illness; the less active a person is, the more medical problems increase and the less satisfied the person becomes with leisure. In addition, free time physical activity is associated with an individual's longevity (Dishman, 1995). Based on a review of the literature, Sobel (1995) concluded that lifestyle behaviors, more than human biology, the environment, and the healthcare system combined, account for the number and quality of years lived.

Several researchers (Caldwell, Smith, & Weissinger, 1992; Iso-Ahola, 1994) have concluded that leisure is associated with psychological health, that leisure helps reduce the effects of stressful life (Coleman, 1993; Coleman & Iso-Ahola, 1993). Iso-Ahola and Park (1996) noted that the social support derived from leisure participation is important in that it is the activity and things done with friends or companions that buffer the adverse effects of stress on physical and mental health (p. 169).

Wankel (1993) proposed that enjoyment may have direct health implications through counteracting stress and facilitating positive psychological health. For example, specific leisure experiences have been documented to improve mood (Berger & Owen, 1992), to increase life satisfaction (Krause & Crewe, 1987), to improve self-esteem (Berryman, 1988), and to decrease depression (Dishman, 1994; Greenwood, Dzewattowski, & French, 1990; Wassman & Iso-Ahola, 1985; Weis & Jameson, 1988), anxiety (Dishman, 1994; Long, 1984; Sachs, 1984), stress (Berk et al., 1988) and loneliness (Osgood, Meyers, & Orchowsky, 1990; Riddick, 1985). These findings imply that the use of leisure education to enhance one's leisure lifestyle is an important way to promote good health.

Regarding the economic value of an active leisure lifestyle, Iso-Ahola (1994) reported that each person with a sedentary lifestyle costs society because of higher medical expenses and work loss. Despite the detrimental effects of a sedentary lifestyle, 80% of the population is considered sedentary (Dishman, 1995). In addition, even though people are considered healthier, more affluent, and technologically advanced than a few years ago, more accounts of stress and anxiety-related illness, depression and boredom have been reported (Dishman, 1995; Seligman, 1990). Seligman (1990) found that depression is 10 times more common now than 50 years ago. As people improve their mental and physical health so that they can experience longer, happier lives with less illness, they will contribute to society's overall reduction in healthcare costs and time away from work due to illness. Accordingly, this provides social and economic rationale for the provision of leisure education across a variety of settings.

Why This Book?

People's ability to develop through leisure is important for both individuals and society. Unfortunately, for many people active leisure involvement is often overshadowed by the amount of time they spend on passive activities such as watching television (Csikszentmihalyi, 1997). Passive entertainment provides minimal opportunity for growth and frequently promotes boredom (Wlodkowski & Jaynes, 1991). For example, Wlodkowski and Jaynes reported that television, although entertaining in moderation, has a negative effect when viewed excessively. A study of the effects of activity level on health of individuals found a correlation between watching more than six hours of television and hospital readmission (Anson & Shephard, 1990). This study implies that dependence on nonproductive leisure may result in a decrease in life satisfaction thus causing illness.

It is helpful for leisure service providers to encourage individuals to take charge of their lives and to learn the value of leisure involvement. Through leisure education, leisure service providers can help participants learn from challenges in their lives and avoid being passive participants who are disempowered and helpless. In 1993, the World Leisure and Recreation Association stated that:

> In light of the critical evolving role and benefits of leisure in all societies, and of the importance of all agents involved in leisure education, we recommend expanding the development of leisure education programs. (p. 5)

All people can learn ways to experience leisure by developing: (a) an appreciation of leisure, (b) a sense of self in leisure, (c) self-determination in leisure, (d) an understanding of leisure resources, (e) the ability to make decisions about leisure, (f) social interaction skills during leisure, and (g) recreation activity skills. These areas of instruction are some of the components of leisure education presented in this text.

What Is in This Book?

This book contains two distinct sections. In addition to this introduction, the first section contains background information about leisure education. Examples of specific components of leisure education are explored in the second section of the book, identified as the Appendices.

As an introduction to the first section, Chapter 2 provides information related to the foundations of leisure education. An introduction to the complexity of leisure behavior is revealed when consideration is given to the way in which leisure is influenced by society. In addition, the factors which motivate and constrain individuals' leisure behaviors are discussed. Chapter 3 contains a discussion of the potential outcomes of leisure involvement as well as how leisure education can foster the development of opportunities for leisure participation. Recommendations regarding the provision of leisure education services is presented in Chapter 4 and empirical evidence supporting the provision of those services is provided in Chapter 5. Chapter 6 provides a detailed description of seven suggested areas of concentration within leisure education programs which can assist people in developing more satisfying leisure lifestyles.

The first section of the book continues with specific strategies designed to aid leisure service providers in conducting leisure education programs. Toward this end, Chapter 7 contains a detailed format which can be used to develop specific leisure education programs. Chapter 8 provides practical suggestions which may assist in preparing, presenting, and concluding leisure education programs. The final two chapters in the first section of this book were included to assist leisure service professionals in meeting the diverse needs of their participants. In Chapter 9, considerations are given on various ways in which programs can be adapted to meet the needs of all participants, regardless of ability. Chapter 10 contains a discussion of multicultural considerations to enhance practitioners' ability to serve participants who bring to leisure services a variety of different experiences, characteristics, and identities.

While the first section provides the theoretical knowledge and specific strategies needed for the provision of comprehensive leisure education services, the Appendices provide examples of what actual leisure education programs may look like. This section of the book responds to the advice of the World Leisure and Recreation Association's 1993 Charter on Leisure Education to develop modules which transmit values, knowledge and skills to professionals. In this second section of the book, specific goals, objectives, and performance measures associated with six of the components of the leisure education model suggested in this book are presented. Each program provides an in-depth examination of the application of one particular leisure education component.

Although the use of leisure education has been advocated as a means to help individuals develop complete and fulfilling leisure lifestyles for more than 500 years (Mundy et al., 1992), leisure education remains an under-utilized tool within the parks and recreation profession. With the hope of increasing the use of leisure education, this book is designed to provide recreation and leisure service professionals with the knowledge and information needed to develop comprehensive leisure education services.

Conclusion

Leisure, then, is an experience, a process, a subjective state of mind born of psychological involvement. To partake fully in leisure is to express talents, demonstrate capabilities, achieve one's potential and experience a variety of positive emotions as a result of perceived freedom, intrinsic desire, and self-expression. Leisure education is designed to facilitate any individual's leisure expression. Although leisure education typically has been provided to people experiencing severe constraints to their leisure, it is the premise of this book that all people can benefit from leisure education. This premise is consistent with the position of the World Leisure and Recreation Association. For example, in the 1997 Editor's Note in the journal *World Leisure and Recreation* devoted to leisure education, Sivan and Ruskin (1997a) stated that:

> With the rapid social and technological changes that the contemporary society is undergoing, preparation of people for the best use of leisure has become an emerging need. Being a life span process, leisure education can develop all-round individuals who utilize the benefits of leisure for their physical, emotional, social, and intellectual development. (p. 3)

It is hoped that this book will assist leisure service providers in developing systematic methods for offering leisure education to all individuals.

Chapter 2
Foundations of Leisure Education

There are three things difficult:
to suffer an injury, to keep a secret,
to use leisure.
-Voltaire

Introduction

To assist the reader in developing a more in-depth understanding of leisure and leisure education, this chapter will briefly review the social and psychological foundations of leisure. Examination of the motivating factors associated with leisure involvement and consideration of constraints which can prevent people from engaging in leisure are presented. To increase knowledge about the complexities of leisure and leisure education, the following three questions are addressed:

(a) How does society influence leisure?
(b) What motivates people to participate? and
(c) What prevents people from experiencing leisure?

How Does Society Influence Leisure?

Regardless of the way in which people choose to conceptualize leisure, an understanding of leisure can be enhanced if consideration is given to the way in which people develop their attitudes. There are many societal factors that influence an individual's attitude about leisure. Frequently, society's influence on a person's attitudes and, subsequently, society's influence on the individual's leisure behavior, occur through the communication of societal norms. Societal norms are communicated through a process of socialization. According to Robertson (1977), socialization is the process of social interaction through which people learn the way of life of their society. The next section of the chapter contains information on the:

(a) development of attitudes; and
(b) social norms and persuasion.

Development of Attitudes

Attitudes reflect "very general evaluations that people hold of themselves, other people, objects, and issues" (Petty, 1995; p. 196). The formation of attitudes is one function of the process of socialization (Robertson, 1977). Typically when individuals form attitudes, they attempt to organize information regarding an issue in a systematic and consistent fashion. Once an attitude is developed, individuals continue to express that attitude through their thoughts, feelings, and behaviors. The particular thoughts, feelings and behaviors of interest to leisure service providers are those associated with leisure participation.

For example, Marcus has been experiencing symptoms associated with multiple sclerosis for several years. During this time, he has heard conflicting information regarding what forms of exercise are beneficial. After careful review of current research, consideration of the advice of friends who have multiple sclerosis, and the advice of his physician, Marcus decided to begin participating in an aquatics exercise program. Since participating in the program, Marcus has developed a positive attitude toward aquatic exercise. Marcus' new attitude toward aquatic exercise is reflected in his consistent attendance of the program. As an indication of his beliefs, Marcus serves as a spokesperson for aquatics exercise at a support group offered by the Multiple Sclerosis Society.

The extent to which attitudes influence behavior depend on the direction (i.e., positive, negative, or neutral) and the intensity of the feeling and thought ranging from weak to strong. In addition, attitudes influence behavior depending on the degree to which the attitude is salient and relevant to the behavior (Robertson, 1977).

For instance, Elaina may feel strongly that meditation is an essential component of her daily routine because it improves her emotional well-being and ability to manage stress. Because Elaina's feelings are positive and strong regarding meditation, she is more likely to be motivated to meditate on a daily basis. The relevance of meditation to improve her emotional well-being and managing her stress is very salient.

Social Norms and Persuasion

According to Robertson (1977), a social norm is a guideline that prescribes behavior for people in a given situation. Social norms reflect accepted ways of thinking, feeling, or acting which are ideas accepted to be true based on community standards. Persuasive messages are a common form of conveying social norms. Social norms can have such an extensive influence over behavior that they "often override personal attitudes to determine social behavior" (Smith & Mackie, 1995, p. 347).

When individuals express their attitude to a group they are creating an opportunity for others to evaluate them. If a group member expresses a dissimilar or conflicting attitude within a group, other group members may attempt to persuade that individual to modify his or her behavior to conform with other members of the group. Therefore, through persuasion, behaviors are frequently changed (Petty, 1995).

> For instance, 16-year-old Nicole enjoyed playing drums in the marching band. Several of her friends encouraged her to quit the band because they felt she was getting too old to participate in this activity and that it limited the amount of time she had to socialize with them. Nicole eventually chose to discontinue her involvement with the band because of the persuasive messages of her friends.

Persuasive messages can transmit information in either a formal or informal manner. Formal and systematic persuasion occurs when an individual carefully considers the arguments and information being presented. Careful consideration typically involves relating the new information to the individual's past and current knowledge, beliefs, and behaviors associated with that situation, person, activity, or object. Situations in which the individual engages in systematic and thoughtful consideration of options can result in feelings of empowerment for the individual.

> For example, after Gloria was provided resources regarding the sport of rock climbing, allowed to watch the sport, then given instructions in rock climbing techniques, she decided that she wanted to pursue this adventure sport. Although Gloria was encouraged to learn the sport by her husband, the persuasion was formal and primarily within her control.

Without completing the aforementioned systematic processing of information, some individuals' may decide to pursue a recreation activity because it is presented in an attractive way through such means as the media even though they may have limited understanding of what participation in this sport entails. In this situation, persuasion influences an individual's attitude in a more informal manner. Informal messages consist of emotional appeals which are minimally processed by the individual but which become information used to form an attitude. Many advertisements on television and in magazines may glamorize a variety of recreation activities including rock climbing.

> As an example, while watching television Taylor observes that youth whom he finds attractive are skateboarding. The advertisement presents the activity in an appealing manner. Taylor may decide to buy a skateboard and attempt this activity based on the television advertisement.

Typically, social norms are so ingrained in a person's social world that individuals are not conscious of the influence that these norms have on their behavior. According to Smith and Mackie (1995), the ability of norms to influence behavior stems from individuals' motivation to feel a sense of connectedness with others and to master their environment. Achieving a sense of connectedness and mastery of one's environment promotes a sense of personal value and acceptance in individuals. Often norms are so subtle that people are not aware of the persuasion that is occurring. People's behaviors can reflect the norm without their being aware that they are complying with the norm (Shaw, 1994).

> As an example, one social norm which is commonly valued in our society is that of honesty. When Matt and Laura play tennis in a mixed doubles league they pride themselves in making line calls honestly. By playing fair, Matt and Laura derive a heightened sense of satisfaction and accomplishment from playing tennis.

Often, individuals are exposed to group and social norms within the context of leisure (Shaw, 1994). In addition to Figure 2.1, the following example illustrates how attitudes and social norms work together to influence leisure behavior.

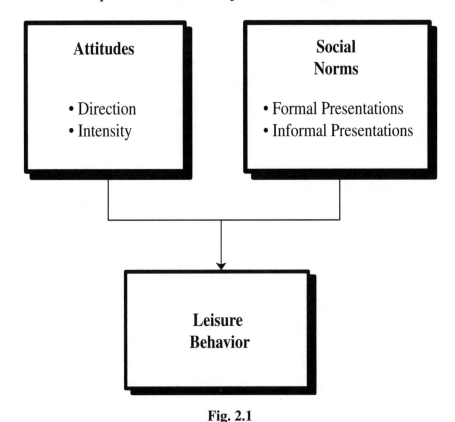

Fig. 2.1

Terry is an adolescent who has taken a drink of alcohol with friends on occasion. She attended a wedding where her parents offered her a glass of champagne to toast the bride and groom. She accepted the drink with the intention of finishing the glass; however, she soon noticed several friends behaving inappropriately because of drunkenness. She decided not to drink the champagne so she would not get drunk and act in the same manner as her friends. However, her friends ridiculed her decision. In this example, Terry's original intention of finishing the glass of champagne was reinforced by social norms (that is, accepting underage drinking in certain situations). However, the behaviors of others influenced a change in her attitudes, and, as a result, she modified her behavior (that is, deciding not to drink). Unfortunately for Terry, this resulted in her being socially isolated.

Summary

Social norms and attitudes can influence thoughts, feelings, and behaviors related to leisure in positive and negative ways. Ultimately, to develop healthy and satisfying leisure lifestyles, it is helpful for individuals to understand the underlying processes which influence their leisure behavior and to develop strategies to overcome problematic leisure participation patterns. Leisure education can help individuals make informed leisure decisions by helping them identify the potential influence of social factors on their leisure participation and attitudes. For example, Backman and Mannell (1986) were successful in changing leisure attitudes and encouraging greater leisure participation by simply providing participants with the chance to think about and discuss their attitudes and values toward leisure with other people.

People's attitudes toward leisure and their behavior to achieve leisure are the result of a complex process involving the interaction between individuals and their environment. In most situations, attitudes guide behavior; however, in some instances attitudes conflict with motivation to participate or actual participation (Ajzen & Driver, 1991). In addition to the influences of attitudes and social norms, it is helpful to consider an individual's motivation to engage in leisure (Iso-Ahola, 1980).

What Motivates People to Participate?

Throughout history, philosophers have discussed the topic of leisure and have attempted to present reasons why people engage in leisure. For example, to Aristotle human striving, achievement, and drives to action were all based on a desire for happiness as an end (Cooper, 1989). Later, Spinoza, a European philosopher born in 1632, contended that life's pleasures and leisure are not inherently worthwhile but are worth pursuing as a means to happiness (Popkin & Stroll, 1993). Spinoza's beliefs supported writings of Epicurus, who believed that all activities are directed toward achieving pleasure and avoiding pain (Shiver, 1981). More recently, Cooper (1989) stated that pleasure through leisure requires a cognitive challenge and a person's intrinsic desire to be satisfied.

Neulinger (1974) described perceived freedom and motivation as key dimensions of the leisure experience. The dimension of perceived freedom denotes the "prime distinction between leisure and nonleisure" (Neulinger, 1974, p. 18). Individuals perceive they are experiencing leisure when their participation is a result of a deliberate choice, rather than from coercion (Neulinger, 1974).

Neulinger identified three categories of motivation that can be used to classify leisure and nonleisure. These three categories of motivation include intrinsic, extrinsic, and intrinsic/extrinsic. Intrinsic motivation, often associated with leisure participation, refers to motivation to participate based on the positive feeling derived from participating in the activity. Conversely, extrinsic motivation, often associated with work-like tasks, refers to the decision to engage in an activity based on external rewards associated with participating in the activity. Neulinger (1974) noted that because behaviors are multidetermined and complex, sometimes a person's decision to engage in a given activity is both intrinsically and extrinsically motivated.

For example, Steven enjoys the sport of golfing but finds that, depending upon the situation, he receives a variety of rewards from the experience. When Steven has an available weekend and is intrinsically motivated to play golf with his friends, he experiences the most satisfaction from the game. When Steven is extrinsically motivated by his supervisor to play golf with potential business clients, he finds that he enjoys the experience less. When Steven was encouraged by his supervisor to represent his company in a local fund-raising golf tournament, he found that although he was extrinsically motivated to play, he enjoyed his participation in the tournament because he knew that the proceeds would go to a charitable cause. Steven found playing in the golf tournament to be quite satisfying.

Intrinsic motivation occurs when the individual is aware of the potential benefits that may be derived from participation in various activities. As individuals encounter enjoyment associated with the leisure experience, they will be intrinsically motivated to participate (Dattilo & Kleiber, 1993). Although people seek leisure experiences to achieve positive feelings associated with participation, rather than for some external outcome, individuals differ in the degree to which they are intrinsically motivated to participate in various activities.

Intrinsically motivated behaviors have a particularly important role in the development of an individual's self-concept (Smith & Mackie, 1995). Self-concept refers to those feelings and beliefs individuals hold about their personal qualities. Activities that facilitate the leisure experience have the potential to allow individuals the freedom to explore their thoughts and feelings about themselves. In this regard, leisure has the potential to help individuals develop their self-concept. Improved self-concept results from a deeper understanding of self (Csikszentmihalyi, 1990). When individuals are uncertain as to how they feel regarding behaviors or attitudes, they are more likely to seek knowledge regarding how they feel by observing their own behaviors (Bem, 1972).

> For example, David may question the degree to which he is creative and, therefore, enroll in a painting class in an effort to evaluate his degree of creativity.

Deci and Ryan (1985) elaborated on individual differences in intrinsic motivation. According to Deci (1975), individuals are motivated to seek intrinsically rewarding experiences due to their desire to:

(a) develop competence, and
(b) become self-determined.

Develop Competence

As individuals succeed in an activity, they begin to feel competent which can increase their motivation to continue the activity. Although individuals' relative competence is important, the perception that they have about their competence plays a major role in their motivation. According to Deci (1975), people use two different types of standards to evaluate their feelings of competence: internal and external. Dattilo (1994) reported that internal competence occurs when people receive a sense of satisfaction from performing according to standards which they have adopted for themselves. Feelings of internal competence are more likely to surface when people achieve their goals in activities which encourage individuals to be self-determined (Harackiewicz & Sansone, 1991).

> For example, Mahu enjoys painting. She decided that she was going to paint a picture for herself. She attended a leisure education class to improve her painting skills and ultimately painted a picture which she has hanging in her apartment. Mahu achieved her goal and gained a sense of competence.

Mobily and colleagues (1993) reported that external competence is derived from individuals' evaluation of their abilities as compared to that of their peers. Because it can result in feelings of personal control (Iso-Ahola, 1980), external competence is an important component of leisure (Smith, Kielhofer, & Watts, 1986). Much of the information used to determine an individual's competence comes from comparisons with other people. To a certain extent then, the degree to which people perceive themselves as competent is based on the degree to which they are able to fulfill social norms

(Festinger, 1957). Even intrinsically motivated behavior is influenced by other people (Iso-Ahola, 1980).

For example, Martin, who is retired, may be motivated to volunteer at a hospital because of the feelings of competence, satisfaction, and enjoyment he is likely to receive from participation. His desire for competence in a particular area is mediated through social norms which inform him that accomplishment in that activity is valued.

Become Self-Determined

According to Mannell and Kleiber (1997, p. 110), "Self-determination is theorized to be an essential ingredient of intrinsic motivation." Self-determination refers to the flexibility and capacity of an individual to choose from available options and to adjust to those situations in which only one option is available (Deci, 1980). Since cognition, affect, and motivation mediate self-determination (Dattilo & Kleiber, 1993), self-determined behaviors are intentional and are acted on out of choice.

For instance, Maria, a single mother, chose to join a health club to maintain her fitness, develop friendships with others who belong to that club, and use the childcare services for her children. When her children became ill and were not eligible to receive childcare, she felt disgruntled about missing her exercise and socializing with her friends. When Maria discovered an exercise program on television, she chose to continue her fitness program at home.

Because self-determined behavior stems from one's free will and is consistent with the individual's goals, individuals engage in the behavior based on their choice (Deci, Eghrari, Patrick, & Leone, 1994). Thus, choice is the underlying regulatory process of self-determination, whereas compliance underlies behaviors that are not self-determined.

One way to respond to people's leisure needs is for professionals "to respect the rights and dignity of every individual they serve and set the stage for enjoyment by providing opportunities for people to enhance their perceptions of self-determination" (Dattilo & Kleiber, 1993, p. 72). Self-determination can be enhanced through the implementation of leisure education programs.

Summary

In this section of the chapter, information was presented which identified that an individual's motivation to engage in leisure can be either intrinsically, extrinsically, or simultaneously intrinsically and extrinsically derived. When individuals engage in an activity because they are extrinsically motivated to do so, they are not experiencing the freedom characteristic of leisure.

Intrinsically motivated behavior is highly reflective of leisure experiences and may stem from an individual's desire to derive feelings of competence and self-determination. As indicated in Figure 2.2, feelings of competence and self-determination contribute to a person's self-concept and in-

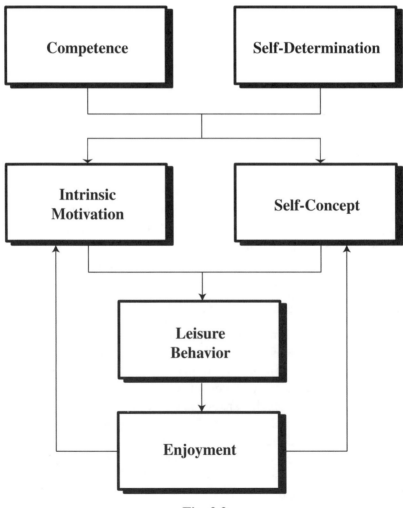

Fig. 2.2

trinsic motivation. Leisure has "the potential to provide opportunities for the satisfaction of needs such as competence, self-determination, and other biological and social needs which appear to be important for human health and well-being" (Mannell & Kleiber, 1997, p. 282). As individuals experience the enjoyment associated with leisure participation, they will be more intrinsically motivated to engage in that activity, and their self-concept will be enhanced. Through leisure education, individuals can gain the awareness, knowledge, and skills required to regain a sense of freedom to participate in enjoyable activities of their choosing.

What Prevents People From Experiencing Leisure?

Feelings of competence and one's perception of freedom to engage in activity may be hampered by internal and external forces which constrain leisure participation. The word "constraint" is used to refer to the subjective feeling individuals experience when obstacles inhibit their ability to engage in an activity of their choosing (McGuire & O'Leary, 1992). Constraints operate on a variety of levels. A conceptual framework developed by Crawford and Godbey (1987) and later articulated by Crawford, Jackson, and Godbey (1991) illustrates the relationship between leisure preferences and leisure participation. The following three categories of constraints were described by Crawford and colleagues:

  (a) intrapersonal constraints;
  (b) interpersonal constraints; and
  (c) structural constraints.

Intrapersonal Constraints

According to Jackson, Crawford and Godbey (1993), intrapersonal constraints represent a person's psychological state and characteristics which interact with, or influence, leisure preferences. Leisure preferences reflect the individual's interest in seeking or avoiding leisure experiences. Therefore, an intrapersonal constraint serves as a reflection of a person's overall disposition and current demeanor which influences his or her leisure preferences.

> For instance, Jamica, an adolescent who is anxious about developing tennis skills because she is afraid of embarrassing herself in front of her peers, is experiencing an intrapersonal constraint.

According to Mannell and Kleiber (1997, p. 349), "The most difficult intrapersonal constraint or psychological disposition to deal with when helping people with their leisure is lack of interest in participating." However, these authors warn that sometimes what is expressed as a lack of interest in participating in leisure activities is a reflection of a lack of confidence in one's ability to engage successfully in an activity, or a negative attitude toward an activity.

Interpersonal Constraints

Interpersonal constraints influence a person's leisure preferences and can influence participation by intervening between an individual's preference and participation. Interpersonal constraints typically involve the social interaction between an individual and his or her friends, family, partner, or relevant social groups.

> For example, John experienced an interpersonal constraint when he lacked a suitable tennis partner and chose to go to the beach because his best friend, Anne, would rather sunbathe than play tennis.

Structural Constraints

Structural constraints influence participation by intervening between preferences, capabilities, and participation (Jackson et al., 1993). Structural constraints include tangible, often physical or geographic constraints located within the environment which inhibit participation.

> An example of a structural constraint might be the lack of an accessible tennis court for Natasha, a tennis player who uses a wheelchair.

Constraints to leisure participation occur because individuals perceive that they are not free to engage in an activity of their choosing because they are experiencing constraints within themselves, with people around them, or with the physical environment. As depicted in Figure 2.3, as people experience intrapersonal (psychological), interpersonal (social), and structural (environmental) constraints, their ability to experience leisure is reduced.

Although the model of constraints developed by Crawford and colleagues is a helpful way to examine constraints, intrapersonal, interpersonal

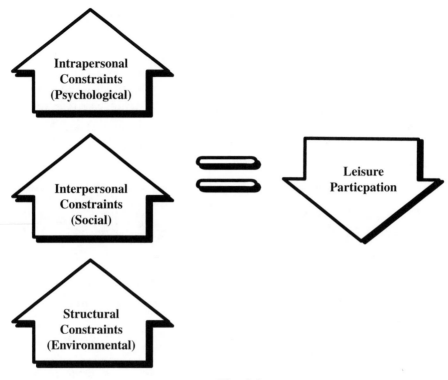

Fig. 2.3

and structural constraints rarely occur in isolation from one another.
Hultsman (1995) concluded that constraints do not act alone to restrict leisure participation. Often, what prevents individuals from engaging in leisure pursuits is a complex condition which involves various types of constraints occurring simultaneously. Some of the conditions which occur as a
result of an interaction between constraints within and outside of the individual include:

    (a) experience reactance;
    (b) learn to be helpless; or
    (c) become bored.

Experience Reactance

When people are prevented from participating in their chosen activities they
may experience reactance, a desire to regain freely chosen behaviors that
are threatened or eliminated (Brehm, 1977). When reactance occurs, the
threatened or eliminated behavior becomes more attractive to the individual,
and, as such, the individual will be motivated to remove the threat to the
behavior or regain the lost behavior (Dattilo & Kleiber, 1993).

For instance, Jason's mother asked him to choose among a pizza party, a pool party, and a skating party for his tenth birthday. He liked all of the choices and had difficulty deciding, but eventually chose a pool party. However, it rained on the day of the party. His mother then asked him to choose again between the pizza party and the skating party. Rather than make the choice, he pleaded with his mother to let him have the pool party in the rain despite the original attractiveness of the other options.

When people expect that they can influence a given outcome, but find their freedom and control threatened, they will experience reactance. That is, they will try harder to establish control. However, after repeated unsuccessful attempts to gain control, they may begin to believe the outcome is uncontrollable and, thus, experience helplessness. This may lead the person to relinquish freedom and develop the condition known as "learned helplessness" (Peterson, Maier, & Seligman, 1993).

Learn to Be Helpless

Learned helplessness occurs when people are exposed repeatedly to uncontrollable events and begin to learn that responding is futile (Seligman, 1975). That is, they begin to believe that no matter what they do in a given situation, they will fail. This influences the individual's intrinsic motivation by reducing the person's desire to respond as well as the ability to learn that responding works.

When people learn that responding does not work, they cease to explore other behavioral options.

For instance, Walter enjoyed watching and reading about baseball. Although he had not received any instruction related to baseball, he decided he wanted to play. He went to the park and asked to join the game. Repeatedly, the other children would not let him play and did not choose him for their team. After trying a variety of different ways to encourage his peers to choose him and failing repeatedly for many days, Walter stopped going to the park and stayed at home and watched baseball and other sports on television.

An important aspect of people learning that they are helpless relates to how it influences their cognition. According to Dattilo and Kleiber (1993), since individuals who believe they are helpless experience difficulty understanding that their behaviors produce meaningful outcomes, they have problems learning to take control of their lives. In addition, the perception of helplessness can influence a person's emotions resulting in depression. When people fail to take control of their lives and are depressed, their ability to experience leisure is reduced (Dattilo & Kleiber, 1993).

For example, Sasha arrives home after school and must wait a couple hours until her grandmother arrives. She has been given explicit instructions to wait inside with the door locked. Outside she sees some neighbors playing kick ball, and wishes she could play. Finally, on a weekend she ventures out to play with the children, but because of her lack of skills she does poorly. In further attempts to play she continues to perform poorly and, subsequently, is not invited to play. Finally, feeling depressed, Sasha stops trying to play with the other children and stays at home even when she is permitted to leave.

Become Bored

Boredom associated with leisure can result from a variety of circumstances. When people have too much time available and too little to do they are prone to boredom (Iso-Ahola & Weissinger, 1990). In addition, if people possess leisure skills greater than the challenge of leisure opportunities they are likely to be bored (Csikszentmihalyi, 1975). Boredom can occur when people perceive that situations are not satisfying, worthless and inescapable (Hamilton, 1981). The view that a situation is monotonous or frustrating can lead to boredom as well (Hill & Perkins, 1985). Finally, boredom can occur when free time is enforced without people having sufficient leisure skills (Patrick, 1982).

Regardless of what causes boredom, Iso-Ahola and Weissinger (1990) found that people who do not have the awareness, attitudes and skills that facilitate leisure involvement, and who perceive constraints to leisure participation, are more likely to be bored and less likely to be intrinsically motivated.

As an example, Laura lives in a rural area. With no peers within reasonable walking distance, Laura has a great deal of time on her hands during the summer and few people with whom to do something fun. The little recreation equipment that her family has is associated with activities Laura has mastered long ago. Laura feels that she can not really get away from her home which offers little that she finds satisfying. She often engages in activities that she feels are worthless or monotonous and is frustrated and bored.

Weissinger and colleagues (Iso-Ahola & Weissinger, 1990; Weissinger, Caldwell, & Bandalos, 1992) identified the following five factors as predictors of perceived boredom: self-determination, competence, leisure ethic, leisure repertoire, and age. As discussed earlier, individuals who lack intrinsic motivation are less likely to have feelings of self-determination and competence and are more likely to experience boredom in their free time. The specific goals of leisure education (to increase leisure appreciation, knowledge of resources, and a sense of self-determination) are designed to empower individuals to avoid boredom and experience the intrinsic motivation associated with leisure participation.

As illustrated in Figure 2.4, there is an inverse relationship between people experiencing reactance, learned helplessness, and boredom with their sense of competence and self-determination. Ultimately, leisure par-

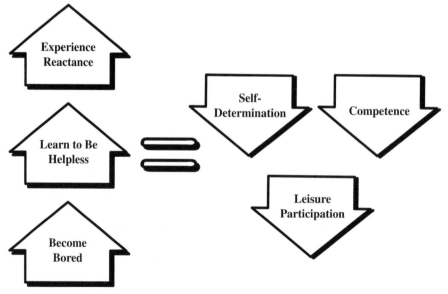

Fig. 2.4

ticipation is negatively impacted when people experience problems associated with reactance, learned helplessness, and boredom.

Summary

In this section of the chapter information about possible reasons for some people encountering problems with leisure has been presented. An understanding of inhibitors to leisure participation can be useful when professionals attempt to design leisure education programs intended to overcome these barriers.

Conclusion

Leisure is characterized by perceived freedom and intrinsic motivation, and is influenced by society. Society's influence comes largely from persuasive messages which influence individuals' attitudes and social norms. The result of these direct or subtle messages can have either a positive or negative influence on individuals leisure attitudes and behavior. The extent of society's influence over leisure may be partially determined by an individual's motivation to engage in leisure.

Leisure experiences are commonly associated with intrinsically motivated behavior. Experiences which are driven by intrinsic motivation may help individuals develop a sense of competence and self-determination. However, intrapersonal, interpersonal, and structural constraints to participation may have an adverse effect on an individual's intrinsic motivation. When individuals experience constraints, they may experience reactance, learn to be helpless, or become bored. Weissinger, Caldwell and Bandalos (1992) suggested that:

> When designing leisure education interventions, it may be useful to directly attempt to increase people's awareness of the potential psychological satisfaction inherent in leisure behavior. It may also be useful to expose individuals to knowledge about intrinsic motivation, the importance of choice and control, the significance of feelings of competence, and so forth. (p. 324)

Therefore, it may be helpful for professionals who are designing leisure education programs to consider how society influences attitudes about leisure, what motivates people to engage in leisure, and the constraints to participation they might experience.

Chapter 3
Potential of Leisure Education

Leisure . . . lifts up all heads from
practical workaday life to look at the
whole high world with refreshed wonder.
-Sebastian de Grazia

Introduction

In the previous chapter, discussions concerning the nature of leisure, societal influence on leisure, and factors motivating leisure involvement were provided. In this chapter attention is directed toward developing an understanding of the possibilities leisure education holds in managing constraints to leisure and facilitating and promoting the leisure experience.

To illustrate that leisure education can assist any individual in developing and maintaining a positive leisure lifestyle, the following questions are addressed:

(a) How can constraints to leisure be managed?
(b) How can the leisure experience be facilitated? and
(c) How can leisure education promote leisure?

How Can Constraints to Leisure Be Managed?

Typically, when people think of their leisure, they define the experience as freedom from responsibilities and obligations such as work commitments, school responsibilities, family obligations, house repairs, or car maintenance. Many people feel that if they had more time, money, and fewer responsibilities they could "really" enjoy themselves. Lee and Mobily (1988) identified this type of freedom as "circumstantial," meaning the ability of individuals to act according to their interests, desires, or wishes. Circumstantial freedom can also be used to refer to the freedom to complete a chosen act. Because most constraints are subjective feelings regarding individuals' perceptions of their ability to engage in an activity of their choosing, the individuals' perceptions govern the degree to which constraints influence leisure behavior (Kay & Jackson, 1991). Therefore, leisure participation is more dependent on an individual's ability to negotiate constraints than it is dependent on the absence of constraints (Jackson, Crawford, & Godbey, 1993).

The presence of real or perceived obstacles does not necessarily result in a person not participating in an activity. Rather, constraints may be managed in such a way that an individual's perceptions of leisure participation are still satisfying and capable of fulfilling his or her leisure desires. Jackson and colleagues (1993) identified the following three key points related to the negotiation of constraints: (a) people find a variety of ways to negotiate constraints; (b) leisure constraints do not necessarily result in nonparticipation; and (c) leisure participation will vary based on the negotiation or absence of constraints.

> For example, when Elizabeth first decided to try out for the hockey team at her high school she was denied the right to play on the team because she was a woman. Being denied the right to play initially left Elizabeth feeling sad and quite angry. Instead of accepting the coach's original decision, Elizabeth sought the support of her family and friends and eventually convinced the coach to let her try out for the team. After the coach saw the extent of her skills he decided that she would be a valuable asset to the team and permitted her to play. Although Elizabeth initially experienced constraints to participation she found a way to overcome that resistance and accomplish her goals.

Although individuals may find a way to negotiate constraints to leisure, the modified leisure experience is likely to be different than an unmodified leisure experience.

> Using the example above to illustrate, Elizabeth was required to expend considerable effort to participate in the leisure activity of her choosing. Because of the support she had to obtain to receive the opportunity to participate, extensive publicity was given to her. As a result of this publicity, she often felt as if there was intense pressure for her to do well. She did not want to disappoint her family and friends who supported her throughout the ordeal. In this instance, although Elizabeth did negotiate through her original constraint and is participating in the activity of her choosing, she may not be having as much fun as she could have if there had not been so much attention devoted to her cause.

Although understanding how to confront constraints and learning about the benefits of leisure may motivate people to initiate participation, there is no evidence that these characteristics promote continued participation (Meichenbaum, 1995). Personal goal attainment, satisfaction and enjoyment of activities appear to be stronger reinforcers of participation than skill development (Shephard, 1994). Methods to promote these experiences can be incorporated into leisure education programs to promote continued participation (i.e., adherence). In addition, enjoyment, influencing intrinsic motivation to continue activity, is implied by Csikszentmihalyi (1990) as a source of adherence. Wankel (1993) stated that enjoyment facilitated through an approach where individuals select an activity or context which appeals to them might help to enhance the probability that a positive experience may result in adherence. However, while important, the author emphasized that enjoyment is an individual perception. Since different people prefer different activities, assessing participants' preferences and offering programs based on what they desire are important aspects of leisure education that can increase the likelihood of adherence.

Although people typically find ways to negotiate constraints to their leisure, it is sometimes necessary to intervene directly and educate for leisure (Mannell & Kleiber, 1997). Leisure education was suggested by McGuire and O'Leary (1992) as a primary means of helping participants understand their leisure participation patterns and possible constraints to participation. These authors discussed the need for leisure service providers to understand constraints and how to facilitate the negotiation process. They suggested that it is helpful for services designed to assist individuals to negotiate leisure constraints that focus on the individual and the environment. Therefore, as seen in Figure 3.1 (see page 36), leisure education can be designed to reduce constraints to leisure, as well as minimize other barriers to leisure such as reactance, learned helplessness, and boredom.

How Can the Leisure Experience Be Facilitated?

To reduce the feelings of reactance, learned helplessness, and boredom which may result from not being able to participate in chosen leisure activities, leisure professionals can provide services designed to facilitate the leisure experience. Facilitating the leisure experience is not necessarily achieved when individuals are provided with recreation activities or encounter additional free time. Rather, professionals may help facilitate the leisure experience by considering the following principles when developing leisure services:

(a) get into the flow;
(b) achieve optimal arousal; and
(c) become socially connected.

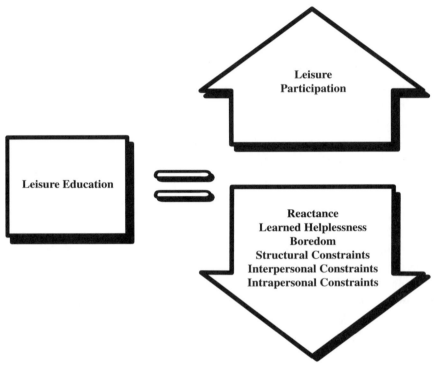

Fig. 3.1

Get Into the Flow

To move beyond boredom and anxiety, individuals may participate in activities that provide challenges that are commensurate with their skills (Csikszentmihalyi, 1975). Achieving a balance between the degree of challenge and skill required for an activity is referred to as "flow" by Csikszentmihalyi (1990). According to Csikszentmihalyi (1997, p. 29), "the metaphor of 'flow' is one that many people have used to describe the sense of effortless action they feel in moments that stand out as the best in their lives." Typically, flow experiences do not occur in periods of relaxation; rather, flow occurs when the activity requires the individual to "stretch" his or her physical and mental abilities (Csikszentmihalyi, 1993). In addition to the need to be challenged and have skills to meet the challenge, conditions which set the stage for flow include clearly identified goals and specific feedback associated with success. Therefore, in summary, Csikszentmihalyi (1990) stated that an activity is conducive for flow to occur if it: (a) presents a set of challenges matched to the person's level of skills; (b) has rules; (c) has clear goals; and (d) provides immediate feedback.

"Games are obvious flow activities, and play is the flow experience *par excellence*" (Csikszentmihalyi, 1992; p. 12). Csikszentmihalyi (1990) described those activities that create flow, such as games and play, that often result in the narrowing of a person's attention on a clearly defined goal. The focusing of an individual's attention creates a state of deep concentration and loss of conscious attention to the surrounding environment and one's own actions; thus, the person is able to focus attention exclusively on the task at hand (Csikszentmihalyi, 1992). If people engage in activities that produce flow they concentrate, expend effort and take control of the situation. Therefore, Dattilo and Kleiber (1993) suggested that professionals work on enhancing participants' involvement, concentration, effort, and a sense of control while promoting freedom of choice and the expression of preference.

A result of "getting into the flow" is that people experience intrinsic motivation and enjoyment (Csikszentmihalyi & Csikszentmihalyi, 1988). Although the word "enjoyment" is often used colloquially as the equivalent of fun or simple positive effect, in this usage it involves a considerable degree of psychological involvement as well (Dattilo & Kleiber, 1993). In addition, Massimini, Csikszentmihalyi, and Delle Fave (1988) observed that participants' desire to repeat an activity (adherence) is closely tied to whether they experienced flow during their participation. In addition to enhancing people's intrinsic motivation and enjoyment, Csikszentmihalyi, Rathunde, and Whalen (1997) noted that flow can result in improved cognition associated with complex thinking, self-actualization, and satisfaction.

People who are able to maintain and create flow situations in everyday life and from ordinary activities, thus enhancing their quality of life, are identified as people who are "autotelic" (Csikszentmihalyi, 1993). These individuals are believed to enjoy life more fully and develop a more complex sense of self than individuals who are not autotelic. Although flow is a desirable state associated with positive feeling, not all individuals are aware of how to create flow experiences within their current lifestyle. Therefore, individuals who are not autotelic may benefit from leisure education so they may learn how to experience flow and enhance their leisure lifestyle.

The conditions which set the stage for flow, experiences which occur while engaged in flow, and the consequences of flow are depicted in Figure 3.2 (see page 38).

As an example, Malcom "gets into the flow" when he sketches. He begins each drawing with a clear idea of what he would like to develop and receives immediate feedback on his efforts based on what he sees on the paper. As he sketches he must focus his attention and exhibit considerable effort when he moves the pencil across the paper. When Malcom draws he forgets about himself, his worries, and the time and becomes absorbed in the activity. After he completes a drawing, Malcolm experiences enjoyment associated with overcoming the challenge of drawing a picture which he finds pleasing. He views his artistic expression as an important part of who he is and is satisfied with the drawings he creates. The positive feelings Malcom has associated with drawing result in intrinsic motivation to engage in this pursuit and continue sketching in the future.

Fig. 3.2

Achieve Optimal Arousal

Iso-Ahola (1980) noted that optimal arousal which is depicted in Figure 3.3 is based on the degree of stimulation an individual derives from engaging in an activity. Either a person is motivated to seek arousal if the current situation is lacking stimulation, or escape arousal if the environment presents too much stimulation.

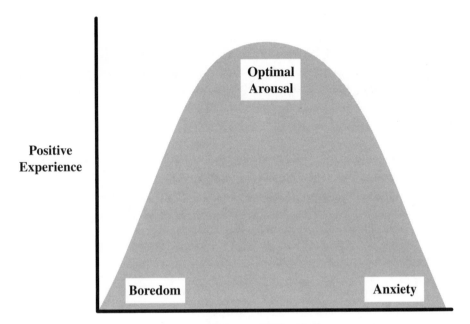

Degree of Stimulation

Fig. 3.3

    The degree of arousal an individual derives from participating in an activity changes daily, as well as over the course of the life span. This change in the ability of an activity to arouse a person occurs because the level of stimulation an activity provides will change from situation to situation and as the individual's skills develop. Participating in the same activity, with the same friend, in the same manner, may eventually no longer pose a challenge to a person.

    Individuals can alter the degree of stimulation they need to be optimally aroused by seeking (a) stability which is associated with security, and (b) change which involves novelty in activities in which they participate (Iso-Ahola, 1983). The desire to achieve a balance between stable and novel experiences can be accomplished within a particular activity.

> For example, Michele has enjoyed playing racquetball for more than five years. Although she continues to play on a regular basis with her friend, Jerry, she decided to begin participating in tournaments to alter the degree of challenge she receives from the sport.

Furthermore, a balance between stable and novel experiences can be achieved with recreation activities.

> For instance, Larry has participated in sports since he was an adolescent. In an effort to add variety to his free time, he recently enrolled in a photography class offered at the YMCA.

By balancing stable and novel leisure interests across the life span, individuals encounter increasingly complex interactions (Iso-Ahola, 1980). The importance of increased complexity in a person's life is that complexity encourages personal growth, happiness, and enjoyment, which can lead to an enhanced quality of life for the individual.

Become Socially Connected

Ashton-Schaeffer and Kleiber (1990) reported that because leisure provides individuals with the opportunity to interact with others in ways that are not coercive, individuals derive emotional value and a sense of well-being from participating. Furthermore, sustained participation in familiar activities may benefit participants by providing them with a sense of "connectedness" with others and their community. Connectedness with others may provide individuals with feelings of security and social competence (Smith & Mackie, 1995). Becoming socially connected in leisure is important because it helps people meet the need for "relatedness." According to Deci and Ryan (1991), relatedness refers to the need for individuals to feel they are loved and connected to others, that others understand them, and that they are meaningfully involved in the broader social world.

Kelly (1987) asserted that leisure can have a central role in individuals' lives throughout the life course, and may provide them with a sense of continuity. During leisure individuals may maintain social networks as well as build friendships. Particularly during periods of transition, leisure activity can offer a buffer against discomfort and stress associated with the experience and facilitate the development of new friends. Therefore, during moments of leisure, individuals may develop and maintain connections with other people and their community which can result in feelings of connectedness.

> For example, Diane recently graduated from college and is beginning a new career in a town far away from her family and friends. Immediately after settling into her new apartment, Diane was glad to learn that the local parks and recreation department offered a volleyball league. Having enthusiastically participated in the sport in college, Diane joined the league. Participation in the league has afforded Diane the opportunity to make several friends whom she now socializes with on a regular basis.

Summary

In summary, leisure service providers can help facilitate social interactions during leisure by creating an environment in which individuals are afforded an opportunity to make connections with others. Through leisure education people can be encouraged to become involved in recreation activities which challenge their existing skills, thus creating flow experiences. Finally, leisure service providers may be able to facilitate optimally arousing situations by providing a variety of consistent and unique programs in which participants may choose to be involved.

Addressing the questions raised in the introduction of this chapter has illustrated the complexities surrounding leisure participation. Given the aforementioned complexities of leisure participation, the potential role of leisure education in enhancing and developing optimal conditions which facilitate leisure participation for everyone is presented in the next section of this chapter.

How Can Leisure Education Promote Leisure?

In this section of this chapter four ways in which leisure education may foster the development of leisure opportunities are presented. Leisure education encourages leisure participation by:

(a) creating opportunities;
(b) building options;
(c) empowering individuals through a dynamic process; and
(d) developing relevant skills.

Leisure Education Creates Opportunities

It is important for people to have freedom, autonomy, choice, and self-determination (Murphy, 1975). Within the context of Lee and Mobily's (1988) assertion that natural freedom involves the irrevocable power that humans have for self-determination, and Bregha's (1985) position that leisure is the most precious expression of our freedom, a convincing case can be made that leisure is an inherent right of all humans. Therefore, attempts made to help people become involved in active leisure participation are considered important.

According to Kelly (1990, p. 385), "The main issue is that of opportunity: If leisure is the element of life in which unique opportunities for expression, development, and relationships are found, then should not a full range of opportunities be available for everyone?" The underlying assumption is that everyone should have opportunities for leisure experiences (Austin, 1989). According to Halberg (1989), all people have the right to a desired leisure lifestyle and optimal independence through the highest quality of coordinated services possible. Therefore, leisure education is based on the premise that all individuals, regardless of race, socioeconomic status, gender, color, religion, or ability, possess the right to experience leisure.

Wade and Hoover (1985) identified a lack of education and training as a major constraint to developing a sense of control during leisure participation. To overcome many people's lack of knowledge related to their leisure participation, leisure service professionals may wish to assist participants in exploring their leisure attitudes, increase their understanding of leisure, and enhance their awareness of available opportunities. As discussed previously in this chapter, one challenge in providing leisure services for many people is helping them identify and overcome constraints to their leisure participation. Another important challenge is to provide them with opportunities to develop the skills, awareness, and understanding needed to participate in freely chosen activities.

Leisure Education Builds Options

The intent of leisure education is to facilitate an individual's ability to choose to participate independently in meaningful leisure experiences. Hopefully, the outcome of this action will result in increased enjoyment and satisfaction. Leisure service professionals who want to facilitate their participants' ability to perceive the freedom associated with leisure experiences may consider developing programs that enhance options for participants (Lee & Mobily, 1988). Often through leisure education, people gain the awareness, appreciation, knowledge, and skills necessary for them to choose to be involved in leisure. Schleien, Tuckner, and Heyne (1985) identified self-initiated, independent leisure functioning in ordinary environments as the ultimate goal of leisure education.

A critical component of the provision of leisure services is the incorporation of choice. Unfortunately, choice making among many individuals continues to receive limited attention. As a result, some recreation activities are offered as passive stimulation, with limited thought to providing opportunities that allow individuals to express their preferences for participation. Participants' preferences are a major concern when developing leisure programs.

Central to the concept of building options, is the notion that individuals develop an awareness of the internal and external forces which influence leisure decisions. Because leisure is often a social experience, it can be useful to increase participants' awareness of the influence others have on their leisure choices. Individuals encounter constraints to leisure participation that remain outside their control such as work commitments, family obligations, financial constraints, physical barriers, and availability of services. To negotiate these constraints people can learn a variety of strategies that help them regain a sense of control over the situation (Jackson, Crawford, & Godbey, 1993).

Leisure Education Empowers Individuals

Leisure education is far from stagnant; it is a dynamic process involving continuous enhancement of leisure-related knowledge, skills, and awareness. The process requires the presentation of information intended to help individuals identify and clarify their leisure participation patterns. A purpose of leisure education is to instill a leisure ethic within people, so that they may freely and willingly participate in activities that can bring them satisfaction and enjoyment with the ultimate goal of having their participation in these activities enrich and enhance their lives.

One goal of leisure education is to help individuals develop an increased sense of awareness of themselves as they experience leisure (Peterson & Gunn, 1984). Development of an awareness of self in relation to leisure and of methods to facilitate involvement enhances the possibility that people will experience leisure. An important element of leisure education involves participants accepting responsibility for their leisure. Ultimately, people must feel that their ability to be happy and to have fun is up to them.

Leisure education also implies that individuals accept the idea that they can change and improve their current leisure participation patterns. Beliefs associated with phrases such as "I cannot do this," must change to "I do not do this now, but I will learn how to do it," and further evolve into "I will be able to do this!" To become self-determining, individuals must make choices, demonstrate preferences, and ultimately make decisions related to their leisure participation. Therefore, leisure education teaches individuals that they have the power to improve their lives through rewarding and fulfilling leisure participation.

Leisure Education Develops Relevant Skills

Among the major challenges facing leisure service providers is determining what to teach the people whom they serve. To manage this challenge, leisure service professionals can work with participants to teach them those skills which they have the most desire to learn and which have the greatest potential for increasing the quality of their lives. Ideally, one of the major outcomes of a leisure education program is for individuals to develop skills that can be used throughout life. Kelly (1987, 1990) contributed information which may help leisure service professionals develop the most effective and efficient leisure education programs.

Providing Balance. Human development spans the entire life cycle and individuals' leisure skills, interests and abilities are likely to change over time. Kelly advocated for a balanced approach to leisure through the development of a broad leisure repertoire. This recommendation was made in response to the observation that people pursue a variety of leisure experiences for many different reasons. Most individuals tend to select recreation activities that result in a balance between social and solitary, active and restful, high and low intensity, and engagement and escape environments. People often seek different combinations of environments, investments, and outcomes. Therefore, leisure education programs that teach individuals to posses a variety of skills should be helpful to many people. To teach participants several types of skills, leisure service providers can consider offering leisure education programs which contain multiple goals. Some leisure education programs might include goals such as: (a) increasing social skills required to develop new friendships, (b) attaining a sense of awareness and appreciation useful in self-development, (c) expressing individuality, and (d) developing philosophical positions. A lack of variety and balance in people's leisure involvement may create serious obstacles to participation in community leisure programs. The development of effective leisure education programs might help to alleviate this obstacle.

Although it is important for individuals to develop a repertoire of leisure skills to provide them with the flexibility to experience leisure in a variety of contexts and circumstances, another consideration is important. Frequently, the time practitioners have available to spend with individuals is limited. In addition, some people learn at a slower rate than others. As a result, professionals may teach only a few skills to any given person. Therefore, it is helpful if the skills which leisure service professionals teach participants are selected with care and in collaboration with participants, and, at times, with their families and friends.

Providing a Core. Professionals may need assistance in selecting skills to be taught in leisure education programs. One important source of reference is the desires and aspirations of participants. In addition, professionals can help identify those common day-to-day skills that impact the quality of an individual's life most significantly. Kelly (1983) identified a set of core activities that are typically low-cost, accessible, common to most adults, and do not vary greatly across the life span. By incorporating Kelly's model of developing core leisure education programs designed to foster and support the development of core recreation activities, leisure services may teach individuals how to: (a) interact informally with other household members; (b) converse in a variety of settings; (c) develop relationships and experience intimacy; (d) enhance living environments; and (e) maintain fitness. This core of leisure experiences occupies a great deal of time, especially those periods of time between scheduled events. Since people have diverse interests, it can be useful for leisure service providers to recognize that core recreation activities will vary depending upon participants' cultural and social histories.

Providing leisure services which combine a balance and core approach to leisure education may be useful. Consideration of core experiences increases the likelihood that leisure professionals will provide relevant leisure services that can be used immediately and consistently by consumers. Inclusion of a balance of experiences in a leisure education program expands the opportunities for participants to experience diversity and variety in their leisure lifestyles.

Summary

As illustrated in Figure 3.4 (see page 46), leisure education can create opportunities for all individuals to experience leisure. In addition, leisure education can be designed to build options for people so that they can make choices between meaningful leisure pursuits. As people experience opportunities and make choices they will then become empowered through leisure education to enhance their lives through leisure. Finally, through leisure education individuals can develop relevant skills which allow them to achieve a balanced and focused lifestyle which embraces leisure.

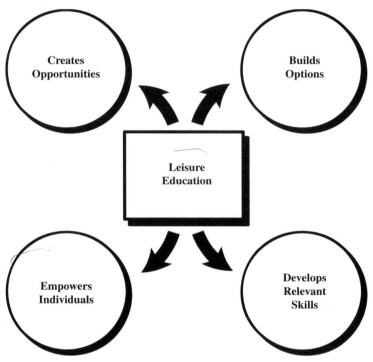

Fig. 3.4

Conclusion

Leisure education programs which focus on the individual and the environment may assist individuals in negotiating leisure constraints. Once constraints to leisure participation are negotiated, leisure experiences may be enhanced by facilitating flow, optimal arousal, and social connectedness through leisure. Leisure education represents a comprehensive approach to facilitating leisure experiences. Leisure education promotes leisure participation by creating opportunities for individuals to engage in various activities. In addition, leisure education may help build options and choices available to individuals. If individuals feel as if they have the freedom and opportunity to participate in activities of their choosing, they may experience a sense of empowerment. Finally, leisure education may enhance individuals' leisure lifestyle by assisting them in developing a balance of skills and core activities from which to draw.

Chapter 4
Recommendations for Leisure Education

Treat people as if they were what they
ought to be and you will help them
become what they are capable of becoming
-Johann von Goethe

Introduction

Although the topics of leisure and education have been debated for centuries, it was not until the late 1970s that the literature began to contain descriptions of how to systematically provide leisure education. This chapter is intended to familiarize readers with writings which are devoted to describing models, curricula and manuals on leisure education, and recommendations to follow when developing these programs. The following description of texts and articles devoted to leisure education is not intended to be exhaustive. However, it is hoped that the reader will gain an appreciation for the literature associated with leisure education. In addition, the resources identified in this chapter can be obtained and utilized so that an understanding of leisure education is enhanced, and other methods to facilitate the delivery of leisure education can be explored. In the past many useful articles and texts have been developed that are devoted specifically to leisure counseling (e.g., Compton & Goldstein, 1977; Dowd, 1984; Epperson, Witt, & Hitzhusen, 1977; McDowell, 1976); however, since the focus of this text is on leisure education and most of the literature since that time has been devoted to leisure education, detailed analysis of this body of literature will not occur.

This chapter is divided into three parts. The first section contains models for leisure education programs. The second describes the content presented in leisure education curricula and program manuals, many of which have been field-tested. The final section of this chapter outlines various recommendations that have been made concerning leisure education.

Leisure Education Models

In their text on leisure education Mundy and Odum (1979) suggested that leisure education provides a vehicle for developing an awareness of activities and resources, and for acquiring skills necessary for participation in leisure throughout life. According to the authors, as a result of leisure education, individuals enhance their experiences in leisure and understand the opportunities, potentials, and challenges that are available through leisure. The authors suggested that the impact of leisure education can be seen in the development of individuals' ability to understand the influence of leisure on the day-to-day pattern of their lives. Further, the authors wrote that as individuals with disabilities acquire the knowledge, skills, and appreciation that enable them to participate in broad leisure experiences, they will improve the overall quality of their lives. To implement leisure education services Mundy and Odum developed a systematic process intended to stimulate leisure awareness, self-awareness, decision making, social interaction, and leisure skill application.

Beck-Ford and Brown (1984) developed a systematic leisure education model that provided a logical sequence of learning experiences. The project that was reported in the text incorporated opportunities available in the community and provided guidelines for the development of individual step-by-step programs. Based on the early work of Mundy (1976), the authors explained that the leisure education process includes awareness of self and leisure, decision making, social interaction, and leisure and related skills.

Peterson and Gunn (1984) identified leisure education as a critical component of comprehensive leisure services that is focused on the development and acquisition of leisure-related skills, attitudes, and knowledge. They emphasized the need for professionals to offer more than activity skills instruction, and stated that practitioners must facilitate satisfying leisure involvement for participants by providing opportunities for participants to develop leisure awareness, social interaction skills, leisure resources, and leisure activity skills. They described the importance of individuals developing leisure awareness, which included knowledge of leisure, self-awareness, leisure and play attitudes, and decision-making skills. A major component of their leisure education model was identified as leisure resources. It included activity opportunities, as well as personal, family, home, community, state, and national resources. The authors also highlighted the importance of developing social interaction and leisure activity skills.

Witt, Ellis, and Niles (1984) developed a model of leisure education based on the belief that freedom is a critical element in leisure involvement and, therefore, efforts to reduce deficiencies in functioning require careful examination of individuals' perceptions of personal freedom. The authors recommended that practitioners work to increase participants' control and to enhance their perceived competence in leisure experiences, and they encouraged professionals to promote the development of intrinsic motivation in their participants and stimulate their participants' depth of involvement and playfulness. Throughout their presentation of leisure education, they emphasized optimizing leisure functioning in the appropriate environmental circumstances through a shared responsibility between participants and leisure service providers. Leisure education, as conceptualized by Witt and colleagues is reflected in the Leisure Diagnostic Battery (LDB). The LDB (Ellis & Witt, 1986), identified by Dunn (1984) as a comprehensive assessment, contains the following components: (a) leisure preferences, (b) playfulness, (c) knowledge of leisure opportunities, (d) leisure barriers, (e) depth of involvement, (f) leisure needs, (g) perceived competence, and (h) perceived control. Dunn reported that conceptualization of the LDB is well-established and provides a basis for construct validity, absent in many other assessment procedures.

Aguilar (1986) presented a four-phase framework for development and evaluation of leisure education programs. The first phase requires professionals to define leisure and identify education needs, to identify desired outcomes of the leisure education program, to design a feasible program, and to consider unique characteristics of participants. During the second phase, educational content is identified in the areas of leisure resources, knowledge of recreation opportunities, recreation skills, leisure skills, and leisure appreciation. The third phase involves identification of educational approaches requiring specification of intervention techniques, learning tools, conducive environment, and appropriate modeling behavior. Finally, Aguilar recommended systematic evaluation of the leisure education program, characterized by thorough examination of program design, employment of practical procedures, provision of outcomes, application of the triangulation approach, and useful information resulting in program enhancement.

Howe-Murphy and Charboneau (1987) supported application of integration and normalization principles in all aspects of leisure education programs and presented a model that included perceived competence, self-awareness, decision making, leisure skill development, resource utilization, and social skill development. They emphasized that leisure education programs should be facilitating social integration and interaction.

Hultsman, Black, Seehafer, and Hovell (1987) described the development of an implementation strategy for leisure education based on the Purdue Stepped Approach Model. This model increases the intensity of intervention presented in five steps which include minimal assistance, media-assistance, regular brief contact, group counseling, and individual counseling. The model is based on Neulinger's (1981a, 1981b) paradigm of leisure and its criteria of perceived freedom and intrinsic motivation. The initial step involves minimal assistance involving the simplest and least costly intervention that works for the individual. Next, the media-assisted instruction step incorporates the implementation of a self-help treatment program that requires participants to read and complete assignments independently.

The third step involves minimal contact resulting in brief and infrequent, but regularly scheduled, counseling contacts that are not necessarily face-to-face. Regularly scheduled group counseling sessions are contained in the fourth step of the model. Finally, the fifth step employs regularly scheduled individual counseling sessions. The authors' intention was to encourage the application of the Purdue Stepped Approach Model to leisure education to produce a potentially cost-effective alternative to traditional resource-intensive counseling approaches.

The Rehabilitation Research and Training Center in Mental Illness (1987) in cooperation with a number of organizations developed a training module on recreation and leisure designed to help a wide range of people in all age groups become more self-reliant and resourceful in the use of their free time. The recreation and leisure module contains a trainer's manual, a videotape, and a workbook. In each of these learning materials the following four skill areas are presented: (a) identify benefits of recreational activities; (b) obtain information about recreation activities; (c) determine what is needed for a recreation activity; and (d) evaluate and maintain a recreational activity. The general concept of problem solving is addressed throughout every aspect of the module.

Dattilo and Murphy (1987) presented a model containing the following five guidelines designed to assist practitioners with the task of developing effective leisure education programs on adventure recreation: safety consideration, resource identification, skill mastery, decision making, and participation. The first guideline involved participants learning about safety measures designed to protect them without detracting from the sense of challenge and adventure. The authors suggested that participants learn about available opportunities and resources for further participation. Mastering the skills required to engage successfully in specific adventure activities was identified as another important aspect of a leisure education program. An additional component required participants to develop the ability to make appropriate decisions based on their skill level, requirements of the activity, and possible consequences of participation. Finally, practitioners were encouraged to help people participate in the actual adventure experiences.

Bedini and Bullock (1988) presented a model of leisure education that was taught within the school system and through cooperative community-based programs. This model was based on the premise that the leisure education program would contribute to successful transition into the community of youth and young adults and the maintenance of appropriate leisure skills. Bedini and Bullock included the following three phases in their model: establish foundation; test and modify; and follow-up. To establish a foundation, professionals were encouraged to review records, conduct leisure classes, and meet with families. In addition, the authors identified the need for testing and modifications of leisure knowledge and skills within the classroom and community. Finally, follow-up services were identified as important to encourage families to support integration by emphasizing areas such as motivation, transportation, interaction with peers, and personal choice. The authors concluded that leisure education is an effective process to aid in the successful integration of young adults into their communities. Specifically, Bedini and Bullock emphasized the importance of cooperative programming among all related professionals.

Dattilo and St. Peter (1991) proposed a model for systematic and comprehensive leisure education services designed to overcome the barrier of limited leisure awareness, knowledge, and skills of young adults that prevent them from making successful transitions into active community living. The authors suggested development and implementation of a leisure education course. This course should be supplemented with community support by a leisure coach and active participation of individuals' families and friends. The leisure instruction was designed to instill the following into the lives of young adults, thus assisting them in making the transition to community living as an adult: (a) self-determination; (b) leisure appreciation; (c) self-awareness; (d) decision making; (e) social interaction; (f) knowledge and utilization of leisure resources; and (g) recreation participation.

In an effort to address the leisure related concerns of families, Malkin, Phillips, and Chumbler (1991) developed The Family Lab leisure education model. Through this program, adolescents and their families are provided instruction in the areas of communication, trust, values clarification, role playing, and enjoyment of leisure activities. Particularly in light of the fact that dysfunctional leisure patterns such as focusing recreational activities around drug use, withdrawal, isolation, or lack of participation can disrupt the entire family, the authors strongly advocated the use of family-based leisure education.

Based on the premise established by Dattilo and St. Peter (1991) that self-determination is at the foundation of leisure education, Wall and Dattilo (1995) discussed the importance of creating option-rich environments to heighten participants' self-determination. The authors explained that people frequently experience constraints to self-determination, such as limited opportunities for choice, unresponsive or controlling environments, and that there are strategies to enhance self-determination including: (a) developing goals for self-determination; (b) providing transdisciplinary services; (c) involving individuals in planning; (d) accessing individual preferences; (e) creating a responsive environment; (f) providing opportunities for self-determined behavior; (g) responding to self-determined behavior; and (h) teaching self-determination. It was concluded that option-rich environments can help facilitate empowerment.

In 1993 the World Leisure and Recreation Association through its Commission on Education sponsored an international seminar intended to formulate a common international platform for leisure education. Following the meeting, a book edited by Ruskin and Sivan (1995) was published which included the full text of the International Charter for Leisure Education, six keynote addresses, poster session articles, and an annotated bibliography. The leisure education models described in two of the chapters based on the keynote addresses are presented in the next two paragraphs.

Ruskin and Sivan (1995) specified goals, objectives, and strategies for infusing leisure education into school curricula. They presented a model for using leisure as a focus of learning activities which specified level of approach, objectives, learning activities, learning techniques, and expected outcomes. The objectives of this model include developing skills, knowledge of concepts, development of curiosity, use of information resources, development of thinking and appreciation, emotional openness, and development of creative capabilities. Ruskin and Sivan discussed the importance of learning activities and learning techniques such as discussions; reading and writing; out-of-school visits; listening, observing and spectating; trial and error; and play, drama and painting.

Fache (1995) suggested that, historically, a variety of leisure service and other community systems have included education for leisure as an integral part of their mission. According to the author, "One of the largest problems in implementing leisure education is the formulation of goal and strategy definition" (p. 73). Fache identified the following seven goals for leisure education that, according to the author, have received insufficient attention: (a) to diversify and widen a person's leisure repertoire; (b) to increase awareness of community opportunities/resources; (c) to bring about favorable attitude toward "leisuring;" (d) to encourage social contact and networks of friends; (e) to increase awareness of and ability to reduce constraints; (f) to enhance self-initiative and self-reliance; and (g) to increase ability and responsibility in time planning.

Later, Fache (1997) recommended that leisure education be systematically included in school curricula so that people's leisure repertoires will diversify and widen. He proposed that such efforts should bring about attitudes favorable to "leisuring" and Fache suggested that leisure education programs be designed to increase awareness of the variety of leisure opportunities and resources for leisure available in the community, develop social interaction skills to encourage social contact and integration in networking with friends, enhance self-initiative, self-organization and self-reliance, foster identity development in and through leisure, and bring about an environmentally sensitive behavior and culturally appropriate leisure behavior in other cultures.

Bullock and Mahon (1997) presented a conceptual model for person-centered leisure education designed to contribute to an individuals' satisfaction. The three domains of leisure education identified by the authors included awareness, skill learning, rehearsal, and self-determination. They suggested that leisure service providers encourage participants to develop an awareness of leisure, themselves, and resources. In addition, leisure education instruction can focus on developing leisure activity skills, community skills, and social/communication skills. Finally, the authors focused on self-determination by suggesting that practitioners provide opportunities for participants to learn to make decisions, plan their leisure, and independently initiate leisure participation.

Curricula and Program Manuals on Leisure Education

Joswiak (1979) developed a leisure education program manual emphasizing development of an awareness of leisure resources within the home and community. Implementing a systems approach to program design, Joswiak presented a program intended to increase awareness of three important aspects of leisure involvement such as the meaning of play and leisure, leisure resources in the home, and leisure resources in the community. The author recommended the application of systematic assessment and evaluation procedures to determine participant and practitioner success as well as identifying strategies for enhancing future programmatic effectiveness.

In their book Wuerch and Voeltz (1982) developed a leisure curriculum that outlined a process for leisure education designed to encourage extensive leisure involvement. The structure for an initial assessment to determine leisure activity selection, appropriateness of activities, preferences, and skill performance levels was described. Based on results of the initial assessment, the authors strongly encouraged practitioners to provide "choice training" designed to permit individuals to exert control over their environment.

McDowell (1983) published a set of ten booklets designed to assist readers in gaining an understanding of the concepts and helping strategies associated with developing "leisure wellness." The author leads readers through an exploration of self and leisure wellness by having them: (a) learn about the concept of leisure wellness; (b) understand wellness and associated principles; (c) develop intimate relationships; (d) explore self-identity and social roles; (e) develop strategies for fitness; (f) assess leisure lifestyle and formulate strategies; (g) develop coping strategies and manage stress; (h) manage attitudes, affirmation, and assertion; (i) manage economics, time, and cultural forces; and (j) establish a new model for leisure. The information was presented in booklet format in an attempt to increase readability and practical use by professionals.

Gushikin, Treftz, Porter, and Snowberg (1986) described a leisure education program to help individuals safely achieve self-initiated, meaningful leisure. The authors stressed the importance of identification of leisure interests and deficiencies which should then be matched with existing leisure opportunities. The value of teaching individuals new skills and conducting sessions identifying barriers that inhibit leisure involvement was highlighted. An important thrust of the program developed by Gushikin and colleagues was inclusion of follow-up appointments to ensure that participants were receiving the assistance necessary to engage in leisure activities.

Stumbo and Thompson (1986) compiled a manual of activities and resources associated with leisure education. The leisure education activities were categorized as mixers, social interaction skills, leisure awareness activity skills, and resources. The authors included specific information relevant to implementing these activities such as space requirements, equipment and materials, type of group, program goals, description and procedure, leadership considerations, and variations. They included a variety of activities associated with leisure education with the intent that the activities would be used to initiate or expand leisure services.

Wittman, Kurtz, and Nichols (1987) developed a booklet based on a model which was intended to be a frame of reference for leisure education, that contained activities, techniques, and resources. The authors used a sequential approach to organize the booklet into sections containing activities associated with reflection, recognition, and reaffirmation. Initially, readers were provided with activities which encouraged them to consider leisure as something unique to them. Following this portion of the booklet, activities were presented that allowed readers to clarify the role of leisure in their lives. In the final section, activities were provided to help readers determine the directions in which to proceed following instruction. The authors' approach to leisure education was founded on the principles of quality education for adults that include such aspects as collaborative planning, respect for "learned experience" of participants, and emphasis on processing and support.

Keller, McCombs, Pilgrim, and Booth (1987) developed a booklet designed to help practitioners encourage older adults to develop active leisure lifestyles. The authors presented a step-by-step process that was designed to assist professionals in helping their clientele to develop leisure habits and lifestyles which promote wellness. The six step process included: discovering leisure time activities and interests, exploring leisure interests, selecting a leisure activity, beginning the activity, checking on participant's progress, and investigating additional leisure pursuits.

Kimeldorf (1989) developed a workbook intended to help create what the author identified as "a spirit of playfulness within its readers." To achieve this state of playfulness, the author compiled games, exercises, daydreams, and scripts to facilitate people's search for leisure. He organized the workbook into the following five sections: examine leisure, explore leisure, decide about leisure, research leisure, and connect to leisure. The first portion of the booklet was devoted to having readers examine leisure by answering questions. The next part of the booklet contained activities that encouraged readers to explore what they have done in the past, examine their current patterns, and project into the future relative to leisure participation. Activities that provide readers with assistance in making decisions about specific leisure participation choices were provided in the third section. The fourth section described a seven-step process to assist people in researching new leisure possibilities. Finally, the booklet concluded with a section connecting participants with leisure opportunities by having them phone or visit with people to get information. The book is arranged in a logical progression to assist readers in developing a more meaningful leisure lifestyle.

Two publications from the G. Allan Roeher Institute focused on what Dattilo and Bemisderfer (1996) identified as an important component of leisure education, that of developing friendships. In the first manual, *Making Friends,* the following four areas were addressed: the importance of friends, obstacles to friendship, ingredients of friendship, and different approaches to building friendships.

Based on the premise that ". . . the desire to be with another person in particular leisure activities appears to be the most important aspect of leisure to the majority of people . . ." (p. 1), the manual, *Leisure Connections,* takes the reader through the following ten steps to develop meaningful leisure relationships: reflections on leisure, a dream is a wish, difficulties in achieving a dream, how important is friendship, leisure and companionship, overcoming difficulties in leisure and friendship, planning, generating realistic options and taking action, changing and adapting roles, and beyond the plan.

The Center for Recreation and Disability Studies at the University of North Carolina—Chapel Hill developed several manuals on leisure education. The Center developed the *Wake Leisure Education Program* to be included in public schools. The curriculum contained elements concerning leisure awareness, self-awareness in leisure, resources, barriers, planning, and outings (Bullock, Morris, & Garrett, 1991). The program included appendices such as a discussion of relevant legislation, an assessment guide, and a sample of a leisure education contract between a teacher and a facilitator.

The next year as a result of a federally funded three-year demonstration project, the Center developed a leisure education curriculum guide written by Bullock, Morris, Mahon, and Jones (1992) to facilitate independent community functioning. The program included detailed instructions for transition services, examples of charts, miscellaneous information such as crisis policy, resource information, evaluation methods, case studies, and a leisure education program. The project managers deemed the project a success and encouraged others to consider instituting the program in their communities. In 1992 the Center developed a comprehensive leisure education program that gave suggestions for a leisure educator's role in the school, community, and home. The program contained a curriculum with six units including leisure awareness, leisure resources, leisure communication skills, decision making, leisure planning, and leisure skills. Each unit contained recommendations for actions that could be taken in the classroom, community, and school. Also included were examples of how the curriculum has been used with various classes, programmatic suggestions, and teaching materials that might be useful in leisure education lessons such as illustrations of different activities.

Stumbo (1992) revised and updated Stumbo and Thompson's (1986) manual by adding additional activities in the areas of leisure awareness, social skills, activity skills, and leisure resources. In addition, the author included suggestions for designing leisure education activities, a review of various relevant assessments, and a discussion of Peterson and Gunn's (1984) model for leisure education.

Similar to the text *Making Friends* developed by the G. Allan Roecher Institute, Heyne, Schleien, and McAvoy (1993) compiled a document devoted to friendship. The handbook is based on the results from a three year friendship program and a comprehensive statewide survey of best practices in inclusive recreation conducted in Minnesota. The handbook contains information on what friendship means for children, what inhibits friendships, how to encourage friendships, and how to facilitate friendships in recreation.

Owen and Gannon (1994) developed a recreation and leisure choice-making training manual. The manual included lesson outlines, suggested narratives, and teaching aids such as prepared overhead transparencies. Training included such topics as making choice a reality, understanding recreation and leisure, considering learning and behavior principles, services and supports, sexuality, and health and wellness.

Dehn (1995) designed a leisure education program with an instructor's manual and a workbook for participants. Each of the eleven steps toward achieving a satisfying leisure lifestyle was divided into several lessons. The lessons contained written exercises, instructions from the leisure educator, and practice exercises for using the leisure skills. The program has been used as part of a wellness education program and in a variety of settings. The eleven steps which organized Dehn's manual encouraged participants to gather information, leisure plan, leisure education, recreation participation, leisure of the past, leisure of the future, community participation, expressive leisure participation, physical leisure participation, cultural leisure participation, and post discharge leisure participation.

As a sequel to the text by Wuerch and Voeltz (1982), Schleien, Meyer, Heyne and Brandt (1995) provided detailed, field-tested task analyses accompanied by instructional support procedures for ten recreation activities which included aerobic warmups, the vertical checkers game "Connect Four," the game "Jenga," the catch and throw game "Magic Mitts" ("Scatch"), "Nintendo Game Boy Compact Video System," pinball, pottery, remote control care, the electronic game "Simon" and target games using Velcro, beanbags, and other similar objects. In describing what to teach in leisure education Schleien and colleagues identified the following six major types of activities: (a) at school and extracurricular; (b) alone at home or in neighborhood; (c) with family and friends at home or neighborhood; (d) physical fitness; (e) with family and friends in the community; and (f) alone in the community.

In the text by Schleien and colleagues (1995), Dattilo recommended instruction in choice-making to enhance to the leisure of people with disabilities. The goal of such instruction was identified as to "provide direct programming to teach people how to make activity choices during their free time and to generalize leisure skills from a highly structured instructional environment to one more closely approximating naturally occurring leisure environment" (p. 135). To that end, the author encouraged professionals to create environments supportive of self-initiated communication, select appropriate leisure activities from which participants can choose, understand free time and activity options, and select a teaching method.

McGill (1996) reported on the development of a leisure education program focused on facilitating leisure identities in people with mental retardation. The program contained elements of self-exploration, relationship skills, self-image, exploration of personal competence, rhythms and routines of leisure activities, and the development and maintenance of leisure identities. The author proposed that promotion of leisure identities would lead to "a new vibrance and gentleness developing in ourselves and in our communities" (p. 107).

Riches (1996) proposed a social skills program and presented both programming skills such as needs assessment and objective setting and specific training manual units. The training units included relational competence, greetings, nongreetings and partings, requests and inquiries, handling refusals, social courtesies, apologies, conversation skills, conversation topics, handling praise and criticism, and friendships. Riches suggested that social skills competence is essential for people who experience a positive quality of life.

Dattilo and Bemisderfer (1996) developed a leisure education curriculum containing 54 one-hour lessons covering the following five units: leisure appreciation, social interaction and friendship, leisure resources, self-determination, and decision making. The curriculum was field-tested using three different sets of participants with lessons conducted approximately three times per week over an 18-week period. The content and process for each lesson was provided with each lesson containing a review, introduction, assessment, presentations and discussions, learning activities, debriefings, an evaluation, and conclusion. Because the curriculum focused on adolescents, much of the instruction focused on identification and utilization of resources as well as developing social skills need for making friends.

General Recommendations for Leisure Education

Since many people fail to adjust to community living because of inappropriate use of their leisure, Hayes (1977a, 1977b) recommended implementation of a program combining leisure education and recreation counseling intended to help individuals select and participate in recreation activities and develop necessary skills for meaningful leisure involvement. Hayes proposed a leisure education model designed to involve participants in meaningful recreation activities within the community which would result in the development of positive feelings. He suggested that procedures must be developed to adequately prepare individuals to cope with free time and facilitate their involvement in total community living.

Based on observations that public schools have done little to develop social leisure skills and attitudes for individuals with disabilities, Collard (1981) identified ways to support interdisciplinary cooperation for leisure education in the schools. After presenting a rationale for inclusion of leisure education in the public schools, the author proposed potential roles for the recreation professional and the classroom teacher. Specific guidelines on becoming an advocate for leisure education were presented. These identified the right people to approach (e.g., parent groups, educators, administrators, nonprofit organizations, governmental agencies) and what to say to these people once their attention is obtained.

As an alternative to the provision of diversional recreation activities, Dunn (1981) encouraged practitioners to employ leisure education strategies that facilitate increased leisure independence. Possible leisure education goals, objectives, and program processes were outlined. The author suggested various ideas intended to promote community adjustment.

Voeltz, Wuerch, and Wilcox (1982) stated that a rationale for leisure education can be provided by examining its effects not only in the area of leisure but also in the participant's entire life patterns. The effects of leisure education can be enhanced by the acquisition of skills that prepare individuals for community adjustment in least restrictive environments. According to the authors, it is important to involve family members and relevant professionals as well as the individual when developing a leisure education plan.

Development of age-appropriate, community-based leisure skill repertoires that facilitate successful integration into the community is extremely important for all individuals. Ford and colleagues (1984) suggested that leisure service professionals encourage participants to acquire leisure skills that are age-appropriate and comparable to their peers. Practitioners should ensure the teaching of those leisure skills that have the potential of being performed in the presence of, or in interaction with, peers (Schleien & Ray, 1988).

Dealing with the increased free time associated with retirement can be a difficult adjustment for some older adults. Mobily (1984) suggested that leisure education can be a useful tool in helping older adults adjust to retirement. Leisure education may help individuals overcome the perception that leisure can only be earned through productive work and may help individuals increase their awareness of and change their attitudes toward leisure. In addition, many individuals faced with retirement are confronted with feelings of helplessness which result from a drastic change in daily life patterns (Mobily, 1984). Leisure can provide an excellent avenue to increase an individual's feelings of control because he or she is free to decide what activity to participate in, with whom, and how often play will occur. Leisure education aimed at enhancing older adults' attitudes toward leisure and reducing their feelings of learned helplessness may be helpful in easing their transition into retirement.

Wehman and Moon (1985) recommended inclusion of fun and enjoyment when designing and implementing leisure programs. They stated that leisure education programs should stimulate constructive or purposeful behavior, accompanied by participation in activities. Programs that are most effective encourage self-initiated behavior and choice. More specifically they emphasized the importance of considering age-appropriateness when selecting leisure skills for instruction. Practitioners are encouraged to consider the attitudes of family members when developing programs intended to reduce barriers to leisure participation. The availability of leisure materials in the home and the types of community resources that are available is another important consideration. Consulting with consumers is critical to any leisure program designed to allow practitioners the opportunity to respond to the attitudes, aptitudes, and skills of the participants.

Putnam, Werder, and Schleien (1985) made suggestions for developing leisure services based on qualitative aspects of leisure involvement and participants' individual preferences. Practitioners are encouraged to give attention to the implications of participation on people's quality of life. The authors identified several recent trends to be addressed when developing a leisure curriculum. Community-referenced instruction that incorporates environmental inventories is an important step in validating leisure instruction and preparing people for active leisure participation within the community. All leisure programs are to be appropriate for the age of the participants regardless of skill level. Recreation departments which incorporate leisure education into their programs are encouraged to attempt to individualize the programs to respond to individual participant preferences. In addition, they strongly advocated leisure participation in community settings and provided useful guidelines to facilitate this participation. An investigation of community leisure services and identification of inhibitors and facilitators of leisure participation was recommended. Development and support of leisure programs fostering community involvement should utilize all community programs that provide leisure services.

Bregha (1985) suggested that leisure understanding, awareness, and control can be accomplished through leisure education. The goal of leisure education is to encourage people to make effective leisure choices. A comprehensive leisure education program can help participants develop skills and behaviors and allow them to realize that their behaviors can have an effect on the environment.

Falvey (1986) identified many activity dimensions to consider when designing, developing, and implementing leisure education programs. She, too, suggested that leisure opportunities be chronologically age-appropriate. Professionals are encouraged to provide opportunities for social interaction. A variety of skills and knowledge should be presented to individuals and efforts should be made to increase accessibility to leisure services. Preferences of participants and their families should be considered as well as relevance of specific leisure skills to a variety of environments. When specific skills are targeted for instruction, the potential for adaptation should be examined. To facilitate implementation of an effective leisure curriculum, Falvey recommended inclusion of components originally identified by Williams, Brown, and Certo (1975) who suggested the components for instructional programs should be focused on the following questions: (a) What activity should be taught? (b) Why should an activity be taught? (c) Where should an activity be taught? (d) How should an activity be taught? (e) What performance criteria should be sought? (f) What materials should be used? and (g) What measurement strategies should be used?

Schleien and Ray (1988) (and in a second edition, Schleien, Ray & Green, 1997) identified the importance of teaching leisure skills that are naturally occurring, frequently demanded, and have a specific purpose. In addition, the authors encouraged instruction of leisure skills that are typically performed by peers while participating in the leisure education program.

After interviewing 19 adults who resided in group homes, Malik (1990) noted participants limited understanding of the terms "recreation" and "leisure." In response to this observation, she recommended that service providers offer leisure education programs that focus on knowledge and aware-ness of leisure and recreation. In addition, the author reported that respon-dents indicated that friendships and social interaction were extremely im-portant to them. This result prompted Malik to suggest the provision of leisure education programs that also include social interaction training and facilitation of friendships.

In the process of describing the emerging challenge of serving older adults with mental retardation, Boyd and James (1990) reported that leisure education is usually a prerequisite for independent recreation participation. The authors warned that professionals should not interpret this as implying that a once-in-a-lifetime program would be sufficient to eradicate learned helplessness in many of the lives of people receiving intensive clinical ser-vices. The authors strongly advocated the provision of leisure education to empower individuals with disabilities to voice preferences and make deci-sions. These recommendations are especially true for older adults with dis-abilities who may have spent many years in protective and highly structured environments that resulted in repeated circumstances that denied most op-portunities for choice and control.

Strachan (1995) suggested that practitioners consider the importance of leisure education for middle-aged adults. Strachan highlighted the need for such programs to fit the individual needs of their customers rather than fit the individual into an already existing program. Strachan suggested a three-phase leisure education program to accomplish this objective. Initially it is helpful to consult with a participant to discern his or her individual needs. Once the trust of the individual has been gained, the focus of the discussion can focus on self-awareness and community awareness. The next step of the program is to pair the participant with a volunteer who could provide indi-vidual support and assistance in reaching the set goals. Finally, Strachan suggested that the leisure education program focus on facilitating commu-nity involvement by having participants make a list of barriers to participa-tion and systematically working though each barrier with the participant.

Kelland (1995) outlined a leisure education treatment protocol with the goal of the development of leisure skills, knowledge and attitudes. Leisure education topics suggested by the protocol included understanding and ap-preciation of leisure, barriers, resources, and time management. The author recommended a wide range of facilitation techniques including discussion groups, experiential learning, lectures, pen-and-paper exercises, audio-visual aids, and discussion.

Leitner, Leitner, and Associates (1996) identified leisure education as important to the well-being of society. The authors equated leisure with psychological well-being and suggested that leisure education should be a "continuous, lifelong process" (p. 32), especially in light of a constantly changing world. Leisure planning was suggested as one way to enhance leisure lifestyles. Among the authors's suggestions were goal setting, time management techniques, and reducing the amount of time spent in sleep.

Sivan and Ruskin (1997b) described techniques and strategies associated with leisure education which have been used successfully. They suggested focusing on leisure when conducting any type of learning activity. In addition, they recommended incorporating leisure education into the schools during recess, school trips and outings and extended day programs. The focus of their suggestions were on incorporating leisure education within the educational system.

Conclusion

This review of leisure education models, curricula, manuals, and recommendations is intended to provide a representative of the current level of knowledge related to leisure education. Such knowledge can be incorporated into a cohesive foundation supporting the provision of quality leisure education. Leisure education programs may vary in content, frequency, duration, format, participants, and other factors. They may also vary in the resources required to implement them. The thread that connects all leisure education programs is the goal of providing assistance to participants to enable them to add meaning to their lives through leisure.

Chapter 5
Effects of Leisure Education

*Education is what survives when
what has been learnt has been forgotten.*
-B.F. Skinner

Introduction

This text has been written from a leisure-oriented perspective on leisure education. According to Peterson (1989), a leisure-oriented perspective implies that the ultimate outcome of leisure services is related to leisure behavior and the orientation draws on existing knowledge relevant to leisure. In this chapter, a summary of selected studies drawn from the literature on leisure behavior is presented which provides insight into the effects of leisure education. The studies summarized in this chapter are intended to assist practitioners in developing defensible rationales for the leisure education programs they might devise. In addition, it is hoped that this chapter will enable instructors to justify leisure education to administrators, supervisors, staff, program participants, and other interested parties.

Typically researchers have examined the impact of leisure education programs on individuals experiencing obvious constraints to their leisure: people who are older, have been abused, have social constraints due to chemical dependencies, have cognitive limitations, have mental health problems, and are incarcerated. In addition, studies have identified problems associated with studying leisure education such as programs of limited duration and those which raise expectation beyond resources. Finally, research has been conducted which has explored the overall support for leisure education. To organize the studies reported in the literature the following categories are used in this chapter:

(a) programs for older adults;
(b) programs for people who have been abused;
(c) programs for people with chemical dependence;
(d) programs for people with cognitive impairments;
(e) programs for people who are incarcerated;
(f) programs limited in duration;

(g) programs which raised expectations; and

(h) support for leisure education.

Programs for Older Adults

Lifestyle changes often associated with aging (e.g., increased discretionary time, health issues) can bring about constraints to leisure that have been addressed by researchers. Backman and Mannell (1986) compared the effectiveness of using a traditional approach to teaching recreation activities, and exposing people to new activities with a leisure education approach focused on changing the attitudes and awareness of leisure of 40 residents of a senior citizens' facility. The residents involved in the program were encouraged to explore their feelings about work, leisure, and free time and to plan for themselves. The authors reported that residents changed their attitudes to become more positive about leisure. However, the residents provided with the traditional approach exhibited no change in their attitudes. The investigators observed that the development of more positive attitudes toward leisure appeared to allow higher levels of satisfaction to be derived from participation.

Searle and Mahon (1991) examined the effects of a leisure education program for older adults whose mean age was 77 years. The participants resided in a day hospital where 26 of the adults were assigned to an experimental group and 27 to a control group. The experimental group participated in one-hour leisure education sessions once a week for eight weeks. Results of the analysis of covariance for the dependent variables (i.e., locus of control, perceived competence, and self-esteem) were all statistically significant. The authors concluded that the study provided further evidence of the effectiveness of leisure education, specifically as a technique for enhancing the ability of older adults to sustain themselves in an independent living environment.

Keller and Hughes (1991), in their work with caregivers of older adults with impairments, concluded that when caregivers are provided with leisure-based information, awareness, resources and skills, the caregivers are more likely to use leisure as a coping mechanism for dealing with the stress which is inherent in the occupation.

Searle and Mahon (1993) suggested that older adults may benefit from learning to use their free time effectively through their participation in leisure education programs. Specifically, they tested the effects of a leisure education program on respondents' perceptions of leisure competence, self-esteem, and internal locus of control. A three-month follow-up measure revealed that leisure education did affect respondents' perceived leisure competence. Although changes in self-esteem and internal locus of control were not statistically significant, the authors contended that leisure education can be beneficial to older adults.

In another study, Searle, Mahon, Iso-Ahola, Sdrolias, and Van Dyck (1995) used an experimental design to investigate the effects of a leisure education program. Participants were assigned to either an experimental group containing 13 people that participated in a leisure education program based on Bullock and Howe's (1991) model or a control group containing 15 people. Although participants in the experimental group completed the 12-unit self-study program at their own pace, it took an average of 17 weeks (working approximately one hour per week) to complete the program. Results indicated that participants in the experimental group significantly improved leisure control and satisfaction and reduced leisure boredom. It was concluded that leisure education can be an effective means to improve individuals' perceived locus of control and competence, each of which is an important aspect of independence in leisure.

Lovell, Dattilo, and Jekubovich (1996) conducted a study to determine the effects of leisure education on aging women with disabilities. Half the participants received leisure education for approximately one hour per day, five days per week for a period of three weeks (15 total hours of leisure education) while the other half did not. The leisure education program consisted of the content areas outlined by Dattilo and Murphy (1991). Two separate data collection methods were used in the investigation: participant interviews and the Leisure Diagnostic Battery (LDB). Results of the LDB were largely inconclusive with the exception of the finding that the women who had received leisure education were more aware of barriers to leisure involvement. However, the interviews revealed that the participants in both groups had common concerns related to leisure involvement. Themes that emerged from the interviews included: (a) reduced leisure repertoires; (b) requirements to make decisions; (c) desires for control; and (d) importance of personal goals.

Dunn and Wilhite (1997) developed an eight-week leisure education program conducted twice per week with evaluation sessions lasting approximately one hour. The Community Reintegration Program Leisure Education Model was used (Bullock, Morris, & Garrett, 1991) and sessions were designed based on the format developed by Dattilo and Murphy (1991). The authors examined the effects of a leisure education program on the leisure behavior and emotional well-being of older adults who were home-centered. Using a single-subject multiple-baseline across participants design, Dunn and Wilhite found that the frequency and duration of leisure participation was positively affected by the leisure education program. The program had no apparent effect on the emotional well-being of participants.

Programs for People Who Have Been Abused

Both systematic and acute occurrences of abuse can lead to constraints to leisure lifestyles. Some leisure education programs have been designed and evaluated that attempt to address such constraints. Sheffield, Waigandt, and Miller (1986) investigated the postrape leisure behavior of sexual assault victims by analyzing data relative to leisure and social activity. Leisure behavior in the areas of physical and social activity appeared to be a factor in the successful recovery of participants. The authors suggested that leisure education programs intended to assist the adjustment of sexual assault victims should include counseling for appropriate skills in the areas of social interaction, self-control, and relaxation.

McDonald and Howe (1989) developed a challenge/initiative program using a leisure education approach for 38 child abuse victims. They supplemented a 40-minute activity period with a required 20-minute debriefing discussion that emphasized group dynamics and self-awareness. The program ran for 28 consecutive days. Results indicated the educational program significantly enhanced self-concepts of participants and supported the model for leisure education in adventure recreation proposed by Dattilo and Murphy (1987a). McDonald and Howe suggested further examination of the use of debriefing sessions in association with recreation activities focused on self-concept and other leisure-related factors.

Programs for People with Chemical Dependence

Rancourt (1991) conducted a qualitative study that described the participation of 40 women in a leisure education program. Participants were residents in a substance abuse treatment facility. By the conclusion of the program, many participants reported several benefits gained in the leisure education program including a new ability to choose "leisure experiences that could meet their needs" (p. 17) and newfound knowledge of the importance of leisure to families. Participants listed several benefits of leisure to the recovery process including drug-free stimulation, having fun while being sober, an ability to cope with stress, and an openness to novel experiences.

Although no leisure education intervention was used with respondents in their study, McCormick and Dattilo (1992) discussed the potential benefits of leisure education for individuals who were alcoholics. In their study with members from Alcoholics Anonymous, the authors found that respondents had difficulty structuring free time. Respondents identified three factors which affected their leisure and/or free time: (a) they saw themselves as being "different" from those around them; (b) they believed that their drinking affected free-time use; and (c) they experienced a loss of social interaction due to recovery from alcoholism. The authors suggested that leisure education can assist individuals who abuse substances by teaching them how to restructure free time use, how to increase social interaction skills, and how to improve self-awareness.

Aguilar and Munson (1992) suggested that leisure education could be an integral element of substance abuse intervention and prevention programs. The authors recommended grounding leisure education programs in theoretical frameworks such as Bandura's (1977) theory of self-efficacy, and substitutability theory (Iso-Ahola, 1986). Self-awareness, leisure awareness, social interaction, decision making, resource awareness, and leisure skills were suggested as potential areas of leisure education program content. The authors suggested several instructional formats but noted that active involvement of participants might enhance learning. They suggested that since an ideal length for leisure education programs does not exist, they recommended that leisure educators focus on other elements such as intensity. The authors concluded that leisure should "no longer be ignored as a critical component to substance abuse intervention and prevention programs" (p. 30).

Measuring the efficacy of a leisure education program can be complicated. One way to address the complexities involved is to use multiple research methods. One method of investigation may miss important results that other methods might reveal. For instance, Jekubovich, Dattilo, Williams, and McKenney (in press) studied the effects of a leisure education program on 30 adults in treatment for chemical dependencies. Three methods of data collection were used: open-ended questions, field observations, and scores from the Leisure Diagnostic Battery. The four-week leisure education intervention consisted of 12 one-hour sessions following the format developed by Dattilo and Murphy (1991) and the content included the following areas: (a) defining leisure; (b) barriers to leisure; (c) overcoming barriers; (d) personal leisure interests; (e) benefits of leisure; (f) community resources; and (g) meeting personal needs through leisure. Although according to results of the Leisure Diagnostic Battery, the leisure education intervention had no effect on the participants, the open-ended questions and the field observations yielded support for the effectiveness of the intervention.

Programs for People With Cognitive Impairments

People with mental retardation who reside in the community often experience constraints to leisure participation. Constraints to participation may stem from a lack of recreational skills, lack of adequately trained staff, lack of care provider support, and attitudinal and transportation barriers.

Anderson and Allen (1985) conducted an investigation incorporating Joswiak's (1979) leisure education program using two 80-minute sessions per week for nine weeks (totaling 24 hours of instruction) for 40 individuals with mental retardation. Anderson and Allen used the dependent measure of activity involvement. They found that participation in a leisure education program that emphasized knowledge of leisure resources increased the frequency of activity involvement. The program, however, did not appear to affect duration of activity involvement, frequency of social interaction, or duration of social interaction. The investigators recommended that social skill development become a priority in leisure education and that training should continue beyond the brief program they used. Although the results of their investigation were mixed, they strongly supported the inclusion of planned intervention following activity involvement.

Schleien and Larson (1986) determined that a leisure education program designed to teach two adults with severe mental retardation how to use a community-based recreation center was helpful in overcoming these constraints. Specifically, the authors found that leisure education helped these individuals develop age-appropriate leisure skills, independently access a community-based recreation facility, and partially, but effectively, independently communicate their leisure preferences to community recreation center staff.

Lanagan and Dattilo (1989) demonstrated that a leisure education program for adults with mental retardation can produce a higher incidence of involvement than a recreation participation program. They reported favorable results for a leisure education program for 39 adults with mental retardation, consisting of 30-minute periods for 55 sessions across a two-month time span. In addition, the results indicated that many participants retained some of the information they learned. Therefore, professionals should consider the inclusion of leisure education programs when attempting to provide comprehensive leisure services.

Bedini, Bullock, and Driscoll (1993) determined that a leisure education program can help individuals with mental retardation develop skills required in the transition from school to adult life. Thirty-eight high school students in special education classes participated in the Wake Leisure Education Program. Information covered in the program included leisure awareness, self-awareness in leisure, leisure opportunities, community resource awareness, barriers, personal resources and responsibility, planning, planning an outing, the outing, and outing evaluation and future plans. An analysis of the quantitative and qualitative data revealed that individuals who participated in this program had substantial changes in a variety of behaviors and attitudes. Strong positive changes were observed in the areas of competence, perceived control, communication barriers, social barriers, self-esteem, leisure satisfaction, life satisfaction, assertiveness, and choice-making.

Although Bedini and colleagues (1993) reported positive effects of a leisure education program for high-school students with mental retardation, they observed that some participants expressed dissatisfaction with leisure after the intervention. Similar to the findings of Caldwell, Adolph, and Gilbert (1989), they suggested that increased information and awareness of leisure may be constraining if individuals increase their expectations regarding leisure but do not act on their intentions to participate in leisure. Feelings of dissatisfaction may also result from parents and teachers verbally supporting leisure education, but lacking the time, resources, money, and understanding of the benefits of leisure to provide limited support to leisure education programs. The authors suggested that efforts to improve leisure education services for individuals with mental retardation should focus on offering leisure education to individuals when they are in elementary school rather than high school since many of their patterns have already been set by that time, and these efforts should advocate for policy changes in schools and developing materials that will help parents and teachers pursue education for leisure.

Mahon and Bullock (1993) suggested that leisure education is valuable because it helps individuals achieve their goals. Moreover, in a study with teachers and parents of young people with mental retardation, they concluded that those who work with and care for youth with mental retardation believe that leisure education programs are important and valuable.

Mahon (1994) used a multiple-baseline design to study the effects of a leisure education program that focused on self-determination. Four adolescent males with mental retardation participated in the study. Results indicated that participants learned techniques that helped them become more self-determined in leisure than they were before the program. Mahon concluded that self-determination in leisure can be facilitated.

Mahon, Bullock, Luken, and Martens (1996) developed a leisure education program for adults with severe and persistent mental illness titled "Reintegration Through Recreation." Mahon and colleagues administered three surveys to determine the social significance of goals for the leisure education program, the social appropriateness of the leisure education program, the social appropriateness of the leisure education intervention strategies, and the social importance of the effects of the leisure education program. The authors reported that, in general, participants, family members, and service providers considered the goals, interventions, and outcomes of a leisure education program to be socially valid. They concluded that the "results underscored the importance of including consumers and persons closely associated with them in the process of refining leisure education interventions" (p. 211).

Mahon and Martens (1996) examined the effects of a three-phase leisure education program on the leisure satisfaction of a convenience sample of nine adults with developmental disabilities using quasi-experimental, pretest, posttest, field-based design. The three phases of the leisure education program included: (a) leisure awareness and decision making; (b) planning alternative tomorrows with hope; and (c) leisure initiation. Participants demonstrated significant increases in leisure satisfaction, as measured by scores on the Leisure Satisfaction Scale (Hoover, Wheeler, & Reetz, 1992), following the completion of the leisure education program as compared to their leisure satisfaction levels prior to the introduction of the intervention. Overall, Mahon and Martens concluded that the participation demonstrated increased integrated recreation participation, enhanced leisure satisfaction, an increase in friendships, and, for some, self-confidence.

Primarily employing a single-subject multiple baseline across participants design, Williams and Dattilo (1997) examined effects of an eight-week leisure education program on self-determination, social interaction, and positive affect during the discretionary time of young adults with mental retardation. The leisure education program used was a modified version of the leisure education curriculum titled "Transition Through Recreation and Integration for Life" (Project TRAIL). Results indicated that the leisure education program had little effect on the self-determination and social interaction patterns of participants, but participants exhibited positive affects during discretionary time more frequently after participating in the leisure education program than before.

Based on the components of a leisure education program for youth with mental retardation proposed by Dattilo and St. Peter (1991), Dattilo and Hoge (1999) developed and tested the Project TRAIL system for leisure education. To extend previous research by Bedini and colleagues (1993), effects of the Project TRAIL leisure education program were determined using a single-subject design to examine participants' positive affect; a formative competency testing procedure to assess participants' achievement of objectives; and two face-to-face surveys with participants, family members and teachers to determine the social validity of the program. Dattilo and Hoge concluded that the 19 participants with mental retardation involved in the Project TRAIL leisure education program conducted in the public schools and the community enjoyed themselves as they acquired socially valid leisure knowledge and skills.

Programs for People Who are Incarcerated

Aguilar and Asmussen (1989) suggested that leisure education can be used with adults in correctional facilities and conducted a study with 165 men who were incarcerated in a state penitentiary. They used a survey questionnaire to try to understand respondents' current and previous (prior to incarceration) leisure participation patterns. Based on their findings, the authors concluded that leisure education enhanced respondents' leisure awareness by teaching them to develop strategies for using their time effectively.

Programs Limited in Duration

Some investigations have focused on the impact of extremely brief leisure education programs. Five such programs will be reviewed in this section. In all five studies, the impact of the brief leisure education programs was measured using fairly stable characteristics such as attitudes and self-esteem. All five studies employed a pretest-posttest experimental design and did not assess behaviors or skills specifically taught in the leisure education program.

Munson, Baker, and Lundegren (1985) implemented a program comprising 30-minute leisure education sessions in conjunction with 60-minute strength training sessions, three times per week over a seven-week period (totaling 10.5 hours of leisure education). They examined the effects of the leisure education program on the self-esteem, leisure attitudes, and leisure behaviors of 30 males who had been identified as juvenile delinquents.

Aguilar (1987) investigated the effects of a five-week leisure education program involving a two-hour session per week (totaling 10 instructional hours) on expressed attitudes toward recreation and delinquency by 38 adolescents labeled as delinquent. An instrument designed to measure attitudes toward recreation was developed as the primary data gathering method for the investigation.

Zoerink (1988) analyzed the effects of a leisure education program involving six sequential 90-minute sessions (totaling nine hours of instruction) using value clarification strategies on the leisure functioning of four young people with spina bifida. The Leisure Diagnostic Battery, Long Form Version A, was the primary data collection instrument. He concluded that the leisure education program affected participants differently and, as a result, demonstrated no systematic changes in perceived competence, perceived control, leisure needs, depth of involvement, playfulness, and personal and motivational barriers.

Munson (1988) compared the effects of a leisure education program to the effects of a group engaged in informal discussion and a group involved in physical activities. Each group met one hour per week for 10 weeks (totaling 10 hours of instruction). A variety of instruments were used to measure the self-esteem, leisure functioning, attitudes, leisure participation and satisfaction of 39 youths with behavioral disorders.

Zoerink and Lauener (1991) developed a leisure education program using values clarification strategies which met weekly for eight weeks with sessions lasting 90 minutes (totaling 12 hours of instruction). Impact of the program was assessed using the Leisure Ethic Scale (Crandall & Slivken, 1980), Leisure Satisfaction Scale (Beard & Ragheb, 1980), and the Leisure Diagnostic Battery (Witt & Ellis, 1987). Twelve adults with traumatic brain injury were randomly assigned to the leisure education program or to an informal discussion group.

In all five studies, the impact of the leisure education programs was not deemed to be significant. Each investigator acknowledged that the brevity of the programs might seriously limit the ability to positively influence leisure-related behaviors. Aguilar (1987) reported that amount of time for a leisure education program will require considerable attention in the future. Munson (1988) identified several factors influencing program length including staff availability, facility scheduling, client attendance, and administrative support. The others agreed that the issue of duration of leisure education programs has not been addressed in the literature.

Programs That Raised Expectations

While many researchers report positive outcomes of leisure education, others urge caution. Caldwell, Adolph, and Gilbert (1989) presented an interesting study providing some useful recommendations for practitioners implementing leisure education programs. The researchers found that when 155 individuals discharged from a rehabilitation hospital were interviewed over the telephone, the people who received leisure counseling reported being more bored and less satisfied with their leisure than people who had received no leisure education. The people who received leisure education perceived more internal barriers to recreation participation than those respondents who did not receive leisure education. The authors offered many possible explanations for the differences between groups other than the intervention effects such as the sample receiving leisure education was different from the onset than those who did not receive the training. In addition, the authors speculated that perhaps raised expectations and enhanced skills that were not realized upon discharge into the community contributed to the results. Based on this possibility, the authors recommended that professionals conducting leisure education programs should not only raise expectations about abilities and opportunities but also should educate participants as to what might prevent them from experiencing leisure after discharge. Caldwell and colleagues agreed that leisure education should be an important component of leisure service delivery but cautioned professionals to be aware of short-term and long-term effects of such programs.

Support for Leisure Education

According to Iso-Ahola and Weissinger (1987), there is a need for leisure education programs that build positive attitudes toward leisure. Weissinger and Caldwell (1990) replicated the previous work by Iso-Ahola and Weissinger and concluded that there is an obvious need for the provision of leisure education services designed to address the psychological and sociological barriers that inhibit functional behaviors. According to Weissinger and Caldwell, the factors most significant in the development of boredom perceptions are potentially amenable to remediation. Weissinger and Caldwell provided support for the reliability and validity of the Leisure Boredom Scale that could be used in clinical and practical situations involving examination of leisure dysfunctions. The authors reported that professionals can use the scale to conduct individual participant assessments that may result in the prescription of various leisure education programs.

Bedini (1990) provided an examination of the status of leisure education by reporting the results of a questionnaire mailed to 133 chairs of recreation and leisure departments at colleges and universities and 52 facilities with therapeutic recreation departments identified in the American Hospital Association's Directory of Hospitals. Results indicated that leisure education instruction has increased in recreation and leisure curricula and the existence of leisure education programs in therapeutic recreation is high. The author concluded that leisure education is an area of intervention that can have a positive impact on the quality of life of individuals, and specifically addresses their needs as they leave a treatment facility and attempt to integrate into their communities.

Conclusion

Although some empirical investigations demonstrating the effects of leisure education have been conducted, more are needed to improve leisure services for all individuals. After an extensive review of the literature, Dunn and Wilhite (1997) suggested that evidence is mixed on the ability of leisure education to contribute to desired outcomes with efficacy research resulting in: (a) inconclusive findings (Aguilar, 1987; Zoerink & Lauener, 1991); (b) lack of effect (Anderson & Allen, 1985; Bedini, Bullock, & Driscoll, 1993; Munson, 1988; Zoerink, 1988); (c) negative effects (Wolfe & Riddick, 1984) such as increases in leisure dissatisfaction (Caldwell, Adolph, & Gilbert, 1989); or (d) positive effects (Aguilar, 1987; Aguilar & Asmussen, 1989; Anderson & Allen, 1985; Hughes & Keller, 1992; Lanagan & Dattilo, 1989; Rancourt, 1991; Skalko, 1990). "Additional investigations are needed which confirm the contribution of leisure education interventions to specific outcomes, and identify which components of these interventions appear to contribute most to these outcomes" (Dunn & Wilhite, 1997, p. 55).

Ellis (1989) suggested that professionals continue to search for answers to fundamental questions about leisure in the lives of all people. He strongly urged practitioners to continue their search for applications of this knowledge and to develop assessment and intervention techniques that create positive changes. More specifically, Bullock and Mahon (1997) stated that more research is needed to help efforts at leisure education to respond to people's changing needs.

Although research typically has examined the effects of leisure education on people who are experiencing several constraints to their leisure such as people who have chemical dependencies, cognitive limitations, mental health problems, people who have been abused or incarcerated, and people who are older, additional research examining the effects of leisure education on other populations is needed. If our society begins to respond to the recommendations stipulated in the World Leisure and Recreation Association's International Charter for Leisure Education (1993) to expand and develop the scope of leisure education programs to all agents of education including schools and community agencies, research examining the effects of such programs on all citizens is surely needed.

Chapter 6
Areas of Concentration for Leisure Education

I never let my schooling
get in the way of my education.
-Mark Twain

Introduction

Leisure education has the potential to exert a positive influence on the lives of all people who engage in the process. It provides a vehicle for developing an awareness of leisure activities and resources, and for acquiring skills for participation throughout life (Howe-Murphy & Charboneau, 1987). Leisure education is a process through which individuals can develop and enhance their knowledge, interests, skills, abilities, and behaviors to a level where leisure can make a significant contribution to the quality of their lives. It can enable individuals to determine for themselves the importance of leisure in their lives, to establish their own leisure goals, to plan the steps needed to achieve those goals, to choose the activities in which they wish to be involved, and to participate in those activities. As a result of leisure education, individuals can understand the opportunities, potentials, and challenges in leisure and the impact of leisure on the quality of their lives and can develop skills that enable broad leisure participation (Mundy & Odum, 1979).

Although leisure education is important to everyone, it assumes an added significance in the lives of individuals who are experiencing constraints to their leisure participation. Many individuals not only have to cope with the constraints that are a direct result of their specific limitations, but also they experience constraints of various kinds imposed by our society. These constraints include physical, attitudinal, and programmatic barriers that work against the achievement of full and satisfying involvement in many aspects of life, including leisure.

Some individuals within our society are likely to be confronted with larger amounts of unobligated time than others because of the scarcity of education and employment opportunities available to them. These large blocks of time can be both unfilled and unfulfilling. They may be unfulfilling because the lack of leisure knowledge, skill, ability, awareness, and opportunity for participation prevent or inhibit a meaningful level of involvement in leisure. An effective leisure education program lessens these problems and has the potential to result in the development of skills, competencies, and attitudes such as problem solving, responsibility for self, and increased awareness that can be useful in other aspects of life.

To develop opportunities for people to experience leisure, information describing the content of a leisure education program is presented in this chapter. The content is based on previous suggestions identified in articles and texts reported in Chapter 3. The writings of many authors provided the impetus for conceptualizing this model. In addition, since writing the first edition of this book, several studies have been implemented which examined leisure education programs which contained various aspects of the content presented in this chapter (e.g., Dattilo & Hoge, 1999; Dunn & Wilhite, 1997; Hoge, Dattilo, & Williams, in press; Jekubovich, Dattilo, Williams, & McKenney, in press; Lovell, Dattilo & Jekubovich, 1996; Williams & Dattilo, 1997). The following components are included in the model which are labeled as the desirable characteristics people have when preparing to participate in leisure:

(a) appreciate leisure;
(b) be aware of self in leisure;
(c) be self-determined in leisure;
(d) interact socially during leisure;
(e) use resources facilitating leisure;
(f) make decisions about leisure; and
(g) acquire recreation activity skills.

Education in these areas can assist people in developing leisure attitudes, knowledge, and skills that can be matched with suitably challenging opportunities which facilitate a sense of competence and satisfaction (Ewert & Hollenhorst, 1989). Figure 6.1 depicts the characteristics of an individual who has a comprehensive awareness, appreciation, understanding, and skills associated with a given leisure pursuit.

Appreciate Leisure

Another significant component of leisure education is the development of a sense of appreciation relative to leisure and its potential contribution to the quality of life for individuals. To develop an appreciation of leisure, people can be encouraged to:

(a) understand leisure;
(b) consider leisure benefits;
(c) realize flexibility of leisure; and
(d) identify contexts for leisure.

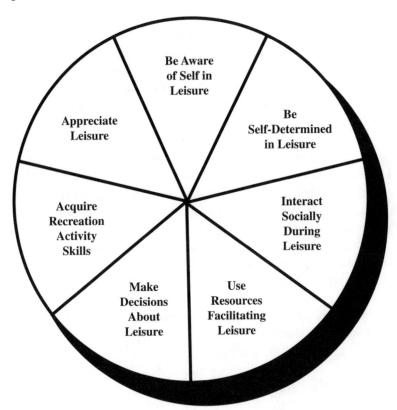

Be Aware
of Self in
Leisure

Be
Self-Determined
in Leisure

Appreciate
Leisure

Acquire
Recreation
Activity
Skills

Interact
Socially
During
Leisure

Make
Decisions
About
Leisure

Use
Resources
Facilitating
Leisure

Fig. 6.1

Understanding the concept of leisure is an important part of developing a sense of appreciation. This sense of appreciation for leisure lends itself to an openness to issues related to cross-cultural communication (Cappel, 1990). Cappel encouraged professionals to facilitate nonjudgmental exploration and discussion of the origin and impact of cultural, societal, and personal attitudes via leisure education sessions emphasizing leisure awareness.

Iso-Ahola and Weissinger (1990) observed that people who do not have the awareness that leisure can be psychologically rewarding are those who are most likely to experience feelings of boredom during periods of leisure. Therefore, an important facet of leisure appreciation is to *consider the benefits that come from leisure participation.* By considering these benefits, participants may learn that leisure is a legitimate source of pleasure and satisfaction and should be available to everyone. Development of a sense of appreciation may require the subsequent elimination of the notion that leisure can be enjoyed only after it has been earned by gainful employment. Leisure education can assist in the removal of guilt associated with vestiges of the work ethic. Appreciation of leisure can be based on understanding the central position leisure occupies in contemporary society.

Another aspect of leisure appreciation is acceptance of the idea that *leisure is flexible* and does not require a special time frame in which to occur but that leisure can be experienced whenever the opportunity presents itself during the normal course of the day. This is the embodiment of the concept of leisure lifestyle. If people begin to understand and embrace the concepts of leisure and leisure lifestyle, their ability to participate in recreation activities that result in satisfaction and enjoyment will be enhanced. By having leisure appreciation as a focus, leisure education can assist individuals in the development of a sensitivity for the uniqueness of leisure.

Leisure appreciation means more than liking or approving of leisure as a social or personal experience; it also means understanding the experience. People may require help in becoming aware of different possibilities that can promote leisure experiences. Leisure education can help individuals *identify a variety of contexts*, possible circumstances, environments, and activities likely to promote the leisure experience. Understanding the way our society views leisure and its impact on total life experiences can assist individuals in enriching their leisure patterns. In summary, people's appreciation of leisure may be enhanced by encouraging them to develop the skills depicted in Figure 6.2.

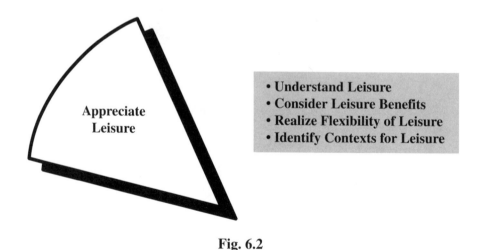

Appreciate Leisure

• **Understand Leisure**
• **Consider Leisure Benefits**
• **Realize Flexibility of Leisure**
• **Identify Contexts for Leisure**

Fig. 6.2

Be Aware of Self in Leisure

According to Barry (1997, p. 6), "basic to all learning, growth and positive behavioral change is awareness;" therefore, an important ingredient of leisure education programs is in assisting participants to explore, discover, and develop knowledge about themselves in a leisure context. Garner (1990) observed that people who monitor their thoughts are likely to solve their problems. "Such self-examination and self-knowledge must be accurate and comprehensive if one is to make effective life choices autonomously" (Sands & Doll, 1996, p. 61). An important aspect of developing a meaningful leisure lifestyle is to engage in self-examination (Hoge, Dattilo, Schneider, & Bemisderfer, 1997). Awareness of self in leisure can be enhanced through teaching individuals to:

(a) identify preferences;
(b) reflect on past participation;
(c) consider current involvement;
(d) project future leisure;
(e) understand skills;
(f) examine values and attitudes; and
(g) determine satisfaction.

Part of self-awareness is for people to have *knowledge of their preferences* relative to leisure activity and involvement. This knowledge is necessary to make appropriate choices regarding leisure participation and is a preliminary step toward independent functioning. Knowing their preferences enables individuals to think about what is required to fulfill their needs and to begin formulating steps to work toward reaching fulfillment.

Awareness of self in leisure can be enhanced by encouraging participants to *reflect on past leisure experiences*. Attention can be given to identifying the factors that encouraged a person to participate in an activity or, conversely, to decline to participate. Recollection of one's behavior while participating in activities, and consideration of its appropriateness, can contribute to an increase in self-awareness. Thinking about the context of one's leisure participation can be of value. For example, was participation with family or friends enjoyed more than participation alone?

For many individuals, another part of developing self-awareness is *examining current leisure involvement*. Such reflection can bring into focus the activities that provide enjoyment, as well as the skills that individuals possess that enable them to participate in activities of their choosing. Reflecting on leisure involvement can help to identify constraints of various kinds that deter participation. In addition, such reflection may assist individuals in thinking about their attributes that aid in coping with those constraints.

Individuals can be encouraged to use their reflections of past and current involvement to help them *consider what they would like to do in the future* regarding leisure participation. By projecting what they would like to do, participants can better understand who they are and who they would like to become.

Another facet of self-awareness is working toward the achievement of a *realistic perception of one's skills and abilities* and how they match with the requirements of specific activities. It is helpful when considering their competencies that participants recognize the existence of limitations and constraints, as well as those assets that aid participation. As individuals gain an understanding of their preferences and abilities, they can be encouraged to take a realistic view of their abilities in terms of what they want to achieve in their leisure participation. Unrealistic perceptions of competencies can lead to disappointment and failure if the demands of an activity greatly exceed the skills that are actually possessed by an individual. Conversely, unrealistic perceptions can discourage individuals from participating in activities that they could, in fact, master and in which they could experience success.

Examination of skills and abilities is an important part of gaining knowledge of oneself. An equally important aspect of developing self-awareness is *examining one's values and attitudes toward leisure* and participation in leisure activities. The degree of interest and involvement in activities may be related closely to the degree to which leisure is valued by an individual. In a leisure education program, examination of attitudes might appropriately precede an examination of skills and abilities. Whatever its place in the sequence of a leisure education program, it is often useful to recognize the influence of attitudes on skills, abilities, and participation. Johnson and Zoerink (1977), as well as Connolly (1977), recommended the use of values clarification techniques to help individuals learn about themselves. Once people become aware of their values and the implications these values have on choice of activities, people can make leisure choices thus retaining the power and responsibility for making their own decisions (Tinsley & Tinsley, 1984).

Satisfaction can be linked with the leisure participation patterns of individuals. People can be encouraged to *determine if they are currently satisfied* with the scope of their leisure participation. Perhaps identification of quality leisure by each individual will assist them in developing a sense of life satisfaction. In addition, participants can be encouraged to examine their leisure choices to determine if those choices are compatible with their values.

Arriving at an adequate level of self-awareness is a task that requires thoughtful, purposeful action. Different people may require different degrees of assistance in this task. Leisure education programs can be designed to provide participants the opportunities needed to achieve greater knowledge of self by encouraging the actions depicted in Figure 6.3.

Be Aware
of Self in
Leisure

• Identify Preferences
• Reflect on Past Participation
• Consider Current Involvement
• Project Future Leisure
• Understand Skills
• Examine Values and Attitudes
• Determine Satisfaction

Fig. 6.3

Be Self-Determined in Leisure

According to Wehmeyer (1996), self-determination involves acting as a primary causal agent in one's life and making choices and decisions regarding one's life free from external influence or interference. Self-determination, which includes the perception of freedom to make choices and the ability to initiate chosen leisure activities, is an important consideration in facilitating leisure (Dattilo, 1995; Dattilo & St. Peter, 1991). Wall and Dattilo (1995) suggested that by creating environments that are option-rich, responsive, and informative, both participants and professionals will increase the likelihood of becoming self-determined. In short, the condition of self-determination occurs when people take control of their freedom.

The fundamental goal of many recreation programs is to "set the stage" for people to enjoy themselves (Dattilo & Light, 1993; Dattilo & O'Keefe, 1992). Because self-determination contributes to enjoyment (Dattilo & Kleiber, 1993), it is important for leisure service professionals to provide services that foster self-determination. To encourage self-determination, Wehmeyer and Schwartz (1997) suggested that professionals provide (a) activities that optimally challenge the person and promote autonomy by supporting initiation of activities, and (b) opportunities to express preferences, make choices, and experience outcomes based on those choices. Since expressing preferences and making choices are important self-determination skills (Foxx, Faw, Taylor, Davis, & Fulia, 1993), leisure education programs can be developed to provide participants with opportunities to learn these skills (Faw, Davis, & Peck, 1996). For example, Devine, Malley, Sheldon, Dattilo and Gast (1997) taught people to make meaningful choices during free time and initiate chosen leisure activities which could enhance their self-determination and reduce learned helplessness.

There are many strategies that leisure service professionals can use to enhance self-determination in the people who attend their programs. Since ". . . opportunities to express preferences and make choices based on those preferences pervade virtually every aspect of daily life" (Faw, Davis & Peck, 1996, p. 173), providing opportunities for choice and respecting the choices made by program participants are important. "The strength of a leisure education intervention may lie in its addressing the issue of choice" (Searle, Mahon, Iso-Ahola, Sdrolias & Van Dyck, 1995). A person's sense of self-determination can be enhanced by encouraging the person to:

(a) take responsibility;
(b) make choices;
(c) terminate involvement; and
(d) become assertive.

Some individuals have been sheltered and overprotected from decision-making. As a result, their ability to take personal responsibility for their own leisure involvement may be drastically reduced. If the essence of leisure is freedom of choice, it follows naturally that it must be accompanied by taking *responsibility for making appropriate choices*. Therefore, leisure education can include an emphasis that leisure participation requires taking responsibility for one's enjoyment and satisfaction (Scheltens, 1990). To aid in the development of a sense of responsibility, individuals may need assistance in understanding the potential outcomes of their decisions regarding leisure participation. According to Pawelko and Magafas (1997, p. 32):

> A particular point of focus in leisure education might include the notion that life involves a series of choices, and it requires evaluating the consequences of alternative choices, in order to select the most satisfying outcomes.

An example of a leisure curriculum focusing on choice was developed by Wuerch and Voeltz (1982). Their leisure training project was dedicated to providing people with opportunities to *make choices* during their free time with the ultimate goal of encouraging development of self-initiated leisure skills. Dattilo and Barnett (1985) demonstrated that when recipients of leisure services are provided opportunities and the means to select activities freely, spontaneous initiation of activity, engagement with elements of the environment and assertion of a degree of control over one's surroundings often result. Development of a sense of self-determination in leisure facilitates the ability of individuals to make choices and sets the stage for acquisition of more complex decision-making strategies (Dattilo, Kleiber, & Williams, 1998). Teaching individuals to make choices has several benefits,

including (a) increasing interactions with materials that can encourage leisure, especially during times when other people are unavailable; (b) improving the quality of life for individuals by allowing them to participate in
the services they receive; and (c) increasing quality of programming by
having participants indicate their likes and dislikes (Realon, Favell, &
Lowerre, 1990). Since leisure service providers are concerned with facilitating participants' involvement in freely chosen activities, ". . . choices of
individuals are front and center in the leisure education process" (Bullock &
Mahon, 1997, p. 383).

Reid (1975) observed that some professionals often choose the activity
in which the person participates rather than allowing the individual to decide. It is likely that the omission of choice in the participation process prevents the individual from experiencing leisure and obtaining the maximum
benefit that is potentially available. It is likely that continuous involvement
in situations failing to provide opportunities for choice will result in feelings of helplessness (Seligman, 1975). People who experience helplessness
have difficulty in learning that their actions produce outcomes. This tends to
reduce voluntary participation and exploration on their part. Further, it is
likely that learned helplessness occurs because some participants are not
afforded opportunities to learn and exhibit self-determined behaviors. To
prevent learned helplessness, it is recommended that individuals be afforded
exposure to controllable situations (DeVellis, 1977); they should be taught
to initiate and *terminate their leisure experiences* (Nietupski & Svoboda,
1982). Leisure services that include elements of choice may be critical in
the prevention and treatment of learned helplessness and the encouragement
of future leisure participation (Iso-Ahola, MacNeil, & Szymanski, 1980).
Incorporation of the concept of choice in leisure education programs is not
only justifiable; it is necessary. If the perception of self-determination in
leisure is to be achieved, it must be built on a foundation that includes a
sense of freedom of choice (Dattilo, Kleiber, & Williams, 1998).

Establishment of a sense of self-determination in leisure can be assisted
by the development of *assertive* behaviors. According to Alberti and
Emmons (1995, p. 6):

Assertive behavior promotes equality in human relationships, enabling us to act in our own best interests, to stand up for ourselves
without undue anxiety, to express honest feelings comfortably, to
exercise personal rights without denying the rights of others.

People must understand their rights and needs, as well as respect the
rights and needs of others. Understanding that personal preferences relate to
what one would like to have, not what one must have, is important for individuals to feel satisfied on a regular basis.

By expanding leisure repertoires and increasing competence, people have more activities to choose from when they have free time and are in a better situation to experience leisure than those who do not. Additionally, Iso-Ahola (1980) stated that increased competence in an activity can lead to feelings of personal control. Having a variety of activities in which a person feels confident to choose can enhance self-determination. Self-determination allows people to have primary choice and control in the decisions and actions taken in their lives (Brotherson, Cook, Cunconan-Lahr, & Wehmeyer, 1995; Cunconan-Lahr & Brotherson, 1996). According to Johnson, Bullock, and Ashton-Schaeffer (1997), making self-determined leisure choices is central to every individuals' growth and development. Participants that can exhibit the actions depicted in Figure 6.4 are likely to experience a sense of self-determination in their leisure.

Be Self-Determined in Leisure

- **Take Responsibility**
- **Make Choices**
- **Terminate Involvement**
- **Become Assertive**

Fig. 6.4

Interact Socially During Leisure

According to Leitner, Leitner, and Associates (1996, p. 19), "one important aspect of life in which leisure education can contribute to societal well-being is socialization." Leisure education programs can focus on assisting participants in developing skills and abilities that will facilitate their participation in social groups and the community (Lord, 1997). Stumbo (1995) stated that although people experience different problems that prevent them from developing a satisfying leisure lifestyle, a somewhat prevalent problem is the lack of social interaction skills. An absence of social skills is particularly noticeable during leisure participation and frequently leads to isolation and an inability to function successfully (Chadsey-Rusch, 1992). According to Terman, Larner, Stevenson and Behrman (1996), social skills training programs are important components of services because people "who have strong recreational interests that can be shared with others are more likely to be integrated in a meaningful way in social settings" (p. 11).

Development of social skills used in leisure situations appears to be important because acquisition of these skills facilitates individuals' acceptance by their peers. For example, Salisbury, Gallucci, Palombaro, and Peck (1995) reported that social relationships with peers provide individuals with a range of supports and acknowledgment of their acceptance. Social interaction skills are relevant to people continuing their leisure participation in different activities. Coleman and Iso-Ahola (1993) concluded that social interaction is one of the most important reasons people participate in and continue their leisure involvement. Therefore, the following areas of social interaction training are an important focus of leisure education programs:

(a) communicate nonverbally;
(b) communicate verbally;
(c) understand social rules;
(d) acquire social competence; and
(e) develop friendships.

Communication is a key element in social interactions. Both verbal and nonverbal behaviors play an important role in communication. *Nonverbal communication skills* influence perceptions of social competence. Mastery of basic skills such as gesturing, facial expressions, posture, and voice volume and pitch all affect an individual's ability to communicate and consequently develop social relationships. People need to develop the ability to maintain an appropriate amount of eye contact, judge adequate physical proximity, and handle physical contact. Each of these skills varies according to the activity, environment, and the people involved, which makes the development of these skills all the more difficult. When a particular situation requires people to play together, the participants will benefit from being able to share equipment and materials, engage in cooperative tasks, and develop friendships.

Attempts at mastery of basic *verbal communication skills* will enhance the likelihood of success in a given leisure environment. The ability of individuals to greet other people, ask questions, wait their turn to speak, and contribute to a discussion are a few examples of verbal skills that are helpful in developing friendships.

A problem-solving approach to help individuals learn and generalize social interaction skills holds some promise. Based on the earlier writings of McFall (1982) and Trower (1984), who proposed a process approach to social skills training that relied on the person's *understanding and acting upon the rules of a social situation*, Park and Gaylord-Ross (1989) developed and tested a four-step training process. In their successful attempt at teaching social interaction skills, the authors taught participants to first interpret or decode the meaning of social situations. Next, participants learned to describe possible alternative ways to interpret a situation and then select one of these choices to cope successfully with the social situation. Last, they evaluated their performance. Park and Gaylord-Ross reported that if individuals learn general rules of social conduct, their ability to transfer learning across different settings may be heightened.

Meyer, Cole, McQuarter, and Reichle (1990) reported on the importance of *acquiring a sense of social competence*. The authors identified a series of functions that appear to be crucial in determining social competence. In addition, Meyer and colleagues presented definitions of these functions, analyses of levels of the functions, and specific items associated with each function. The following eleven functions indicative of social competence were identified: (a) joins an ongoing interaction or starts a new one; (b) manages own behavior without instruction from others; (c) follows rules, guidelines, and routines of activities; (d) provides positive feedback and reinforcement to others; (e) provides negative feedback and consequences for others; (f) obtains and responds to relevant situational cues; (g) provides information and offers assistance to others; (h) requests and accepts assistance from others; (i) makes choices from among available and possible alternatives; (j) exhibits alternative strategies to cope with negative situations; and (k) terminates or withdraws from an interaction and/or activity. Mastery of these social interaction skills can lead to development of positive social relationships that produce enjoyment and satisfaction.

Along similar lines to Meyer and her colleagues, Chadsey-Rusch (1990) examined the social interactions of youth and discussed her findings in reference to facilitating individuals' transition from school to work. Chadsey-Rusch identified eleven behaviors that represent social competence including the ability to direct others, question, criticize, praise, request assistance, offer assistance, be polite and demonstrate social amenities, greet/depart, tease or joke, converse/comment/share information, and get attention. Identification of these behaviors provides practitioners with possible areas that could lead to development of individualized social interaction objectives for their constituents. Chadsey-Rusch provided specific delineation of these behaviors that would facilitate both the development of behavioral objectives and associated performance measures.

To provide leisure service providers with suggestions on dealing with participants who demonstrate anger and aggression, Mundy (1997) proposed "an anger and aggression control management program that could be implemented in recreation, park, and leisure service systems" (p. 66). After reviewing the literature, Mundy selected the following 24 social skills for development in leisure service settings so that a person's social competence could be enhanced: (a) listening; (b) starting a conversation; (c) keeping a conversation going; (d) introducing oneself; (e) joining in; (f) following instructions; (g) apologizing; (h) knowing one's feelings; (i) expressing one's feelings; (j) understanding the feelings of others; (k) dealing with someone else's anger; (l) dealing with fear; (m) giving a compliment; (n) sharing something; (o) helping others; (p) negotiating; (q) standing up for one's rights; (r) sportsmanship; (s) dealing with embarrassment; (t) dealing with being left out; (u) responding to failure; (v) solving problems; (w) dealing with group pressure; and (x) making decisions. Mundy's list of social skills illustrates the importance of these skills and the many behaviors of participants that can be addressed with systematic leisure education.

Closely tied to the ability of people to develop a sense of social competence is their ability to use social skills so that they can *develop friendships*. According to Prager (1998, p. 157), "for most people friends are crucial to happiness." Similarly Csikszentmihalyi (1997) stated that:

The importance of friendships on well-being is difficult to overestimate. The quality of life improves immensely when there is at least one other person who is willing to listen to our troubles, and to support us emotionally. National surveys find that when someone claims to have five or more friends with whom they can discuss important problems, they are 60 percent more likely to say they are "very happy." (p. 43)

Perhaps more than any other aspect of development, friendships are an expression of a person's inclusion in a community (Guralnick, Conner & Hammond, 1995). Attention to social networks and the support they provide has resulted in a recognition of the value of friendships (Romer, White & Haring, 1996). Green, Schleien, Mactavish and Benepe (1995) explained that it is through joint participation in recreation activities that friendships flourish. Furthermore, Schleien, Ray and Green (1997) reported that the number and quality of social interactions strongly influence the ability of individuals to develop meaningful relationships.

An absence of meaningful friendships is a frequent barrier experienced by many people and leads to isolation and withdrawal from community life (Heyne, Schleien & McAvoy, 1993). According to Ashton-Schaeffer and Kleiber (1990), social leisure skills appear to be essential for individuals to form and maintain friendships. Development of meaningful friendships and effective social interaction skills can be taught through systematic leisure education programs (Heyne, 1997).

The development of social interaction skills through leisure education is complex, yet important. Leisure education can create optimal environments for encouraging social skill development, social interaction, and friendships. Instruction related to increasing the actions depicted in Figure 6.5 (see page 88) can help participants participate effectively in many leisure pursuits.

Interact
Socially
During
Leisure

• **Communicate Nonverbally**
• **Communicate Verbally**
• **Understand Social Rules**
• **Acquire Social Competence**
• **Develop Friendships**

Fig. 6.5

Use Resources Facilitating Leisure

The failure of some people to engage in meaningful leisure activities may be the result of a lack of awareness of recreation resources and the inability to use them. Although numerous leisure resources are available to most people, not knowing how to access these resources can be a barrier to leisure involvement (O'Dell & Taylor, 1996). As a result of a needs assessment, Sable and Gravink (1995) identified problems with leisure resources which included lack of information and lack of knowledge about equipment and modifications. Similarly, Hoge and Dattilo (1995) concluded that there is a need to include individuals in a variety of community recreation activities and leisure education programs designed to increase exposure to recreation activities.

Therefore, knowing about the existence of leisure resources and how to use them can be an important element of leisure education programs. There are instances when recreation programs assist individuals in acquiring and developing the skills necessary to participate in specific activities and, as a culminating experience, provide opportunities for actual participation in those activities. Participation in the activities is the pinnacle of the program. After individuals have participated in the program, frequently the program is terminated or their involvement in it is terminated. It is unfortunate, but true, that when the program is ended, participants may not possess sufficient knowledge regarding potential leisure resources to continue their involvement in the activities they have just been taught. Therefore, a helpful consideration in a comprehensive approach to leisure education is the provision of information relative to leisure resources. Some people who want to make decisions about their leisure can be encouraged to do so by having them:

(a) identify people who could serve as resources;
(b) locate facilities providing recreation activities;
(c) understand participation requirements;
(d) match skills to activity requirements; and
(e) obtain answers to questions relevant to resources.

To enhance their ability to experience leisure, individuals can develop an understanding that other *people can be valuable resources* for leisure participation. Personnel associated with community enterprises such as fitness clubs, bowling alleys, or movie theaters that provide leisure services can provide useful information about the recreation activities they sponsor. People associated with agencies or organizations that serve as clearing houses identifying community leisure opportunities such as travel agencies, chambers of commerce, or park and recreation departments can also provide helpful information. Knowledge of organizations promoting a membership of active participants which might include bridge clubs, outing associations, or track clubs can greatly enhance the ability of individuals to continue or expand their leisure participation. Identification of experts in a particular area of interest, such as naturalists, artists, or musicians, may allow for increased education, mentoring, and skill development permitting more active and, perhaps, more meaningful leisure participation.

If individuals are interested in a particular recreation activity, they can be taught to identify and *locate facilities or environments* providing opportunities to participate in that activity. Accurate identification of relevant locations can be accompanied by the ability to reach those sites. Reaching destinations requires people to identify their current location and to understand directions to a desired location. If people know where a desired facility or environment is located, they are in a position to walk there or to arrange alternative methods of transportation. The use of alternative forms of transportation may require specific skill development such as learning to drive, using public transportation, or asking family or friends for transportation.

Prior to arriving at a destination, participants can be encouraged to *acquire knowledge of the requirements associated with participation* in a desired activity. One requirement may be a specific cost for participation. Knowledge of entry fees and funds required for continued participation is important to planning for leisure involvement such as those fees associated with fitness clubs. An understanding of the schedule of events is needed to plan for active participation when going to the movie theater or other similar activities. Participation in a particular recreation activity may be contingent on specific eligibility requirements that can be known prior to attempting entry to programs such as advanced swimming lessons. Individuals with mobility limitations can identify the degree of accessibility associated with a given environment associated with entrance ramps, accessible rest rooms, and other types of physical structures.

Participation in recreation activities may require a minimum level of proficiency that can be identified prior to attendance. Knowledge of activity requirements allows individuals the opportunity to prepare for their participation and *develop realistic expectations regarding their ability* such as participating in ballet. Understanding the rules associated with a particular event may encourage people to actively participate or encourage them to become interested spectators for recreation activities such as basketball or football. If people become knowledgeable about the equipment and apparel associated with different activities, they will then be able to prepare better for participation in those activities. Some equipment such as a skateboard may be required for participation while other equipment such as hiking boots may simply improve performance. Use of appropriate apparel such as a helmet may prevent injuries while other apparel may prevent embarrassment such as an appropriate swimming suit. Although these factors may not be central to the development of the specific recreation activity skill, they may be the determining factor between successful, enjoyable participation and failure.

Knowledge of leisure resources and the ability to utilize those resources appears to be an important element in the establishment of an independent leisure lifestyle (Peterson & Gunn, 1984). Therefore, Dattilo and Murphy (1987a) recommended that practitioners teach participants not only how to participate in an activity but *how they can find answers to questions* associated with the activity. For example:

(a) Where can one participate?
(b) Are there others who participate?
(c) How much will participation cost?
(d) What type of transportation is available? and
(e) Where can a person learn more about a particular recreation activity?

In addition to the need for people to acquire knowledge of community leisure resources, it is helpful for them to be given opportunities to access those resources. If feasible, they can be given assistance until they acquire the skills needed to utilize the resources independently and, thus, become active participants in community life (Richler, 1984). The ability of participants to utilize leisure resources can be enhanced through the actions depicted in Figure 6.6.

- Identify People
- Locate Facilities
- Understand Participation Requirements
- Match Skills to Activity Requirements
- Obtain Answers

Use
Resources
Facilitating
Leisure

Fig. 6.6

Make Decisions About Leisure

Encouraging the acquisition and development of decision-making skills can be a valuable component of leisure education (Lord, 1997). If it is accepted that one of the goals of leisure services is to foster independence in individuals, it is imperative that the ability to make appropriate decisions regarding specific tasks be encouraged during recreation participation (Dattilo and Murphy, 1987a). According to Dattilo and Murphy, an intended benefit of recreation participation is an increase in personal effectiveness that can result from the making of timely and correct decisions. People who do not possess the appropriate appraisal and judgment skills needed for activity involvement will be more likely to acquire these skills if they participate in actual recreation activities. Practitioners can encourage participants to evaluate their decisions, determine the effectiveness of their decisions, and, given similar circumstances, decide whether they would act in a similar fashion, or change their behavior in some manner (Mahon & Bullock, 1992).

Some individuals encounter difficulty in making decisions related to many aspects of their lives. This problem is often evident in relation to their leisure lifestyle. Hayes (1977b) recommended that practitioners teach the decision-making process to individuals and encourage them to select and engage in appropriate recreation activities. McDowell (1976) identified the importance of using rational problem-solving and decision-making techniques to promote the independent responsibility of individuals for making wise decisions about their leisure involvement. According to McDowell, successful decision making can be enhanced by an assessment of leisure interests and attitudes, identified as leisure appreciation and self-determination. Making a decision related to leisure participation is facilitated by an individual's:

(a) awareness of self in relation to leisure;
(b) appreciation of the value of leisure;
(c) development of a sense of self-determination related to leisure involvement;
(d) ability to identify goals; and
(e) ability to solve problems.

The first three aspects of decision making, *become aware of self in lei-sure, appreciate value of leisure,* and *develop self-determination,* have been addressed in detail in previous portions of this chapter. Therefore, the remaining portion of the decision-making section will be devoted to discussing the implications of identifying goals and problem solving. *Identification of realistic leisure goals* and determination of needs met through goal attainment are also important aspects of the decision-making process. Murphy (1975) identified removal of constraints that impede or prohibit participation as a primary goal of leisure services. Many people experience intrinsic and environmental constraints to leisure involvement. Therefore, decision-making training can focus on the identification of constraints preventing leisure involvement and the development of strategies for overcoming these barriers. To make decisions effectively, people can be taught to identify alternatives for their leisure goals and reasonably predict participation outcomes. McDowell concluded his description of decision making with the recommendation that individuals establish a plan for leisure participation.

A potential plan for leisure participation for individuals may involve the development of *problem-solving skills* (Bouffard, 1990). To solve a problem, it is first necessary to clarify and define the problem. An analysis of possible forces influencing the circumstances may be useful in placing the problem in the correct perspective. After the problem and its associated forces are identified, the generation of possible solutions can occur in a free and accepting environment, such as through brainstorming. Solutions generated during the brainstorming process can then be analyzed and evaluated, using predetermined criteria to assess the feasibility and ramifications of different solutions. After a solution is agreed upon, roles and responsibilities of relevant parties, as well as procedures to implement actions to solve the problem, can be clearly delineated. Following this logical preparation for solving a problem, participants can be encouraged to take the actions necessary to implement their decision. Implementation of a decision, however, does not mean the process is completed. As a final step, individuals evaluate the success of their actions. Information obtained from the evaluation can strongly influence participants' future leisure participation patterns.

One type of problem solving that has been used effectively is "collaborative" problem solving. Turiel (1987) determined that children learned problem-solving processes, applied guiding principles, and engaged in moral reasoning that allowed for democratic group decisions. In addition, Salisbury, Evans, and Palombaro (1997) found that a collaborative problem-solving process which was developed by Salisbury, Palombaro, and Evans, (1993) promoted an inclusive community through the identification and elimination of physical, social, and instructional instances of exclusion. Through collaborative problem solving, participants learn tolerance for diversity of opinion, perspective taking, and the value of consensus (Johnson & Johnson, 1994). The ability of participants of leisure education programs to make decisions relative to their leisure may be enhanced by the action depicted in Figure 6.7.

Make Decisions About Leisure

- **Awareness of Self**
- **Appreciation of Leisure**
- **Development of Self-Determination**
- **Ability to Identify Goals**
- **Ability to Solve Problems**

Fig. 6.7

Acquire Recreation Activity Skills

The core of many leisure education programs is the development of the participant's ability to choose and successfully engage in recreation activities of sufficient scope and variety to experience satisfaction and enjoyment. Therefore, when participants acquire recreation activity skills they are encouraged to:

(a) choose meaningful and enjoyable activities; and
(b) participate with support to overcome fears.

If it is believed that choice is a critical aspect of leisure participation and choice involves options, it appears logical that an array of recreation activities and opportunities should exist from which individuals *could choose to experience meaningful leisure* (Peterson & Gunn, 1984). Participants in recreation programs can be encouraged to select and develop recreation skills having the most potential for providing them with enjoyment and satisfaction. Selection of recreation activity skills should be contingent on the needs, interests, motivations, and aspirations of the person (Howe-Murphy & Charboneau, 1987), and it is important to remember the role the participant should play in the choice of activities.

Howe-Murphy and Charboneau reported that recreation activity skill development can provide physical and emotional support assisting participants in overcoming fear of the unknown and failure. Reduction of fear associated with leisure participation should lessen the hesitancy of people to become active participants in community life. The ability of participants to choose and engage in leisure activities may be enhanced by the action depicted in Figure 6.8.

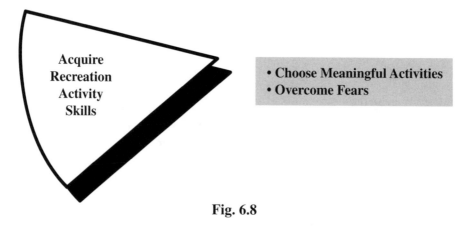

Fig. 6.8

Conclusion

The quality and success of leisure education programs is dependent on many factors, not the least of which is program content. The program components that have been presented in this chapter meet the test of logic and have a research foundation that merits their inclusion in leisure education efforts. Practitioners preparing people to live successfully within their communities are encouraged to consider the incorporation of these components in their programs aimed at educating individuals for active leisure participation. The intent of this text is to present comprehensive and feasible leisure education procedures to practitioners dedicated to expanding leisure opportunities for all persons. It is hoped that professionals will not only include leisure instruction in their services but will also provide educational opportunities that move beyond skill development to a more comprehensive strategy. This strategy can attempt to instill an appreciation of leisure, awareness of self, self-determination and decision making relative to leisure, knowledge and utilization of leisure resources, and development of skills in the areas of social interaction and recreation activities.

Chapter 7
Systematic Programming for Leisure Education

Though this be madness,
yet there is method in it.
-William Shakespeare

Introduction

It is helpful for departments or agencies providing leisure services to have a clearly delineated purpose statement to guide their service delivery. Based on this purpose statement, goals can be generated that further specify the intent of the department or agency. After a statement of purpose and goals has been generated, leisure service providers can develop specific programs that make the goals operational (Peterson & Gunn, 1984). According to Peterson and Gunn, a *specific program* is defined as a set of activities and their corresponding interactions that are designed to achieve predetermined objectives selected for a given group of participants, implemented and evaluated independent of all other specific programs.

Specific Programs

The specific leisure education programs included in this text are provided to assist practitioners in generating programs which help participants to develop a satisfying leisure lifestyle. Programs which facilitate increased leisure involvement enhance the opportunities for participants to improve the quality of their lives (Hopper & Wambold, 1978). Therefore, it is necessary that leisure service providers teach participants a comprehensive range of leisure skills (Nietupski & Svoboda, 1982).

To assist practitioners in achieving this goal, six leisure education programs have been completed and presented in the Appendices of this text. The specific programs were developed based on experiences of the author with input from practitioners and students. Variations of the specific programs reported in this text have been tested and were reviewed in Chapter 4 (Dattilo & Hoge, 1999; Dunn & Wilhite, 1997; Hoge, Dattilo & Williams, in press; Jekubovich, Dattilo, Williams & McKenney, in press; Lovell, Dattilo & Jekubovich, 1996; Williams & Dattilo, 1997). The second portion of this book contains one specific program for each of the six leisure education components identified in the first chapter of the text:

(a) appreciate leisure;
(b) be aware of self in leisure;
(c) be self-determined in leisure;
(d) interact socially during leisure;
(e) use resources facilitating leisure; and
(f) make decisions about leisure.

Format for Specific Programs

The format for the specific leisure education programs in this text is a revised version of an approach developed by Peterson and Gunn (1984). Each specific leisure education program contains:

(a) a program title;
(b) a statement of purpose;
(c) program goals;
(d) enabling objectives;
(e) performance measures;
(f) content description; and
(g) process description.

To accommodate the varying acquisition rates of different participants, sequencing of the individual sessions is not included in this text. Practitioners are encouraged to sequence the material according to the needs of the people they serve. The specific programs in this book are intended to be a starting place for the implementation of a leisure education program. Practitioners are encouraged to make changes to the programs in this text to meet the individual needs and interests of participants receiving their services. This text provides practitioners with information required for developing a leisure education program. The components of the format for each specific program that are presented in this section have been described in detail by Peterson and Gunn (1984).

Each specific leisure education program is identified by *a title* that reflects the program purpose. The six specific programs contain a concise, one-sentence *statement of purpose* describing the intent of the leisure education program from the point of view of the leisure service department, and each statement is comprehensive, yet concise and clear.

Program goals which were identified by Peterson and Gunn (1984) as Terminal Program Objectives are included in each program to further delineate the purpose of the program. The program goals are written as general participant outcome statements that specify what participants should gain from participating in the program. The goals specify whether the intent is to increase awareness and sensitivity of a particular concept, to develop an understanding of knowledge associated with a specific area, or to acquire specific skills related to successful leisure participation.

The program goals for each specific leisure education program have been divided into a number of behavioral units identified as *enabling objectives.* An "objective is a collection of words and/or pictures and diagrams intended to let others know what you intend your students to achieve" (Mager, 1997, p. 3). According to Busser (1990), objectives are the specific intended measurable outcomes of the program that serve as the anchor for the design of the program. The objectives are written using behavioral terms that describe the outcome that is desired from the participant. Mager (1997) stated that an instructional objective is related to intended outcomes rather than process for achieving outcomes, is specific and measurable rather than broad and intangible, and is concerned with students rather than teachers.

Performance measures have been developed that correspond with each enabling objective. "The performance measure is a statement of the exact behavior that will be taken as evidence that the intent of the enabling objective has been achieved" (Peterson & Gunn, 1984, p. 101). Performance measures specify the exact criteria and conditions under which the behavior identified in the objective must be achieved. The measurement procedure that will be used to determine if participants completed the objective is described in the performance measure. Therefore, the performance measure must permit examination of a sufficient amount of the desired behavior, a representative sample, to increase confidence that the person achieved the objective. The performance measure combined with the objective answers the following questions identified by Mager (1997, p. 46): (a) What should the learner be able to do? (b) Under what conditions do you want the learner to do it? and (c) How well must it be done?

The majority of information contained in the specific programs describes the content and process required to conduct the program. The *content* contained in the specific program "is what is to be done in the program to achieve the intent of the enabling objectives" (Peterson & Gunn, 1984, p. 113). An attempt has been made to specify a sufficient amount of material to act as a starting place for program delivery. Frequently, tasks associated with the objectives were analyzed, and the components were presented in a step-by-step fashion.

Although identification of the material for content is extremely important, it is not sufficient when planning a leisure education session. The *process,* or way in which the material is presented, is an important consideration (Peterson & Gunn, 1984). Many of us have experienced a teacher who obviously had command of the material (the content) but was an ineffective educator. Educational experiences which fail to maintain a participant's attention may limit the degree of knowledge, skill acquisition, and retention of material by that participant. Each specific program included in the Appendices of the text contains process sections. A process section may be found in all levels of the educational stages including the orientation and learning activities, presentations, discussions and debriefings, and conclusions. The process sections provide information which may help practitioners create an enjoyable, organized environment that results in development of awareness and appreciation, knowledge acquisition and retention, and skill enhancement.

An important part of developing the process of a leisure education program is presenting information to answer the question "How do I prepare for a session?" Preparation is a key ingredient in conducting successful programs and will be discussed in detail in the following chapter. To help practitioners prepare for some of the learning activities presented in the specific programs located in the Appendices, a section titled "preparation" is included. Therefore, the process section focuses specifically on what to do when conducting the activity and the information on preparation is included at the beginning of the

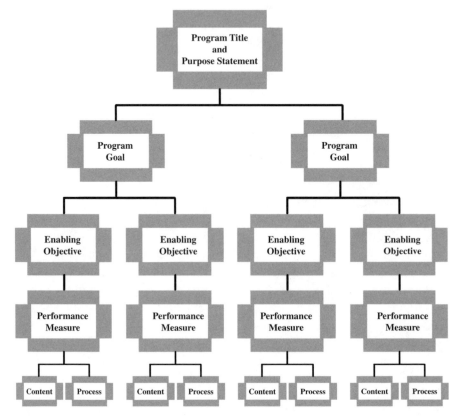

Fig. 7.1

learning activity. The information about preparation is presented at the beginning of the activity to communicate the need to develop and collect materials before it is time to conduct a session. An icon labeled PREPARE FOR SESSION identifies this section.

The information contained in the format for the six specific programs is designed to encourage practitioners to provide systematic leisure education for the people whom they serve. The format for specific leisure education programs described in this section of the chapter is depicted in Figure 7.1.

As stated at the beginning of this chapter, it is anticipated that practitioners will change some aspects of the programs provided in the Appendices to accommodate the unique talents of the people whom they serve. For example, the number of objectives established in a specific program may be too many to complete during the amount of time participants will be available to attend the program. Therefore, practitioners may choose only the most relevant objectives for the participants and not implement aspects of the program associated with the other objectives. In another situation, some performance measures may appear too rigorous for people enrolled in one of the specific programs. Practitioners then can modify performance measures to meet the individual needs of the participants. In addition, when considering the needs of a particular group of individuals, leisure service professionals may choose to present more detail associated with the content described in a specific program. Professionals may wish to add to the existing information presented in this book. In general, practitioners are encouraged to use whatever they feel is useful from the examples presented in the Appendices. It is expected that leisure service professionals will use their professional judgment in selecting teaching strategies, making modifications, and considering the diversity of participants so that they can produce the most effective leisure education program for the people they serve.

Educational Structure for Specific Programs

In an attempt to develop an effective leisure educational environment, each of the specific leisure education programs follows a similar structure. Each program begins with an orientation activity that is followed by an introduction of the topic. The specific programs contain descriptions of presentations that are immediately followed by discussions that actively solicit participant involvement. In addition, learning activities are presented with associated debriefings. Finally, conclusions are provided at the end of each objective. Therefore, each specific leisure education program contained in the Appendices includes:

(a) an orientation activity;
(b) an introduction;

(c) presentations;
(d) discussions;
(e) learning activities;
(f) debriefings; and
(g) a conclusion.

To provide a systematic teaching strategy, instruction on each objective within every specific program begins with an *orientation activity* to introduce participants to one another and to the leisure education material. The orientation activity is included to create an atmosphere of fun and enjoyment, as well as one that will stimulate learning and development. As a result, the orientation activities not only introduce the participants to each other but also provide a preview to the participants of what is to come in the program. These orientation activities are designed to set the learning climate. Since the first few minutes of an educational session are crucial in establishing a learning environment, it is essential that these initial moments be interesting, relevant, and pleasant (Davis, 1974).

The orientation activity is followed by an *introduction* of the leisure education program. The introduction briefly acquaints the participants with the topic and the objective to be covered in the session. The intent of the introduction is to provide participants with a preview of what is to come. According to McKeachie (1986), if people know what they are expected to learn from an educational session, they learn more of the material.

Once an introduction is provided, each objective contains a series of *presentations* and associated *discussions.* The combination of these two procedures allows the rapid dissemination of material during the presentation, complemented by discussions requiring participants to contribute actively to the learning process. McKeachie (1986) recommended the use of a lecture to communicate information and model problem solving as well as the use of discussion to allow participants to practice problem-solving skills.

Enjoyable *learning activities* are incorporated into the educational program associated with each leisure education objective. The learning activities are developed to allow participants to practice the information they acquired during the presentations. The activities are designed to be fun while encouraging participants to assimilate the relevant material. Immediate communication of their understanding of the material is required via the learning activities. Participants are placed in situations where they are actively involved in an experience that encourages them to use the skills provided in the presentation.

Learning activities are followed immediately by *debriefings.* Typically, debriefings consist of a series of questions that require participants to reflect upon, describe, analyze, and communicate about the learning activity

(Brackenreg, Luckner, & Pinch, 1994). Debriefings are designed to encourage participants to identify accomplishments and difficulties experienced during the learning activity and the relevance of that experience to their everyday life. Individuals who internalize the meaning associated with the experience are in a better position to apply that learning to other aspects of their lives (Knapp, 1990). To conduct meaningful debriefings, Brackenreg and colleagues (1994) suggested that practitioners prepare and plan for the debriefings, create a caring environment, carefully sequence the learning activities, develop effective communication and questioning skills, and provide focused feedback to participants.

Several authors have identified the benefits of conducting systematic debriefings. McDonald and Howe (1989) reported that debriefings encourage self-expression, enlightenment, and empathy among participants. According to Gass (1993), processing activities through debriefings can help participants reflect, analyze, describe, or discuss an experience after it is completed, reinforce their perceptions of change, and encourage the integration of their learning into their lives after the experience is completed. Processing activities of this sort can help participants incorporate the learning that occurred in a given leisure program to their lives at home, school or work (Luckner & Nadler, 1995).

The learning structure associated with each objective contains a *conclusion* that attempts to make sense of the entire educational process associated with a particular leisure education objective. By recapitulating the major points, proposing questions, and creating an anticipation for the future, the practitioner can help participants learn (McKeachie, 1986). The conclusion brings closure to the objective and provides an opportunity for participants to ask questions and reflect on what they have learned. A conclusion can encourage participants to become more aware of their accomplishments.

Each of the six specific leisure education programs presented in this book contains the components depicted in Figure 7.2 (see page 102). These components are included to communicate as clearly, completely, and concisely as possible the intent of each program. The information in the specific programs is only a beginning in developing complete and specific leisure education programs.

Specific Program Outreach Into the Community

Typically, specific programs are conducted with the intent of encouraging participants to be actively involved in their communities. O'Dell and Taylor (1996) suggested that educating for leisure is a long-term project with people being "exposed early and often to experiences that help them develop appreciations and skills" (p. 18). After assessing attitudes of community recreation participants, Sparrow, Shinkfield, and Karnilowicz (1993)

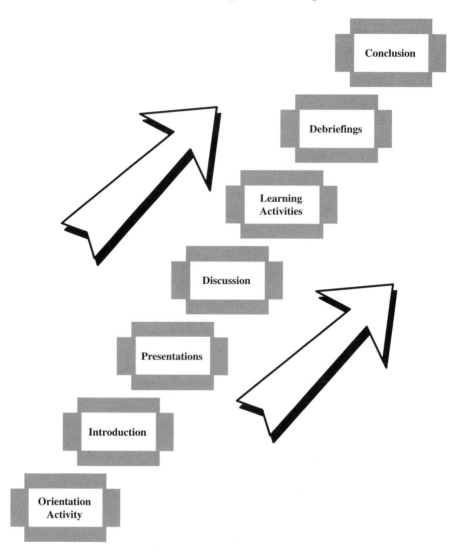

Fig. 7.2

concluded that gaining entry into a recreation program may not be sufficient to promote peer acceptance; supports such as a leisure coach can help facilitate success. Researchers report that positive attitudes are more likely in the presence of sufficient resource support (Janney, Snell, Beers, & Raynes, 1995; Minke, Bear, Deemer & Griffin, 1996). For leisure education to heighten perceived leisure control, opportunities must exist for participants' involvement in chosen activities with support from people such as a leisure coach (Searle, Mahon, Iso-Ahola, Sdrolias, & Van Dyck, 1995).

Systematic follow-up procedures for some participants may be developed to place participants into existing community recreation programs with the assistance of leisure coaches. Dattilo and St. Peter (1991) developed a leisure education model involving the development of a specific structured leisure education program. This model has been suggested by Williams and Dattilo (1997) and tested by Dattilo and Hoge (1999) and Hoge, Dattilo and Williams (in press) who demonstrated support for the model.

Community-based instruction and education of significant people in the lives of individuals can be incorporated into the leisure education specific programs, or it may occur immediately following formalized instruction. Ideally, a leisure education specific program is accompanied by systematic community-based leisure instruction with a leisure coach. In addition to a leisure education course containing content described in Chapter 6, the following sections contain a description of supportive services that include:

(a) leisure coaching; and
(b) family and friend involvement.

Leisure Coaching. A leisure coach can meet with community leisure service professionals and provide consultation and support. Leisure coaches can be available to respond to the questions and concerns of the community leisure service providers and act as advocates for both leisure service professionals and the participant. In addition, leisure coaches may provide assistance to participants who engage in inclusive community recreation activities (Dattilo, 1994). As the environment begins to respond to individual needs and the person gains skills and confidence, the leisure coach can be phased out.

Family and Friend Involvement. Based on compelling evidence that sociocultural factors outside the classroom influence development and acceptance, Sontag (1996) stated that family functioning and community context are critical issues for professionals. After reviewing 25 parent surveys, Westling (1996) recommended making programs and information available to parents. In addition, Kaplan and Saccuzzo (1993) concluded that involving families in service delivery helps professionals serve people. Although leisure services focus on the person's needs, Mactavish (1997) recommended a strategy that acknowledges the importance of families in facilitating recreation experiences.

Examination of the leisure of adolescents helps to clarify that families and friends are important aspects of leisure participation. For example, Hultsman (1993) concluded that parents are perceived to have greater influence than other people in the decision of adolescents not to join an activity. Although friends and others outside the family become increasingly important with age, family support remains critical to the developing adolescent's optimal adjustment (Wenz-Gross & Siperstein, 1996, p. 177).

A major component of the model developed by Dattilo and St. Peter is the involvement and participation of family members and friends. Family support of participants' active leisure participation within their communities can be stimulated through the provision of meetings and workshops designed to increase the ability of family members to promote, rather than discourage, independent leisure participation. All people have needs for companionship and emotional support that are best met through contact with a person's peers and family (Romer, White, & Haring, 1996).

Conclusion

This chapter provides an overview of the format, structure, outreach capability, and areas of concentration related to the specific programs contained in this text. The suggested format for the specific programs follows a systems approach to the provision of leisure education services. To provide an organized educational structure to the specific programs, each objective for every program contains an orientation activity, introduction, presentations, discussions, learning activities, debriefing, and a conclusion. A model is presented to encourage practitioners to stimulate inclusion of all citizens through leisure education within the community that incorporates a leisure education course, leisure coaching, as well as family and friend participation.

Chapter 8
Teaching Techniques for Leisure Education

*The world cares very little about what
a man or woman knows, it is what
a man or woman is about to do that counts.*
-Booker T. Washington

Introduction

This text provides information about the conceptualization of leisure education and some examples of specific leisure education programs. The specific programs contained in this book are not intended to be depictions of complete programs. Because they provide a starting point to begin systematic instruction of leisure education, leisure service providers are encouraged to develop additional leisure education goals, objectives, content, process, and any strategies that increase their ability to educate the people they serve. While this additional information is being developed, careful consideration relative to teaching leisure education sessions may be useful. In this chapter some suggestions to consider when developing and conducting leisure education programs are provided.

Sections of this chapter are based on the work of Dattilo and Sneegas (1987) who presented suggestions to practitioners attempting to lead recreation activities. The material has been adapted, revised, and expanded to address the concerns of conducting effective leisure education sessions. This chapter provides information on the preparation and planning of a leisure education session, and suggestions for effective service delivery. Concerns related to the appropriateness of leisure education sessions, the environment, and knowledge of the program are featured in the section devoted to preparation and planning. Suggestions for presentation of sessions are divided into introduction and explanation, actual implementation of sessions, use of prompting strategies to promote skill acquisition, and bringing closure to sessions devoted to leisure education; therefore this chapter is divided into the following sections:

(a) prepare an appropriate session;
(b) prepare the environment;
(c) gain knowledge of the session;

(d) present introduction;
(e) implement the activity;
(f) prompt behaviors; and
(g) present conclusion.

Prepare an Appropriate Session

When preparing and planning to lead a session on leisure education, it is helpful for the leisure service professional to determine the appropriateness of the session both for the participants and for achieving preestablished goals and objectives. If, for example, the instructor wished to select a leisure education session for a group of teenagers, the session would contain leisure education content and be developed at a level appropriate for adolescents.

To assist in preparing for an appropriate leisure education session the following strategies are described to:

(a) determine program content;
(b) assess participant skills;
(c) match program to participants;
(d) develop program process;
(e) consider time; and
(f) ensure safety.

Determine Program Content

After establishing the goals and objectives associated with a specific leisure education program, the degree of rigor associated with the content can be determined. That is, the professional determines the degree of challenge that will be used when teaching.

Assess Participant Skills

In conjunction with a thorough examination of the program content, the instructor can conduct an accurate assessment of the participant to determine the appropriateness of the content. Assessment information may be compiled relative to the participants' skills, interests, and needs.

Match Program to Participants

After analysis of the program has been conducted, the assessment of the participant has been performed, and the goals of the program have been determined, the appropriate match of aspects of a program with the participant can be made. The ability of the instructor to match the session content with the skills of the participants is strongly influenced by the manner in which the practitioner plans to present the content.

Develop Program Process

The intended presentation strategy (the process) requires the leisure service professional to determine how the material will be presented. Concerns as to how the material is presented include the level of material to be communicated, the rate of information dissemination, the amount of practice for the participants, the use of audiovisual aids, the number and type of learning activities, and the amount of participant involvement.

Consider Time

In addition to matching program content to participants' skills after a thorough examination of both, the instructor can consider issues of time and safety to help determine the appropriateness of a leisure education session. One of the more difficult aspects of conducting leisure education programs is determining the amount of time required for presentations, discussions and learning activities. It is important to choose those activities that can be properly initiated and completed. The practitioner may examine the time allotted for the session and then determine the approximate length of time needed to conduct the session successfully.

Ensure Safety

Safety is monitored continuously by the professional. A proactive posture can be assumed to anticipate and prevent problems. Prevention is the most effective form of safety; however, when problems arise related to unsafe conditions, immediate remediation is suggested.

By preparing for an appropriate session as illustrated in Figure 8.1 (see page 108), leisure education programs can be enhanced. To determine if a session is appropriate, it is helpful to determine program content and assess participant skills so that the program challenge can be "matched" to the participants' skills. In addition, determining the strategy for presentation of the material, the amount of time needed for a session and safety concerns can all improve the quality of a leisure education program.

Prepare the Environment

As practitioners plan to conduct a session devoted to leisure education, consideration of characteristics of the existing environment may be useful. Environmental concerns may be considered which include:

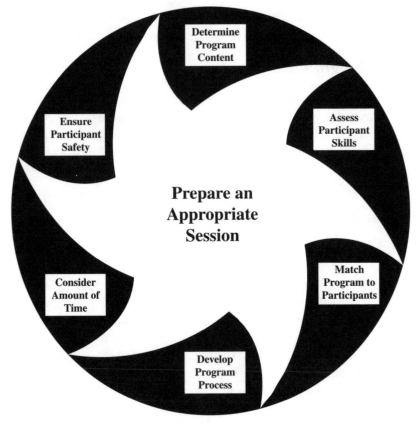

Fig. 8.1

(a) arrange environment; and
(b) examine equipment.

Arrange Environment

Thoughtful consideration of the environment can aid in creating an enjoyable atmosphere for learning and active participation. Arrangement of furni-
ture and recreational and educational equipment and the establishment of
boundaries prior to the arrival of participants may alleviate confusion and
boredom. Another approach is to engage participants in these prepara-
tory tasks. This may increase their sense of involvement in the overall experience.

Examine Equipment

Examination of equipment to be used during the session in advance of
actual implementation can prevent confusion and embarrassment for the

instructor. Electrical devices such as cassette tape players and compact disc players can be tested as well as the tapes and compact discs to be used. Examination of resources at the session site, such as electrical outlets, can be made to increase the likelihood of the equipment working when needed. Alternative plans should be developed in the event of equipment failure.

Gain Knowledge of the Session

A thorough understanding of the activities which comprise a leisure education session is helpful. To effectively gain knowledge about the session instructors may wish to consider the following ideas:

   (a) understand content and process;
   (b) plan sequence of events;
   (c) consider formation; and
   (d) rehearse session.

Understand Content and Process

Another important step in planning and preparing to conduct a leisure education session is to have a thorough understanding of the content and process employed in that session. Reviewing the content and process associated with the particular leisure education objective and practicing communicating the information to other people can improve the delivery of the program.

Plan Sequence of Events

Planning the sequence of events fosters a cohesive session. The use of transitions from one portion of the session to another allows participants to better understand how components of the leisure education session relate to each other. A sequence can be applied that initially uses introductory activities if the participants do not know each other, and then alternate between presentations, discussions, learning activities, and debriefings.

Consider Formation

When preparing for a session on leisure education, the most appropriate formation for the participants can be considered. A circle may be a more appropriate formation for discussion while rows may be used for observation. The nature of the content and the proposed process, along with the intended outcomes, determine the chosen formation.

Rehearse the Session

Many practitioners have shared the experience of believing they have a thorough understanding of a session until they actually attempt to engage the participants. Communication of the intent of the session and specific directions provided during the session may not be as clear to participants as they are to the practitioner. Therefore, once the instructor has considered all of the aforementioned steps, it is useful to rehearse the session.

Present Introduction

Getting a session off to a good start helps everyone relax and begin to enjoy themselves. To begin sessions effectively the following steps can be used:

(a) signal participants;
(b) identify session purpose;
(c) adjust voice volume;
(d) change proximity;
(e) group creatively;
(f) position self;
(g) consider the four Cs; and
(h) provide chance for questions.

Signal Participants

A leisure education session can begin with an effective introduction and explanation. Regardless of the skills practitioners may possess, if the attention of the participants is not obtained, it is unlikely that the educational session will be successful. The instructor can develop a consistent signal allowing participants to know when the session is ready to begin. A signal may involve the playing of background music prior to a session and then stopping the music when the session is to begin. Another signal that can be used is flickering the lights.

Identify Session Purpose

Once a signal is given, it can be useful for the instructor to recite the title of the leisure education program, the goals and objectives to be addressed, and the name of any learning activities employed during the session. The naming of the leisure education program, possibly accompanied by some instruction related to the name, can allow participants to refer to the program more accurately in the future.

Adjust Voice Volume

Sometimes the instructor may feel the need to raise his or her voice to gain participants' attention. However, at times, the instructor can attract the participants' attention by lowering his or her voice instead.

Change Proximity

If some participants are not yet paying attention to the practitioner, the proximity of the participant to the practitioner may be considered. The instructor can often gain participants' attention by moving closer to these individuals. This action allows the leisure service professional to gain participants' attention without disrupting introduction of the session. Moving closer to a participant also allows the practitioner to avoid accidentally reinforcing the behavior of an inattentive participant.

Group Creatively

An exciting aspect of any program can occur during the grouping of participants. This critical component of leadership is often not adequately considered and may result in some participants being bored, embarrassed, or feeling rejected. Alternatives to the traditional method of "number call" and "choosing sides" should be employed to stimulate interest and eliminate cliques.

Grouping is an excellent time to provide opportunities for leisure education by having participants group and regroup according to how they perceive themselves relative to leisure. For instance, the instructor might ask all participants who consider themselves to be more like "leaders" during their leisure to form one group and those who consider themselves "followers" to form another. Once they are arranged in these groups, participants may be encouraged to discuss why they chose that group. This technique may not be feasible when it is important to develop groups of equal number.

Providing participants with a playing card is another possible way to group people. Participants will then be asked to form a group with those people with the same card color which would make two groups, the same suit making four groups, or the same number establishing groups containing four participants. By providing them with the concrete cue of a playing card, participants are less likely to forget to which group they belong when compared to other grouping strategies that do not provide participants with a concrete cue. The use of playing cards allows the leisure service professional to regulate the size of the group. The number of ways an instructor groups participants is limited only by the person's imagination.

Position Self

When explaining a session, practitioners can consider how they are positioned relative to the participants. Proper positioning may allow each participant to adequately observe the practitioner and hear what is being said.

Consider the Four Cs

The practitioner can use the four "Cs" when providing directions for a session. The directions for a session include being *clear* to participants, being *concise* by stating only information critical to comprehension, being *complete* so as to give participants all information needed to perform identified tasks successfully, and *comparing* the identified activity and learning tasks to activities and tasks familiar to participants.

Provide Chance for Questions

One of the most difficult skills to master when conducting a leisure education session is the ability to provide opportunities for questions and then to respond effectively to the questions. The act of frequently pausing during instructions can provide a greater opportunity for participants to raise concerns. An instructor can evaluate participants' understanding of the directions. To evaluate their understanding, the instructor can either ask specific questions or provide the participants with the opportunity to ask questions. During a question and answer exchange, it is important for the practitioner to respond accurately to a question posed by a participant. If practitioners are unable to answer relevant questions, they can acknowledge the fact that they do not know and describe to participants what actions can be taken to answer the question.

The beginning of any session often sets the tone for the entire session. To assist professionals in starting the session in a positive manner, suggestions illustrated in Figure 8.2 were made in this section.

Implement the Activity

After a session on leisure education has been explained and introduced, it is time to implement the session. When implementing the session, consideration of the following may be of assistance:

(a) to encourage participants;
(b) to provide assistance;
(c) to monitor voice; and
(d) to focus eyes and body on participants.

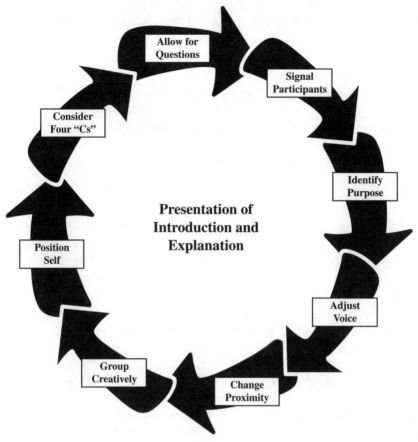

Fig. 8.2

Encourage Participants

Throughout the implementation process, the practitioner can provide adequate encouragement to participants. More encouragement is typically given when individuals are first learning a skill, as opposed to practicing a skill that has previously been mastered. The instructor can attend to those individuals who demonstrate understanding, as well as those participants who may require additional instruction. The type of acknowledgment can be systematically altered to maintain the interest of the participants.

Provide Assistance

The instructor may provide participants with assistance when needed. It can be useful to maintain a balance between providing participants with assistance and encouraging independent behavior. If participants are encountering difficulty completing a task, the practitioner may provide feedback to the participants about their performance. Often, it is less embarrassing if group corrections are made rather than singling out individuals. For instance, if during an aerobics class the instructor were to notice one of the participants performing a skill incorrectly, the instructor could obtain the entire group's attention and demonstrate the correct skill with all participants modeling the instructor's behavior. Such a strategy is preferable to identifying the person performing the skill incorrectly. Group corrections allow the practitioner to maintain participants' attention without focusing on a participant who is experiencing difficulties.

Monitor Voice

Practitioners can continuously monitor their verbal delivery style. It is helpful if the instructor's voice is loud enough to be heard and at an appropriate pitch. Some people have difficulty hearing higher tones while many other people find a high-pitched voice to be distracting. In addition, the pitch and volume of the practitioner's voice can be varied to avoid monotony. The delivery speed of speech can be closely monitored by the instructor. Often the participants' attention will be lost if the speech is too slow (boredom) or too fast (confusion).

Focus Eyes and Body on Participants

By establishing eye contact, a practitioner can make participants feel as if they are being spoken to directly. A sense of concern and interest can be communicated by directing one's gaze at an intended audience. In addition, Tauber (1994) observed that looking directly at participants whose interest appears to be wavering can rekindle their attention.

The directions of the instructor's body and stance can also communicate interest. His or her movements can either accentuate the presentation by providing helpful embellishments and visual representations of speech, or detract from the presentation if the actions are idiosyncratic and irrelevant to the presentation.

Prompt Behaviors

Prompting procedures are teaching procedures in which leisure service professionals provide a prompt prior to participant's responses to increase the probability of the participant responding correctly (Snell, 1992). These procedures are both effective and efficient ways to assist individuals in acquiring skills (Wolery, Ault, & Doyle, 1992). A "prompt" is an action made by an instructor that cues an individual to a behavior. The most effective prompts are those that occur naturally in the person's environment and are easily faded.

Types of Prompts

When a prompt is used the ultimate goal is that the prompt will help a person learn a skill, be faded, and eventually be withdrawn so that the individual performs the skill independently. There are a variety of prompts:

(a) verbal;
(b) gestural;
(c) pictorial;
(d) partial physical; and
(e) full physical.

Verbal Prompts. Verbal prompts are verbal statements of how to perform a task. They differ from a task direction which tells individuals what to do. For instance, when an instructor says, "Play golf," the statement is a verbal cue. When the instructor says, "Put the golf ball on the tee on the ground directly in front of your feet," the statement is a task direction. A practitioner may deliver verbal prompts indirectly or directly. During the instruction for hitting a softball, the instructor may ask, "What do you need to do after stepping into the batter's box?" as an indirect verbal prompt. A direct verbal prompt would be asking the participant to turn his or her nose toward to the pitcher.

Gestural Prompts. Gestural prompts are nonverbal behaviors that include hand movement, facial expression, or body movement (Wolery, Bailey, & Sugai, 1988). An advantage of gestural prompts is that these prompts are natural. Individuals use a variety of gestures every day without realizing that they are using gestural prompts. For example, a baseball coach may point to the third base to direct a player to run to the base. Similar to verbal prompts, it is helpful to assess whether the participant understands the meaning of the gesture (Wolery, Ault, & Doyle, 1992).

Pictorial Prompts. Pictorial prompts include pictures, drawings, or written words. Instructors may take pictures of the proper posture for tennis and teach participants about the posture using these pictures. Other instructors may write words on index cards describing the expected behavior.

Model Prompts. Model prompts are an instructor's demonstration of the correct behavior (Wolery, Ault, & Doyle, 1992). For example, when an instructor teaches participants to play Frisbee, the instructor may provide all participants with a Frisbee and keep one. Using the Frisbee, the instructor can demonstrate the proper ways to throw the Frisbee and encourage participants to imitate the motions. In addition, model prompts can be used if a desired behavior is a verbal response. In this case, participants imitate what the instructor says. For instance, an instructor may ask participants to identify different sports equipment by name. When participants fail to answer, the instructor can name the equipment and then ask participants to repeat the response.

Partial Physical Prompts. Partial physical prompts involve the practitioner's physical contact with a participant. Partial physical prompts do not entirely control participants' behavior (Wolery, Ault, & Doyle, 1992). The physical contacts include nudging, tapping, soft pulling, or pushing. For instance, when teaching a child how to use a tape player, an instructor may hold and direct the participant's index finger.

Full Physical Prompts. Full physical prompts involve an instructor's control over a participant's behaviors. Most of the time, the practitioner stands behind a participant, holds the participant's hands, and moves the participant through the desired behaviors (Wolery, Ault, & Doyle, 1992). In the example of operating a tape player, the instructor may put his or her hands over the participant's hands, having full control of the participant's hand movement to push the play button. The instructor must be careful not to harm participants by forcing their movements.

Prompting Procedures

Prompting procedures, which are described in the next section of the chapter, incorporate strategies to fade prompts, and are shown to be effective in teaching a variety of tasks to different people (Demchak, 1990). Some examples of prompting procedures include:

(a) constant time delay;
(b) system of least prompts;
(c) graduated guidance; and
(d) most-to-least prompting.

Before describing these four prompting procedures, a brief discussion of task analysis is provided. Typically when providing prompts, the leisure service professional decides what needs to be taught. Next, the skills are divided into discrete or chained behaviors. Discrete behaviors involve a single response and have a clear beginning and ending (Wolery, Ault, & Doyle, 1992). Chained behaviors are a composition of many behaviors, such as throwing a Frisbee, hitting a softball or turning on a tape player, and involve several responses to perform a behavior. To teach a skill composed of chained behaviors, instructors divide the skill into teachable units of behaviors.

Constant Time Delay. A constant time delay procedure limits the chances for participants to make errors during instruction. Low error rates are attractive because errors tend to be repeated. Errors decrease the amount of time devoted to instruction, and some people demonstrate negative behaviors when they commit an error (Demchak, 1990). Also, near-errorless learning helps avoid feelings of helplessness while promoting a sense of competence. This procedure is relatively quick and easy to implement and has been used successfully to teach leisure skills to adolescents (Zhang, Gast, Horvat, & Dattilo, 1995) and parents of adolescents (Wall & Gast, 1997).

When using constant time delay, an instructor systematically delays a prompt to promote a participant's independent leisure participation. The procedure requires that a participant wait for the instructor's prompt when the participant does not know how to perform a task. In this way, participants are taught to wait if they are not sure of their ability to complete a task.

Procedures for Constant Time Delay. Steps in implementing this procedure include:

(a) determine length of prompt delay interval;
(b) determine time to complete a task;
(c) select a controlling prompt; and
(d) begin instruction.

After the task analysis is completed, the amount of time needed for a participant to begin and complete a task is selected. These times will likely vary from one participant to another because of varying skill levels. It is important to select an appropriate time because intervals that are too short may lead to frustration while intervals that are too long may lead to boredom. Next, the least intrusive prompt that will influence a participant's behavior is selected. After a prompt is selected, the instructor is ready to begin instruction.

To begin, the participant is asked to complete the first step in the task analysis. For the first few times using constant time delay, the instructor will immediately prompt the participant. After the prompt, the instructor waits the predetermined amount of time for the participant to begin the task. If the participant correctly completes the task, the participant is praised, but if the participant incorrectly completes the task, the instructor correctly completes the task and proceeds to the next step in the task analysis. As instruction continues over several sessions, the instructor begins to delay the prompt so that the participant will have the opportunity to perform tasks independently.

Example of Constant Time Delay. Josh is interested in arts and crafts. He knows that one of the staff members at the recreation center, Mary, is skillful at origami, the Japanese art of paper folding. Josh asks Mary to teach him origami. Mary agrees and decides to start with something simple, and decides to teach Josh how to make a paper airplane. She divides the task into steps. Next, Mary decides how many seconds she needs to complete a step in the task analysis. It takes three seconds for Mary to complete each step. Because Josh is younger and has not had the experience with origami that she has, Mary estimates that it will take him five seconds to complete each step. Mary chooses to use a model prompt because she thinks that Josh will correctly perform the skills by imitating what she does during each step and because she thinks that the independent Josh will resist physical prompts.

To initiate instruction for Josh, Mary gives two pieces of paper to him and keeps two pieces for herself. Mary reminds Josh that he should wait for her direction if he does not know how to perform a task. Mary tells him to make an airplane and immediately models the first step, paired with the descriptive verbal direction, "Hold one edge of your paper."

After Mary completes the first step with her paper, she waits five seconds for Josh to imitate the step. He begins to perform the step within five seconds after Mary's prompt and completes the step within five seconds after the initiation. Seeing that he has correctly performed the first step, Mary praises Josh and immediately begins to show him how to perform the second step. Unfortunately, Josh has some difficulty and does not complete the step within five seconds. Mary takes his paper and completes the second step for him. As soon as she completes the second step with Josh's paper, she shows him the third step. She continues this procedure through all the steps of the task analysis.

System of Least Prompts. Heyne and Schleien (1994) recommended the use of system of least prompts to leisure service providers because it has been documented to be an effective procedure to teach leisure skills (Collins, Hall, & Branson, 1997). The system of least prompts is a procedure in which the leisure service professional provides different levels of prompts to assist participants in the performance of a task. In this procedure, the instructor selects more than two levels of prompts and begins instruction using the least intrusive prompt. If a participant fails to respond to the least intrusive prompt, the instructor will use increasingly more intrusive prompts until a participant performs a task.

Procedures for the System of Least Prompts. Steps in implementing this procedure include:

(a) determine time to complete task;
(b) select prompts; and
(c) begin instruction.

Primarily, the procedure is used to teach simple and one step tasks because the procedure is too involved for teaching more complex tasks. After the selection of a single step from a task analysis, the instructor identifies at least three levels of prompts and the length of time allotted for participants to begin and complete the skill.

To begin, the practitioner provides a task direction, and waits the predetermined amount of time for the participant to respond to the direction. If a participant responds correctly, the instructor praises the participant. If a participant responds incorrectly, the instructor interrupts the participant and provides the second-level prompt. If the participant still does not respond correctly, the instructor interrupts again and uses the third-level prompt.

Example of System of Least Prompts. Using this procedure to teach Josh one of the steps in making a paper airplane, Mary selects the third step from the task analysis, which reads, "Fold the paper so that two adjacent edges meet each other." As before, she determines that it will take Josh five seconds to complete the step. Mary selects three prompts: verbal, gestural, and pictorial. Mary gives Josh verbal instructions to complete the task. When Josh begins to fold the paper incorrectly, Mary interrupts him and uses the next level prompt (gestural) by pointing to the two edges of the paper that he should fold together. When Josh correctly completes the task, Mary praises him. In this case, there is no need for Mary to use the third level prompt (pictorial) that she had selected.

Graduated Guidance. A graduated guidance procedure is similar to the system of least prompts in that the leisure service professional provides several levels of prompts to participants. However, graduated guidance differs from system of least prompts in the prompt fading system. As previously discussed, in the system of least prompts the instructor provides the least intrusive prompt at the beginning and increases the level of prompt until the participant responds. In graduated guidance the instructor uses the most intrusive prompt at the beginning of instruction and decreases the intrusiveness of the prompting as participants become more skilled. This procedure almost always involves physical contacts with participants. For instance, instructors put their hands over the hands of the participants when teaching a manual skill such as holding a bow and arrow. Physical prompting can be faded in terms of the amount of pressure and locations of assistance.

Procedures for Graduated Guidance. Steps in implementing this procedure include:

(a) select prompts;
(b) decide how prompts are faded; and
(c) begin instruction.

After selecting a target skill, the practitioner decides how to fade prompts. At the beginning of each session, the practitioner provides a verbal direction. Immediately after the delivery of the verbal direction, the instructor provides full physical assistance. When participants do not resist the instructor's assistance, the instructor provides verbal praise. Immediately after a participant performs the first step from the task analysis, the instructor provides full physical assistance for the second step. The frequency of providing verbal praise is dependent on an instructor's discretion.

When participants perform two or three consecutive steps in the task analysis without resistance, a less intrusive prompt may be provided. There are no clear criteria regarding the change in level of prompt. The instructor attends to participants' ability to perform a skill and adjusts the assistance according to the ability of the participants.

Example of Graduated Guidance. Returning to the example of teaching Josh to make a paper airplane, Mary decides to instruct Josh using graduated guidance. She completes a task analysis then selects several levels of physical prompts to use during instruction. What distinguishes one prompt from another is the amount of physical assistance she uses such as the amount of pressure she applies to Josh's hands. Mary decides to fade from one level of prompting to another when Josh performs two steps consecutively without resisting her prompting. Mary instructs Josh to perform the first step in the task analysis and immediately provides full physical assistance. Josh does not resist her assistance, and Mary praises him. After Mary instructs Josh to perform the second step, he again offers no resistance, so Mary praises him and fades to a lesser level of physical prompt. As the instruction continues, Mary adjusts her level of physical assistance according to Josh's behavior.

Most-to-Least Prompting Procedure. The most-to-least prompting procedure is called a decreasing assistance procedure. Leisure service professionals select levels of prompts and provide appropriate amounts of assistance, depending on the performance of participants. This procedure shares a common procedure with the system of least prompts in which the instructor selects several levels of prompts. However, there are distinctions between the two procedures. In the most-to-least prompting procedure, the practitioner provides the most intrusive prompt first and works toward the least intrusive prompt, which is the reverse sequence of the system of least prompts procedure. In addition, instructors identify a criterion for moving from one to another level of prompt.

Procedures for the Most-to-Least Prompts. Steps in implementing this procedure include:

(a) select prompts;
(b) select length of intervals for responses;
(c) decide on criterion for moving to less intrusive prompt; and
(d) begin instruction.

After a leisure skill is selected and a task analysis is completed, the practitioner selects at least three prompts and decides how long to wait for a participant to respond to each prompt. The behavior of a participant serves as the criteria in determining whether or not an instructor moves to a less intrusive prompt. These criteria can be expressed in terms of number of consecutive correct responses (Colozzi & Pollow, 1984) or percentage of correct responses. Finally, the instructor is ready to begin instruction.

Example of Most-to-Least Prompts Procedure. Using this procedure to teach Josh to fold a paper airplane, Mary completes a task analysis. She then selects three prompts: model, full physical, and partial physical. She chooses an interval of five seconds for Josh to initiate an action after a prompt is given. Mary decides that if Josh correctly responds to the full physical prompt twice in a row, she will reduce the level of prompt to a partial physical prompt. She gives Josh verbal instructions to perform the first step of folding a paper airplane, and she immediately uses a full physical prompt by placing her hands on Josh's hands to guide him through the first step. When Josh does not resist her assistance, she praises him and instructs him to move to the next step. Once again Mary uses a full physical prompt, and Josh does not resist. Mary praises him again and begins to use a partial physical prompt since Josh met the criterion for moving to a less intrusive prompt. Mary continues to instruct Josh in this way until he has finished folding a paper airplane.

At times, leisure service providers can help participants learn skills by systematically providing prompting procedures. Four methods for administering prompts were presented in this section and are illustrated in Figure 8.3. It is hoped that knowledge of these techniques will help professionals choose the most effective prompting procedure.

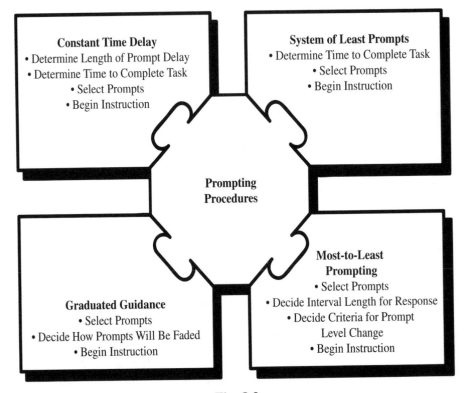

Constant Time Delay
• Determine Length of Prompt Delay
• Determine Time to Complete Task
• Select Prompts
• Begin Instruction

System of Least Prompts
• Determine Time to Complete Task
• Select Prompts
• Begin Instruction

Prompting Procedures

Graduated Guidance
• Select Prompts
• Decide How Prompts Will Be Faded
• Begin Instruction

Most-to-Least Prompting
• Select Prompts
• Decide Interval Length for Response
• Decide Criteria for Prompt Level Change
• Begin Instruction

Fig. 8.3

Presentation of a Conclusion

Just as it is important for the leisure service professional to introduce a concept effectively, it is equally important to terminate a session thoughtfully. To provide a successful conclusion, instructors may wish to consider the following suggestions:

(a) end while interest is high;
(b) provide a warning;
(c) summarize events; and
(d) restore environment.

End While Interest Is High

Adequate closure provides participants with a sense of accomplishment, while encouraging participation for future involvement. It is generally helpful to end a session while interest is high rather than allowing participation to gradually fade.

Provide a Warning

Instead of ending a session abruptly, the practitioner may provide warnings to participants that the session is coming to a close. For example, the professional might say that a few minutes remain in the session and encourage participants to begin completing their assigned tasks. In another situation, the professional may announce that there is only time for two more questions, again notifying the participants that the session is winding down.

Summarize Events

A useful technique for providing adequate closure is to summarize the preceding events. Helping the group to reconstruct what was done and the purpose therein allows for continued participant involvement to the end of the session.

Restore Environment

A final consideration in ending a session is environmental restoration. Leaving the area where a leisure education program was completed in better condition than when people arrived can leave participants as well as instructors with a positive feeling. Participants can be encouraged to become actively involved in restoration and cleaning activities. With a little creativity, cleaning tasks can be effectively incorporated into a leisure education session.

Conclusion

The chapter provided information on how to prepare and plan for a leisure education session as depicted in Figure 8.4 (see page 124). Suggestions for effective service delivery were presented. Concerns related to appropriateness of leisure education sessions, the environment, and knowledge of the program were featured in this chapter. Suggestions for presentation of sessions were made relative to introducing and explaining information, conducting sessions, using prompting techniques, and bringing closure to sessions devoted to leisure education.

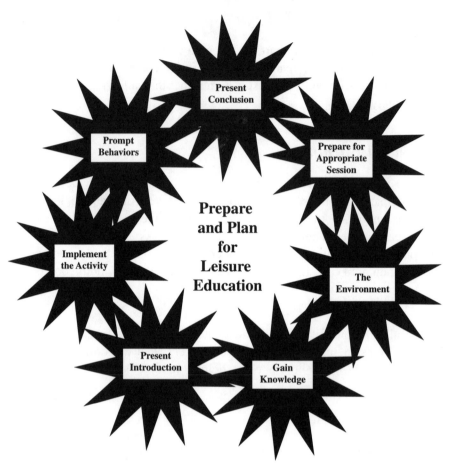

Fig. 8.4

Chapter 9
Adaptations of Leisure Education Programs

Things do not change, we do.
-Henry David Thoreau

Introduction

The specific leisure education programs presented in this text have been designed generically; that is, the programs were not developed with a particular population in mind. Instead, they were designed for any group of people experiencing barriers to a satisfying, enjoyable, and meaningful leisure lifestyle. The programs were designed in this fashion to facilitate greater application by practitioners working in a variety of settings attempting to provide leisure education for people possessing different abilities.

"If leisure is a profoundly human phenomenon and not just a trivial option in life, then no person should be arbitrarily cut off from it" (Kelly, 1996, p. 400). This aspiration by Kelly is particularly important given the passage of the Americans with Disabilities Act in 1990. The Americans with Disabilities Act is a civil rights law that is intended to end the discrimination against people with disabilities by providing them the right to equal opportunities to participate in community-based services (Dattilo, 1994). Consequently, more than ever in the past, all leisure service professionals who are aware of program adaptations can design and implement programs which facilitate individuals of all abilities to participate in programs together.

The absence of the identification of a particular group of individuals associated with each specific program does have its shortcomings. Some practitioners may need to adapt the programs to meet various individuals' needs. Although the programs in this text will not be used as is by all leisure service providers, they do provide a starting point from which practitioners can adapt and expand their leisure education services.

This chapter on adaptations is designed to encourage leisure service professionals to adapt the information presented in the specific programs as necessary. When needed, these adaptations should permit professionals to meet the varying needs and abilities of the people receiving leisure services. The suggestions for adaptations are not intended to be all-inclusive. They are, however, intended to describe some options available to practitioners to make adjustments intended to facilitate active leisure participation for all people.

General Considerations

When making adaptations to leisure education programs there are some general suggestions that are helpful to consider. The suggestions presented in this section of the chapter are divided into the following four broad guidelines:

(a) focus on the person first;
(b) encourage participant autonomy;
(c) involve participants in adaptation process; and
(d) evaluate adaptations.

Focus on the Person First

To focus on the person first, it can be helpful for professionals to consider the unique characteristics of the program participants. Three strategies are identified in this section to help encourage a "person-first" approach:

(a) individualize adaptations;
(b) concentrate on abilities; and
(c) match challenge and skills.

Individualize Adaptations. A key to adapting leisure education programs is to consider the individual needs of each participant. Because people possess differing levels of skills, practitioners must individualize their adaptations.

Concentrate on Abilities. A person-first philosophy requires practitioners to focus on participants' abilities. Too often, assessments associated with leisure education content areas are such that they initially identify what participants cannot do, and adaptations are designed to accommodate this limitation. Perhaps a more useful procedure may be to focus initially on the skills and abilities of participants and then make adaptations building upon these skills. When people's abilities become the focus of attention, practitioners are more likely to allow participants to be as independent as possible; they will tend to avoid stifling these individuals by making unnecessary adaptations that fail to capitalize on skills they possess.

Match Challenge and Skills. Each leisure education program contains learning experiences that possess a certain degree of challenge. In addition, prior to conducting a leisure education program, practitioners can systematically assess the skills and interests of the people for whom the leisure education program is designed. Then, when conducting leisure education programs, professionals will be in a position to better achieve the delicate balance between the challenge of specific activities and the skills of the participants.

If an imbalance exists between the degree of challenge of a program and the participants' skills, barriers may be created to leisure participation. For instance, if a specific leisure education learning activity is too easy for participants, boredom often results. Conversely, if a learning activity is too difficult, frustration can occur. One way to reduce these barriers is through adaptation. Adaptations permit modification of the challenge associated with a leisure education program to meet the abilities of the participants. Once adaptations are made, they must continually be adjusted to meet the changing skills of the participants.

Encourage Participant Autonomy

Since perceived freedom is a critical element of leisure, encouraging participant autonomy is a natural extension of leisure expression. The following three strategies are provided to assist professionals in instilling a sense of autonomy within their participants:

(a) facilitate independence;
(b) determine necessity of adaptation; and
(c) view adaptations as transitional.

Facilitate Independence. When practitioners adapt a leisure education program to permit participation, they can design the adaptation to encourage the individual to participate as independently as possible. Therefore, modifications can decrease the need for participants to rely on others for assistance while providing individuals with increased opportunities to participate actively in leisure as independently as possible. Since leisure education is designed to increase independence, practitioners are encouraged to adopt the goal of independence when adapting leisure education programs.

Determine Necessity of Adaptation. Because some people experience barriers to leisure participation, some practitioners may be quick to change a leisure education program. In addition, changes may be readily made to a given program because leisure service professionals are often highly skilled at modifications. Sometimes these changes are made with the knowledge of the general characteristics of a group rather than with explicit information about the specific participants. Although this practice may be practical in some situations, it may create a problem. Some aspects of leisure education programs may be changed when they need not be. Consequently, it is important for practitioners to examine each adaptation and decide if it is actually necessary.

View Adaptations as Transitional. Adaptations to leisure education programs can permit active participation for people with a wide range of knowledge and skills. The very nature of leisure education implies that individuals will learn and change. As learning and change occurs, skills and knowledge fluctuate. Many individuals receiving leisure services will develop skills and knowledge associated with leisure participation. Therefore, if an adaptation was made at one time, it may no longer be appropriate because the individual has now acquired the abilities to participate without any adaptations. At that point, the adaptations may impair, rather than encourage, leisure participation. Other people participating in leisure education programs may possess degenerative or progressive conditions that require continual modifications. A previous slight adaptation to a particular learning activity may be insufficient later to provide the person with the opportunity to participate. In any case, practitioners must be willing to adopt the view that any adaptations they make to a given situation may need to be altered in the future.

Involve Participants in Adaptation Process

A valuable resource for all leisure service providers is the participants of their programs. Three suggestions are provided to encourage professionals to include participants in the adaptation process:

(a) discuss adaptations;
(b) determine feasibility of adaptation; and
(c) ensure safety of adaptations.

Discuss Adaptations. In almost every aspect of leisure planning, practitioners are encouraged to consult with consumers regarding their opinions and desires. A critical task in motivating people to take part in leisure education programs is to encourage them to perceive that they have input into their program. Active involvement in shaping a leisure education program can provide individuals with a sense of investment that may increase their motivation to initiate and maintain participation. This principle applies as well to adapting aspects of the leisure education program. Discussions with participants may provide practitioners with valuable information on methods to adapt the activity and instill feelings of control and commitment by the participants. When participants do not currently possess the skills to communicate their feelings and ideas toward an adaptation effectively, observations can be used to obtain input from these consumers.

Determine Feasibility of Adaptation. Involving participants in the process of adapting leisure education programs can provide practitioners with a means to determine the feasibility and usability of the adaptation. If participants feel that the adaptation detracts from the program, their motivation may be reduced. Therefore, asking participants their opinions of adaptations and encouraging them to make suggestions for different adaptations can enhance the ability of leisure service professionals to make feasible adaptations. Sometimes, practitioners may go to great lengths to adapt a specific learning activity only to find that as a result of the adaptation people are no longer interested in participation. Discussion with consumers prior to and during adaptations can help encourage active leisure participation following adaptations.

Ensure Safety of Adaptations. The most critical element to remember when making changes to any recreation program is safety. Commercially available equipment, materials, games and many other aspects of a leisure education program typically have been tested and retested to determine their safety for potential participants. When an adaptation is made, the previous research conducted by the manufacturers is compromised and associated safety claims change. Therefore, practitioners must examine and evaluate any program they adapt and must consider the safety of participants. One strategy to help practitioners evaluate the safety of an adaptation is to encourage participants' input regarding ways to ensure and increase the safety associated with a given aspect of a leisure education program.

Evaluate Adaptations

Participant skills and environmental situations often change frequently. To accommodate these changes, the following suggestions are provided to encourage professionals to evaluate adaptations:

(a) conduct observations;
(b) make adjustments; and
(c) consider original task.

Conduct Systematic Observations. When adaptations are made to specific aspects of a leisure education program, practitioners can continuously observe individuals participating in the program. Observations of individual participation should allow practitioners to determine if the adaptations are achieving their intended goals. These observations provide practitioners with the ability to examine unanticipated difficulties participants may be experiencing relative to the adaptations. Continuous observations put practitioners in a position to understand the effectiveness of the adaptations.

Make Necessary Adjustments. Observations provide practitioners with the opportunity to discover problems with adaptations. When problems are identified, practitioners must then be willing to respond to any difficulties associated with adaptations. This willingness to change an adaptation may stem from the belief that even if a great deal of time and energy is put into a given task, it may need to be altered to permit active leisure participation for persons with disabilities. A slight adjustment to an aspect of a leisure education program may make the difference between active and meaningful participation or failure.

Consider Resemblance to Original Task. Each time an adaptation is made, that aspect of the program becomes less like the original task. Therefore, adaptations can tend to limit the ability of individuals to participate in different programs that do not contain such adaptations. Practitioners who keep aspects of the program as close to the original program as possible tend to encourage participants to generalize their ability in order to participate in the activities in other environments and situations.

Four broad guidelines for making adaptation to leisure education programs, as illustrated in Figure 9.1, have been presented in this section of the chapter. As leisure service providers focus on the people they serve, encour-

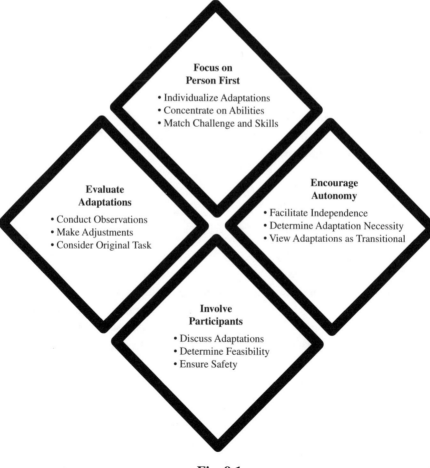

**Focus on
Person First**

• Individualize Adaptations
• Concentrate on Abilities
• Match Challenge and Skills

**Evaluate
Adaptations**

• Conduct Observations
• Make Adjustments
• Consider Original Task

**Encourage
Autonomy**

• Facilitate Independence
• Determine Adaptation Necessity
• View Adaptations as Transitional

**Involve
Participants**

• Discuss Adaptations
• Determine Feasibility
• Ensure Safety

Fig. 9.1

age their autonomy and involvement in the adaptation process and closely evaluate any adaptation, they should develop meaningful leisure education programs for all participants.

Areas of Adaptation

When adapting existing leisure education programs to meet the unique needs of participants, practitioners should consider the many aspects of a given program. A multitude of facets associated with leisure education programs can be examined for possible adaptations intended to increase participation. For the purposes of this text, identification of possible adaptations of leisure education programs are divided into four major areas:

(a) materials that are used;
(b) activities;
(c) environment in which the activity is conducted; and
(d) instructional strategies employed by practitioners.

These four areas are not necessarily mutually exclusive and are intended to help organize the suggestions on adaptations.

The following information should encourage practitioners to consider a variety of aspects of the leisure education programs when attempting to make adaptations facilitating leisure participation. The *materials* used during a leisure education program can be adapted to meet the needs of the participants. In addition, the specific requirements associated with the learning *activities* may be changed. The *environment* provides another alternative for practitioners to adapt to bring about active involvement of participants. Finally, practitioners are encouraged to turn their focus of adaptations inward and examine possible ways to modify *instructional strategies* to teach persons with disabilities about leisure. The descriptions related to these five areas are not intended to be all-inclusive but are designed to assist practitioners in beginning to develop plans for adaptations for leisure education programs. Examples given in many of the following situations are made with recreation activities, rather than leisure education activities, to provide instances with which readers are familiar and to enable visualization of the suggested adaptation.

Materials

Many aspects of materials used in leisure education programs can be adapted. Examples of methods for adapting materials are presented here relative to the following areas:

(a) size;

(b) speed;

(c) weight;

(d) stability;

(e) durability; and

(f) safety.

Size. The size of materials should be adjusted for participants by making objects, such as puzzle pieces, larger for those having difficulty grasping small objects. Tape can be wrapped around handles to increase their size
and permit manipulation. Conversely, other people who may have difficulty
grasping larger objects, such as felt tip markers, need smaller ones. Decreasing the size of objects that are intended to be inserted into an opening,
such as a basketball, can increase success, while making the opening larger,
such as a basketball hoop may also lessen the requirements of an activity.
Large colorful cards can assist individuals with visual problems in playing
table games designed to teach about leisure. If individuals are participating
in racquet sports, the racquets can be shortened for more control or length-
ened to allow participants to cover more ground.

Speed. Some individuals with disabilities may experience problems
associated with gross motor coordination. A coordination problem can be
quickly spotted as individuals respond to moving objects. One way to increase the success of a person's response is to reduce the speed of the moving object. Air can be removed from a ball so when struck it will move at a
slower speed. Wedges can be placed under any angled surface to reduce the
incline on which a ball may be placed to slow the ball.

Weight. The weight of objects can be adjusted to meet the strength of
the participants. Wooden and metal materials can be exchanged for those that
are made from plastic or rubber. For instance, plastic balls, sponge balls and
balloons can be substituted for heavier balls in some situations, while lighter
plastic or sponge bats can be used in lieu of heavier metal or wooden bats.

Stability. People who have unsteady movements may be prevented
from using some expensive technology because they are apt to break the
equipment. Suction cups and clamps can be used to stabilize the item, such
as a tape recorder, so that the person can use it without fear of accidental
damage. In craft projects people who possess grasping skills with only one
hand can be assisted by securing the project to a board or table.

Durability. Material for leisure education programs should be made
durable. Duct tape is often helpful in reinforcing many different pieces of
equipment. Game boards and playing cards should be laminated to prolong
their use. Velcro can also be used to secure objects that need to be removed
at different times.

Safety. When making any adaptations to objects it is critical to evaluate continuously each adaptation in reference to safety. No toxic substances should be added. If changes to objects occur, they should be examined and any sharp edges removed. The dangers of ingestion of objects and suffocation should be anticipated. In all cases, problems should be anticipated and steps taken toward prevention of injuries.

Activities

Many traditional recreation activities can be adapted to encourage more active participation by all individuals. Some examples of methods for adapting activities are presented below relative to the following areas:

(a) physical aspects;
(b) cognitive requirements; and
(c) social conditions.

Physical Aspects. Individuals receiving leisure services vary a great deal in terms of physical strength, speed at which they move, endurance, energy level, gross motor coordination, eye-hand coordination, flexibility, agility and many other physical skills. To adapt a physical requirement of a program, the typical *number of people* associated with a game can be changed. For instance, the number of people participating in volleyball can be changed from six to ten people for persons with limited speed and agility.

People with limited endurance and strength may benefit from making the requirements to complete an activity not as strenuous by reducing either the *number of points* needed such as 8 points to win a table tennis game rather than 21. In addition, the *length of time* a game lasts can be changed such as reducing the time to complete an activity from 30 to 15 minutes.

While learning some activities, the *physical movements* can be changed by requiring participants to walk instead of run such as when playing basketball. For those individuals who have reduced mobility, changing the required *body position* from standing to sitting may provide opportunities for participation such as when throwing a ball. Since some people receiving leisure services may have limited physical endurance, incorporating opportunities to rest during certain events, such as hiking, might be effective.

Cognitive Requirements. Some people may encounter problems associated with cognitive requirements. To accommodate these individuals, the *rules* associated with different games can be changed. For instance, if short-term memory appears to be a problem for some participants, the number of cards used in a card game can be reduced (i.e., rather than using all cards in a deck in a game of concentration, only the face cards can be used). People who do not yet possess counting skills may be able to play a game by substituting matching of colors, instead of requiring the recognition of numbers or words to move game pieces.

If the requirements for *scoring* during an activity are too difficult for some participants, changes can be made such as having people initially keep track only of the number of pins they knock down, rather than using scoring procedures associated with calculating spares and strikes. Some individuals may require some minimal assistance with reading cards used for a table game. Practitioners may wish to change the game from requiring individuals to play alone to participation with *partners*. Often, teams of participants can be developed that allow the individual team members to complement each others' skills and abilities. In addition, friendships may be developed from the team interaction.

Social Conditions. People participating in leisure education programs are doing so because they may be experiencing barriers to their leisure involvement. Frequently, these barriers are related to problems encountered in a social context. Some individuals may be intimidated by activities requiring larger groups. A reluctance to participate in larger groups may be a result of previous experiences associated with failure and perhaps ridicule. To assist people in gaining the confidence needed to participate in large group activities, practitioners may initially choose to *reduce the number of people* required to participate in an activity and to begin instruction and practice of an activity in small groups or, if resources are available, on a one-to-one basis. For instance, social skills instruction related to learning how to make friends may be conducted initially with a few individuals. As participants acquire the necessary social skills, the context could be expanded to include more participants.

The pressure involved in some activities involving direct competition against another team may be extremely threatening for some people. A person's failure to perform may result in the entire team losing to an opponent. This failure can decrease confidence and self-esteem and contribute to a reduced motivation to participate. One approach to adapting an activity could be changing the activity so *cooperation is emphasized* and direct competition against another team is eliminated. To accomplish this cooperative atmosphere, practitioners may decide to eliminate the opposing team. The opposing team would be replaced by a series of established goals to be achieved by the team. For instance, in place of the traditional game of basketball, one team could participate by establishing goals related to making a basket. By beginning at the opposite end of the court, all five team members could be required to dribble the ball as it is brought down the court, attempting to make a basket in the least amount of time.

Environment

The environment can play an important role in the ability of individuals to actively pursue leisure involvement. Practitioners may be in a position to adapt the environment in which leisure participation is intended to occur or to make recommendations for changing the environment. Because practitioners are attempting to provide leisure education in a variety of contexts, possible adaptations to the environment are suggested in this section that relate directly to:

(a) sensory factors; and
(b) the participation area.

Sensory Factors. Participation can be enhanced for some individuals by simply manipulating the *sounds* occurring within the environment during participation. For instance, when playing a leisure education learning activity, some people who are easily distracted may have difficulty concentrating when the game is being played in a multipurpose room with other people present talking to one another as they engage in other activities. Moving the leisure education learning activity to a small, quiet room where only the people participating in the learning activity are present may facilitate more active participation for some individuals. In addition, some people can experience difficulty hearing when participating in a gymnasium because of the echoing effect. Placement of drapes and sound absorbing tiles near the ceiling may muffle some distracting sounds while allowing all participants to hear and follow directions more easily.

An environment that permits people to see as much as possible is and should be provided. Practitioners should examine the context of an activity and determine if adequate *lighting* is available. Completion of craft projects located at a table may be made easier by simply placing a lamp on the table. Some people's vision, however, may be substantially impaired as a result of glare. Therefore, professionals must consider the angle of the lights realizing the possibility that some lights may be too bright and inhibit participation.

Participation Area. The area in which an activity is played can be adapted to facilitate more active participation. To accommodate individuals with reduced mobility, the *playing area* used for an activity can be changed. Rather than using an entire baseball field to play kick ball, participants can be required to keep the ball in play within the infield. In softball, participants can be required to hit to one side of the pitchers mound allowing more individuals to cover a small area. Reduction of the playing area can allow participants with limited speed to participate successfully.

Boundaries designating the end of the playing areas can also be changed to make people more aware of these designations. Wider chalk marks can be used on a soccer fields to allow people to see more clearly when they are approaching an area designated as out-of-bounds. Ropes can be placed along a walking trail to permit individuals with visual limitations to follow the trail and maintain their awareness of boundaries associated with the walking trail.

The *surface area* can also be changed to permit people to more easily access activities. A person who uses a wheelchair may be able to join a hiking expedition when some firm foundation has been applied to a trail. Children with visual impairments who are using playground equipment may be signaled that they are moving toward different equipment by changes in textures on the ground and adjacent walls.

The *facility* where the activity is conducted may be changed. For instance, ramps may be placed in a swimming pool to permit access by people with limited mobility. In addition, the water in the swimming pool could be lowered to only two or three feet to accommodate initially those people with significant fears associated with water.

Instructional Strategies

The three areas to consider when making adaptations mentioned previously have required practitioners to focus their attention away from themselves and onto the activity, materials and environment. The fourth area of consideration encourages professionals to examine their practice of leisure service delivery. If people receiving leisure services are not developing leisure skills and knowledge at a rate consistent with their potential, there may be ways to improve the instructional strategies employed by the professionals to allow individuals to meet their needs more effectively and efficiently. Although many teaching techniques were described in the previous chapter, the next section of this chapter briefly addresses the following instructional strategies that directly relate to making adaptations:

    (a) establish goals;
    (b) develop instructional steps;
    (c) provide chances for practice;
    (d) include instructional prompts;
    (e) give reinforcement; and
    (f) consider personnel.

Establish Goals. At times, participants of leisure services may find it difficult to achieve preestablished goals. Practitioners may continue to focus on the inability of individuals to achieve these goals and thus create further difficulty. A possible problem may have occurred during the establishment of goals resulting in tasks that may be too difficult to master. If this occurs, practitioners can reassess the goals and change them to meet the needs of participants. This is not to say that practitioners should develop goals that are not challenging. In fact, participants should be monitored closely for the possibility of having goals that are too easily completed. Rather than create frustration for both participants and practitioners as with overly rigorous goals, the development of goals demanding too little of the individuals can create an environment conducive to boredom and apathy.

Develop Instructional Steps. As mentioned in the previous chapter, an extremely useful tool in providing leisure services is task analysis. Task analysis involves the segmenting of a task into components that can be taught separately. The instructional components can then be sequenced together to allow individuals to complete an identified task. The procedure of task analysis is used when attempting to teach a multifaceted task that may appear complex for participants. Although task analysis requires identification of components that, when accomplished in sequence, permit completion of the task, the number of components identified for any given task may vary considerably. For instance, in one situation the act of swinging a table tennis paddle to hit the ball may be divided into four steps, while in another circumstance the task may be divided into ten steps. The skills of individual participants should determine the level of specificity associated with a task analysis. Therefore, if people are encountering difficulty learning a skill, practitioners may examine the components being taught. They can determine if further delineation is needed for those individuals stuck on a particular component or if some components should be combined or removed to accommodate people who feel they are not being sufficiently challenged.

Provide Chances for Practice. To educate people about leisure, practitioners develop content and then attempt to present this content in a systematic fashion. Sometimes people enrolled in leisure education programs fail to progress at the rate practitioners expect. One reason people may not acquire skills and knowledge associated with a particular aspect of leisure education is that they may not have received sufficient opportunity to practice the information presented in the program. Another way to adapt the instructional strategy is to change the amount of practice associated with a particular activity. If participants are not acquiring the skills and knowledge, they may benefit from more practice. Repetition through practice can allow individuals to integrate the newly acquired knowledge and skill into their existing leisure repertoire. Continuous practice of previously learned skills can increase the likelihood that individuals will maintain the skills over time. When planning practice sessions, practitioners can be creative and make these opportunities as interesting and fun as possible. Frequently, people do not acquire an understanding of a concept the first time they are presented with the idea. Practice provides experiences that permit repetition of concepts and ideas that enable people to retain that information more easily.

Include Instructional Prompts. As practitioners provide instruction, they may observe that participants are not responding to their directions. In this case, they may wish to use prompts described in the previous chapter to assist participants. Prompts can provide auditory cues for individuals, typically through verbal instructions. There are, however, other forms of prompts that can be used. Environmental prompts can encourage participants' involvement by simply manipulating the context in which an activity is provided. For instance, one way to encourage use of leisure education table games in a recreation lounge may be for the practitioner to place the games on tables in the room or open the closets where they are stored so that participants entering the area will see the games. Additional visual cues may be provided to stimulate participation. Modeling appropriate behaviors and providing systematic demonstrations may allow participants to see more clearly the desired leisure behavior. In addition, as mentioned in the chapter on teaching techniques, hand-over-hand physical guidance involving partial or full physical contact may permit individuals to feel the specific movements associated with participation and thus increase their ability to perform the skill correctly. Because people may respond differently to various prompts, practitioners are encouraged to examine the established procedures and be willing to modify the way they are prompting participants to learn and apply new leisure skills.

Give Reinforcement. Sometimes practitioners mistakenly assume that the object or event they provide individuals to encourage the acquisition of leisure skills and knowledge is a positive reinforcer. The object or event, however, may not be perceived by the participant to be a reinforcer. Dattilo and Murphy (1987b) reported that reinforcers differ from one person to another. According to the authors, "selection of an object or event to serve as a positive reinforcer must be person specific; that is, it must be something that will effectively influence that individual's behavior" (p. 54). Practitioners should monitor the response of participants to a consequence in order to determine if it is truly a powerful enough reinforcer to influence behavior. If, over time, behaviors do not improve in response to administration of a specific item or activity, practitioners should be willing to make adaptations. Testing various items and activities until reinforcers are identified may provide practitioners with a systematic procedure for identification of reinforcers.

Although the use of reinforcement can be a helpful adaptation, the discussion on intrinsic motivation in Chapter 2 is worth considering here. If trophies, prizes or other consequences associated with external rewards are assigned as indicators of learning and successful participation, these same rewards can tend to undermine the intrinsic motivation previously associated with learning and spontaneous participation in recreation and activities (Lepper, Green, & Nisbett, 1973). Mannell and Kleiber (1997, p. 138) warned that

"When people are rewarded for listening to music, playing games or volunteering, their behavior can become overjustified, that is, they may begin to attribute their participation to extrinsic motives. Research has suggested that such overjustification can be dangerous. The introduction of extrinsic rewards tends to undermine people's experience of self-determination . . . ."

Consider Personnel. Interaction between participants and practitioners is a highly complex process. Some participants may respond to some practitioners more enthusiastically than to others. Failure of some participants to progress at an anticipated rate may be influenced by the professionals who are delivering the services. Practitioners can closely monitor their interactions with participants as well as other personnel delivering leisure services. In-service training can be provided in an attempt to improve the skills of practitioners. In addition, adapting schedules to accommodate both staff and participant needs may encourage more effective implementation of leisure education programs.

Specific suggestions for making adaptations to materials, activities, environments, instructional strategies, as illustrated in Figure 9.2, have been

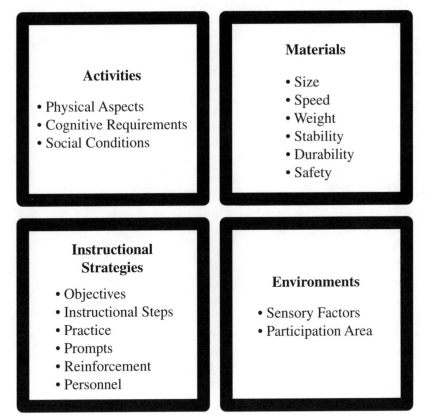

Fig. 9.2

presented in this section of the chapter. It is hoped that as professionals implement these strategies their leisure education programs will be enhanced.

Conclusion

This chapter focuses on ways to make adaptations. These adaptations make it possible for practitioners to meet the varying needs and abilities of the people attending leisure education programs. The suggestions contained in this chapter identify some options available to practitioners to make adjustments needed to facilitate active leisure participation for all participants. Initially, general considerations are presented in the chapter to provide guidelines when making any adaptation intended to promote leisure involvement. The remaining portion of the chapter is devoted to providing suggestions on adaptations related to materials that are used, the activity, the environment in which the activity is conducted, and instructional strategies employed by practitioners.

Chapter 10
Multicultural Considerations for Leisure Education

*No culture can live
if it attempts to be exclusive.*
-Mahatma Gandhi

Introduction

Many people raised in the United States have been told the nation's founders envisioned a "melting pot" ideal. Immigrants were encouraged—sometimes even forced—to "cast . . . off, to the extent possible, one's ethnic or minority identity" (Berger, 1995, p. 140) including various customs, traditions, and languages in order to become assimilated with the homogeneous mass, the so-called "melting pot." Today, however, the emphasis is on maintaining subcultural identities and embracing the value of difference (i.e., heterogeneity). The earlier "melting pot" metaphor has been replaced by the more multicultural metaphors of a "mosaic" (Kraus, 1994, p. 88), "salad bowl" (Bete, 1994, p. 1), "quilt" (Jackson, 1992, p. 23) or "'beef stew'. . . in which the essential elements in the stew maintain their discrete identities yet are part of something that includes, and is flavored by, all" (Berger, 1995, p. 140).

The term used to describe such a heterogeneous whole is "pluralism: a condition of society in which numerous distinct ethnic, religious, or cultural groups coexist within one nation" (Soukhanov et al., 1992, p. 1394). Today our national motto, *e pluribus unum*, is no longer interpreted to mean one custom, one tradition, one language, but a single *nation* representing a model of cultural pluralism (Godbey, 1991). According to Shoultz and McBride (1996), pluralism assumes that "race, gender, ethnicity, sexual orientation, class, and so on deeply shape the experiences of each one of us in relation to how we view ourselves, and how we view and are viewed by others." Cultural pluralism is now generally recognized as an organizing principle of our society and is an important consideration for leisure service professionals (Kraus, 1994).

Holland (1997) concluded that "a more diverse society will have a direct impact upon the recreation field . . ." (p. 48). Therefore, an understanding of cultural diversity issues is crucial for leisure service delivery (Malkin, Voss, Teaff, & Benshoff, 1994). If professionals are to provide leisure education services equitably in a pluralistic society, awareness of cultural diversity can be helpful (Lee & Skalko, 1996) so as to avoid focusing on "traditional white, male, middle-class, able-bodied, heterosexual perspectives" (Henderson, 1995, p. 2). According to Godbey (1991), leisure service professionals will increasingly be required to develop programs to enhance the quality of life and leisure in pluralistic societies.

Based on the beliefs of many professionals, including Henderson (1997, p. 34), that "all populations need a long-term approach to leisure education," this chapter was developed. Much of this chapter is based on an earlier writing by Sheldon and Dattilo (1997) and is designed to provide information on multicultural issues. In response to confusion over terms associated with multicultural issues by leisure service providers (Peregoy, Schliebner, & Dieser, 1997), terminology pertinent to multicultural understanding is defined and explained. In addition, specific suggestions are given for communicating sensitivity to the diversity of participants. This chapter is intended to promote multicultural awareness, without which, according to Hetzroni and Harris (1996), professionals cannot begin to serve people from diverse backgrounds adequately. Helping to create a multicultural society is an important goal for leisure service professionals (Russell, 1996).

Understanding the Vocabulary of Multiculturalism

Although many terms associated with multiculturalism are used commonly, many people cannot provide a clear definition of these terms. This section will define and explain terms selected because they appear frequently in writing related to multiculturalism. The terms include:

(a) culture;
(b) stigma;
(c) cultural diversity;
(d) acculturation;
(e) minority;
(f) race; and
(g) ethnicity.

Culture

Culture, according to Berger (1995), has multiple definitions that vary according to one's discipline. For example, anthropologists may define culture in a different way than would a sociologist or historian. Most definitions share the following: culture is a pattern of beliefs, values, and behaviors that is socially transmitted from generation to generation through the spoken and written word, the use of certain objects, customs, and traditions (Berger, 1995). Geertz (1983) summarized culture as whatever people need to know or believe so that they can operate in a way acceptable to members of a particular society. Thus *culture,* by definition, is learned behavior. Further, culture affects communication patterns, methods of conveying messages, and the comprehension of information (Hetzroni & Harris, 1996), and exists not in the artifacts or festivals, but in how people think and feel (Geertz, 1983). Kelly (1996) stated that "culture . . . includes language as well as art, styles of movement as well as dance, and ways of caring for children as well as literature" (p. 328).

Wlodkowski and Jaynes (1991, p. 57) wrote, ". . . cultural factors, including racial and socioeconomic differences, can contribute to ongoing alienation when certain behaviors are misread and unfairly judged." The conclusion of Wlodkowski and Jaynes were supported by Malaney and Shively (1995) who found that students of color in schools with a majority of Caucasians reported that it was more difficult to meet people with similar backgrounds and interests and that they generally encountered social isolation. Wlodkowski and Jaynes explained that participants who may have experienced rejection or exclusion because of their culture may choose not to attend programs. The individual's absence may be interpreted by leisure service professionals as disinterest.

According to Saville-Troike (1989), culture is what people need to know to be members of a community and to regulate interactions with other members of the same community as well as people from backgrounds different from their own. Every person has cultural identity; most people have multiple cultural memberships. Most individuals readily identify race (or races, for those who are multiracial), nationality, ethnicity, and religion as cultural groups. Other examples include gender, sexual orientation, social class, education, level of ability, and the region of the country, part of a city, or rural area in which an individual resides. Therefore, culture involves ways of living that evolve from the process of thinking, perceiving, believing, and evaluating within a particular group (Saville-Troike, 1989).

Stigma

Individuals who belong to certain racial, religious, or other groups may perceive *stigma:* an attitude by others that the individual is marked, tainted, or discounted. Goffman (1959) described three categories of stigma: abominations of the body, blemishes of individual character, and tribal stigma. Those who have the first category, abominations of the body, include individuals with visible disabilities, individuals of races other than the majority, and those who have tattoos, scars, or other identifying marks. The second category, blemishes of character, are assigned to those who have a history of addiction, alcoholism, homosexuality, imprisonment, radical political behavior, suicidal attempts, or unemployment (Goffman, 1963). The final category, tribal stigma, includes attributes that can be passed down through the family, such as race, nationality, and religion.

Discrimination against individuals who are stigmatized occurs because people "believe the person with a stigma is not quite human" (Goffman, 1963, p. 5). Having recognized one characteristic, such as race, people then ascribe other attributes and imperfections to the person, a situation known as the "spread phenomenon" (Tripp & Sherrill, 1991). Unthinkingly, an individual may stereotype the woman who is African American as a welfare mother, the man who is Hispanic as an illegal alien, or assume that the student who is Asian plays chess and the violin. In response, the person who is stigmatized may battle feelings of shame, inferiority, and confused identity.

Cultural Diversity

Diversity is defined as "difference . . . variety" (Soukhanov et al., 1992, p. 543) and is simply the recognition that two or more things have different characteristics or elements. Therefore, "'cultural diversity' refers to the differences among cultures and the influences and implications of these differences that must be recognized if cross cultural understanding is to be accomplished and mutual respect for those cultural differences engendered" (Henderson, 1995, p. 2). This position is not without critics: there are those who believe that we should simply teach that all human beings are basically the same and no group should be singled out for special examination (Henderson, 1995). To focus on studies specifically associated with people who are women, African American, aging, gay or lesbian, or who have a disability—according to this school of thought—is to create division, rather than unity. Conversely, proponents of diversity studies argue, we are *not* all the same and our differences should be celebrated, not marginalized (i.e., confined to a lower status or to the edges of society).

Professionals providing leisure education services are cautioned to be accurate when using the words "culture," "uncultured," and "popular culture." The term *culture* is sometimes used to refer only to intellectual and artistic activity, specifically, the fine and performing arts: opera, ballet, classical literature, and music. People who do not know of, or are not fond of, these arts are sometimes called "uncultured," but this is not accurate: as explained in the preceding section, every human being has a cultural identity. The term *popular culture* refers to television, radio, serial novels, popular music, and so on, and is generally used in a way to distinguish it as different or less worthy than "culture" (Berger, 1995).

Acculturation

The degree of difference that influences a person often depends on the extent to which he or she is acculturated. *Acculturation* is the process by which individuals "absorb, learn, acquire, and integrate the overt and covert cultural characteristics of the host culture" (Valdés, Barón, & Ponce, 1987, p. 204). The word *assimilation* is a synonym for acculturation and, according to Soukhanov et al. (1992, p. 112) is "the process whereby a minority group gradually adapts the customs and attitudes of a prevailing culture." *Overt* cultural characteristics might include clothing choices, eating habits, entertainment choices, and language usage, including local slang. These overt traits are usually easily adopted and prove functional for the individual. *Covert* characteristics which are more subtle and more difficult to adopt include attitudes, beliefs, affective reactions, and values (Valdés, Barón, & Ponce, 1987). Therefore, cultural differences can be both visible and invisible to the casual observer.

Acculturation has occurred and continues to occur at varying rates for different immigrant groups and for specific individuals. Factors influencing acculturation include such conditions as the degree of acceptance by the dominant culture, the amount of social support by the ethnic community, and the degree to which the individual is personally motivated to become integrated into the host culture (Valdés, Barón, & Ponce, 1987). Further, some families may maintain their traditional dress, language, and values indefinitely, while others may adopt new customs immediately. When meeting an individual from a racial or ethnic group other than one's own, it can be helpful to consider that the person may have come to this country very recently or may be a second or third generation American.

Minority

People of different groups are sometimes referred to as minorities. *Minority* literally means smaller or fewer in number (Soukhanov et al., 1992, p. 1151): the Navajo Nation is a minority group because there are fewer of them than of the larger society. The categories of people most often referred to as minorities are those of certain racial backgrounds such as Polynesian, religious practices such as the Quakers, economic status such as people without homes, political affiliations such as Libertarian, sexual orientations such as lesbian, and disability groups such as mental retardation. The term *minority* is problematic because a person can be a member of a minority group in one culture but when in another culture be a member of the majority. In addition, the proportion of people associated with different cultures can change over time. For example, White (1997) reported that "if current demographic trends persist, midway through the 21st century whites will no longer make up a majority of the U.S. population" (p. 33). The term *minority* is currently less-preferred than terms or phrases that are more precise. For example, the phrase "people of color" has:

> . . . been revived for use in formal contexts to refer to members or groups of non-European origin (e.g., Black people, Asians, Pacific Islanders, and Native Americans) . . . Many people prefer "people of color" as a rough substitute for "minorities" because these groups are not in fact the minority in many parts of America. (Soukhanov et al., 1992, p. 375)

Race

Race is the term used to describe a group of people having genetically transmitted physical characteristics (Soukhanov et al., 1992, p. 1488). Such characteristics might include skin, eye, and hair color, facial features, height and body type. At times, leisure service providers are required to identify the racial, ethnic, and/or religious membership of a client on an assessment form. In such an event, Dattilo and Smith (1990) suggested that, "in all situations, professionals listen to their constituents to determine the terms and phrases they most prefer and attempt to understand their reasons for these choices" (Dattilo & Smith, 1990, p. 15).

Historically, individuals who have more than one racial background were identified by such terms as "Eurasian," "half-breeds," "mixed," or "mulatto" (Root, 1990). At present, the preferred terms are either "biracial" or "multiracial" (e.g., having one parent who is Asian and Caucasian and the other parent Native Hawaiian). For example, the advocacy group, Multiracial Americans of Southern California, have lobbied for a multiracial category on government forms (White, 1997).

As the number of individuals who are multiracial increases (White, 1997), professionals will have a greater chance of providing leisure education services to people who have more than one racial background. Root (1990) stated that being multiracial is complicated by a "hierarchy of color" based on two underlying assumptions: first, that Caucasian is considered superior to all other races; and second, that the privileges and power accorded to Caucasians are desired by those who are of other races. The hierarchy of color further dictates a social status system based on ethnic features and skin tone. Traditionally, an individual has been considered to belong to the racial group of the darker skinned parent (Root, 1990). A child who has a parent who is Caucasian and a parent who is Asian is usually identified as Asian, whereas a child with a parent who is African American and a parent who is Asian would be considered African American. Unfortunately, in many cases, these biracial classifications have been written into law (Root, 1990).

According to Root (1990), individuals with a multiracial background may have unique problems with identity. For example, they may not racially identify with the way they look, and may not automatically be accepted by the racial group with which they do identify. People with a multiracial background may actively reject the culture of one of their parents or may choose to identify with a different racial group than do their siblings. And they may change their racial identity over the course of their lifetime.

Ethnicity

The terms *race* and *ethnicity* are sometimes used interchangeably when their meanings are different. While race is genetically transmitted, ethnicity is socially communicated. The word *ethnicity* "refers to an individual's membership in a group sharing a common ancestral heritage . . . (including) the biological, cultural, social, and psychological domains of life" (Buriel, 1987, p. 134). Of these, the psychological dimension of ethnicity is the most important since individuals can accept or deny their ethnicity (Buriel, 1987). To self-identify, then, is to be willing to be perceived and treated as a member of the group such as Polish American, Gypsy, or gang member. Again, whenever possible, it is useful to ask an individual how he or she self-identifies (Dattilo & Smith, 1990).

As people begin to acquire knowledge of the words and phrases associated with any idea, often they improve their understanding of the idea. Although the aforementioned descriptions of words and phrases may be helpful, Henderson's (1997) sentiments about diversity are worth considering here. Henderson stated that ". . . although all of us have many group characteristics (e.g., gender, race, class, physical or mental disability, geography, religion), frequently as much difference exists among groups as between them" (p. 26).

The words depicted in Figure 10.1 (see page 148) were defined in this section to help professionals who are developing leisure education learn more about multiculturalism. Rather than thinking about what is "politically correct," it can be helpful to think about our use of words as an indicator of our understanding and sensitivity to the people we serve.

Working in Multicultural Settings

The next section of this chapter is intended to move from discussing the vocabulary of multiculturalism to specific, practical suggestions for providing more culturally sensitive leisure education programs. The suggestions

Fig. 10.1

provided are intended to encourage movement away from global consider-ations of bias to specific case-by-case respect for individual differences. Although these suggestions are by no means complete, they are intended to assist professionals to provide leisure education services in a multicultural environment. This section of the chapter is divided using the following headings:

(a) examine biases;
(b) learn about the community;
(c) use sensitive language;
(d) think about families; and
(e) focus on individuals.

Examine Biases

Attitudinal biases are both the most difficult to identify and the most difficult to overcome (Dattilo, 1994). As professionals who are committed to providing inclusive leisure education services, it can be beneficial to scrutinize personal beliefs about and attitudes toward people. Among other things, stereotypes "keep us from knowing the individual, cut us off from fresh ideas, limit the person's opportunities" (Bete, 1994, p. 7) and can lead to the individual adopting the stereotype as true.

For example, a child may think, "Kids of my race are supposed to like rap music and basketball but I don't—I wonder if something is wrong with me?" To begin examining personal biases, questions such as the following could be asked: (a) What do I believe about people who are Asian? (b) What do I believe about people who are Jewish? (c) What do I believe about people who have been incarcerated? (d) What do I believe about single women who choose to have children? (e) What do I believe about people who are HIV-positive? or (f) What do I believe about children who are "at-risk?"

Learn About the Community

Some agencies which have established effective leisure education programs in the past may continue delivering services while the communities surrounding them change.

For example, a senior program may experience dwindling attendance because the program does not meet the needs of the older adults who are Spanish-speaking who have settled nearby. In another example, recreation departments may be offering afternoon arts and crafts programs despite the fact that the average family in their service area now consists of teens and young adults. Changing demographics, economic, and other factors contribute to the composition of a community and can influence leisure education programming.

Recognizing and responding to the religious patterns of the surrounding community may enhance leisure education services.

> For example, if individuals in the community attend religious services on Saturday, programs offered on Sunday may be well-received. In addition, it may be helpful for leisure service departments to recognize and perhaps help celebrate the religious holidays of participants, including Ramadan, Rosh Hashannah, or Tet. In some communities, there is an unwritten rule that Wednesday evening is kept open for midweek religious services, choir practice, or Family Home Evening. Sensitivity to these traditions may result in better attendance for leisure education programs.

In addition to examining program offerings, it may be helpful to ask peers or an advisory board for assistance. Professionals may benefit from assembling an expert panel of community members who represent the diverse racial, ethnic, and other cultural groups in the area. Such an advisory board can provide suggestions related to community needs, outreach, publicity, service provision, follow-up, and inservice training. Fellow professionals or advisory boards help examine agency offerings by determining if: (a) advertisements are in languages used by individuals in your service area; (b) publicity materials are reflective of the cultural groups targeted for services; or (c) staff or volunteers are available to assist people who use languages other than English.

Use Sensitive Language

Politically correct language has been misunderstood by many in our society. The primary intent of using sensitive language is to refer to all individuals in a manner that will build mutual respect and understanding. It can be helpful to be alert to language and images that may be offensive to ethnic or cultural groups.

> For instance, naming teams the "Redskins," "Cannibals," or "Hillbillies" may embarrass and offend some participants. Sensitivity can be demonstrated by asking clients to sit "cross-legged," rather than "Indian style," by advertising a "no-host" meal rather than "Dutch treat," and referring to the "Lunar New Year" rather than "Chinese New Year."

Language, like culture, is not static but dynamic and changing. For example, in the past 50 years there has been an evolution of acceptable terms for those of African heritage: from colored, to Negro, to Black, to Afro-American, to African-American, to African American (Dattilo & Smith, 1990). Another group of people presently struggling with a satisfactory label are those who have origins in Spain. According to Legon (1995), the Census Bureau used seven classifications for the 1990 census: Chicano, Spanish, Mexican-American, Mexican, Cuban, Puerto Rican, and "other." Notably missing were the terms "Hispanic," and "Latino." The Census Bureau created the word "Hispanic" in the 1970s to emphasize the common denominator of language. The 1992 *American Heritage Dictionary* described the term as "widely used in both official and unofficial contexts and entirely acceptable" (Soukhanov et al., 1992, p. 856). However, because the term is of English origin and ignores the Indian heritage of people in the West and Southwest, it is rejected by many people (Legon, 1995). The term "Chicano" was used by some Mexican Americans during the civil rights movement of the late 1960s as a symbol of ethnic and political pride. Since other Mexican Americans reject it as derogatory, it may be safer to avoid the term unless an individual expresses a preference for it. The term "Latino," which is Spanish in origin (Buriel, 1987), is considered less formal than "Hispanic" and emphasizes an individual's Latin American ethnic descent (Soukhanov et al., 1992, p. 1018). It too has been rejected by some who "do not like the word because Portuguese-speaking Brazilians are included" in Latin America (Legon, 1995). In light of the variety of terms available to describe ethnicity in general whenever possible, identify people specifically and sensitively: Cuban American, Mexican American, Puerto Rican (APA, 1994). Since preferred terminology can change rapidly, professionals who wish to remain on the cutting edge of best practice will be prepared to adapt with equal rapidity.

Think About Families

According to Shaw (1992, p. 13), "home-based activities and family-oriented activities outside the home are the most common forms of leisure activity." A question arises, however, as to how "family" is defined. The "traditional family," one in which the father worked outside the home, while the mother stayed at home with the children, is now the exception, rather than the rule (Coontz, 1996). Instead, "families" have become increasingly diverse. Social and economic conditions of American society have increasingly led to multigenerational families (Burton, 1992). In addition, immigrants to North America may bring with them the living arrangements that were typical in their mother country, including the division of household tasks by gender, arranging marriages for young adult children, and the allocation of family resources (Burr & Mutchler, 1993).

Sensitivity is suggested when asking people about their home, spouse, partner, parents, or family.

> For example, individuals who refer to themselves as "single" may, in fact, be involved in discreet gay or lesbian relationships, however there is little reliable data to indicate just how many same-sex relationships there may be in the United States (Kimmel, 1992). Furthermore, such partnerships frequently function very much as do heterosexual couples: they may raise natural or adopted children, may maintain solid relationships with their biological families, and may create a network of friends and others who serve as social support. Another example of family diversity is the "skipped-generation families" those families who have children living in the custody of one or more of their grandparents (Jendrek, 1995).

To use inclusive language when speaking to individuals about residence-related issues can be helpful.

> For example, children may live in a homeless shelter, with one or more of their adult siblings, or in a foster home for a variety of reasons. Factors influencing families can be helpful to consider before planning a Father-Daughter Banquet, Father-Son Sleepover, or similar events. Instead of saying "your parents," it may be more helpful to refer to "the people who raised you" or "the people with whom you live." Likewise, "the place you live" is more inclusive than "your house," "your trailer," or "your room at the shelter" (see also Kunstler, 1991).

Focus on Individuals

Differences in individuals' daily living patterns may be important factors which can influence the delivery of leisure education. As leisure service professionals become familiar with individuals' cultural expressions, they are more likely to gain knowledge about their differences. To illustrate, consider the implications of differences in dressing and eating.

Examining an agency's dress code by asking the following questions may be beneficial: Does the code require that people wear tennis shoes and remove headgear when in the gymnasium, exercise in sweatpants or shorts, cover the midriff, remove all jewelry, or wear a swimsuit in the swimming pool? Such rules, while typical in recreation settings, may be perceived as insensitive by some participants.

For example, some women will wear only skirts or dresses in accordance with their religious customs such as women who are Pentecostal, while other women will wear only a midriff-revealing sari in accordance with their cultural customs such as women from India or Pakistan. Likewise, many religions require that both men and women keep their heads covered at all times such as those individuals who are Orthodox Jews. Some people believe that the removal of a protective medal, symbol, or amulet such as a St. Christopher medal, cross, or medicine pouch worn round the neck or wrist will subject the owner to bad luck or to an accident. Some cultures prohibit men and women from using a swimming pool at the same time such as people who are Moslem. Finally, some people do not have the luxury of multiple clothing changes and can only participate in their street shoes and pants. Professionals can accommodate individual attire preferences by providing alternatives or adaptations as needed. Jewelry can be taped down to the skin for safety and to prevent its loss. Swimming pool time can be adjusted to protect the dignity of all who wish to participate. As with other situations in providing leisure education, the key to success is sensitivity and flexibility.

At times refreshments may be served during a leisure education program. In addition to considering the medical need for low-fat, high-fiber, or diabetic diets, consideration can be given to religious food restrictions, regional food preferences, and cultural differences associated with food preferences, preparation, and serving (Capitman, Hernandez-Gallegos, & Yee, 1991).

For example, some cultures believe that a proper balance of "hot" and "cold" food and beverages is needed to restore good health (Evans & Cunningham, 1996). In addition, food restrictions may be related to religious beliefs. For example, Mormons avoid coffee, tea, cola beverages and other products containing stimulants such as caffeine; Catholics may eat a self-restricted diet during the 40 days of Lent each year; Seventh Day Adventists may eat a meat-free vegetarian diet; and Jewish or Moslem individuals may eat a pork-free diet.

The aforementioned suggestions as illustrated in Figure 10.2 are provided to encourage instructors to develop an appreciation for the diversity associated with the people who attend leisure education programs and to encourage respect for individual differences. The suggestions are intended to be a starting point for sensitivity with the recognition that many additional considerations are needed when working in a multicultural society. "Generally, all individuals may want the same things in their recreation experiences, such as choice, enjoyment, and social interaction, but they may want to access those outcomes in different ways" (Henderson, 1997, p. 26).

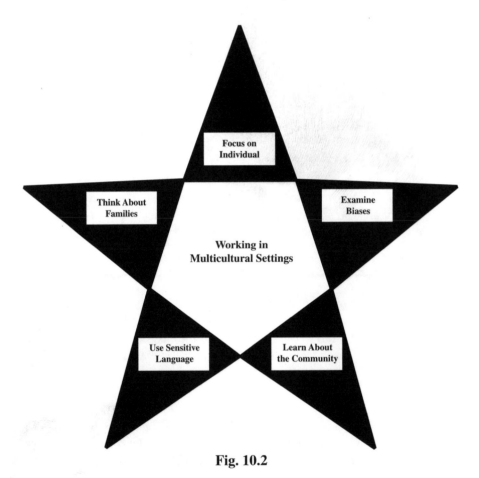

Focus on
Individual

Think About
Families

Examine
Biases

Working in
Multicultural Settings

Use Sensitive
Language

Learn About
the Community

Fig. 10.2

Conclusion

"More than ever recreation professionals will be expected to work with, and have significant knowledge and understanding of, individuals from many cultural, racial and ethnic backgrounds" (Holland, 1997, p. 42). The purpose of this chapter is to provide information on multicultural issues. Hetzroni and Harris (1996) concluded that the identification of multicultural influences is important to the future of professional service delivery. When discussing multicultural issues and diversity, professionals are encouraged to begin with shared vocabulary. The terms most often associated with multiculturalism are defined and discussed in the first section of this chapter. Specific suggestions for working in multicultural settings are given in the latter portion of the chapter.

According to Ivey (1987), effective professionals integrate an understanding of individual differences and use various techniques and interventions to be as effective as possible as they work within a diverse society. Such an understanding of individual differences can help leisure educators respond to the challenges put forth by Levy (1997) when he stated that leisure service providers must:

> . . . reach out and embrace all human beings whose present status makes them marginalized and disenfranchised as a result of gender, race, age, socioeconomic status, or other unique categories of humanity. (p. 11)

Proper use of multicultural vocabulary, sensitivity to culturally based differences, and outreach to previously neglected groups may expand and enrich leisure education programs. Perhaps, Beth Harry (1997) said it best, "If we can just get to a point where we can bear in mind that the values we so cherish are not necessarily universal, then I believe we can begin to do a better job" (p. 11).

Appendix A
Leisure Education
Specific Program #1

APPRECIATE LEISURE

Purpose, Goal, and Objectives

Purpose: Provide opportunities for participants to learn definitions of leisure and leisure lifestyle, become familiar with outcomes of leisure participation, identify barriers to leisure participation, and determine ways to overcome barriers to their leisure.

GOAL 1: DEMONSTRATE AN APPRECIATION OF LEISURE.
Objective 1.1: Demonstrate knowledge of definitions of leisure and leisure lifestyle.
Objective 1.2: Demonstrate knowledge of the outcomes of leisure participation.
Objective 1.3: Demonstrate knowledge of barriers to leisure participation.
Objective 1.4: Demonstrate knowledge of strategies to overcome barriers to leisure.

Goal and Objectives: Performance Measures

GOAL 1: DEMONSTRATE AN APPRECIATION OF LEISURE.

Objective 1.1: Demonstrate knowledge of the definitions of leisure and leisure lifestyle.
Performance Measure: When provided with paper and pencil, within one minute and with 100% accuracy on three consecutive occasions, participant will:
  (a) write a description of leisure that includes at least five of the nine following concepts: freedom, choice, control, enjoyment, satisfaction, growth, responsibility, preferences, and self-determination; and
  (b) write a description of leisure lifestyle that includes four of the five following components: day-to-day, expression of leisure appreciation, leisure awareness, leisure skills, and in context of entire life.

Objective 1.2: Demonstrate knowledge of the outcomes of leisure participation.
Performance Measure: When provided with paper and pencil, within 10 minutes and with 100% accuracy on two consecutive occasions, participant will:
  (a) identify five possible outcomes of leisure participation (e.g., fun, self-esteem, relaxation, release of tension, acquisition of skills, increase in fitness, sense of freedom, perception of mastery); and
  (b) for each of the five outcomes, identify one recreation activity that could facilitate that outcome (e.g., increase in fitness: jogging; fun: telling jokes; self-

esteem: helping others in need; relaxation: yoga; release of tension: participating in martial arts).

Objective 1.3: Demonstrate knowledge of barriers to leisure participation.
Performance Measure: When provided with a list of six factors affecting leisure participation (e.g., existing funds, free time, availability, societal role expectations, health, and skills), and paper and pencil, within 10 minutes and with 100% accuracy on two consecutive occasions, participant will:
  (a) describe how these factors can be barriers to leisure involvement (e.g., existing funds: "not enough money;" free time: "not enough time"); and
  (b) identify one example of how each of the six factors may be a barrier in an individual's life (e.g., existing funds: "I only have $1.00, so I cannot go bowling;" free time: "It takes me so long to get dressed that I do not have enough time to go bowling.").

Objective 1.4: Demonstrate knowledge of strategies to overcome barriers to leisure.
Performance Measure: When provided with a list of six barriers to leisure participa-tion (e.g., existing funds, free time, availability, societal role expectations, health, and skills), and paper and pencil, within 10 minutes and with 100% accuracy on two consecutive occasions, participant will:
  (a) identify two ways that each barrier could be reduced (e.g., lack of skills: "attend a class to learn the skill" or "adapt the materials associated with an activity"); and
  (b) provide an example for the two ways identified to reduce barriers (e.g., lack of skills: "I do not know how to paint, but I am going to enroll in a painting class;" adapt the materials associated with an activity: "I do not have the strength to make a basket in basketball, so I am going to use a smaller, lighter ball and lower the hoop.").

Goal and Objectives: Content and Process

GOAL 1: DEMONSTRATE AN APPRECIATION OF LEISURE.

Objective 1.1: Demonstrate knowledge of the definitions of leisure and leisure lifestyle.

1. Orientation Activity

Content: "We are going to participate in an activity that will help us to meet one another and get us started thinking about leisure. Please arrange your chairs in a circle. When it is your turn to participate, state your first name and a recreation activity that begins with the first letter of your first name. For example, if your name is John you could say jogging; if your name is Anne, you could say angling. Each person will repeat the preceding name and activity that was stated and then give his or her name and activity. I will select a person to start the activity and we will proceed clockwise until everyone has had his or her turn."

Process: Use this activity as an icebreaker. When participants enter the room, have them arrange chairs in a circle. Once everyone has arrived, explain activity. Activity contin-ues until everyone in the group has had opportunity to introduce himself of herself.

2. Debriefing

Content:
   a. Was it difficult to think of recreation activities when it was your turn? If so, why?
   b. How do you think recreation activities relate to your leisure?
   c. What did you learn about other group members?

Process: Conduct debriefing using above questions. Provide opportunity for each person to respond. Encourage those who did not contribute.

3. Introduction

Content: "Leisure and leisure lifestyle can be difficult ideas to understand. But if we can develop an understanding and appreciation of these ideas and act on the new knowledge that they will bring us, it can result in additional opportunities for us to get satisfaction and joy from our lives. The place for us to start is to examine the meaning of leisure and lifestyle."

Process: Introduce topic of defining leisure and leisure lifestyle.

4. Presentation

Content: "One of the reasons that leisure is difficult to understand is because it can be thought of in several different contexts and there is a lack of agreement about which context is correct. The absence of a precise definition will not stand in the way of us understanding leisure. In fact, the flexibility that is associated with leisure, the room for different interpretations of its meaning, may be one of its most appealing features. Leisure may be regarded as (a) activity, (b) as free time, (c) as a state of mind or being, or as (d) a combination of activity, time, and state of mind.

"When leisure is regarded as activity, it is the activity that is the determining factor as to whether or not it is thought to be leisure. For example, washing the dishes, dusting, mowing the lawn, and doing laundry are activities that must be accomplished but they are not regarded as leisure. On the other hand, playing cards, swimming, going to the movies, and bowling are things that do not have to be accomplished and are usually thought to be leisure activities. The first examples are associated with a sense of obligation. They are things that must be done; they are like work. The examples in the second set are not associated with any sense of compulsion; they are generally thought to be fun.

"The difficulty associated with thinking of leisure as activity is that sometimes activities that are thought to be fun do not turn out that way and activities that are thought to be compulsory (like work) can turn out to be fun. It appears that it is not the activity that is leisure; it is how we feel about the activity that helps determine whether or not it is leisure."

Process: Present information. Use board to list four ways of thinking about leisure. Underline the word "leisure" on the chalkboard as it is being discussed and list the following:

LEISURE

- activity
- free time
- state of mind or being
- combinations of all three

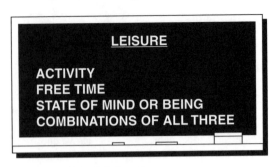

5. Discussion

Content:
   a. What determines whether or not an activity is leisure?
   b. Can an activity be leisure for some people but not for others? How so?
   c. Can an activity be leisure at one time for a person but not at another time for the same person? How so?
   d. Who determines whether or not an activity is leisure?

Process: Conduct discussion using above questions. Encourage all participants to contribute to the discussion.

6. Learning Activity

Content: "Each of you has pencil and paper. Think about recreation activities in which you like to participate and which you think of as leisure. List five such activities on your paper. When you are finished, we will put the activities on the board and ask some questions about them."

Process: Provide pencil and paper. Explain activity. Allow sufficient time for thinking and writing. When participants are finished, ask them to take turns and read their activities aloud. List activities on board. Move to debriefing.

7. Debriefing

Content:
   a. Are there activities on the board that you do not consider to be leisure for you? If so, which ones? Why?
   b. How should other people's opinions influence your choice of activities?
   c. What is your opinion of the diversity of activities that are listed?

Process: Conduct debriefing using above questions. Encourage all participants to contribute to the debriefing.

8. Presentation

Content: "Leisure can be thought of as free time, the time an individual has remaining after work and self-maintenance requirements have been met. That is, when you are finished with work, school, family, hygiene, house and car maintenance and other similar responsibilities. This free time is sometimes referred to as discretionary time. It is the time when an individual is free to choose what to do. The notion of choice is important. Choosing to participate in an activity that brings enjoyment and satisfaction is fundamental to this and other concepts of leisure."

Process: Present information on leisure as free time. Circle the word "time" on the chalkboard as the content is being presented.

9. Discussion

Content:
   a.   Is any time really free from obligation? How so?
   b.   How often do we have the chance of making choices to please ourselves?
   c.   Did you have a choice of whether or not to come to this session?
   d.   What would have been the consequences if you had chosen not to come here?
   e.   Does this have any application in making choices for leisure? How so?
   f.   How much time do you choose to take for leisure?

Process: Conduct discussion using above questions. Encourage all participants to contribute to the discussion.

10. Learning Activity

Content: "We have an activity period now but some of you are needed to help us get some work done. I am going to divide you into two groups, which we will call Group A and Group B. I need Group A to help me pull some weeds. Group B may remain inside and play with any of the games or equipment that is here."

Process: Explain activity. At beginning, do not reveal the purpose of the activity is to emphasize the difference between being required to do something and having a choice of what to do. Do not actually go to pull weeds but facilitate discussion of the feelings of each group towards each activity. Choose a task that has the connotation of work (e.g., pull weeds, wash dishes, sweep floors, shovel snow from sidewalk).

11. Debriefing

Content:
   a.   How did you feel when you were told you were required to do a task?
   b.   How did you feel when you were told you were free to choose what you wanted to do?
   c.   Can you compare the two feelings?
   d.   How important is choice to the concept of leisure?

Process: Conduct debriefing using above questions. Encourage all participants to contribute to the debriefing.

12. Presentation

Content: "Leisure can be thought of as a state of mind or a state of being. It is characterized by feelings of freedom, of independence, of choice, of being in control, of creativity, reward and self-fulfillment, and of being competent.

"Often leisure is associated with intrinsic motivation. People are intrinsically motivated when they do things for their own sake, not for some type of external reward (like money).

"Both the perception of freedom and intrinsic motivation are important parts to the concept of leisure as a state of mind. It focuses on the feelings one experiences (the state of mind) rather than the activity or when participation takes place. This concept provides the flexibility needed to allow individuals to vary widely in their choice of activities and the time frame in which those activities occur. It is the perception of the individual that is the basis of leisure."

Process: Present information on leisure as a state of mind. Make sure that each participant understands what is meant by the words "freedom," "independence," "creativity," "self-fulfillment," "competence," and "free." Take time to assess their knowledge of these important concepts. Perhaps reviewing the definitions of these words may be useful for some participants.

13. Discussion

Content:
a.   What is the meaning of intrinsic motivation?
b.   What are some of the feelings that are the basis for intrinsic motivation?
c.   Are you intrinsically motivated by any activities? If so, which ones?
d.   How does leisure as a state of mind differ from leisure as activity or free time?

Process: Conduct discussion using above questions. Encourage all participants to contribute to the discussion. Be sensitive to the terminology used. Review definitions of key terms, checking to see if participants understand the words associated with leisure as a state of mind.

14. Learning Activity

Content: "Chances for leisure are all around us. We are going to divide into groups of three or four and each group will go for a 15–20 minute walk in the area. Each group will be supplied with pencil and paper and one person in each group will be the recorder. As you walk, take note of the potential leisure opportunities you see. Each group should make a list of at least 10 opportunities. When you return, we will share the lists."

Process: Explain activity. Provide pencil and paper, designate one person in each group as recorder. If necessary, assign staff supervision for each group's walk. When groups return, ask them to read their lists. Put activities on the chalkboard. Proceed to debriefing.

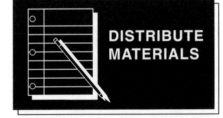

DISTRIBUTE
MATERIALS

15. Debriefing

Content:
a.   In which of the listed activities have you participated?

LIST
ON
BOARD

   b.   Which new ones would you like to try?

   c.   Are any of your favorite activities listed? If so, which ones?

   d.   What is your opinion of the diversity of activities listed?

Process: Conduct debriefing by using above questions. Encourage each participant to respond to at least one of the questions.

16. Presentation

Content: "If leisure is regarded as a state of mind, then leisure is more than special activities or events or free time. It can be the little things we enjoy in our day, such as talking to a friend, reading a newspaper, listening to a bird, or enjoying a sunset or a starry night. Leisure can be all the enjoyable things that we experience from day to day. This is referred to as a leisure lifestyle. Leisure lifestyle can be regarded as the way you approach daily living to get satisfaction from it. A leisure lifestyle can grow and develop or it can wither away. Your leisure lifestyle requires attention. A positive leisure lifestyle can provide additional opportunities for you to enhance the quality of your life."

Process: Present information on leisure lifestyle.

17. Discussion

Content:

   a.   What is meant by leisure lifestyle?

   b.   How would you describe your leisure lifestyle?

   c.   Would you like to change your leisure lifestyle? If so, how?

Process: Conduct discussion using above questions. Encourage all participants to contribute to the discussion.

18. Learning Activity

Preparation: Develop a handout containing ten lines, with each line numbered in succession. To the right of the space for the activities, 14 columns should intersect the lines, forming a grid pattern. The columns should be headed as follows: (1) Something I Enjoy Doing; (2) Have Been Doing For Less Than Two Years; (3) Will Probably Do Two Years From Now; (4) Will Probably Be

Doing After I'm 65; (5) Expensive; (6) Inexpensive; (7) Requires Risk; (8) Requires No Risk; (9) Group Activity; (10) Individual Activity; (11) Advanced Planning; (12) Spontaneous; (13) Requires Equipment; and (14) Requires No Equipment.

Content: "We are going to do an activity entitled '10 Things I Enjoy.' This activity should help you become more aware of your leisure lifestyle. Each of you will receive a pencil and a handout that has spaces for 10 activities. List as many activities as you enjoy that you can think of. After you have completed this, return to each activity and check the appropriate columns to its right. When you are finished, we will have a discussion focused on the activities you chose and any leisure patterns you may have noticed."

Process: Participants remain seated for this activity. Explain activity. Distribute pencil and handouts. Instruct participants to list their activities on these lines and check the columns that are appropriate for each activity. When participants are finished, proceed to debriefing.

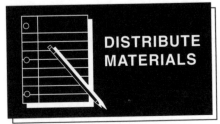

DISTRIBUTE MATERIALS

19. Debriefing

Content:
    a.   Did you notice any patterns after you checked the columns? If so, what were they?
    b.   Does this give you any insight into your leisure lifestyle? How so?
    c.   How will you make use of this information?

Process: Conduct debriefing using above questions. Encourage each participant to respond to at least one question.

20. Conclusion

Content: "Leisure and leisure lifestyle are important concepts. Although leisure can be thought of in several different ways, the two essential ingredients are freedom of choice and intrinsic motivation. If an individual can develop an appreciation for leisure and the potential benefits that can be derived from it, the possibility exists for an increase in the quality of that person's life. This could be a very significant accomplishment."

Process: Make concluding statements. Provide opportunities for questions.

Objective 1.2: Demonstrate knowledge of the outcomes of leisure participation.

1.   Orientation Activity

Content: "We are going to participate in an activity that will help us to know each other better and get us started in thinking about the benefits of engaging in leisure activities. A benefit is something good that is derived from participation. In addition, a benefit is something that serves to the advantage of an individual. Please arrange yourselves in a circle. As we go around the circle, individuals will take turns in stating their first name, a recreation activity he or she enjoys, and a benefit personally derived from participating in that activity."

Process: Explain activity. Arrange participants in a circle. Provide opportunity for each participant to have a turn. Move to debriefing.

2. Debriefing

Content:

a. What did you learn during this exercise about the benefits you obtain from leisure?

b. Did anyone mention the same benefit as someone else, but indicate that it came from a different activity? If so, what was it?

c. Did anyone mention the same activity as someone else, but indicate a different benefit? If so, what was it?

d. Can an individual obtain more than one benefit from a single activity? If so, how?

Process: Conduct debriefing using above questions. Emphasize diversity of benefits. Encourage each participant to respond to at least one of the questions.

3. Introduction

Content: "Engaging in leisure activities can result in a variety of outcomes, depending on the activity chosen, the reason for which it was chosen, and the manner in which an individual participates. For example, an individual may choose to go walking in order to relax and enjoy the sights and sounds of nature. The pace of the walk would not be hurried and there would probably be frequent stops along the way. At another time, an individual may choose to walk in order to release some tension and anxiety. The pace of the walk would probably be vigorous and nonstop. Having a knowledge of the outcomes of leisure can help an individual make decisions about participation."

Process: Introduce topic on the outcomes of leisure participation.

4. Presentation

Content: "The positive outcomes of leisure participation can be regarded as benefits that come to an individual. These benefits can, for the sake of discussion, be placed in one of four categories: social, emotional, mental, or physical. As we discuss these benefits, remember that many of them could fit into more than one category.

"Some benefits derived from leisure participation are regarded as social. Social refers to the relationships that exist among people and the things people do to shape those relationships. It ranges from the behaviors that influence an intimate relationship between two individuals in a familiar environment to the behavior of one person surrounded by a crowd of strangers in an unfamiliar place. Leisure participation can help you obtain skills that are of value in building social relationships of all kinds.

"Examples of social benefits derived from participation in leisure include: (a) ability to work toward a common goal as a member of a group; (b) ability to exert leadership as a member of a group; (c) ability to recognize group interests as well as individual interests; (d) ability to develop confidence in capacity to meet and work with strangers; (e) opportunities to make new friends; (f) opportunities to gain acceptance and recognition by peers; (g) opportunities to develop respect for and understanding others; (h) ability to develop self-confidence and feel comfortable in unfamiliar surroundings; and (i) ability to recognize types of behavior required in diversity of circumstances.

"The acquisition and development of social skills through leisure participation can lead to feelings of independence and control."

Process: Present information on social benefits of leisure participation. Use chalkboard or overhead projector to list benefits. Emphasize that the list is incomplete. Some examples include:

- common goals
- confidence
- recognition
- leadership
- new friends
- respect
- group interacts
- acceptance
- comfortable

5. Discussion

Content:
a. Are there other social benefits that we should list? If so, what are they?
b. Do you have any social skills that were acquired or enhanced through leisure participation? If so, what are they and how were they acquired or enhanced?
c. Are there any social benefits that you hope to gain from participating in this program? If so, what are they?
d. What will you have to do to gain these benefits?

Process: Conduct the discussion using the above questions. Encourage all the participants to contribute to the discussion.

6. Presentation

Content: "A second category of leisure participation outcomes is emotional benefits. Emotional refers to feelings that arise within us as a reaction to various kinds of external sensory stimuli, such as what we see, hear, smell, touch, or taste. Emotions may also be stimulated by internal sources, such as remembering a significant personal event or anticipating involvement in something that is yet to happen.

"It is important to recognize that all people experience a range of emotions and emotions cannot be categorized as 'good' or 'bad.' All feelings that exist are valid. The manner in which people respond to their emotions is an indication of their character and control.

"Examples of emotional benefits derived from leisure participation include: (a) happiness at being able to participate; (b) satisfaction of doing something well; (c) sense of reward from helping others participate; (d) opportunity to release tension and anxiety; (e) feelings of self-esteem from successful completion of project; (f) appreciation of the beauty and wonder of nature; (g) satisfaction of the urge to create; (h) opportunity to express oneself; and (i) contentment after a good physical workout.

"Leisure is capable of providing opportunities to experience the entire range of emotions known to us. If leisure is approached with a positive attitude, the emotional benefits are likely to be positive."

Process: Present information on emotional benefits. List benefits on chalkboard or use other visual aids. Move to discussion.

LIST ON BOARD

7. Discussion

Content:
a. Should we specify additional emotional benefits? If so, what are they?
b. What emotions have you experienced from leisure participation?
c. In what other aspects of your life have you experienced this same emotion?
d. Does leisure provide the best chance to feel emotions you like? Why or why not?
e. Are most emotions you experience from leisure positive? If not, why not?

Process: Conduct discussion using above questions. Encourage all participants to contribute to the discussion. Some examples of discussion topics are:

- happiness
- satisfaction
- reward

- release tension
- success
- appreciation

- create
- expression
- contentment

8. Presentation

Content: "A third category of benefits available through leisure participation is mental. Mental refers to the mind and the processes that are used to learn, remember, and solve problems. A common belief among many people is that learning is often unpleasant and required, leisure is enjoyable and the result of freedom of choice, and therefore, the two are incompatible. This does not have to be the case. Leisure provides many chances to obtain mental benefits in a pleasant and enjoyable atmosphere.

"Examples of mental benefits obtained by participating in leisure include: (a) learning the rules of a new activity; (b) opportunities to focus attention on the accomplishment of a single task; (c) learning to identify and make use of various community resources; (d) applying ideas learned in leisure to other aspects of living; (e) opportunities to set goals and determine how to best achieve them; (f) opportunities to participate in activities demanding timely decisions; (g) learning to devise and apply strategy in various activities; and (h) determining the best course of action from several possible options.

"The mental benefits of leisure participation should not be overlooked. They are real and readily available."

Process: Present information on mental benefits. List benefits on chalkboard. Once presented, review the concepts and check them off the chalkboard as you review them. Move on to discussion.

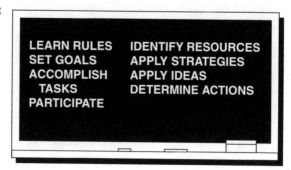

LEARN RULES   **IDENTIFY RESOURCES**
SET GOALS   **APPLY STRATEGIES**
ACCOMPLISH   **APPLY IDEAS**
  TASKS   **DETERMINE ACTIONS**
PARTICIPATE

- learn rules
- accomplish tasks
- identify resources
- apply ideas

- set goals
- participate
- apply strategies
- determine actions

9. Discussion

Content:
a. Are there additional mental benefits we should list? If so, what are they?
b. Have you gained any mental benefits from leisure participation? If so, what were they and how did you do it?
c. Can you relate a leisure experience where you learned something that was useful in another aspect of your life? If so, what was it?

Process: Conduct discussion by using above questions. Encourage all participants to contribute to the discussion.

10. Presentation

Content: "The last category of benefits from leisure participation we will discuss is physical. Physical refers to the body and its operations. When most people think of the outcomes of leisure involvement, one of the first things that comes to their mind is physical benefits. Many Americans today do not have occupations that demand enough in the way of physical activity. Because exercise is important to health and fitness and, in many cases, is available primarily through leisure, the physical benefits of leisure participation are important. They are of equal importance with the other benefits of leisure.

"Examples of physical benefits that can be derived from leisure participation include: (a) an increase in the efficiency of the cardiovascular system; (b) improvement in muscle tone; (c) increase in strength; (d) improvement in eye-hand coordination; (e) increase in flexibility; (f) improvement in endurance; (g) increase in agility; and (h) improvement in weight control. The physical benefits of leisure are dependent on the type of activity chosen and the frequency and duration of participation. In an age of sedentary living for many Americans, vigorous participation in leisure is recommended and encouraged."

Process: Present information on physical benefits of leisure. List benefits on chalkboard. Show pictures or slides of people engaged in activities that appear to be providing physical benefits. Show these pictures or slides as you present the benefits:

- cardiovascular
- flexibility
- muscle tone
- endurance
- strength
- agility
- coordination
- weight control

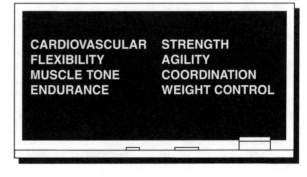

CARDIOVASCULAR STRENGTH
FLEXIBILITY AGILITY
MUSCLE TONE COORDINATION
ENDURANCE WEIGHT CONTROL

11. Discussion

Content:
    a.   What are other physical benefits of leisure participation?
    b.   Have you obtained physical benefits from leisure? How so?
    c.   What physical benefits would you now like to obtain from leisure?
    d.   What activities will help you obtain these benefits?

Process: Conduct discussion using above questions. Encourage all participants to contribute to the discussion.

12. Learning Activity

Preparation: Prepare slips of paper prior to session. Examples of activities could include reading, going for a walk, visiting a sick friend, stitching a quilt, baking a cake, bowling, and playing bingo.

PREPARE FOR SESSION

Content: "We are going to participate in an activity that will help us think about the benefits we can get from leisure involvement. I am going to divide you into two groups of equal numbers. I have a paper sack containing several slips of paper. On each slip of paper is written a recreation activity. The sack will be presented to one group and a member of that group will take one slip. The group will then have two minutes to say aloud all of the benefits that could be derived from participating in that activity. The benefits will be listed on the chalkboard. The sack will then be presented to the second group and the process will be repeated. Groups will alternate until each group has had five chances. We will then count the number of benefits identified by each group. We will see how many benefits we come up with as a total group. The object is to beat the previous record set by the last group."

LIST ON BOARD

Process: Explain activity. When slip is taken, do not return it to sack. Monitor the listing of benefits to ensure fairness. Examples of benefits could include learning new things, relaxation, meeting new people, feeling good, fun, creating something, and sharing time with friends. Tally benefits and declare winner. Emphasize and summarize benefits generated by participants.

13. Debriefing

Content:
    a.   What is your impression of the variety of benefits that were identified?
    b.   Which of these benefits would you like most to obtain? Why?
    c.   What will you need to do to obtain them?

Process: Conduct debriefing using above questions. Encourage each participant to answer at least one of the questions.

14. Learning Activity

Preparation: Prepare questionnaire with the following starting points:

1. If I had a free weekend, I would want to:
2. I have decided to finally learn how to:
3. If I were to buy two magazines, I would choose:
4. I feel most bored when:
5. If I used my free time more wisely, I would:
6. I feel best when people:
7. On weekends, I like to:
8. I get real enjoyment from:
9. If I had a tankful of gas in a car, I would:
10. What I want most in life is:
11. I have never liked:
12. When my family gets together:
13. I do not have enough time to:
14. I would consider it risky to:
15. My greatest accomplishment in leisure has been:

Content: "You are going to have a chance to complete an open-ended questionnaire that will help you think about the benefits of leisure and, at the same time, learn something about your own leisure involvement. Please take the time to think carefully about your answers to the questions. There are no 'right' or 'wrong' answers. Be honest and write exactly what you feel. When the questionnaires are completed, we will use them as the basis for a group discussion."

Process: Explain activity. Distribute questionnaire and pencils. Provide sufficient time for completion. Move on to debriefing.

DISTRIBUTE MATERIALS

15. Debriefing

Content:
    a. How did you complete question 1? What benefits would you get from doing this?
    b. What is your answer to question 2? What benefits would you get from this?
    c. How did you answer question 3? Why did you to choose the magazines you did?
    d. How did you answer question 4? What could you do to keep from getting bored?
    e. What did you put for question 5? What category of benefits would your answer fit?
    f. How did you answer question 6? Is your answer a social or emotional benefit?
    g. What was your response to question 7? When was the last time you did this?

h. How did you complete question 8? When was the last time you experienced this?

i. How did you answer question 9? How would this benefit you?

j. What did you say for question 10? What will you do to help you get it?

k. What was your response to question 11? What does this say about you?

l. How did you complete question 12? When was the last time your family was able to do this? Could you do anything to help in this area?

m. How did you answer question 13? What could you do to have more time to do the things you want?

n. What did you say for question 14? What could you do to change this?

o. How did you complete question 15? Do you feel like your greatest accomplishments are yet to come? How can you help it happen?

Process: Conduct debriefing using above questions. Ask questions of each participant. Encourage more than one participant to respond to any given question.

16. Conclusion

Content: "There are many benefits available through participation in leisure but these benefits do not automatically come to everyone. It sometimes takes purposeful effort to obtain benefits. The benefits of leisure can play a very important role in our lives."

Process: Make concluding statements. Provide opportunities for questions.

Objective 1.3: Demonstrate knowledge of barriers to leisure participation.

1. Orientation Activity

Preparation: Prepare cards prior to session. The first set of cards could include the following words or phrases:

- existing funds
- free time
- availability
- societal attitudes
- health
- skills

The second set of cards could include barriers such as:

- I want to go bowling but I do not have enough money.
- I would like to go for a walk tonight but I have to clean the house.
- I would like to play on a soccer team but there are no programs in the community.
- Theater owners do not want me to attend their movies because I use a wheelchair.
- I want to participate in the race but I do not have the stamina.
- I would like to go on the river trip but I do not know how to canoe.

Content: "I am giving each of you a card with a word or phrase that is relevant to leisure participation. Another person will have a card explaining how this word or phrase can be a barrier that inhibits or prevents leisure participation. You should try to find this person, introduce yourself, and discuss the barrier. After you have found the person and discussed the barrier, together the two of you should look for another pair of people that have succeeded in finding one another. When you find another pair, introduce yourselves and present your barrier to them, and allow them to tell you about their barrier. Continue moving about the room, finding pairs of people until I give the signal to end the activity."

Process: Explain activity. Agree on a signal (e.g., music starts) to end the activity. Distribute cards. Monitor activity. Provide assistance where needed.

2. Introduction

Content: "A barrier is something that stands in the way of our doing something we want to do. Therefore, a barrier may stop us from experiencing leisure as often as we would like. Sometimes we may plan or want to do something and we discover that, at that time, we are not able to engage in the activity. We may not be able to participate for many reasons. These reasons are 'barriers' to satisfying and enjoyable experiences. Each factor influencing leisure participation, such as existing funds, free time, availability, societal attitudes, health, and skills, may at some time or another be a barrier."

Process: Introduce topic of barriers to leisure participation.

3. Presentation

Content: "Lack of money can be a barrier to leisure participation. Many recreation activities require money to participate or enjoy. This means that those of us wishing to participate must make sure we have enough money to pay for the activity. If we do not have enough money and are not permitted to participate as a result of this lack of resources, money has become a barrier to leisure participation for us."

Process: Present information on existing funds. List the first barrier on the chalkboard as "money."

4. Discussion

Content:
- a. What are some examples of how money may be a barrier to leisure participation?
- b. How do you feel when a lack of funds prevents you from engaging in an activity?
- c. Have you ever observed people being turned away from recreation activities because they did not have enough money? If so, how did that make you feel?

Process: Conduct discussion using above questions. Encourage all participants to contribute to the discussion.

5. Presentation

Content: "Lack of free time is another possible barrier to leisure participation. All activities require some amount of time. As a result, we must possess the time to participate. If we do not have sufficient time to participate in recreation activities, we may not experience leisure as frequently as we would like. In addition, there are instances when we do not manage our time very well and, as a result, we use time in ways that might not make us feel very good. We may feel that we 'wasted' time and missed out on opportunities for enjoyable, satisfying and meaningful experiences. When we do not have enough time or do not take advantage of the time we do have, time becomes a barrier to leisure participation."

Process: Present information on free time. Record the phrase "free time" on the chalkboard after the previous barrier of money.

MONEY
FREE TIME

6. Discussion

Content:
a. Have you ever had problems finding enough time to enjoy yourself? If so, why do you think this happened?
b. Are there instances when you have mismanaged your time? If so, when?
c. Why do you think you have mismanaged some of your time in the past?
d. What was the result of your mismanaged time?
e. How do you feel when you have mismanaged time?

Process: Conduct discussion using above questions. Encourage all participants to contribute to the discussion.

7. Presentation

Content: "Lack of resources is another possible barrier to leisure participation. Sometimes we would like to participate in activities but we cannot because we do not have adequate transportation. For example, a bus may not have a route running near a park you would like to go to. It also might be true that we want to participate in an organized activity that no one is providing in the community. For example, there does not seem to be an organized volleyball league in our community. Sometimes an activity can be present in a community and due to our work schedule and other responsibilities we can not get there at the times the activity is available. For example, because I work in the evening, I cannot participate in the evening bridge program. If you have limited mobility, you may encounter physical obstacles in the form of architectural barriers or ecological barriers. Architectural barriers are built by people, such as steps and heavy doors, while ecological barriers include those that are in the natural world, such as hills and snow."

Process: Present information on resources. List on an overhead projector or a chalkboard the major concepts discussed such as:

- transportation
- programs
- scheduling
- architecture
- ecology
- facilities

> TRANSPORTATION
> PROGRAMS
> SCHEDULING
> ARCHITECTURE
> ECOLOGY
> FACILITIES

8. Discussion

Content:
  a. Are there activities in the community that are unavailable to you? What are they?
  b. Why do you think these activities are unavailable to you?
  c. Have you seen people that could not attend an activity because it was not available to them? If so, what happened?
  d. How do you feel when you want to do something and you cannot participate because the activity is not available to you?

Process: Conduct discussion using above questions. Encourage all participants to contribute to the discussion.

9. Presentation

Content: "Societal attitudes can be another possible barrier to our leisure participation. We will now talk about attitudes that constitute barriers to participating in recreation activities. Sometimes people who provide programs refuse to let us participate because they think we will hurt ourselves or that we are not skilled enough to have fun. If we encounter these negative attitudes enough times, we may begin to believe we cannot do the things people keep telling us we cannot do. Other times, we might attend a program and the other participants may make us feel uncomfortable or actually tell us that we are not welcome. If enough people make us feel uncomfortable and not many people make us feel welcome, we may stop doing something we really enjoy."

Process: Present information of societal attitudes. Add the possible barrier of "societal attitudes" to the list of barriers on the chalkboard.

> MONEY
> FREE TIME
> SOCIETAL ATTITUDES

10. Discussion

Content:
  a. Were there times when people's attitudes affected your participation? If so, how?
  b. How did you feel when people's attitudes became a barrier to leisure expression?
  c. What have you done in response to people's negative attitudes?

Process: Conduct discussion using above questions.

11. Presentation

Content: "A person's health can be another barrier to leisure participation. At times we may not be healthy. This lack of good health may inhibit our participation in recreation activities. Because of our temporary or permanent poor health, we may have to cope with limited physical abilities. For example, emphysema may prevent participation in aerobic activities, such as walking. In addition, we may have to deal with reduced mental awareness. For example, certain medications taken when we have an illness may result in confusion, preventing us from engaging in certain table games we enjoy. Social isolation may also result from health problems. For example, an observable disability may make some people feel uncomfortable, reducing chances for informal conversations. In addition, health problems may result in considerable pain and discomfort that may create barriers for us to concentrate on activities or have fun. For example, people receiving rehabilitation for severe burns may find concentration or even reading difficult. All the examples we have just talked about are situations where poor health has become a barrier to leisure involvement."

Process: Present information on health. Add "poor health" to the list of potential barriers. Present pictures or slides of each example of health problems.

MONEY
FREE TIME
SOCIETAL ATTITUDES
POOR HEALTH

12. Discussion

Content:
    a. Have there been times when health conditions have prevented your leisure participation? What were your problems?
    b. What activities have you been unable to enjoy due to health problems?
    c. How have you felt when you could not participate due to health reasons?
    d. Are the health conditions creating barriers to you still present? If so, what are they?

Process: Conduct discussion using above questions. Encourage all participants to contribute to the discussion.

13. Presentation

Content: "Lack of skills can be another possible barrier to leisure participation. There are going to be times when you do not possess the skills required to participate in an activity. Sometimes, it is possible to work hard and acquire the needed skills, but there will be other times when the desired skills will not be attained despite the strongest efforts. Whether the lack of skills is temporary or permanent, if you do not have them, their absence creates a barrier for you. For example, if someone asks you to play tennis and you do not know how to hold a racquet, hit the ball, or keep score, your lack of skills will prevent you from sharing time with this person. Some activities will have prerequisite skills for participation. Therefore, you may need to demonstrate a certain level of competence to be eligible to participate. For example, water skiing requires you to be able to swim. If you do not possess these skills, an absence of these abilities becomes a major barrier to your leisure involvement. For example, because you cannot swim, you should not water ski."

Process: Present information on skills as a barrier to leisure. Add the word "lack of skills" to the list of potential barriers to leisure participation. If possible, provide visual aids such as pictures or slides of people participating in the recreation activities (e.g., tennis, swimming) as they are presented in the discussion.

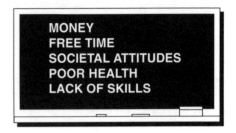

14. Discussion

Content:
- a. Have you been asked to participate in recreation activities but were not able to because of a lack of skills? If so, what activities?
- b. Have there been times when you knew people did not ask you to participate because they knew you were unable? If so, when?
- c. How did you feel when the absence of skills limited your participation?

Process: Conduct discussion using above questions. Encourage all participants to contribute to the discussion.

15. Learning Activity

Preparation: Cut out pictures from magazines that depict people engaged in a variety of recreation activites. Place a large piece of paper on the wall. Attach the pictures to the paper on the wall with tape.

Content: "We are now going to participate in an activity that helps us identify barriers to leisure participation. I am going to divide you into two teams: A and B. I have placed on the wall a number of pictures of people engaged in many different recreation activities. Team B will choose a picture. Team A must then identify a barrier that may prevent people from engaging in the activity. If Team A can identify a barrier, then Team B has the chance to identify a barrier. If Team B can identify a barrier, then Team A will continue. The teams will take turns identifying barriers until one team runs out of ideas. When a team can no longer come up with any barriers, the other team will be awarded the picture. If at the beginning of the turn, Team A cannot identify a barrier, Team B can take a turn. If Team B identifies a barrier, it may take the picture off the wall and keep it. If neither team can identify a barrier, I will identify possible barriers. The picture will remain on the wall and can be chosen later. Team A will point to a new picture and Team B will begin. The game will proceed in this fashion until one team has obtained five pictures. Once a team has five pictures, we will go around the room and review the barriers we have identified during the game."

Process: Explain activity. Monitor activity; be prepared to assist if disagreements arise.

16. Debriefing

Content:
   a. Was it difficult for you to identify barriers?
   b. Have any barriers identified in the game been barriers to your leisure participation?
   c. Which of the pictures is your favorite? Why?
   d. Do you experience barriers limiting your participation in any of the activities in the pictures? If so, what are they?
   e. Did you like the game we just played? If so, why? If not, why not?
   f. Why do you think we did this activity?

Process: Conduct debriefing using above questions. Encourage each participant to respond to at least one of the debriefing questions.

17. Conclusion

Content: "A first step in solving any problem is to recognize that a problem exists. The same is true when we think about our leisure participation. If there are barriers to our participation, the first step is to identify what they are. We can then take steps to eliminate, reduce, or otherwise cope with those barriers."

Process: Make concluding statements. Provide opportunities for questions.

Objective 1.4: Demonstrate knowledge of strategies to overcome barriers to leisure.

1. Orientation Activity

Preparation: Prepare lists prior to session. Include items such as:

BARRIERS:
I do not have enough money for activity; I do not have enough time; I do not know about community activities; I do not have the skills.

SOLUTIONS: Save money and spend less on other items; Get organized and budget your time; Call recreation professional on the telephone; Enroll in course teaching you a leisure skill.

Content: "We are going to look at ways we can overcome leisure barriers. Each of you has been given one-third of a piece of colored paper. Find the other two people with the same color piece of paper, introduce yourself, and find out their names. Put together the pieces of paper to form one solid sheet. Use scotch tape on the side of the paper that does not have any words typed on it and fasten the three pieces together. Turn the paper over to discover two columns. In the left column is a list of barriers to leisure. In the right column is a list of possible solutions. One person from the group draws the first line to connect one barrier with one possible solution. The next player will match the next barrier and solution. Then the third takes a turn. Continue in this way until all barriers and solutions have been matched. Use only one barrier per solution and do not use a solution or barrier twice."

Process: Explain activity. Arrange participants in small groups. Distribute lists. Monitor activity. Follow with debriefing.

DISTRIBUTE MATERIALS

2. Debriefing

Content:
a.   Was it difficult to match strategies to overcome the barriers that were presented?
b.   Did you have any problems in matching the items?
c.   Were there any strategies you did not understand? If so, what were they?
d.   What did you like about this orientation activity?

Process: Conduct debriefing using the above questions. Encourage all participants to contribute to the discussion.

3. Introduction

Content: "Strategies to overcoming leisure barriers are in demand. In order to participate actively in recreation activities, we must develop these strategies. In turn, we hope to reduce barriers that challenge us so that we can have more fun and be satisfied with our leisure participation. Strategies to overcome leisure barriers may include participating in recreation activities that are free of charge, developing time management skills, using leisure resources at home, learning necessary skills to participate in activities, and adapting materials to meet your needs."

Process: Introduce importance of strategies in overcoming leisure barriers.

4. Presentation

Content: "Participating in recreation activities that are free of charge is an excellent way to benefit from leisure and overcome the barrier of limited money. Free programs are offered by parks and recreation departments, community organizations, state parks, and cultural centers. The media, which includes television, newspaper and radio, advertise these programs and the media can be used to find free programs that meet your needs. Programs change over time, and new ones that are offered can be as interesting and exciting as those that charge fees. Lack of funds does not have to be a barrier to your leisure participation."

FREE ACTIVITY

Process: Present information on free activity. List the phrase "free activity" on the chalkboard.

5. Discussion

Content:
   a. What agencies offer free recreation?
   b. What sources are available to find activities that are cost-free?
   c. Will free programs be offered to meet your needs?
   d. Are free programs as interesting and exciting as other programs?

Process: Conduct discussion using above questions. Encourage all participants to contribute to the discussion.

6. Presentation

Content: "Developing efficient time management skills is a positive approach to overcoming the barrier of not enough free time. Time management is a step-by-step process in which you prioritize and chart your responsibilities. In managing your time effectively, you include free time for recreation activities. If a situation arises whereby your scheduled free time is no longer free, reschedule it as soon as you can. Once you have developed a high level of time management skills, it becomes a natural process and leisure time improves."

FREE ACTIVITY
TIME MANAGEMENT

Process: Present information on developing time management skills. List "time management" on the chalkboard.

7. Discussion

Content:
   a. What are you doing when you are charting your responsibilities?
   b. When you develop a time management plan, do you schedule free time?
   c. How long must you use a schedule before free time becomes part of daily life?
   d. What happens when leisure is planned and situations occur that prevent it?

Process: Conduct discussion using above questions. Encourage all participants to contribute to the discussion.

8. Presentation

Content: "Using leisure resources at home is an easy way to overcome transportation barriers. Many leisure activities can be enjoyed at home and around your neighborhood. You may decide to use your basement or an extra room as a recreation area. It is easy to set up an area for games and hobbies that you enjoy. Just about any activity that you like can be done at home if you can get the equipment you need.

"There may be people in your neighborhood that are interested in these close-to-home activities. Talk with people in your area to see what they might be interested in doing. Whenever transportation is a barrier, use your home or yard as a place for leisure."

Process: Present information on leisure resources at home. Record "leisure at home" on the chalkboard.

9. Discussion

Content:
    a.   What are some recreation activities that can be done at home?
    b.   What can you do at home to set it up for leisure?
    c.   Can free time be enjoyable at home?
    d.   What are some ways to get neighbors involved?

Process: Conduct discussion using above questions. Encourage all participants to contribute to the discussion.

10. Presentation

Content: "Acquiring needed skills to participate in activities reduces the skills barrier. There are many strategies to develop introductory skills without participating in the activity. These techniques can be practiced at home, with videotapes, with skilled peers, or with a private instructor.

    "Videotapes are usually easy and fun to learn from. You can imitate the skills and review them many times. Skilled peers are enjoyable to work with. They tend to understand your position and they want to help you. They can tell you what you are doing wrong and offer you assistance when you need it. Private instructors are also willing to give you the help you need. They are skilled in their area, and they can teach you methods to improve your ability. Any strategy you choose will lead you toward participation."

Process: Present information on acquiring skills. Record the phrase "acquiring skills" on the chalkboard.

11. Discussion

Content:
    a.   What is the benefit of acquiring needed skills?
    b.   How can videotape instruction improve skills?
    c.   What are some advantages of learning skills from experienced peers?
    d.   How can private instruction help?
    e.   How can practicing at home prepare you for the activity?

Process: Conduct discussion using above questions. Encourage all participants to contribute to the discussion.

12. Presentation

Content: "Materials required for leisure may be adapted or changed to meet your needs. Adaptive equipment is available for many recreation activities. Pools may have ramps or lifts to help you enter the water. Heavy or large equipment can be replaced by light or small equipment to help you learn skills. If you do not have access to these resources, you may contact people in the community to assist you in making special equipment or you may use substitute equipment.

"Rules can also be changed to allow you to participate in activities. Scores, distances, time limits, and so forth, can be altered to meet your needs. Lack of equipment or hard rules do not have to keep you from experiencing leisure."

Process: Present information on adaptive equipment. List "adaptive equipment" on the chalkboard.

FREE ACTIVITY
TIME MANAGEMENT
LEISURE AT HOME
ACQUIRING SKILLS
ADAPTIVE EQUIPMENT

13. Discussion

Content:
    a. Can substitutions be used to replace required materials in order to remove or lessen a barrier?
    b. Is it possible to make special equipment on your own?
    c. Can equipment be adapted to meet your needs?
    d. What other ways are there to modify activities?

Process: Conduct discussion using above questions. Encourage all participants to contribute to the discussion.

14. Learning Activity

Preparation: Have leisure barrier symbols prepared before session. Some possible symbols would be:

PREPARE FOR SESSION

- No money—indicated by dollar sign.
- No time—indicated by clock face.
- No transportation—indicated by automobile.
- Lack of skills—indicated by wrecked bike.

Content: "We are now going to participate in an activity that helps us develop strategies to overcome leisure barriers. First, I will help you get into pairs. Each pair will receive a card with a symbol of a leisure barrier pictured on it. Using your knowledge and imagination, develop a strategy to overcome the barrier. Then, try to explain your strategy on the other side of your card. After everyone is finished, we will join in a circle. One partner will be asked to share the symbol and explain the barrier to the group. The other partner will then describe the strategy to overcome the barrier. We will continue until everyone has taken a turn."

Process: Explain activity. Monitor activity and assist when needed.

15. Debriefing

Content:
   a.   Was it hard to identify the leisure barrier by the symbol provided?
   b.   What were some difficulties in developing a strategy to overcome the barrier?
   c.   Do you think you can develop strategies to overcome barriers on your own?
   d.   When faced with a leisure barrier, what is your first reaction?
   e.   Do you think this activity helped you improve your skills to overcome barriers?

Process: Conduct debriefing using above questions. Encourage each participant to respond to one of the questions.

16. Conclusion

Content: "Leisure barriers do not always have to keep us from participating. We can use various resources to help us develop strategies to overcome them. We must first identify what the barrier is, and then start to think of solutions to overcome the problem. Developing strategies will allow us to participate in many fun activities that we may have thought were impossible."

Process: Make concluding statements and provide opportunity for participants to ask questions.

Appendix B
Leisure Education
Specific Program #2

BE AWARE OF SELF IN LEISURE

Purpose, Goal, and Objectives

Purpose: Provide opportunities for participants to become aware of their attitudes toward leisure, understand factors that may affect their leisure participation, examine their past recreation involvement, consider their current recreation involvement, and identify possible preferred future recreation activities.

GOAL 2: DEMONSTRATE AN AWARENESS OF SELF IN LEISURE.
Objective 2.1: Demonstrate knowledge of personal attitudes toward leisure.
Objective 2.2: Demonstrate knowledge of past recreation involvement.
Objective 2.3: Demonstrate knowledge of current recreation involvement.
Objective 2.4: Demonstrate ability to identify possible preferred future recreation activities.

Goal and Objectives: Performance Measures

GOAL 2: DEMONSTRATE AN AWARENESS OF SELF IN LEISURE.

Objective 2.1: Demonstrate knowledge of personal attitudes toward leisure.
Performance Measure A: Given paper and pencil, within five minutes and with 100% accuracy on two consecutive occasions:
  (a) identify five recreation activities that you like to do (e.g., fishing, painting, cycling, reading, kayaking); and
  (b) give one reason why you like each activity (e.g., fishing: peaceful; painting: creative expression; cycling: physical fitness; reading: choices of books; kayaking: adventure).
Performance Measure B: Given paper and pencil, within five minutes and with 100% accuracy on two consecutive occasions:
  (a) identify five recreation activities that you do not like to do (e.g., jogging, card playing, boating, football, attending opera); and
  (b) give one reason why you do not like each activity (e.g., jogging: tiring; card playing: boring; boating: afraid of water; football: rough; attending opera: too confusing).

Objective 2.2: Demonstrate knowledge of past recreation involvement.
Performance Measure: Given paper and pencil, within 15 minutes and with 100% accuracy on two consecutive occasions:
  (a) list 10 past recreation activities resulting in enjoyment and satisfaction (e.g., horseback riding, jogging, basketball, reading, bird watching, bowling, volleyball, gardening, swimming, cross-stitch); and
  (b) provide examples of participation in three of the activities listed (e.g., horseback riding) by identifying at least three of the following considerations:
      (1) where (e.g., when I lived in the country),
      (2) when (e.g., as a young adult),
      (3) why (e.g., I rode for pleasure),
      (4) who (e.g., with my sister), or
      (5) how often (e.g., at least three times per week).

Objective 2.3: Demonstrate knowledge of current recreation involvement.
Performance Measure A: Given paper and pencil, within 10 minutes and with 100% accuracy on two consecutive occasions:
  (a) list 10 current recreation activities resulting in enjoyment and satisfaction (e.g., watch television, attend sporting events, movies, visit art galleries, play video games, gardening, swimming, archery, fishing, macramé); and
  (b) provide examples of participation in three of the activities listed (e.g., watch television) identify at least one of the following considerations:
      (1) where (e.g., when I am home),
      (2) when (e.g., at night),
      (3) why (e.g., I watch television to relax),
      (4) who (e.g., by myself), or
      (5) how often (e.g., every evening).
Performance Measure B: Given a list of 10 past and 10 current recreation activities resulting in enjoyment and satisfaction, and paper and pencil, within 10 minutes and with 100% accuracy:
  (a) identify all activities on the list previously engaged in but that you are no longer doing (e.g., horseback riding, jogging, basketball, reading, bird watching, bowling, volleyball, gardening, and cross-stitch); and
  (b) specify reasons why you are no longer engaging in those activities (e.g., jogging: "I now experience pain in my knees when jogging");
OR
  (a) identify that no discrepancies exist, and
  (b) specify reasons for consistency ("Over the years, I have found ways to continue doing the things I like").

Objective 2.4: Demonstrate ability to identify possible future recreation activities.
Performance Measure: Given paper and pencil, within five minutes and with 100% accuracy on two consecutive occasions, list 10 recreation activities in which future participation is desired (e.g., horseback riding, jogging, basketball, dating, traveling, bowling, volleyball, gardening, swimming, mountain climbing).

Goal and Objectives: Content and Process

GOAL 2: DEMONSTRATE AN AWARENESS OF SELF IN LEISURE.

Objective 2.1: Demonstrate knowledge of personal attitudes toward leisure.

1. Orientation Activity

Content: "Please arrange yourselves in a circle so we can participate in an activity that will help us start to think about our attitudes toward leisure. We will introduce ourselves by our first names, state a leisure activity which we have enjoyed, and tell what it was about the activity that we liked. For example, a person could say, 'My name is Larry. I went on a camping trip and I enjoyed being in the natural environment.' Telling others what we like about something will begin to provide us with insight into our attitudes about it."

Process: Explain activity. Help arrange participants in circle. Provide each person with an opportunity to participate.

2. Introduction

Content: "Attitudes have a major effect on actions. This is as true of leisure as it is of other aspects of life. Your attitude toward leisure is important in deciding whether or not to participate in an activity, with whom, for how long, what is expected from it, and other factors. If leisure is valued, you will be willing to expend the resources and make the commitments necessary to have a chance to participate. If leisure is not valued, you will make little or no effort to be involved in it. Developing an awareness of self requires clarification of your personal attitudes toward leisure."

Process: Introduce topic of personal attitudes toward leisure.

3. Presentation

Content: "Examining your attitude about leisure requires careful thinking. It calls for a high degree of honesty. It means that you must search yourself for your true feelings about leisure and attempt to develop an understanding of why you feel the way you do. One way this may be done is for you to ask yourself questions related to leisure. Care must be taken in answering questions to ensure that your response is an accurate reflection of your feelings and not merely what you believe others may expect to hear.

"Another way for you to investigate your attitudes is to place yourself in situations where you are confronted by choices regarding leisure. The choices that are made will be an indication of your attitude. Reflecting on why a choice was made may result in even better insight into to your attitude.

"There is nothing mysterious about gaining a knowledge of your attitudes toward leisure. It simply requires a little thought relative to some very basic questions. For example: (a) Is leisure valued? (b) Why is it (or is it not) valued? (c) Which activities are desired more than others? (d) Why is this so? (e) What types of leisure environments are preferred and why? and (f) How often do you like to participate and with whom? Responding to these and similar questions will help individuals learn a great deal about their attitudes toward leisure."

Process: Present information on personal attitudes toward leisure. List the questions that can
be asked of self on a chalkboard or easel.

LIST ON BOARD

- Is leisure valued? Why?
- Which activities are desired more
  than others? Why?
- What types of leisure environments are preferred? Why?
- How much involvement is preferred?
- With whom is involvement preferred?

4. Discussion

Content:
  a. Why is it important to understand your personal attitudes towards leisure?
  b. How does making choices help you learn about your leisure attitude?
  c. What additional questions can be asked to learn about one's attitude toward
      leisure?

Process: Conduct discussion using above questions. Encourage participants to contribute to the discussion. At the end of the discussion, inform participants that they will
engage in several learning activities to investigate their attitudes towards leisure.

5. Learning Activity

Preparation: Gather a pair of scissors, three
envelopes, and a pencil for each participant.
Provide group with a selection of magazines
to clip pictures from (1 or 2 magazines per
participant that show various activities that
could be considered leisure).

PREPARE FOR SESSION

Content: "We are going to begin to learn more about our attitudes towards leisure. Each
of you has a pair of scissors, three envelopes, and several magazines. Browse through
the magazines and cut out pictures of recreation activities. Select activities in which you
have participated and experienced enjoyment and satisfaction, activities in which you
have participated but had a negative experience, and activities in which you have not
yet participated but think might interest you in the future. Label your envelopes in some
way to reflect these three categories. For example, you could draw a happy face on the
envelope that will contain pictures of activities you enjoyed, a sad face on the envelope
containing activities that were negative experiences, and a question mark on activities
you have not yet experienced. Try to get four or five activities in each envelope.

"When you are finished, I am going to put you in pairs and ask you to exchange
envelopes with your partner. Your partner will select an envelope, withdraw one picture,
and hand it to you. When you see the picture, tell your partner why you liked the activity, disliked it, or might be interested in it in the future. When you are finished, take a
picture from one of your partner's envelopes and your partner will discuss the picture.
Take turns drawing pictures from envelopes, making sure that you use all three envelopes
during your discussion. As you participate in the discussion, think about why you liked
or disliked an activity."

Process: Explain activity. Provide scissors, pencils, envelopes, and magazines. Divide into pairs. Allow ample time for discussion. Move about the room providing assistance as needed.

DISTRIBUTE MATERIALS

6. Debriefing

Content:
a. Did you find pictures of your favorite activities? If so, what were they?
b. Did you learn anything about your partner's attitude toward leisure? If so, what?
c. What did you learn about your own attitude?
d. Was it difficult to think of things to say during your discussion? If so, why?

Process: Conduct debriefing using above questions. Encourage each participant to respond to at least one of the questions.

7. Learning Activity

Preparation: Obtain five blank index cards per participant, and pencils.

PREPARE FOR SESSION

Content: "We are going to do an activity named 'Reaction.' Please get in a circle. I am going to give each of you five blank cards. Write the name of a different recreation activity on each of the cards. When everyone is finished, I will collect the cards and place them in a basket. I will withdraw a card, read aloud the name of the activity, and point to a person in the circle. That person will have five seconds to say aloud one word that describes his or her attitude toward the activity. We will then go clockwise around the circle and each person will have five seconds to state one word that describes his or her attitude toward the activity. For example, I may draw a card that has 'hang gliding' on it. The first person may say it is 'scary,' the second person may say it is 'exciting,' the third person may say it is 'dangerous.' When you respond, try to use a word that genuinely reflects your attitude toward the activity; it does not matter if someone else has already used that word."

Process: Explain activity. Provide cards and pencils. Arrange participants in a circle. When selecting a person to give first word, go around the circle so that everyone has an opportunity to be first to react.

DISTRIBUTE MATERIALS

8. Debriefing

Content:
a. Do you think the words you used were an accurate reflection of your attitude?
b. Did you use any words that, after reflecting on them, you would like to change? If so, what were they and with what activity were they used?

    c.   Was it hard to react with a five-second time limit? If so, why?
    d.   Did you learn about your attitude toward leisure from this activity? If so, what?

Process: Conduct debriefing using above questions. Encourage each participant to respond to at least one question. Ask participants about the rationale for their answers.

9. Learning Activity

Preparation: Prepare questions prior to session. Questions could include the following. Is your leisure more like:

- the beach or the mountains?
- slippers or running shoes?
- a seven course meal or fast food?
- a sports car or a pickup?
- a basketball or a book?
- a campsite or a hotel?

Content: "This is an activity named 'Either-Or.' Again, it is designed to assist you in knowing more about your attitude toward leisure. Please arrange yourselves in a circle. I will go around the circle and ask each of you a question: 'Is your leisure more like *(first choice)* or *(second choice)*?' I will point in one direction for the first choice and the opposite direction for the second choice. You will have 10 seconds to decide which choice your leisure is more like. You will then tell us why you made the choice you did. For example, I may say 'Is your leisure more like summer or winter?' and then you must choose."

Process: Explain activity. Arrange in circle. Ensure each participant has opportunity to respond to question. Go around circle as many times as desired.

10. Debriefing

Content:
    a.   Was it difficult for you to make a choice? If so, why?
    b.   Can you think of other pairs of choices that we could ask? If so, what are they?
    c.   Did others make choices you thought they would? If not, what does this mean?
    d.   Would you make changes in your choices? If so, what would they be and why?

Process: Conduct debriefing using above questions. Provide an example of how you might change an original choice. Encourage participants to respond to the questions.

11. Learning Activity

Preparation: Obtain pencils and develop the Leisure Values Form. Prepare something similar to the following Leisure Values Form in advance of session:

LEISURE IS:

Exciting	1	2	3	4	5	Boring
Gratifying	1	2	3	4	5	Disappointing
Important	1	2	3	4	5	Trivial
Accepting	1	2	3	4	5	Rejecting
Bold	1	2	3	4	5	Timid
Positive	1	2	3	4	5	Negative
Action	1	2	3	4	5	Idleness
Growing	1	2	3	4	5	Stagnating
Expressive	1	2	3	4	5	Passive
Creative	1	2	3	4	5	Repetitious

Content: "Another way to learn something about your attitude toward leisure is to complete a Leisure Values Form. A Leisure Values Form is one that contains a rating scale and pairs of words that describe opposite feelings about leisure. A rating scale has several points on it, indicating different levels of agreement with the idea expressed by the word pair. For example, a rating scale might have five points on it, as follows:

1 = very   2 = slightly   3 = neutral   4 = slightly   5 = very

A word pair might be 'Exciting' and 'Relaxing' and would be shown as follows:

Exciting   1   2   3   4   5   Boring

"If a person was very positive about leisure and believed it was exciting, then '1' would be circled. If a person had no feelings about it, '3' would be circled. The person circles the number that most nearly resembled his or her feelings about leisure as indicated by the word pair. A number would be circled for every pair of words.

"Each of you has a Leisure Values Form. Read it carefully and complete it according to your feelings. When the forms are completed, you will be placed in groups of three or four and discuss your responses."

Process: Explain activity. Use board to show sample scale and word pair. When form is completed, put participants in small groups for discussion.

12. Debriefing

Content:
    a.   Did you feel the rating scale provided you with enough choices? If not, why not?
    b.   Do you have any suggestions for additional word pairs? If so, what are they?
    c.   As you look at your Leisure Values Form, are there more numbers on the left side of the sheet circled? On the right side? In the middle? What does this mean?
    d.   What did you learn from this activity?

Process: Conduct debriefing using above questions. Possibly enlarge the instrument and make an overhead transparency to be used as a visual aid during the debriefing. Encourage all participants to contribute to the debriefing.

13. Learning Activity

Preparation: Obtain pencils and develop the Leisure Satisfaction Form. Prepare forms in advance of the session. The form could include the following questions:

LEISURE SATISFACTION

Complete the following sentences:

    a.   I am happiest when:
    b.   My favorite weekend is when:
    c.   If I could do anything I want, I would:
    d.   In the summer, I like:
    e.   My favorite evening activity is:
    f.   If I could go anywhere I want, I would go:
    g.   When I am alone, I like to:
    h.   If I had more time, I would:
    i.   I like holidays because:
    j.   The thing I like best about being with my friends is:

Content: "Another pencil and paper exercise that can be used to learn about one's attitude toward leisure is the completion of a Leisure Satisfaction Form. A Leisure Satisfaction Form is a series of open-ended questions focused on what individuals like to do with their leisure. For example, a question might be stated as follows: 'When I am in the park, I like to . . . .' Each individual completing the form would then write a response to that question."

"Each of you has been given a Leisure Satisfaction Form. Think carefully and complete each question on the form. When you finish, we will use the forms as a basis for discussion."

Process: Explain activity. Distribute forms and pencils. Allow sufficient time for completion. Move to debriefing.

14. Debriefing

Content:
    a.   How did you respond to the statement (a through j)?
    b.   Are there additional statements that should be on the form? If so, what are they?
    c.   Was there a statement that was easier to answer than the others? If so, which one?
    d.   What did you learn from this activity?

Process: Conduct debriefing using above questions. Encourage each participant to respond to at least one of the questions.

15. Learning Activity

Preparation: Obtain marbles and a cup. Develop a series of questions written on index cards. Examples of questions could include:

PREPARE FOR SESSION

- What does leisure mean to you?
- What leisure activity is your favorite and why?
- What leisure activity would you like to learn and why?
- What was your favorite thing to do as a child?
- Where would you like to travel next year?

Content: "This activity is called 'Lose Your Marbles Over Leisure.' It is an activity designed to help you become more aware of your leisure attitudes and lifestyle and to help you interact with other members of the group. Each of you will receive five cards with a leisure-related question on each card. You will also receive five marbles. The cards will be facedown on the table in front of you and there will be a cup in the center of the table. Play will begin with the person whose next birthday is closest to today's date and will rotate clockwise from that person. When it is your turn to play, draw one of your cards and answer the question on it within one minute. If you answer the question, place a marble in the cup and set the card aside. If you do not answer the question within one minute, return the card to your stack but do not place a marble in the cup. Play will proceed to the next person. Play will continue until one person has placed all five marbles in the cup."

Process: Explain activity. Prepare cards. Distribute cards and marbles. Monitor activity for compliance with one-minute time limit.

DISTRIBUTE MATERIALS

16. Debriefing

Content:
   a. What did you learn about your leisure involvement from this activity?
   b. Was it awkward to answer questions in front of other group members?
   c. What did you learn about other group members?
   d. Why did we do this activity?

Process: Conduct debriefing using above questions. Refer back to the questions. List questions on an easel or chalkboard and point to the questions as they are addressed. Encourage each participant to respond to at least one of the questions.

LIST ON BOARD

17. Conclusion

Content: "We have participated in a variety of activities to help us learn about our attitudes toward leisure. Knowing what we like and dislike and why we feel the way we do is an important part of learning about ourselves. This knowledge can guide us in our choices and help us use our leisure more effectively."

Process: Make concluding statements. Provide opportunities for questions.

Objective 2.2: Demonstrate knowledge of past recreation involvement.

1. Orientation Activity

Content: "We are going to do an activity to introduce ourselves and to share our past recreation involvement with one another. On a sheet of paper, I want you to write one type of recreation that you enjoyed in the past. When all participants are finished, I will ask you to go around the room and introduce yourselves to each other and tell each other about your past recreation involvement. If you find someone with the same recreation involvement, pair up with him or her and introduce him or her to the next person. Once you have met each person and shared your experiences, sit down and wait for everyone to finish."

Process: Explain activity. Provide paper and pencils. Initiate introduction segment. Encourage participation and interaction.

DISTRIBUTE MATERIALS

2. Introduction

Content: "Past recreation involvement provides us with background information that can help us examine our awareness of self in leisure. Past experiences contribute to our knowledge and our present participation. By looking at our past involvement, we will increase our leisure awareness."

Process: Introduce topic of past recreation involvement.

3. Presentation

Content: "Our past recreation involvement can tell us our likes and interests. Several personal factors can cause changes in leisure. These factors can be determined by reviewing our past involvement. We need to look at those factors separately to see how and why they have changed. Personal factors may include age, health, free time, availability of recreation resources, and interest level. Any of these may change over time and cause a change in your recreation involvement.

"The amount of time you spent in recreation participation is also important. If you spent much of your time in recreation, it was probably important to you. You can gain a better understanding of the significance that leisure has had in your life by looking into the past."

Process: Present information on past recreation involvement. Provide examples that are appropriate for the participants.

4. Discussion

Content:
    a. Why is your past recreation involvement important?

    b.   What is important to remember about your past involvement?
    c.   What factors can change over time and change your recreation involvement?
    d.   How can you use your past experiences to increase awareness of your leisure?

Process: Conduct discussion using above questions. Encourage participants to contribute to the discussion.

5. Learning Activity

Preparation: Obtain pencils and develop handouts. Prepare handout with the following headings:

- age
- health
- time
- availability
- interest level

Content: "We are going to do an activity to examine our past recreation involvement and the factors that were present. I am going to give you a handout that has been divided into several columns. In one column, you will make a list of your past involvements. Next to each item, you will describe personal factors considered during participation. These factors are labeled: age, health, time, availability and interest level. Under each heading, record personal data during the time you participated in the recreation activity listed in the first column. Record as follows: your age at the time; your physical health in terms of being good, fair, or poor; hours per week you spent in this area; availability of resources in terms of good or poor; your interest level in this area in terms of high, medium or low. We will then take turns sharing one of our pastimes and our personal factors with the rest of the group. Each person will volunteer and present his or her data."

Process: Explain activity. Distribute handout to the participants. Provide assistance as necessary. Encourage all participants to volunteer and share their data. Move to debriefing when activity is completed.

6. Debriefing

Content:
    a.   Was it hard to remember the personal factors during your involvement? Why or why not?
    b.   Do you think that some of your interests have changed because of these factors? If so, which ones?
    c.   Would you like to change some factors so you can continue to be involved in these activities? If so, which ones?
    d.   How did availability of the resource affect your participation?
    e.   Has your interest level in the areas you listed changed over time, or has it remained the same? Why do you think it has or has not changed?

Process: Conduct debriefing using above questions. Encourage participants to contribute to the discussion by responding to at least one of the questions.

7. Learning Activity

Preparation: Obtain pencils and develop handouts. Prepare paper with following categories:

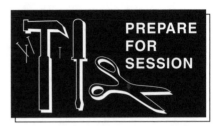

- friend
- TV show
- sport
- games
- hobby

Content: "We are going to look at our past recreation involvements and see if we can determine any patterns through our lives. Each of you will receive a piece of paper with categories on the right-hand side across the paper. On the left-hand side write years 5, 10, 15, 20, 25, 30 . . . up to your current age. Answer each category by the age indicated. For example my favorite TV show when I was 5 years old was "Deputy Dawg," at 10 years old it was "Bonanza," etc. . . . After you have completed all the categories we will discuss your past recreation involvements and look for patterns.

Process: Explain activity. Provide paper with categories and columns listed. Use age intervals that are appropriate for the participants. Provide assistance when necessary. Move to debriefing when activity is completed.

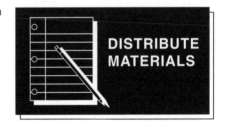

8. Debriefing

Content:
  a. Who was your best friend when you were five? ten? fifteen? Can you recognize a pattern? Did these friends live on your same street or far away?
  b. What was your favorite TV show? Has that changed over the years?
  c. What about in the sports category? Is there a pattern of participation?
  d. What about your favorite games? How has that changed over the years?
  e. What was your favorite hobby? Any patterns through the years?

Process: Conduct debriefing using above questions. Encourage participants to contribute by responding to the questions.

9. Learning Activity

Preparation: Obtain red pencils or pens, develop handout. The handout consists of a piece of paper with a long, narrow oval on it.

Content: "Is leisure significant in our lives? Significance is how important it feels to us.

We are going to make individual significance thermometers to show how important we feel leisure has been in our lives. I will give each of you a paper with a long narrow oval on it. If you feel recreation participation has little importance in your life, make a mark toward the bottom of the long oval. If you feel recreation has been of great importance, make a mark high on the oval. Color in red the area on the scale underneath the mark you made. The picture is now a thermometer of how important you think recreation has been in your life. Each of you will now show your thermometer and tell the group how important recreation participation has been to you."

Process: Explain the activity. Give each person a red pencil or pen and a copy of the handout. Provide assistance as needed. Show two examples of thermometers drawn on an easel, one with a great deal of red to signify high and one with very little red to indicate low. Encourage participation. Move to debriefing.

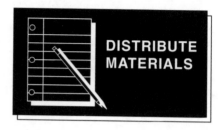

DISTRIBUTE MATERIALS

10. Debriefing

Content:
- a. How is the importance of recreation in your life influenced by past experiences?
- b. Are you happy about the significance of leisure in your life? Why or why not?
- c. How can you make recreation more important to you?
- d. After looking at your scale, do you have a better understanding of the significance of recreation? In what way?

Process: Conduct debriefing using above questions. Encourage participants to contribute to the debriefing by responding to the questions.

11. Conclusion

Content: "Reviewing our past recreation involvement is a great way to look at our interests and is a method to use to find out how much time we have spent in recreation. We can see what has changed over time and what significance leisure has had in our lives. By looking at our past interests, we become more aware of the role that leisure has had in our lives."

Process: Make concluding statements. Provide opportunities for questions.

Objective 2.3: Demonstrate knowledge of current recreation involvement.

1. Orientation Activity

Preparation: Develop card set. Prepare cards with one participant's name on each (total card count will equal number in group).

PREPARE FOR SESSION

Content: "We are going to participate in an activity called 'I see you' to help us start thinking about our current participation in recreation activities. In my hand is a stack of cards. Each card contains the name of one person in this group. Each of you will be given the opportunity to draw one card from the stack. If you draw your own name, return the card and draw again. After everyone has drawn a card, arrange yourselves in a circle.

"We will start at one point in the circle and continue in a clockwise fashion. When it is your turn, look at the name on your card, use that person's first name, and try to guess what that person enjoys doing in his or her leisure participation. For example, the person who is guessing might say: 'Larry, in your leisure I see you flying model airplanes.' or 'Diane, in your leisure, I see you enjoying a walk through the park.' The person who was the subject of the guess must then tell the group whether the guess was correct or incorrect. Now it will be time for the person whose interest was guessed to guess about the person whose name is on his or her card.

"Continue guessing in this way until everyone has had a chance to guess what another person enjoys."

Process: Explain activity and distribute cards. Select person to start activity. Emphasize necessity for guesses to be positive. Monitor process.

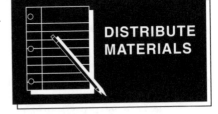

DISTRIBUTE MATERIALS

2. Debriefing

Content:
  a. Were you able to make an accurate guess of a leisure interest of the person whose name you drew? If so, on what did you base your guess?
  b. Was the guess made about your leisure interest accurate? On what basis do you think the guess was made?
  c. Did it make you uncomfortable to have someone guessing about your leisure activities? If so, why?
  d. What did you learn about the leisure interests of other members of the group?
  e. Were you surprised to learn this? If so, why?
  f. Why do you think we did this activity?

Process: Conduct debriefing using above questions. Emphasize how learning about recreation interests can help participants to get to know one another. Encourage all participants to contribute to the debriefing.

3. Introduction

Content: "Developing an awareness of leisure in your life requires an understanding of several related areas. We have spent some time in identifying our personal attitudes toward leisure and learning about factors that influence leisure participation. We have also thought about recreation activities in which we have engaged in the past. It is now time for us to think clearly and carefully about our current recreation involvement."

Process: Introduce topic of understanding one's current recreation involvement.

4. Presentation

Content: "Thinking about our current recreation involvement seems easy. All we need to do is remember the recreation activities in which we participate. But sometimes we do not think as carefully as we should. For example, people might think of backpacking as a recreation activity in which they have recently been involved, but it has really been five years since their last backpacking journey. Would it be accurate to claim backpacking as a form of current recreation involvement? It is also difficult to be objective when we are thinking about ourselves. For example, people may not think of watching television as one of their current recreation involvements, when the truth is that this is how they spend a majority of their free time. It is not that these people are dishonest, they simply have not thought carefully.

"It can become easy to get from day-to-day without knowing how much or how little time is spent on specific activities, with whom time is spent, or how long it has been since participating in a favorite recreation activity. But there are several things you can do to arrive at a better understanding of how your time is actually spent. We are going to do several learning activities to help us understand our current recreation involvement."

Process: Present information on current recreation involvement. Gear examples to the needs and interests of the participants.

5. Discussion

Content:
    a.   Why is it important to have knowledge of your current recreation involvement?
    b.   How is it possible to not know precisely your current recreation involvement?
    c.   What are some suggestions for determining your current recreation involvement?

Process: Conduct discussion using above questions. Encourage participants to respond to at least one of the questions.

6. Learning Activity

Preparation: Obtain pencils and develop Pie of Life form (a piece of paper with a circle that can be divided into segments).

PREPARE
FOR
SESSION

Content: "We are going to complete an exercise entitled 'Pie of Life.' It is a visual exercise designed to help individuals see how much of their time is spent on various activities during a typical day in their lives. You have each received a Pie of Life form. You can see the Pie of Life is represented by a circle and the circle has been divided into four equal quadrants. Each quadrant represents six of the 24 hours in a day. Take some time to think of how you spend a typical weekday. Choose any day, Monday through Friday. Divide the pie into segments (we will call them slices) that show how much time per day is spent on the things you typically do. For example, you may have a pie divided into: sleep, school, homework, household chores, self-maintenance (e.g., eating, personal hygiene), family obligations, and recreation.

"Another person may not have a slice that represents school but would have one that represents working to earn an income. The size of each slice depends on how much time is spent on the activity it represents. The more time that is spent on an activity, the larger the slice of pie; the less time that is spent, the smaller the slice. Try to be as accurate as possible in completing your Pie of Life. There is no predetermined right or wrong amount of time to spend on specific activities. Remember that the pie is to represent how you spend your time. Your pie may not resemble other pies in the group. When everyone has completed his or her pie, we will discuss what they depict."

Process: Explain activity. Distribute Pie of Life form to individuals. Provide assistance as necessary. Move to debriefing.

DISTRIBUTE MATERIALS

7. Debriefing

Content:
  a. Which of your slices is the largest? Which is the smallest?
  b. How many different slices do you have?
  c. Are you satisfied with the relative size of your slices?
  d. If you could change the size of your slices, which ones would you change and what size would you make them?
  e. Is there a realistic possibility that you could change the size of some of your slices? If so, which ones?
  f. What would you have to do to bring about these changes?
  g. What did you learn from your Pie of Life?
  h. If you could step outside your Pie of Life and view it as someone else's, would you think that person had a balanced and interesting life? If not, why not?

Process: Conduct debriefing using above questions. Encourage participants to contribute to the discussion by responding to at least one of the questions.

8. Learning Activity

Content: "Now that you know how to do a Pie of Life, repeat the process, using a typical weekend day. Choose Saturday or Sunday and depict the way you typically spend your time. Again, be as accurate as possible and do not be concerned about what others' pies may look like. Your focus is to be on how you spend your time. When you are finished, compare your two pies."

DISTRIBUTE MATERIALS

Process: Explain activity. Distribute pie forms. Provide assistance as necessary.

9. Debriefing

Content:
  a. Did you have more free time available on a weekday or a weekend day?

b. On which of the two days would you prefer to have free time available?
c. If you could increase your free time on only one of the two days, which day would you choose? Why?
d. What would you do with the increased free time?
e. Are you satisfied with the way you spend your time, as depicted by both pies? If not, how would you change it?
f. If you know how you would like to change the way in which you spend your time, is there anything preventing you from doing it? If so, what is it?

Process: Conduct debriefing using above questions. Encourage participants to contribute to the debriefing by responding to at least one of the questions.

10. Learning Activity

Preparation: Obtain pencils and develop inventory form. Use lined paper. Provide space for 20–25 recreation activities on the left side of the paper. On the remainder of the paper, prepare columns headed by the following questions:

PREPARE
FOR
SESSION

• How often do I participate?
• When was the last time I participated?
• With whom did I participate?
• Where did I participate?
• How much did it cost?
• Was it fun?
• Do I want to do it again?
• Does this activity rank among my ten most favorite activities?

Content: "Another way to think about your current recreation involvement is to complete a recreation activity inventory. Each of you will be given an activity inventory form. The form will provide you with a place to list all of the recreation activities in which you have participated within the past year. The form will also contain columns in which you can respond to specified questions concerning those activities. Complete the form as correctly as possible. Do not include activities if you have not participated in them within the past calendar year. Again, the form should be a reflection of you and your recreation activities. Do not be concerned if it does not resemble other persons' forms. Use as many forms as needed to list your recreation activities in the past year."

Process: Explain activity and distribute activity inventory forms. Remind participants to answer each question for each activity listed.

DISTRIBUTE
MATERIALS

11. Debriefing

Content:
a. Were you surprised at how many (or how few) activities are on your inventory?
b. Are you satisfied with the number of activities on your form?

    c.   What did you learn about your current recreation involvement?

    d.   What additional questions about the activities could be included on the form?

Process: Conduct debriefing using above questions. Encourage participants to participate actively in the debriefing by responding to at least one of the questions.

12. Conclusion

Content: "Thinking carefully about your current recreation involvement is a beneficial
exercise. It can help you focus your thoughts on what you are now doing, rather than
what you have done at times in the past. If you wish to make a change in your leisure
participation, you must first know what your current status is. This type of exercise
helps you to be objective and provides a good foundation for any decisions you may
wish to make regarding your leisure."

Process: Make concluding statements. Provide opportunities for questions.

Objective 2.4: Demonstrate ability to identify possible future recreation activities.

1. Orientation Activity

Preparation: Obtain pencils, poker chips, a
container, and slips of paper, and develop
handouts. Prepare bingo sheet handouts prior
to session by dividing paper into 16 adjoining
squares, four columns with four squares in
each column.

Content: "We are going to play a type of 'leisure bingo' to help us get to know each
other better and to start us thinking about recreation activities in which we would like to
participate in the future. Each of you will be given a small piece of paper and a pencil.
Write your name and one recreation activity in which you do not now participate but
would like to try in the future. I will collect your slips of paper when you are finished
and place them in a small basket.

    "Each of you will also be given a sheet of paper that has been divided into 16
squares. Move about the room and meet other persons. Ask them their names and which
activities they wrote on their slips of paper. Put the name of a person and his or her
activity in one square. Continue this process until all the squares are filled.

    "When everyone has finished, I will give each of you several poker chips. I will
draw the slips of paper from the basket, one at
a time. As I read the name and activity on the
slip, look to see if it is on your sheet. If it is,
place a poker chip on that square. The first
person to cover four squares, vertically, horizontally, or diagonally, will call out 'bingo.'
That person will be the winner."

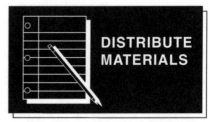

Process: Explain activity. Distribute pencils

and slips of paper. Distribute sheets and poker chips. Allow sufficient time for participants to fill squares. Draw and announce contents of slips. Confirm winner.

2. Debriefing

Content:
a. Did you find anyone who had a future interest that matched yours? If so, who?
b. By listening to others, did you get any ideas of activities in which you might become interested? If so, what were they?
c. Did others list activities in which you already participate? If so, what were they?

Process: Conduct debriefing by using above questions. Encourage contributions from all participants by encouraging them to respond to the questions.

3. Introduction

Content: "Developing a comprehensive awareness of self in leisure is a task that includes several different components. We have examined four of these components. The remaining component is recreation activities in which we would like to participate in the future."

Process: Introduce topic of identifying possible future recreation activities in which they would like to engage.

4. Presentation

Content: "Thinking about which recreation activities you might like to do in the future is not just an exercise in wishful thinking, although dreaming about what you want to do is perfectly acceptable. Thinking about future recreation involvement should also be tempered with *realistic assessments* of the chances of participating in what you wish.

"Leisure, like life, is a dynamic process. It is not something that is static, but rather it changes and evolves as time passes. The things in which you are interested today might become things that are boring in a year's time. It is possible that some activities that may be widespread in the future have not yet been created and developed. Because change is inevitable, you should keep a *flexible attitude* about future recreation involvement.

"This is not to suggest that *long-term interests* should not be developed or that all interests and activities will be short-lived and eventually drop out of favor to be replaced by new ones. On the contrary, some activities that are favorites today may remain as favorites in the future. For example, nature walks are often a life-long interest for many people. There is no good reason for them to be otherwise, unless one becomes disinterested.

"The important focus is to *think seriously* about what you want in the future. Keeping interest and involvement in activities that bring joy and satisfaction is quite natural. But there should also be room for thinking about ideas of new activities that can be rewarding.

"Remember, it is fine to dream about what you want to do, but it often takes *purposeful effort* to make dreams come true. You should not be discouraged about future possibilities, but should understand that those things that are most likely to happen in the future are the things that you work to achieve."

Process: Present information on future recreation involvement. Use the chalkboard to record the following major points identified in the presentation:

- realistic assessments
- flexible attitude
- long-term interests
- serious thought
- purposeful effort

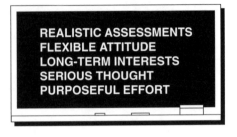

REALISTIC ASSESSMENTS
FLEXIBLE ATTITUDE
LONG-TERM INTERESTS
SERIOUS THOUGHT
PURPOSEFUL EFFORT

5. Discussion

Content:
a. Why is it important to think about future recreation activities in which you want to participate?
b. Do you participate in activities today that you did not do five years ago? Why?
c. Which of your current recreation activities will still be of interest to you 10 years from now? Why?
d. What can you do to increase your chances of participating in what you want in the future?

Process: Conduct discussion using above questions. Encourage all participants to contribute to the discussion by responding to at least one of the questions.

6. Learning Activity

Content: "A good way to begin thinking about future recreation involvement is to become aware of the many possibilities that exist. To start this process, we are going to participate in an activity known as 'Leisure Alphabet.' Get into groups of three. On a sheet of paper, list the letters of the alphabet in one or two columns. Now, try to think of recreation activities that begin with each letter of the alphabet, A through Z. If you think of an activity that begins with the letter A (e.g., archery), write that activity by the letter A. Continue through the alphabet. Be as complete as possible but do not be discouraged if you do not think of an activity for a specific letter (e.g., Z). You will have 15 minutes to complete this activity. Groups will then share results of their lists with the larger group."

Process: Explain activity. Provide pencil and paper. Put letters of alphabet on board. When groups are sharing, list activities by appropriate letter.

LIST
ON
BOARD

7. Debriefing

Content:
a. Were any groups able to complete the entire alphabet?
b. Were there any activities listed that were new to you? If so, what were they?
c. What is your opinion of the diversity of activities?
d. Do you see any activities that strike your interest as future possibilities? If so, what are they? What interests you about them?

Process: Conduct debriefing using above questions. Encourage participants to contribute to debriefing by having each person respond to at least one of the questions.

8. Learning Activity

Preparation: Obtain pencils and develop Leisure Interest Finder forms prior to session. Each form will consist of three columns. The left column will contain a list of words, such as the following:

- active
- passive
- spring
- summer
- autumn
- winter
- indoors
- outdoors

- social
- cultural
- educational
- intellectual
- entertaining
- creative
- physical
- artistic

The middle column will have a header entitled "By Myself" and a corresponding line or space for each word in the left column. The right column will have a header entitled "With Others" and will also have a line or space for each word from the left column.

Content: "Another way to think about possible future recreation involvement is to complete a 'Leisure Interest Finder.' Each of you will be given a form that has a list of words on the left-hand side, a column headed 'By Myself' and a second column headed 'With Others.' For each of the words on the left-hand side, think of a recreation activity that you would enjoy doing by yourself in the future and record that activity in the column headed 'By Myself.' Think of another activity for that same word that you would enjoy doing with others in the future and enter it in the column headed by 'With Others.' Do not use an activity more than once. When everyone has finished, we will discuss the results."

Process: Explain activity. Distribute forms and pencils. Encourage participants to complete both columns. Provide sufficient time to complete. Move to debriefing.

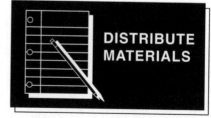

9. Debriefing

Content:
  a. What activities were listed for 'Active' and 'By Myself?' (Use several combination of words and columns.)
  b. Was it easier to think of activities for the 'With Others' column than the 'By Myself' column? If so, why?
  c. Did you get any ideas for future participation from listening to the others? If so, what were they?
  d. What are the possibilities that you will participate in several activities you listed?

Process: Conduct debriefing using above questions. Encourage each participant to contribute to the debriefing by having each respond to at least one of the questions.

10. Learning Activity

Content: "An additional way to think about recreation activities in which you might want to participate is to project yourself into the future to a time where you could do anything you wanted. Imagine that for a 48-hour period, you could do as you wish. The 48 hours could be next week, next month, next year, or any other time in the future. You have no physical or financial constraints; your only limit is the 48-hour time period. What would you do with that time? Construct an ideal 48 hours for yourself and put it in writing. Be as creative as you want; fantasize to your heart's content. When you are finished, be prepared to share your ideal 48 hours with the group."

Process: Explain activity. Distribute pencils and paper. Encourage creative thinking. Create an atmosphere of acceptance to innovative and different ideas.

11. Debriefing

Content:
    a.   What did your 48 hours look like?
    b.   What did you learn about yourself?
    c.   What did you learn about others?
    d.   Is there a chance some of your ideal 48 hours will come to pass?
    e.   What will you have to do to help it come true?
    f.   Was the process of fantasizing fun? How so?

Process: Conduct debriefing using above questions. Encourage participants to be active contributors to the debriefing by having them respond to at least one of the questions. Have as many participants as possible respond to the first question.

12. Learning Activity

Preparation: Obtain magazines, scissors, glue, and construction paper.

Content: "Each of you now has the opportunity to create a future leisure collage. There are plenty of magazines, scissors, glue, and construction paper available to you. Browse through the magazines and cut out pictures of activities you will be doing or want to be doing in the future. Glue these pictures to the construction paper in any pattern you wish. Be as colorful and creative as you can, but remember your collage should represent you and what you want to do."

Process: Explain activity. Supply magazines, scissors, glue, and construction paper. Emphasize future orientation of collage.

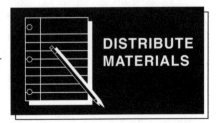

13. Debriefing

Content:
    a. What do you like best about your collage? Why?
    b. How would you describe the majority of the depictions on your collage? Are they Physical? Social? Cultural? Solitary? Group?
    c. If you made a leisure collage five years from now, do you think it would be similar to this one?
    d. What will you do with your collage?

Process: Conduct debriefing using above questions. Encourage participants to contribute to the debriefing by responding to at least one of the questions.

14. Conclusion

Content: "Thinking about possible future recreation involvement is both healthy and necessary. How else will we know what we want to do? Although we have to do more than speculate about the future, speculating is the first step. Once we know where we want to go, then we can plan how to get there."

Process: Make concluding statements. Provide opportunity for participants to ask questions.

Appendix C
Leisure Education
Specific Program #3

BE SELF-DETERMINED IN LEISURE

Purpose, Goal, and Objectives

Purpose: Provide opportunities for participants to learn about their personal successes in leisure, understand the importance of personal growth and responsibility for leisure participation, learn to express preferences, and understand how to be assertive.

GOAL 3: DEMONSTRATE AN UNDERSTANDING OF SELF-DETERMINATION IN LEISURE.
Objective 3.1: Demonstrate knowledge of personal successes in leisure.
Objective 3.2: Demonstrate knowledge of the importance of personal responsibility for leisure participation.
Objective 3.3: Demonstrate the ability to express preferences.
Objective 3.4: Demonstrate knowledge of assertive behaviors.

Goal and Objectives: Performance Measures

GOAL 3: DEMONSTRATE AN UNDERSTANDING OF SELF-DETERMINATION IN LEISURE

Objective 3.1: Demonstrate knowledge of personal successes in leisure.
Performance Measure: Given a list of 30 recreation activities (e.g., making friends, eating out, dancing, hiking, reading, skiing, playing cards, talking, swimming, writing, canoeing, jogging) with an additional three spaces identified as "other" to allow additions to the list, and pencil, within five minutes and with 100% accuracy on two consecutive occasions:
   (a) identify three recreation activities where some level of success was achieved; and
   (b) specify an instance of success associated with each of the three recreation activities (e.g., making friends: "Last year I met this teacher and we see each other at least once a month and have a great time;" eating out: "Yesterday I ate lunch with a friend at an Italian restaurant and had a great time").

Objective 3.2: Demonstrate knowledge of the importance of personal responsibility for leisure participation.
Performance Measure: Upon request, within five minutes and with 100% accuracy on three consecutive occasions, state four possible reasons why personal responsibility for

leisure participation is important (e.g., to allow change, to encourage learning, to avoid feelings of helplessness, to stimulate growth, to reduce impact of barriers, to gain control, to permit freedom, to facilitate engagement).

Objective 3.3: Demonstrate the ability to express preferences.
Performance Measure: Given four lists of five recreation activities (e.g., going to the movie theater, walking outside, talking to a friend on the phone, listening to music, volunteering to help someone; OR playing video games, chatting over dinner, playing tennis, painting, building models), five minutes to speak and with 100% accuracy on three consecutive occasions:
  (a) identify the most preferred recreation activity associated with each list (totaling four activities); and
  (b) identify one reason why you chose each activity (e.g., going to the movie theater: "I like getting out of the house and seeing what many people are talking about" OR playing tennis: "I like to stay fit and enjoy the out-of-doors") by using a different reason for each activity.

Objective 3.4: Demonstrate knowledge of assertive behaviors.
Performance Measure A: Given five minutes to speak and with 100% accuracy on three consecutive occasions, identify three basic assertive rights (e.g., act to promote dignity and respect without violating others' rights; be treated with respect; say no without guilt; express feelings; change one's mind; ask for preferences; ask for information; make mistakes; feel good about self).
Performance Measure B: Given five minutes to speak and with 100% accuracy on three consecutive occasions, make distinctions among the following modes of interaction by identifying two characteristics of each:
  (a) assertive behavior (e.g., honest, direct, respectful, accurate);
  (b) aggressive behavior (e.g., illogical, hurts others, explosive, offensive); and
  (c) nonassertive behavior (e.g., manipulative, dishonest, ulterior motives, hidden agendas, vague intentions).

Goals and Objectives: Content and Process

GOAL 3: DEMONSTRATE AN UNDERSTANDING OF SELF-DETERMINATION IN LEISURE.

Objective 3.1: Demonstrate knowledge of personal successes in leisure.

1. Orientation Activity

Content: "We are going to do an activity to help us meet each other and to help us think about personal successes in leisure. Please arrange yourselves in a circle. I want you to think about a personal success that was a result of a leisure experience. For example, during a visit to the park, you improved your appreciation for nature. When you have a success in mind, stand up in the circle. We will start with the last person who joined the circle and have this person state his or her name and the leisure success. We will continue clockwise until everyone has taken his or her turn."

Process: Explain activity. Arrange participants in a circle. Encourage each person to participate. If appropriate, ask participants to provide some additional detail related to their reported leisure experience.

2. Introduction

Content: "Our ability to determine what we want to do in leisure happens more easily when we become aware of our personal successes. Leisure provides an excellent opportunity for us to experience success. It is very important for us to realize when we are successful because this information will help us decide what we will do in the future. Our success is often related to how we feel about what we did in a given activity and the accomplishments we experienced. Personal successes are, therefore, defined by the individual and are unique to each individual. It is important to recognize your successes in leisure to increase your ability to determine what you will be in the future and gain control of your life. Leisure is a rewarding, self-fulfilling experience during which you can allow yourself the satisfaction of personal successes."

Process: Introduce topic of personal successes in leisure.

3. Presentation

Content: "Personal successes provide us with feelings of pride, self-worth, and personal satisfaction. Leisure gives us the opportunity to experience these qualities. If we allow ourselves to review our leisure experiences, we will become aware of our successes. The successes we experience in leisure are often internally rewarding. These experiences are not determined by external rewards or reinforcement from other people. The successes we experience are determined by the feelings of pride and satisfaction we derive from our participation. We can measure our leisure experiences by comparing our personal successes to the different values we feel are important. Our values include any personal beliefs we have that are related to our wanting to do something that is in the best interest of all people. Such values might include appreciation of nature, respect for other people, making life fun for yourself and others, equal rights and opportunities for all people. These are just a few examples of values that you can think about when you participate in leisure."

Process: Present information on personal successes.

4. Discussion

Content:
    a.   What are some of the feelings we get from personal successes?
    b.   When can we experience personal successes?
    c.   How are these experiences determined?
    d.   How can we measure these successes?

Process: Conduct discussion using above questions. Encourage participants to contribute to the discussion.

5. Learning Activity

Preparation: Obtain paper, pencils, easel with oversized paper tablet, markers, and masking tape.

Content: "Now we are going to list possible successes in leisure. Each of us has our own ideas of success. Success can be anything that provides us with positive feelings. Some examples of success are making new friends, building a bird house, and finishing a race. Together with three other participants, think of 10 successes that can be achieved in leisure. Record these on the paper you have received. Once each group has identified 10 activities, one person from each group will come to the easel and record one of the items from their list. We will take turns. Please try not to repeat any of the successes that are listed before yours. After we have had one contribution from each group, we will move to round two involving a different person from each group to record one response on the easel. We will continue in this way until everyone has had a chance to add to the list."

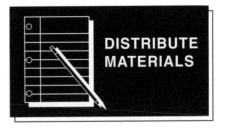

Process: Explain activity. Divide into groups. Provide paper, pencil and markers. Assist participants when necessary. Encourage all individuals to participate and contribute to the list. After the easel paper becomes filled with responses, tear off the page and tape the paper to the wall with masking tape. Have participants continue to write on the next page of the easel tablet. Encourage participants to write large enough for people to see but small enough to get at least a few successes listed on each piece of paper. Draw lines on easel paper to guide participants, if needed.

6. Debriefing

Content:
  a. Was it difficult to think of successes in leisure? If so, why? If not, why not?
  b. Is there a limit to possible successes during leisure? If so, why? If not, why not?
  c. Can one person's idea of success differ from another's idea? Why or why not?
  d. Do differences in ideas mean that one is a success and one is not? Please explain.

Process: Conduct debriefing using above questions. Encourage all participants to answer at least one question. Refer back to the items listed on the easel throughout the debriefing.

7. Learning Activity

Preparation: Obtain art paper, paint, paintbrushes, water for cleaning brushes, and containers for paint.

Content: "We can now look at our own personal successes in leisure. Each of us has our own interests and we each reach different levels of success in these interests. I want you to use the piece of paper you have been given and the paints on the table to paint a picture of what you have achieved in leisure recently. Include paintings of any feelings or improvements you have had that resulted from your leisure participation. You will be able to share the picture with the group."

Process: Explain the activity. Provide paper and paints. Assist participants when necessary. Move about the room to examine the paintings. Provide verbal encouragement and guidance when appropriate. After the paintings are completed, have participants sit in a circle and one at a time stand and describe their painting.

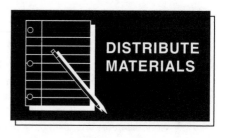

DISTRIBUTE MATERIALS

8. Debriefing

Content:
   a. Was it difficult to paint your successes based on your interests? Why or why not?
   b. Do your personal successes make you feel good about your leisure?
   c. Do these successes make you a better person? If so, how? If not, why?
   d. Can participating in leisure increase chances for you to succeed? Why or why not?

Process: Conduct debriefing using above questions. Prior to the debriefing, tape the pictures on the walls in the room so that they can be viewed by the participants. If needed, pictures can be referred to during the debriefing. Encourage all participants to respond to at least one of the debriefing questions.

9. Learning Activity

Preparation: Obtain pencils and develop handout for rating determination. An example of a possible scale is:

DETERMINATION LEVEL IN LEISURE

HIGH
MEDIUM
LOW

PREPARE FOR SESSION

Content: "Personal successes in leisure contribute to our self-determination. This means that the more we succeed, the more likely we will independently choose what we like to do. If we experience success in leisure, we are more likely to be determined to participate in leisure. With this in mind, we are going to rate our level of determination in leisure based on our successes in leisure. Choose two leisure activities that you frequently participate in. I have a rating form for you to complete. Rate your level of determination on how strongly you wish to engage in leisure to achieve personal successes. Circle the word that best describes your rating."

Process: Explain activity. Provide participants with the scale to rate determination
level from high to low.

**DISTRIBUTE
MATERIALS**

10. Debriefing

Content:
a. Do you feel more determined to
    engage in leisure because of the
    personal successes you achieved during leisure? If so, why? If not, why not?
b. Now that you have experienced some personal successes from leisure, will
    you be more determined for leisure? Why or why not?
c. How does the amount of determination you have in leisure affect your success?

Process: Conduct debriefing using above questions. Encourage all participants to
contribute to the debriefing.

11. Conclusion

Content: "Personal successes are valuable to individual well-being and worth. We can
experience successes during leisure that enhance ourselves and improve our personal
qualities. Leisure provides us with the opportunity for self-accomplishment and
reward."

Process: Make concluding statements. Provide opportunity for questions.

Objective 3.2: Demonstrate knowledge of the importance of personal responsibility
for leisure participation.

1. Orientation Activity

Content: "Let's do an activity to help us meet one another. I will ask each of you a
question, please respond first by giving your name then your answer. The question is:
Who is responsible for your leisure?"

Process: Explain activity. Try to encourage all to respond.

2. Introduction

Content: "It is important for us to take responsibility for our leisure participation. This
means that each one of us is responsible for our own happiness and satisfaction.
Therefore, if we are not enjoying ourselves, we must look closely at what we are doing
and determine ways we can change. This means that we must take credit for our
satisfaction and we must not blame others if we are not satisfied. Personal responsibility
is taking control of a situation. We can control our leisure by learning about our
responsibilities."

Process: Introduce topic of personal responsibility in leisure.

3. Presentation

Content: "To understand our personal responsibility in leisure, we can think about what we must do in a leisure situation. Each of us has responsibilities for leisure. Responsibility involves becoming more aware of what we enjoy and what we can do to help ourselves feel good. Trying to understand our skills and limitations is an example of showing responsibility. When we act in certain ways and accept the consequences of those actions, we are being responsible. Also, we may choose to develop skills and recognize that growth requires effort, time and practice. Responsibility in leisure requires us to know about resources associated with chosen recreation activities. When we take steps to ensure our physical health, we are setting the stage for ourselves to be able to experience leisure more easily and, therefore, we are being responsible for our actions. The following are just a few examples of ways we can be more responsible for our leisure participation.

"If we are to participate in an activity, it is our responsibility to learn the skills necessary for participation. We can develop skills before and during participation, but it is something we must each do. No one can do this for us. People may help and provide guidance, but when all is said and done, we must put forth energy and effort to gain skills. This is what responsibility is all about.

"It is our responsibility to gain knowledge of leisure resources. If we want to be able to participate in leisure, we have to know what is available to us. Not only do we have to know what is available, but we need to learn where the activity is going to take place. Once we determine where it is, we need to consider how to get there next. It is also useful to learn when the desired activity is going to occur. As we consider all of these issues and many other ideas, we are demonstrating responsibility for our leisure participation and, ultimately, our happiness.

"We must maintain our physical health to engage in leisure. Of course, there are some things over which we do not have control. There are, however, many actions we can take that keep us healthy as possible. We can try to get plenty of rest so that we have the energy to do the things that bring joy into our lives. Eating right and ensuring we receive proper nutrition is another action that demonstrates responsibility and can put us in position to experience leisure. Taking any medication we are on at the prescribed times with the recommended dosages is also very important. Staying fit by exercising regularly allows us to have the strength and stamina to do many things that we like. Doing all these things shows that we are acting responsibly and taking control of our lives.

"Each of us is responsible for initiating our own participation. If we have a desire to participate, we have to be the ones to do it. Therefore, we must learn to choose to participate in activities we enjoy without the prodding of other people. To be responsible for our leisure means we must initiate some of our participation. This means it is fine to talk with other people when we are thinking about doing something. We must, however, take responsibility for our choices and contribute to the decision-making process.

"Taking personal responsibility in leisure gives us control over what we do during leisure. Understanding our responsibilities and learning how to meet them makes us more self-determined in leisure."

Process: Present the information described above. Provide as many examples as possible. Expand the list to meet the unique needs of the participants. Present pictures of people demonstrating responsible actions that may lead to enhanced leisure participation. List key words on a chalkboard and write any additional phrases that may help participants retain information.

> **LEARN LEISURE SKILLS**
> **GAIN KNOWLEDGE OF LEISURE RESOURCES**
> **MAINTAIN PHYSICAL HEALTH**
> **INITIATE PARTICIPATION**

4. Debriefing

Content:
    a. How do we have personal responsibility in leisure?
    b. What are some of our responsibilities in leisure?
    c. Who is responsible for developing our skills for participation? Why?
    d. What is the benefit of having knowledge about leisure resources?
    e. How can we become responsible for our physical health?
    f. Do you control your participation in leisure? If so, how? If not, why?

Process: Conduct debriefing using above questions. Encourage all participants to respond to at least one of the questions. Refer to the key words listed on the chalkboard when discussing the concepts.

5. Learning Activity

Content: "We are going to do an activity to learn more about our responsibility in leisure. I want you to find two other people to work with during this activity. The three of you must choose what you all will do together this evening during your free time. You must come up with an activity that you all enjoy and includes one of the following: (a) it allows you to learn leisure skills; (b) it provides you with an opportunity to gain knowledge of leisure resources; or (c) it increases your ability to maintain your physical health. After you choose the activity, devise a plan to make it possible for the three of you to participate in this recreation activity together. When the plan is completed, discuss why it is important to take personal responsibility for your leisure participation. Write your ideas on the paper you have been given. Each group will report to the entire group. One member of the group will describe the recreation activity the group chose. Another member of the group will describe the plan devised to allow them to partici-pate. The final member of the group will state why it is important to take responsibility for leisure participation."

Process: Explain activity. Help participants get into groups of three. Provide paper and pencils to each group. Offer assistance as needed. Write group ideas on the board. List the criteria for the recreation activity on the easel or chalkboard:

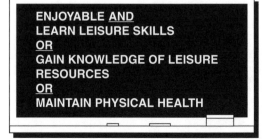

> **ENJOYABLE <u>AND</u>**
> **LEARN LEISURE SKILLS**
> **OR**
> **GAIN KNOWLEDGE OF LEISURE RESOURCES**
> **OR**
> **MAINTAIN PHYSICAL HEALTH**

- enjoyable AND
- learn leisure skills, OR

- gain knowledge of leisure resources, OR
- maintain physical health.

6. Debriefing

Content:
  a. Did you feel like it was your responsibility to help choose a recreation activity all of you liked?
  b. By choosing the activity, how did you demonstrate responsibility?
  c. Did you have control over the situation when working with the other people? If so, how? If not, why?
  d. Will you be more likely to engage in leisure when you are responsible? If so, how? If not, why?

Process: Conduct debriefing using above questions. Encourage each person to respond. Refer to the criteria followed to choose the activity.

7. Learning Activity

Content: "We must take personal responsibility to learn the skills that are required for leisure participation. On the board, I have listed 10 different activities. We are going to list the skills that we would need to learn for each one. Then, we will discuss why it is our responsibility to develop these skills if we want to participate in these activities."

Process: Explain activity. Write the activities on the board and leave space for skills to be recorded under each activity. List activities appropriate for the participants. Refer to the book *Leisure Education: Specific Programs* (Dattilo, 1999), that contains complete leisure education programs for:

- bowling
- camping
- canoeing
- cooking
- gardening
- painting
- playing softball
- playing volleyball
- swimming
- walking

BOWLING	PAINTING
CAMPING	PLAYING SOFTBALL
CANOEING	PLAYING VOLLEYBALL
COOKING	SWIMMING
GARDENING	WALKING

8. Debriefing

Content:
  a. How can a lack of skills prevent us from participating in recreation activities?
  b. How can we take responsibility and learn skills needed to experience leisure?
  c. If we learn the skills needed to participate in a desired recreation activity, are we more determined to participate in an activity? If so, how? If not, why?
  d. What could happen if we do not take responsibility to learn leisure skills?

Process: Conduct debriefing using above questions. Encourage all participants to respond to at least one of the questions.

9. Learning Activity

Content: "It is our responsibility to learn about leisure resources that are available to us. Pair up with one other person. Together, make a list of all the leisure resources you can think of that are available to you related to swimming, bowling, gardening, softball, walking, and volleyball. For example, if you would like to go swimming, there may be a pool in your neighborhood. After each group is finished, we will have each person read a resource from the list to the entire group."

Process: Explain activity. Help participants find a partner. If there is an odd number of people, participate in the activity yourself. Provide paper and pencils. Offer assistance when necessary. Ask each pair to share its list with the other participants.

10. Debriefing

Content:
  a. What are some leisure resources that are available?
  b. Why is it important to know about leisure resources?
  c. Who is responsible for knowing what is available?
  d. How can knowledge of leisure resources improve your self-determination?

Process: Conduct debriefing using above questions. Encourage all participants to respond to at least one of the questions.

11. Learning Activity

Content: "It is our personal responsibility to participate in leisure. Everyone sit down in a circle. I want each person to think of one reason why he or she should be responsible for his or her leisure participation. For example, I think that I should be responsible because sometimes I may be by myself and I will be the only person I can depend on. After you have thought of a reason why it is important to be responsible, raise your hand. When everyone has his or her hand raised, we will have one person at a time tell the group what he or she thought of. There are no wrong or right answers, we are just interested in what you are thinking."

Process: Explain the activity. Help the participants form a circle. Encourage participation. Assist participants in expressing their ideas if they encounter difficulty.

12. Debriefing

Content:
  a. Is it our personal responsibility to participate in leisure?
  b. Will you be more likely to engage in leisure if you know it is your responsibility? If yes, why? If not, why not?
  c. How can you take control of your participation?

Process: Conduct debriefing using above questions. Encourage all participants to respond to at least one of the questions.

13. Conclusion

Content: "We have personal responsibilities in leisure. These responsibilities include, but are not limited to, the decisions we make, the skills we develop, the knowledge we gain about resources, the way we care for our physical health, and the amount of participation we have. It is important for us to take control of our lives in order to experience leisure throughout our lives."

Process: Make concluding statements. Provide sufficient opportunity for participants to ask questions and voice any of their concerns.

Objective 3.3: Demonstrate the ability to express preferences.

1. Orientation Activity

Preparation: Obtain red and blue chips (poker chips), and a small paper bag.

Content: "You have each been given a set of red chips, a set of blue chips, and a small paper bag. We are going to do an activity to help us meet each other and to start thinking about our preferences for leisure. Let's start by everyone finding a partner. Introduce yourself to this person and find out his or her name. Ask the person to tell you one thing he or she likes to do for leisure. If the activity or experience your partner describes is also one that you prefer, place a blue chip into your bag. If the activity or experience is not one that you prefer, place a red chip in your bag. Now it is your turn to state a preferred activity or experience and your partner will place the appropriate colored chip into his or her bag. Once you have both stated a preference, move to other people in the room and repeat the process. If you like, you may change the activity or experience for each person. When I give the signal, stop, sit down and count how many blue and red chips you placed in your bag."

Process: Distribute a set of red chips, a set of blue chips, and a small paper bag to each person. Make sure you distribute enough chips to account for meeting each person in the room. Explain the activity to the partici-pants. Encourage their active participation. In advance determine a signal to stop the activity. When the activity is completed, move quickly to the debriefing.

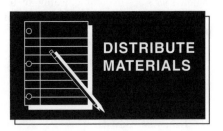

2. Introduction

Content: "Our ability to express preferences often determines what we do. Preferences are what we want to do the most, what we like to do, or what we enjoy doing. Learning to tell others what we prefer will help us do what we want."

Process: Introduce topic of expressing preferences.

3. Presentation

Content: "We can express preferences in a number of ways. To be most effective, we need to learn how to express ourselves to get the best results. Expressing preferences for leisure can be looked at in a number of ways.

"At one time or another you may be given a list of activities to choose from and you need to decide which one you want to do the most. The choices may come in the form of a list of movies in the newspaper, a list of classes or workshops you may enroll in, or a list of recreation activities at a recreation center. Even if you have a preference, you may not know how to tell someone what it is or why it is. First, you must attempt to communicate these preferences to people in positions to respond to your preferences.

"You may want to do an activity that is not readily available to you. The activity may not be considered by others as an option for you, but you prefer to participate in this activity over many other activities. After you communicate your preferences, you can support your preferences by providing reasons for wanting to participate. Although it should not be necessary, many people may be more cooperative if they become aware of the reasons you want to participate.

"You can choose the activity you wish to participate in. Regardless of others' opinions or criticisms, if you have the necessary skills and knowledge to participate safely, you should be permitted to do so. Responsible recreation participation requires that your actions not bring physical or mental harm to others or yourself. We need to express our choices and our desires to be most effective. We should clearly communicate our leisure preferences to people in positions to respond to our requests.

"When we learn how to express preferences to others, we will be on our way to doing what we most want to do. We will also be more in control of our leisure when we do what we prefer. That is to say, we will enhance our ability to determine our leisure lifestyle. Therefore, another step in expressing our preferences is acting on the opportunities that are available to us to participate in our chosen leisure experiences."

Process: Present information on expressing preferences. Provide examples as needed. Present picture or slide of people demonstrating the four steps in communicating their preferences. Write the following key words on the board:

- communicate preferences
- provide reasons
- act on opportunities

4. Learning Activity

Preparation: Develop a list of 10 activities that could include swimming, gardening, volleyball, cooking, canoeing, camping, walking, bowling, softball, and painting.

Content: "Effective communication is necessary to express our preferences. Let's do an activity to improve our communication skills. Each of you will be given a list of 10 activities. Look at the list and choose one or two things that you would prefer to do. If you do not like any of them, pick something else you would like to do. We will go around the room and each person will have a chance to express his or her preference. Tell us exactly what you want to do."

Process: Explain the activity. Provide list to participants. Provide assistance and examples when necessary. Encourage all individuals to participate.

5. Debriefing

Content:

   a. Did you like choosing your favorite activity and giving a preference? If yes, why? If not, why not?

   b. If a preference of yours was not on the list, did you choose a different activity? Why or why not?

   c. Why is it important to communicate our preferences to others about what we want to do?

Process: Conduct debriefing using above questions. Encourage all participants to answer at least one of the questions.

6. Learning Activity

Preparation: Obtain paper and pencils.

Content: "We can support our preferences by giving reasons for them. For example, you may want to go on a walk because it makes you feel relaxed and allows you to enjoy the outdoors. You have a specific reason for wanting to take a walk and you can support it by stating the reason. In this activity, we are going to look at our preferences in leisure and give reasons for them. On a piece of paper, list five leisure preferences. Next to each one, write down at least one reason why you want to do that activity. You may have only one reason, or you may have several reasons. Write them on the piece of paper. After everyone is finished, I will ask each person to tell me one of his or her reasons and I will write them on the chalkboard."

Process: Explain the activity described above. Distribute paper and pencils to participants. Provide assistance when necessary. Write one reason from each individual on the board.

7. Debriefing

Content:
    a.   Was it easy or hard to think of the reasons why you prefer certain activities? Why do you think it was this way?
    b.   Do you feel your reasons support your preferences?
    c.   Did you see similarities between your reasons and reasons why other people participate? If so, what are they? If not, why do you think this is the case?
    d.   What reasons do you think are acceptable for participating in a recreation activity?

Process: Conduct debriefing using above questions. Encourage each person to answer a question. Refer to the reasons listed on the chalkboard.

8. Learning Activity

Preparation: Obtain pencils and develop an activity list for each pair of participants. Some examples of leisurely pairs are:

• talking on the telephone	• play a table game
• watch television	• do some art work
• go for a walk	• use a computer
• go camping	• go shopping
• swim	• read
• play volleyball	• play softball
• garden	• listen to music
• go bowling	• go to the movies

Content: "Our self-determination in leisure is shown by our ability to express preferences. We can measure our self-determination by looking at the process of expressing preferences. If we know what we want to do, we can tell others.

    "To find out how determined we are in leisure, let's look at our ability to express preferences. Find a partner. On the piece of paper I am handing out, your partner will read two leisure choices and you tell your partner your preferred activity and why it is your preference. Continue through the list, then switch with your partner and ask about his or her preferences and reasons."

Process: Explain the activity. Have participants choose partners. Distribute paper with leisure activity pairs and pencils.

9. Debriefing

Content:
    a.   If you have a preference, are you determined to engage in it? If yes, how do you communicate this preference? If no, why not?
    b.   How can you show someone that you are determined to do what you prefer?

   c.   How can your ability to express leisure preferences show your self-determination?

Process: Conduct debriefing using above questions. Encourage all participants to contribute to the debriefing.

10. Conclusion

Content: "Our ability to express preferences often determines what we will do during leisure. To be most effective, communicate your preferences and provide reasons to support them. The more determined you are to participate in an area of interest to you, the more likely you will participate."

Process: Make concluding statements. Provide sufficient opportunities for participants to ask questions and voice concerns.

Objective 3.4:   Demonstrate knowledge of assertive behaviors.

1. Orientation Activity

Preparation: Develop scenario cards. A sample situation may be:

You are waiting in line at the movies and someone breaks in line. Of the following, which response is the closest to the one you would make:
1.   "Hey jerk, no cutting in line."
2.   "Excuse me but you need to go to the end of the line, we have been waiting here a while."
3.   You are mad but you make no verbal response.

Content: "To increase your knowledge about assertive behaviors, I am going to give you a chance to act out your responses to different daily situations. Each of you has been given a colored card with a situation written on it and a list of possible reactions. Please find the other three people that have the same color card as you. Sit in a group with the three other participants. Introduce yourselves to one another. One person will read the situation and possible reactions. Next, each person in the group will respond as if he or she were in that situation. Take turns reading the situation and responding to it."

Process: Explain the activity. Give a set of situations to each group. Move to debriefing when finished. Situations need to include possible reactions that represent aggressive, assertive, and nonassertive reactions to daily situations.

2. Introduction

Content: "Assertive behavior is an important component of self-determination in life and especially in leisure. Indeed, it is as appropriate in a leisure context as it is in any other aspect of living. But before one can behave in an assertive manner, it is necessary to develop an understanding of assertiveness. This requires a knowledge of what is involved in assertiveness and, of equal importance, what distinguishes assertiveness from other types of behavior."

Process: Introduce topic of gaining knowledge about assertive behaviors.

3. Presentation

Content: "Being assertive is based on the assumption that every human being has certain fundamental rights. The manner in which individuals behave in relation to these rights can be placed in one of three categories: nonassertive, assertive, or aggressive. Being able to distinguish among these three types of behavior is essential. Behaving assertively is equally essential. People who learn how to respond in an assertive manner to various situations are accepting responsibility and taking control of their lives.

"Assertive behavior is behavior that helps you to act in your own best interests, to stand up for yourself without fear, to express honest feelings comfortably, and to exercise personal rights without denying the rights of others. It is a style of behavior that recognizes the extent of one's rights, the extent of the rights of others, and works to maintain a balance between the two. For example, you may have just purchased a new softball glove. A friend may ask to borrow it for a week to use in an out-of-town tournament. You could respond assertively by saying, 'I understand your desire to use a new glove, but I just bought this and want to break it in myself.' You would be recognizing both the right of your friend to ask to borrow your glove and your own right to refuse it.

"Nonassertive behavior occurs when individuals are unable to maintain a balance between their rights and the rights of others. Referring to the previous example of the softball glove, you could respond to the request in a nonassertive manner by loaning the glove because you were afraid if you refused, your friend would think you were being selfish and petty. You could then spend the next week worrying that your friend would damage your glove and it would not fit you properly. Nonassertive behavior occurs when an individual allows others to extend their rights by restricting his or her own.

"Aggressive behavior is the third style of responding or reacting to the fundamental rights that all humans possess. It occurs when an person invades the rights of others. In the matter of the softball glove, you could respond to your friend's request to borrow it by saying, 'You can't be serious!' or 'Absolutely not!' You would be acting aggressively because you would be ignoring your friend's right to be treated with respect and courtesy."

Process: Present information on assertive behavior. Use the chalkboard to list major points:

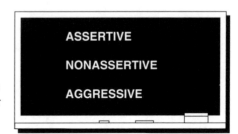

ASSERTIVE

NONASSERTIVE

AGGRESSIVE

- assertive
- nonassertive
- aggressive

4. Discussion

Content:
   a. What are the differences among nonassertive, assertive, and aggressive behaviors?
   b. What are some situations where you have observed others acting in a nonassertive manner? Assertive manner? Aggressive manner?
   c. What are some instances where you have behaved in a nonassertive manner? Assertive manner? Aggressive manner?
   d. How did you feel when you behaved nonassertively?
   e. How did you feel when you behaved aggressively?
   f. Why is it important to learn how to engage in assertive behavior?

Process: Conduct discussion by using above questions. Encourage participation by everyone by having each participant respond to at least one of the questions.

5. Conclusion

Content: "Learning to be assertive is similar to learning anything else. It requires commitment and a willingness to practice, even when it feels uncomfortable. But persistence pays off. Acting in an assertive way allows you to be in control of your life and to assume responsibility in your leisure."

Process: Make concluding statements. Provide opportunity for questions. Allow participants to share any concerns or reservations related to acting assertively.

Appendix D
Leisure Education
Specific Program #4

INTERACT SOCIALLY
DURING LEISURE PARTICIPATION

Purpose, Goal, and Objectives

Purpose: Provide opportunities for participants to learn the dynamics of social interaction, gain knowledge about the appropriateness of social interaction behaviors, demonstrate verbal and nonverbal behaviors encouraging attention to speakers and exhibit verbal behaviors required of an effective speaker.

GOAL 4: DEMONSTRATE KNOWLEDGE OF EFFECTIVE SOCIAL INTERACTION SKILLS.
Objective 4.1: Demonstrate knowledge of the dynamics of social interaction.
Objective 4.2: Demonstrate knowledge of considerations for appropriateness of behaviors during social interaction.
Objective 4.3: Demonstrate verbal behaviors encouraging attention to speaker.
Objective 4.4: Demonstrate nonverbal behaviors encouraging attention to a speaker.
Objective 4.5: Demonstrate verbal behaviors required of an effective speaker.

Goal and Objectives: Performance Measures

GOAL 4: DEMONSTRATE KNOWLEDGE OF EFFECTIVE SOCIAL INTERACTION SKILLS.

Objective 4.1: Demonstrate knowledge of the dynamics of social interaction.
Performance Measure A: Upon request, within two minutes and with 100% accuracy on three consecutive occasions, identify two modes of social interaction (e.g., verbal and nonverbal interaction skills).
Performance Measure B: Upon request, within two minutes and with 100% accuracy on three consecutive occasions, identify two roles associated with social interaction [e.g., speaking (sender) and listening (receiver)].
Performance Measure C: Upon request, within two minutes and with 100% accuracy on three consecutive occasions, specify basic considerations related to behavior when engaging in social interaction.

Objective 4.2: Demonstrate knowledge of considerations for appropriateness of behaviors during social interaction.

Performance Measure A: Given a paper and pencil, within five minutes on two consecutive occasions, write the definitions of the following:
- (a) paying attention (e.g., staying focused on the individuals with whom one is interacting); and
- (b) empathy (e.g., act of projecting one's own consciousness into the situation of another person; act of putting oneself into the position of another in an attempt to understand that person's feelings).

Performance Measure B: Upon request, within five minutes and identifying at least three of the four steps per behavior on two consecutive occasions, describe the steps involved in the following:
- (a) initiating an interaction by exhibiting the following behaviors: (1) approach person; (2) get other person's attention; (3) make an opening statement; and (4) engage in a conversation; and
- (b) interrupting properly by exhibiting the following behaviors: (1) raise index finger or motion with the entire hand; (2) wait until acknowledged; (3) speak; and (4) if speaker does not acknowledge, say "Excuse me . . .".

Objective 4.3: Demonstrate verbal behaviors encouraging attention to speaker.
Performance Measure: Given a paper describing a situation (e.g., Person A is having difficulty learning a recreation activity skill and is telling Person B about the situation), with 100% accuracy on three consecutive occasions, and with 15 minutes to engage in interchange:
- (a) assume the role of Person B; and
- (b) demonstrate attentiveness to person by eliciting each of the following verbal behaviors at least once: (1) agree (e.g., uh-huh, yes) or disagree (e.g., no); (2) paraphrase ("You said that you are having difficulty kicking the soccer ball into the net"); (3) clarify ("I am confused as to how this relates to your brother. Could you help me understand?"); and (4) perception checking ("You appear frustrated. Am I correct?").

Objective 4.4: Demonstrate nonverbal behaviors encouraging attention to a speaker.
Performance Measure A: Given a paper describing a situation (e.g., Person A is having difficulty learning a recreation activity skill and is telling Person B about the situation), 80% of the time on two consecutive occasions, and with 10 minutes to engage in interchange:
- (a) assume the role of Person B; and
- (b) demonstrate attentiveness to person by exhibiting each of the following nonverbal behaviors: (1) looking directly at speaker; (2) sitting or standing upright; (3) gesturing comprehension (e.g., head nods, head shakes); (4) making supportive facial expressions (e.g., smile or frown as appropriate for discussion); (5) maintaining proximity (staying within three yards of speaker), and (6) using voice effectively (volume, tone).

Performance Measure B: Given a paper describing a situation (e.g., Person A is having difficulty learning a recreation activity skill and is telling Person B about the situation), 80% of the time on two consecutive occasions, and with 10 minutes to engage in interchange:

(a) assume the role of Person A; and

(b) demonstrate being an effective speaker by exhibiting each of the following nonverbal behaviors: (1) looking in direction of audience; (2) sitting or standing upright; (3) using gestures (e.g., supportive hand movements); (4) making supportive facial expressions (e.g., smile or frown as appropriate for discussion); (5) maintaining proximity (staying within three yards of audience); and (6) using voice effectively (volume, tone).

Objective 4.5: Demonstrate verbal behaviors required of an effective speaker.
Performance Measure: Given a paper describing a situation (e.g., Person A is having difficulty learning a recreation activity skill and is telling Person B about the situation), 90% of the time on two separate occasions, and with 15 minutes to engage in interchange:

(a) assume the role of Person A; and

(b) demonstrate effective speaking skills by exhibiting the following verbal behaviors: (1) use appropriate vocabulary (avoid slang and offensive terminology); (2) enunciate clearly (pronounce words properly); (3) avoid distracting fillers (e.g., "ummm," "like ya know," "ahh"); (4) present information in a logical sequence; and (5) present relevant content.

Goal and Objectives: Content and Process

GOAL 4: DEMONSTRATE KNOWLEDGE OF EFFECTIVE SOCIAL INTERACTION SKILLS.

Objective 4.1: Demonstrate knowledge of the dynamics of social interaction.

1. Orientation Activity

Content: "Form a circle by linking your arms with each other. Introduce yourself to the person on your right and left. After the circle is formed, drop your arms. Extend your right arms into the circle and join hands with someone across the circle from you. Without releasing your right hand, extend your left arm into the circle and grasp the left hand of someone other than the person whose right hand you are holding. The result of these actions should be a giant human knot. Now, it is your task to untie the knot by directing one person at a time to unwind the knot."

Process: Explain activity. Help form circle. Monitor joining of hands to ensure that no person is joined with only one other person. Emphasize untying of knot by one person at a time. Refrain from giving directions to specific individuals to release hands.

2. Debriefing

Content:
    a. How did communication help untie the knot?
    b. Was the communication that occurred easy to understand or was there some confusion on the part of the speakers, listeners, or both? How so?
    c. Were you a speaker, a listener, or both? Give examples.

Process: Conduct debriefing by using above questions. Encourage all participants to contribute to the debriefing by responding to at least one of the questions.

3. Introduction

Content: "An important aspect of participating in leisure activities is having the skills necessary to interact with other people. It is essential that one be able to establish and maintain friendships, socialize with others, and feel competent to cope with different types of social situations. Having good communication skills is an integral part of the dynamics of social interaction."

Process: Introduce topic on the dynamics of social interaction.

4. Presentation

Content: "Most of us have already acquired some interpersonal skills, simply by the process of having lived among and interacted with other people. But most of us could also improve our interpersonal skills and become more open, more understanding, more caring, and more genuine in our relationships with each other. Communication is the foundation upon which interpersonal skills are based. It is the essential ingredient in all relationships. When clear, caring communication occurs, relationships grow; when communication is incomplete, hostile or ineffective, relationships deteriorate. Few things are more important in social interaction than good communication.

"Communication is the process of *sending* and *receiving* messages. At a personal level, communication may be *verbal* or *nonverbal*. It is important to understand that words are not always needed to send messages. Clear messages are often conveyed by body position (stance) and facial expression. Examples of sending messages without using words include the following: (1) an individual standing with hands on the hips and a frown on the face can clearly send a message of anger or disapproval; (2) an individual can smile broadly to communicate approval or happiness; or (3) a person can wink and use a hand to cover the mouth to communicate the idea of a secret or a shared feeling. There are many other forms of nonverbal communication.

"Sometimes, individuals send unclear messages because their body postures and facial expressions do not fit the words they are using. For example, an individual could emphatically pound a table and frown while saying, 'I am not angry.' Or an individual could have a pinched facial expression and state, 'I am really quite happy about this.' These individuals would be sending mixed signals to their listeners. The likelihood is that clear communication is not present.

"In addition to speakers (senders) sometimes failing to transmit clear messages, listeners (receivers) sometimes fail in hearing and interpreting messages. Misunderstandings can happen when individuals think they have received a clear message but they have not been careful in listening to the message or they have misinterpreted nonverbal clues coming from the speaker. Failure to listen with understanding can result in some serious communication problems. For example, if a listener is preoccupied with something else, it may appear that total attention is being given to the speaker, but in reality, little is being heard. The message did not get through to the receiver. Sometimes, listeners can assume they know what speakers are trying to tell them and they do not bother to listen carefully or check to see if their assumptions are correct. If their assumptions are wrong, there is miscommunication. Sometimes senders and receivers interpret common words or sayings differently. For example, a speaker might say, 'I will be back in a few minutes.' A listener might interpret the phrase 'a few minutes' to mean less than 10 minutes. The speaker might mean anything up to 30 minutes. In this situation, the potential for miscommunication is very high."

Process: Present information on communication. Demonstrate nonverbal messages. Use board to illustrate major points.

COMMUNICATION PROCESS	TYPES OF COMMUNICATION
• sending messages	• verbal
• receiving messages	• nonverbal

5. Discussion

Content:

    a. What are some examples of how you use communication in your everyday routine?

    b. Have you been in situations that were unexpected because of miscommunication with someone? What were the circumstances?

    c. Have you sent nonverbal messages to someone? Please demonstrate.

    d. Have you received nonverbal messages from someone? How were you able to tell if you interpreted them correctly?

    e. What are examples of words or phrases that people might interpret differently?

Process: Conduct debriefing using above questions. Provide opportunity for each person to respond to at least one of the questions.

6. Learning Activity

Content: "We are going to do an activity using verbal and nonverbal communication. Stand, link arms, and form a circle. After the circle is formed, drop your arms. We will go around the circle clockwise. The first player will state his or her name, identify a favorite recreation activity, and briefly act out the activity. The next player will say his or her name, act out the activity, and repeat the previous person's name and activity. Play will proceed until everyone in the circle has had a turn."

Process: Explain activity. Help form circle. Make sure each player has a turn. Move to debriefing when activity is completed.

7. Debriefing

Content:

    a. Was the verbal communication clear? Did you clearly understand what the activities were before they were acted out?

b. Were the nonverbal actions used to illustrate the activities appropriate? Would you have been able to identify the activities if you did not already know what they were?
c. Why do you think we did this activity?

Process: Conduct debriefing using above questions. Provide opportunity for each person to respond to at least one of the questions.

8. Learning Activity

Content: "We are going to do an activity that will focus on the use of nonverbal communication. Now, without speaking or writing, arrange yourselves in a straight line by order of month of birth. Figure out some way to have those people whose birthdays are in January to be in the first part of the line, those with birthdays in February to be in the second part of the line, and continue through December. Remember, do this without speaking or writing a single word."

Process: Explain activity. Monitor to ensure no speaking. When line is formed, check to see if order is correct. Move to debriefing.

9. Debriefing

Content:
a. Was the line in the right order? If not, how far off was it?
b. How many strategies did you use to form the line?
c. Which strategies were the most successful?
d. How can nonverbal communication be used in leisure participation?

Process: Conduct debriefing using above questions. Provide opportunity for each person to respond to at least one of the questions.

10. Learning Activity

Preparation: Obtain paper and pencils. Prepare arrangement of squares ahead of session. If desired, prepare several different arrangements of squares and provide each participant with opportunity to be the speaker. An example of an arrangement of the squares could involve three squares in a diagonal with the top square's bottom left corner touching the middle square's upper right corner and the middle square's lower left corner touching the bottom square's upper right corner.

Content: "We are going to do an activity that will require careful speaking and listening skills. Each of you has paper and pencil. One of you will be selected to study the arrangement of a set of squares and verbally direct the others to duplicate (by drawing) the same arrangement of squares. The person giving the directions will be the only person allowed to see the arrangement of squares and will also be the only person to speak. The person giving the directions should stand with his or her back to the group. The listeners, who will try to duplicate the arrangement as directed, will not be allowed to ask questions about the directions. This activity requires the speaker to be careful and precise in describing the squares and it requires the listeners to be very attentive to the speaker."

Process: Explain activity. Provide paper and pencils. Monitor activity to ensure that listeners do not ask questions or seek clarification of directions.

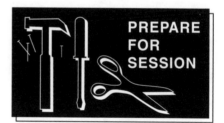

11. Debriefing

Content:
    a.   How close was your drawing to the original set of squares?
    b.   What was the most difficult part of doing this activity?
    c.   Was it easier to give directions or to listen to them? Why?
    d.   What conclusions can you draw from this regarding communication?

Process: Conduct debriefing using above questions. Provide opportunity for each person to respond to at least one of the questions.

12. Learning Activity

Preparation: Obtain paper and pencils. Prepare squares ahead of session. Prepare sufficient number of different arrangements to provide each person the opportunity to be the speaker.

Content: "We are going to repeat the previous activity, but with two important differences. The squares will be in different arrangements and the listeners may ask questions of and seek clarification from the speaker. The speaker may face the listeners, repeat directions, and answer questions. The speaker will still be the only person who can see the arrangement of squares that is being described."

Process: Explain activity. Provide paper and pencils. Try to allow sufficient time for each person to be the speaker. Provide verbal support for their efforts.

13. Debriefing

Content:
    a.   How close were your drawings to the squares that were being described?
    b.   Were the directions easier to follow this time? If so, why?
    c.   What conclusions relative to communication can you draw from this activity?

Process: Conduct debriefing using above questions. Provide opportunity for each person to respond to at least one of the questions.

14. Conclusion

Content: "Communication is a process that requires careful attention from both senders and receivers. If careful attention is given, there is a great likelihood that the communication will be accurate and easily understood. Communication can be verbal, nonverbal, or a combination of both. Being adept in communication is usually a prerequisite for establishing comfortable relationships with others. Communication improves social interaction."

Process: Make concluding statements. Provide opportunities for participants to ask questions and raise concerns.

Objective 4.2: Demonstrate knowledge of considerations for appropriateness of behaviors during social interaction.

1.   Orientation Activity

Preparation: Prepare cards in advance containing the following statements (one per card):

PREPARE
FOR
SESSION

- Pay attention to the person.
- Be empathetic to the person.
- Initiate interaction with the person.
- If necessary, interrupt the person properly.

Select and rehearse with two participants ahead of session. Prepare script to show interaction. Script could be as follows:

Speaker 1: Let me tell you about my weekend. It was so wonderful.

Speaker 2: Oh, I had a good time on the weekend too.

Speaker 1: Yes, well, I've been waiting a long time for this, but I finally got to go to San Francisco. The weather was just beautiful . . . .

Speaker 2: I really like good weather. I can play tennis in good weather.

Speaker 1: Good. Oh, I want to tell you about the Golden Gate Bridge. It was my first experience on a suspension bridge and . . . .

Speaker 2: I haven't had much experience with tennis, but I'm getting better, especially with my backhand.

Speaker 1: That's nice. Anyway, in San Francisco we drove to the top of Nob Hill and we could see the boats in the bay and . . . .

Speaker 2: I like boating too, but tennis is even more exciting.

Speaker 1: Yes. Well, I hope you get to play soon. So long.

Instruct Speaker 2 to abruptly interrupt Speaker 1 at indicated times. Move to debriefing at conclusion of skit.

Content: "Everyone please sit in a circle. I have given each of you a description of something that you could do that would be appropriate and would communicate that you care about the person. If your card is green, turn to the person on your left; if your card is purple, turn to the person on your right.

"Introduce yourself and find out the person's name. Then read the statement to the person and allow him or her to read the statement to you. Once you have completed this, turn to your other side and wait for that person to finish talking and then repeat the process. After you have introduced yourselves to the people on both sides of you, we are going to watch a skit that presents a brief interaction between two people. Observe closely and be prepared to share your observations at the end of the skit."

Process: Explain activity. Encourage everyone to listen carefully to the skit because the group will discuss the skit as soon as it is completed.

2. Debriefing

Content:
    a.   How would you characterize Speaker 2's behavior? Why?
    b.   If you believe Speaker 2's behavior was inappropriate, in what ways was it inappropriate?
    c.   How would you have felt if you were Speaker 1? Why?
    d.   What was the quality of the interaction between the two speakers? Why?
    e.   Based on this observation only, what do you think the quality will be of any future interactions between these two people?

Process: Conduct debriefing using above questions. Emphasize Speaker 2's interruptions and inability to pay attention to Speaker 1. Encourage all participants to contribute to the debriefing.

3. Introduction

Content: "Behaving appropriately is an important part of social interaction. When an individual behaves inappropriately, a negative influence is introduced into the environment in which the interaction is taking place. If the behavior is mildly inappropriate, the interaction may be disturbed but it may also continue. If it is markedly inappropriate, the interaction may simply cease. Making decisions about behavior requires intelligent judgments because what may be inappropriate for one situation may be acceptable in a different situation. The best rule of thumb to follow is to always be conservative in behavior until one learns more about the situation."

Process: Introduce topic on gaining knowledge of considerations for appropriateness of behaviors during social interaction.

4. Presentation

Content: "Although there may be some uncertainty regarding the appropriateness of behavior in certain situations, there are some basic considerations that relate to behavior. Although these considerations are not all-inclusive, they are paying attention (staying focused), being empathetic, initiating interaction, and interrupting properly.

"*Paying attention,* or staying focused, on the individuals with whom one is interacting is fundamental to the establishment and maintenance of good relationships. If one is self-absorbed, unfocused, or inattentive in other ways, one is sending a clear message to the other individuals present that what they are saying is not worth the effort it takes to listen to them. Such behavior is inappropriate and makes it difficult, if not impossible, to engage in meaningful social interaction with others."

Process: Present information on paying attention. List key points on an easel or chalkboard.

- paying attention
- being empathetic
- initiating interaction
- interrupting properly

5. Discussion

Content:
   a. Have you attempted to interact with others who would not pay attention to you?
   b. How did you feel when this happened?
   c. After this happened, did you make other attempts at interaction with them? Why?
   d. Have you been in situations where you ignored others who were trying to interact with you? If so, why?

Process: Conduct discussion using above questions. Provide opportunity for each person to contribute to the discussion by responding to at least one of the questions.

6. Presentation

Content: "*Empathy* is the act of projecting one's own consciousness into the situation of another person. It is an act of putting oneself into the position of another in an attempt to understand that person's feelings. It does not mean that one has to have the same intensity of feeling or emotion that another person is experiencing, but it does mean that one cares enough to listen to the concerns of the other. Empathy is associated with the saying 'Walk a mile in my shoes.' Being empathetic can be an important form of interaction."

Process: Present information on empathy. Use examples as needed.

7. Discussion

Content:
   a. What is empathy?
   b. Why is it important?
   c. Are there empathetic persons among your friends?
   d. Are you an empathetic person? If so, can you provide an example of when you were empathetic?

Process: Conduct discussion using above questions. Provide opportunity for each person to contribute to the discussion by responding to at least one of the questions.

8. Presentation

Content: "*Initiating interaction* is usually an easier thing to do with friends than it is with strangers or people you have just met. Yet, someone must take the first step if interaction is to take place. If you are faced with the prospect of initiating interaction with a stranger, following some simple guidelines will be a great help. These guidelines include:

    a.   Approach the other person.
    b.   Get the other person's attention. Do this by saying 'Excuse me,' gently tapping on his or her shoulder, etc.
    c.   Have an opening statement. A question such as 'How are you today?' a statement such as 'My name is Margaret,' or a request such as 'Can you please tell me the time?' would be appropriate.
    d.   Engage in conversation.

"Making the initial effort to start some interaction will be easier if these simple guidelines are followed."

Process: Present information on initiating interaction. List guidelines on chalkboard.

- approach person
- get other person's attention
- have an opening statement
- engage in conversation

APPROACH PERSON
GET OTHER PERSON'S ATTENTION
HAVE AN OPENING STATEMENT
ENGAGE IN CONVERSATION

9. Discussion

Content:
    a.   When you meet someone for the first time, do you wait for him or her to start a conversation? Why?
    b.   What is an example of when you took the first steps to start an interaction?
    c.   What can you do to improve your ability to initiate interaction?

Process: Conduct discussion using above questions. Provide opportunity for each person to contribute to the discussion by responding to at least one of the questions.

10. Presentation

Content: "As a general rule, it is inappropriate to interrupt others when they are speaking. But there are times when it may be necessary. In those situations, there is a procedure to follow that is appropriate. The procedure for *interrupting properly* in any nonemergency situation is as follows: (a) the listener may raise an index finger or motion with the entire hand to let the speaker know he or she has something to say; (b) the listener waits until he or she is acknowledged and then speaks; (c) if the speaker does not acknowledge the listener and continues speaking, the listener may say 'Excuse me, but I need to say . . . .' This needs to be done politely but firmly. If there is an emergency, one does not need to worry about interrupting improperly, but should immediately take whatever action the emergency requires."

Process: Present information on interrupting properly. List key points on the easel or chalkboard.

RAISE INDEX FINGER
MOTION WITH THE ENTIRE HAND
WAIT UNTIL ACKNOWLEDGED
SPEAK
IF SPEAKER DOES NOT
ACKNOWLEDGE, SAY
"EXCUSE ME . . . ."

- raise index finger
- motion with the entire hand
- wait until acknowledged
- speak
- if speaker does not acknowledge, say "Excuse me . . . ."

11. Discussion

Content:
    a.   How do you feel when you are abruptly interrupted?
    b.   What are some times when it would be appropriate to interrupt a speaker?
    c.   What procedure should be followed when interrupting a speaker?

Process: Conduct discussion using above questions. Provide opportunity for each person to contribute to the discussion by responding to at least one of the questions.

12. Learning Activity

Preparation: Obtain paper and pencils.

Content: "We are going to do an activity that will help us become more aware of behaving appropriately during social interaction. Please get into groups of three. One person in each group will assume the role of observer; the other two participants will engage in a five-minute conversation on a topic of their choosing. The conversationalists will focus on paying attention to each other, being empathetic, and interrupting properly. The observer will make notes about how the conversation was initiated and by whom, any indications of empathy, and if interruptions were made properly. When five minutes have elapsed, the conversation will end and all three participants in each group will use the next five minutes to discuss the notes. The observer will then change roles with one of the conversationalists and the process will be repeated. The activity will continue until each group member has had the opportunity to be the observer."

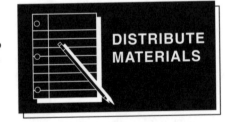

DISTRIBUTE MATERIALS

Process: Explain activity. Divide group into threes. Provide paper and pencil for observers. Monitor five-minute time periods.

13. Debriefing

Content:
    a.   What clues did you use to determine if the conversationalists were paying attention to each other?
    b.   What evidence of empathy did you observe?
    c.   Were the interruptions done properly?
    d.   As a speaker, how did you feel when you were interrupted?
    e.   How did you feel when you interrupted the speaker?

Process: Conduct debriefing using above questions. Provide opportunity for each participant to respond to at least one of the questions.

14. Conclusion

Content: "Appropriate behavior is important to social interaction. It is something that can be practiced and perfected. People who genuinely try to behave appropriately are generally successful."

Process: Make concluding statements. Provide participants with the opportunity to ask questions.

Objective 4.3: Demonstrate verbal behaviors encouraging attention to a speaker.

1. Orientation Activity

Preparation: Develop cards with the following procedures written on different cards:

- listening to the speaker
- paraphrasing what the speaker said
- clarifying responses of the speaker
- checking the perception of the speaker

Preselect and rehearse two people to engage in following interactions:

- First person to talk for one or two minutes about participating in an upcoming recreation activity; the other person to sit silently and make no reaction to what is being said.
- Same person to repeat comments in first situation; second person to respond in timely fashion with comments such as 'I see,' 'That's interesting,' or 'Tell me more about that.' First person to speak with more enthusiasm after hearing listener's comments.

Content: "Everyone please sit in a circle. Now that we are seated in a circle, I have given each of you a procedure that you could follow to show you are paying attention to a person and that you care about the person. If your card is brown, turn to the person on your left; if your card is yellow, turn to the person on your right. Introduce yourself and find out the person's name. Then read the statement to the person and allow him or her to read his or her statement to you. Once you have completed this, turn to your other side and wait for that person to finish talking and then repeat the process. After we have introduced ourselves to the people on both sides of us, we are going to watch a brief skit to help us become aware of the importance of verbal behaviors a listener can use to encourage a speaker. Watch and listen carefully to the interaction between two people."

Process: Explain the activity. Encourage everyone to listen closely to the skit because the group will discuss the skit as soon as it has been completed.

2. Debriefing

Content:
a. What differences did you see between the first and second situations?
b. What do you think the speaker was feeling in the first situation?
c. What else could the listener have done to encourage the speaker in the second situation?

Process: Conduct debriefing using above questions. Provide opportunity for each person to respond to at least one of the questions.

3. Introduction

Content: "Most people would benefit from an improvement in their listening skills. It is important to be an effective listener because of the amount of time most of us spend in listening. The quality of our relationships with others is often dependent on our ability to listen. It may be helpful to think about the difference between listening and hearing. Hearing has been described as a process whereby sound is received by the ears and sent to the brain. It is a physiological process. Listening is a process that involves interpreting and understanding the significance of the sounds. Listening is more than hearing."

Process: Introduce topic on verbal behaviors encouraging attention to a speaker.

4. Presentation

Content: "Learning to be a good listener can be a difficult task for some people. Although most of us spend more time in listening than we do in speaking, we receive very little, if any, training in how to be good listeners. Yet, it is possible to acquire and develop skills that will enhance our abilities as attentive and effective listeners.

"There are five major skills involved in being an active listener. These skills may be categorized as: (a) attending; (b) paraphrasing; (c) clarifying response; (d) perception checking; and (e) listening response. Attending is nonverbal behavior that tells the speaker the listener is paying attention to the speaker and is interested in the message. Attending is the focus of the next objective in this program.

"*Paraphrasing* is a good way for a person to demonstrate active listening skills. A paraphrase is a response by a listener to a speaker, wherein the listener uses his or her own words to state the essence of the speaker's message. A paraphrase has four basic characteristics.

"The first characteristic of a good paraphrase is that it is brief. It should never be longer than the speaker's message. Otherwise, it can result in the listener interrupting the speaker's train of thought and erecting a barrier to communication. Good listeners learn to make brief paraphrases.

"The second characteristic of a good paraphrase is that it is concise. It reflects accurately the essence of the speaker's message and cuts through the nonessential details that are present in many conversations. A good listener develops the ability to be attentive to the heart of the message.

"A third characteristic of a good paraphrase is that it focuses only on the content of the speaker's message and disregards the emotions with which the message is spoken.

Even though nonverbal clues provided by the sender are important, the paraphrase should state only the facts or ideas being communicated. The nonverbal clues can be received and processed in another manner. A good listener learns to focus on the content of the message.

"The fourth characteristic of a good paraphrase is that it is stated in the listener's own words, rather than by repeating the words of the speaker. A paraphrase summarizes the listener's understanding of the message in his or her own words. If a listener simply repeats the words of the speaker, the result is parroting, not paraphrasing. Parroting can be a barrier to communication; paraphrasing can enhance it."

Process: Present information on paraphrasing. Use chalkboard to list four major characteristics:

- brief
- concise
- focuses only on the content of the speaker's message
- state in the listener's words

BRIEF
CONCISE
FOCUSES ONLY ON THE CONTENT OF THE SPEAKER'S MESSAGE
STATE IN THE LISTENER'S WORDS

5. Discussion

Content:
   a. What is a paraphrase?
   b. What are some instances when you have found paraphrasing to be useful?
   c. How do you feel when someone paraphrases something you have just said?
   d. In your opinion, what is the most difficult thing about paraphrasing?
   e. How can you improve your ability to paraphrase?

Process: Conduct discussion using above questions. Provide opportunity for each person to contribute to the discussion by responding to at least one of the questions.

6. Presentation

Content: "Another skill that active listeners can employ to improve communication is the *clarifying response.* A clarifying response is sought from the speaker when a listener is confused or has an inadequate understanding of the message. Listeners can accomplish this by asking speakers to repeat part of the message, to use different words, to illustrate their meaning with an example, or to respond to questions from the listener. A clarifying response can be an integral part of communication but it must be used in a wise manner. If a listener constantly interrupts a speaker to seek clarifying responses, communication will probably be greatly impeded.

"It is usually best to enhance understanding by asking for one clarifying response at a time. When two or more clarifying responses are sought in quick succession, it sometimes means the listener is not attending to the speaker and the communication process is needlessly inhibited."

Process: Present information on clarifying response. Provide examples as the information is presented.

7. Discussion

Content:
a. What is a clarifying response?
b. What are some examples of a clarifying response?
c. Can you give some instances when you have asked for a clarifying response?

Process: Conduct discussion using above questions. Provide opportunity for each person to contribute to the discussion by responding to at least one of the questions.

8. Presentation

Content: "*Perception checking* is another tool that can be used by active listeners. Sometimes it is difficult for people to say precisely what they want to say and sometimes others find it equally difficult to listen without distraction to what is being said. Because this is a rather common occurrence, there needs to be a check for accuracy in communication. Effective listeners frequently reflect back the essence of what they have heard. This process is referred to as perception checking.

Perception checking is basically a three-step process used by effective listeners. It involves (a) the listener paraphrasing the message from the speaker; (b) asking the speaker if the paraphrase is accurate; and (c) providing the speaker with an opportunity to correct any misperception. Perception checking provides a channel through which accuracy of communication is determined and controlled."

Process: Present information on perception checking. List the three steps on the easel or chalkboard:

- paraphrase message from speaker
- ask speaker to confirm or deny accuracy of paraphrase
- provide speaker with opportunity to correct any inaccurate perception

> PARAPHRASE MESSAGE FROM SPEAKER
>
> ASK SPEAKER TO CONFIRM OR DENY ACCURACY OF PARAPHRASE
>
> PROVIDE SPEAKER WITH OPPORTUNITY TO CORRECT ANY INACCURATE PERCEPTION

9. Discussion

Content:
a. What is perception checking?
b. Why is it necessary?
c. When have you used perception checking?
d. How can you improve your ability in perception checking?

Process: Conduct discussion using above questions. Provide opportunity for each person to contribute to the discussion by responding to at least one of the questions.

10. Presentation

Content: "*Using a listening response* is another way to be an attentive listener. A listening response is a very brief comment or action made to the speaker that indicates the listener is interested and wishes the speaker to continue. It is made quietly and briefly to ensure there is no interference with the speaker's train of thought.

"There are at least five types of listening responses. One type is simply nodding the head slightly and waiting for the speaker to continue. A second type is to pause and look at the speaker expectantly, without saying or doing anything. A third is using a casual remark, such as 'I see,' 'Mmmm,' or 'That's interesting,' to demonstrate interest in the speaker and the message. A fourth is the echo, or repeating the last few words of the speaker. A fifth listening response is known as a mirror, which is the listener reflecting his or her understanding of the message back to the speaker."

Process: Present information on listening response. Use board to list types of listening responses:

- nod head slightly and wait for speaker to continue
- pause and look at speaker expectantly
- use a casual remark, such as "I see."
- repeat last few words of speaker
- reflect your understanding of the message back to speaker

> NODDING HEAD SLIGHTLY AND WAITING FOR SPEAKER TO CONTINUE
>
> PAUSE AND LOOK AT SPEAKER EXPECTANTLY
>
> USING A CASUAL REMARK, SUCH AS "I SEE."
>
> REPEAT LAST FEW WORDS OF SPEAKER
>
> REFLECT YOUR UNDERSTANDING OF THE MESSAGE BACK TO SPEAKER

11. Discussion

Content:
  a. What is a listening response?
  b. Are there listening responses that you commonly use? If so, what are they?
  c. What is your feeling when you are speaking and someone provides you with a listening response?
  d. How can you improve your ability to give listening responses?

Process: Conduct discussion using above questions. Provide opportunity for each person to contribute to the discussion by responding to at least one of the questions.

12. Learning Activity

Preparation: Obtain paper and pencils.

Content: "We are going to do an activity that will help you become more aware of listening responses. Please get into groups of three. One person in each group will assume the role of speaker, one the role of listener, and one the role of observer. The speaker will think of a problem he or she has experienced while participating in a recreation activity and relate it to the listener. The listener will make listening responses, as appropriate. The observer will record notes about the listening responses. When five minutes have elapsed, the speaker will end his or her comments and the next five minutes will be spent with all three members discussing the listening responses that were recorded. The three group members will then change roles and repeat the process. The activity will continue until each group member has had the opportunity to act in all three roles."

Process: Explain activity. Divide group into threes. Provide paper and pencil for observers. Monitor five minute time periods.

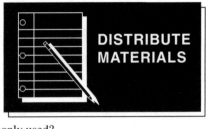

DISTRIBUTE MATERIALS

13. Debriefing

Content:
   a.   What listening responses were commonly used?
   b.   As a speaker, how did you feel when you received a listening response?
   c.   As a listener, was it difficult to find an appropriate moment to make a listening response? If so, how did you deal with it?
   d.   How will you use your knowledge of listening responses in your recreation participation?

Process: Conduct debriefing using above questions. Provide opportunity for each person to respond to at least one of the questions.

14. Learning Activity

Preparation: Obtain paper and pencils.

Content: "We are going to do another activity that will allow you to use paraphrasing, clarifying response, and perception checking. Please get into groups of three again, with one person being the speaker, one the listener, and one the observer. The process will be repeated three times so that each person has the opportunity to fill each role. The speaker and listener will engage in a five minute exchange, with the speaker giving his or her thoughts about a specified topic and the listener using the techniques of para-phrasing, clarifying response, and perception checking as often as appropriate. The observer will record each use of these skills. A five minute discussion, focused on these skills, will occur among the three members of each group before the roles are rotated."

Process: Explain activity. Help divide into groups of three. Provide pencil and paper. Ensure each participant has opportunity to play each role. Move to debriefing.

DISTRIBUTE MATERIALS

15. Debriefing

Content:
   a.   Were the listening skills of paraphrasing, clarifying response, and perception checking used at appropriate moments?
   b.   Were they used at inappropriate times? If so, how could a sense of timing be improved?
   c.   Which skill was used most often?
   d.   As a listener, which skill seemed to be the most effective? Why?
   e.   As a speaker, what was your reaction when the listener utilized these skills?

Process: Conduct discussion using above questions. Provide opportunity for each person to contribute to the discussion by responding to at least one of the questions.

16. Conclusion

Content: "Becoming a good listener requires purposeful effort; it is not something that occurs just by chance. Like most other skills, becoming a good listener takes practice. Consciously utilizing different listening responses and the techniques of paraphrasing, clarifying response, and perception checking will result in being a better listener."

Process: Make concluding statements. Provide participants with the opportunity to ask questions.

Objective 4.4: Demonstrate nonverbal behaviors encouraging attention to a speaker.

1. Orientation Activity

Preparation: Prepare slips of paper prior to session. Slips could contain words such as bored, curious, preoccupied, confused, sad, excited, happy, relaxed, or impatient.

PREPARE FOR SESSION

Content: "We are going to do an activity where each of you will use nonverbal behavior in an attempt to convey the meaning of a word. There are several slips of paper in the little box in the center of the table. Each slip contains one word that describes a feeling or emotion which people often have. One at a time, each of you will draw a slip from the box and go to the front of the group. Introduce yourself to the group and then do not speak. Use actions or facial expressions, but no words, to demonstrate the meaning of the word on your slip. The rest of the group will have one minute to guess the word that is being demonstrated. The activity will continue until each person has had the opportunity to use nonverbal behavior to demonstrate a word."

Process: Explain activity. Ensure that each participant has opportunity to demonstrate word.

2. Debriefing

Content:
   a. Were different facial expressions used by group members? If so, describe some?
   b. What were some other physical actions used to convey meanings of words?
   c. Were some words easier to guess than others? If so, which ones?
   d. Were some nonverbal messages particularly strong? If so, which were they?

Process: Conduct debriefing using above questions. Provide opportunity for each person to respond to at least one of the questions.

3. Introduction

Content: "Nonverbal behaviors are ways that attitudes and feelings can be conveyed without speaking. They can send strong messages and have a significant impact on others. Some experts believe it is not possible to speak without also sending a nonverbal message to the listener. It is also believed that listeners always send nonverbal messages back to speakers. There is a considerable amount of agreement that the nonverbal behavior of a listener can have a powerful influence on a speaker."

Process: Introduce topic of nonverbal behaviors encouraging attention to a speaker.

4. Presentation

Content: "Nonverbal behavior is an essential component of communication. It is behavior that is displayed by speakers and listeners. It can be used by either to enhance or retard communication. When nonverbal behavior is used by listeners to enhance communication, it is often referred to as attending to the speaker. *Attending* means listeners are giving their physical attention to speakers. It is sometimes referred to as listening with the whole body. It indicates that the listener is paying careful attention to the person who is talking. Attending behavior includes eye contact, facial expressions, posture and gestures, body orientation, and physical proximity.

"In our culture, good *eye contact* on the part of the listener expresses interest in what the speaker is saying. Poor eye contact is usually interpreted in a negative way, such as embarrassment, dishonesty, lying, shame, hostility, lack of respect, or disinterest. It is important to know that poor eye contact includes more than a refusal to look at the speaker or looking away whenever the speaker looks at the listener. It also includes staring constantly at the speaker or looking at the speaker in a blank, unfocused manner. Good eye contact means a soft focusing of the eyes on the speaker's eyes, with an occasional shifting to other parts of the face or body, such as a gesturing hand, and then returning to the eyes.

"Some individuals have a difficult time making eye contact, just as some individuals have a difficult time knowing what to do with their hands during conversation. Good eye contact is a skill that may require some hard work to achieve, but it is necessary for effective social interaction. It allows speakers to judge how their message is being received and what steps they may have to take to make their communication more meaningful."

Process: Present information on eye contact. Demonstrate examples of poor and good eye contact. Encourage participants to repeat your behaviors.

5. Discussion

Content:
  a. Why is good eye contact important in a listener?
  b. How does good eye contact enhance communication?
  c. What is involved in good eye contact?
  d. How is poor eye contact perceived?
  e. What are some examples of poor eye contact?

Process: Conduct discussion using above questions. Provide opportunity for each person to contribute to the discussion by responding to at least one of the questions.

6.   Learning Activity

Content: "Establishing eye contact is a skill that can be learned like any other skill. We are going to engage in a brief activity to help us get started. Please pair up with a partner. Face each other at a distance of six feet. Look in the direction of your partner for one minute. Decrease your distance by half. Look at your partner's hair, forehead, ears, chin, and eyes for one minute. You may shift your gaze in a random manner, but return to your partner's eyes every other shift. Try to look at specific features for at least three seconds at a time."

Process: Explain activity. Help divide into pairs, if necessary. Announce beginning and end of one minute periods. Remind participants that this is a skill they can practice whenever they are with another person.

7.   Debriefing

Content:
   a.   From a distance of six feet, could you tell if your partner was looking at your eyes?
   b.   How difficult was it to look into the eyes of your partner?
   c.   How difficult was it to distinguish between your partner looking at your eyes and looking at your forehead?
   d.   When can you practice using eye contact?

Process: Conduct debriefing using above questions. Provide opportunity for each person to respond to at least one of the questions.

8.   Presentation

Content: "*Facial expression* is another important component of nonverbal behavior in communication. The expression on a listener's face should convey a message of interest and attentiveness to the speaker. It is the expression on a listener's face that indicates the speaker is receiving the psychological as well as the physical attention of the listener.

"Attending to a speaker also implies that the facial expression of the listener is appropriate to what is being heard. For example, if a coach called a meeting of the volleyball team and announced that one of the players had suffered a broken leg in an automobile accident on the way to practice, it would be inappropriate to receive that news with a smile on one's face. On the other hand, it is equally inappropriate to receive happy and joyous news with a grim expression on one's face. The expression on a listener's face should tell the speaker the message is not only being heard, it also is being understood and processed in a manner that is appropriate to its content. Facial expressions, like other forms of nonverbal behavior, can enhance or inhibit communication."

Process: Present information on facial expression. Demonstrate examples.

9. Discussion

Content:
a. How is facial expression important in attending to a speaker?
b. Do facial expressions reveal the attitude of the listener? How so?
c. When have you observed inappropriate facial expressions on listeners?
d. Do you believe your facial expressions when listening are always appropriate?
e. If your facial expressions are inappropriate at times, what can you do to improve?

Process: Conduct discussion using above questions. Provide opportunity for each person to contribute to the discussion by responding to at least one of the questions.

10. Learning Activity

Preparation: Obtain magazines, scissors, sheet of construction paper, and paste. Develop the handout with 4 columns containing the headers: HAPPY, SAD, ANGRY, and DETERMINED.

Content: "We are going to do an activity to make us more aware of facial expressions. I have placed a large sheet of construction paper on the wall. The sheet of paper is divided into four major columns. One column is headed by the word *happy,* one by *sad,* one by *angry,* and one by *determined.* There is a large group of magazines on the table in front of you. Browse through the magazines. When you come to a picture that depicts one of the four facial expressions listed on the sheet of paper, ask another person if he or she agrees with you about what the face is expressing. If the two of you agree on the expression, remove the picture from the magazine and paste it in the appropriate column on the construction paper. We will do this activity for 15 minutes."

Process: Explain activity. Place paper on wall. Provide magazines, scissors, and paste. If necessary, demonstrate directions by looking through a magazine, finding a picture of a face, removing it, and pasting it in the appropriate column of the paper.

11. Debriefing

Content:
a. Select one of the pictures on the paper and identify some possible reasons for the facial expression. (Repeat this item as often as desired.)
b. Is there any disagreement about any expression in any of the columns? If so, which one(s)?
c. Which expression(s) seemed to be easy to identify? Why?

Process: Conduct debriefing using above questions. Encourage all participants to respond to the first question. Provide opportunity for each person to contribute to the debriefing by responding to at least one of the questions.

12. Presentation

Content: "*Posture* and *gestures,* like facial expression, can contribute to or detract from communication. Maintaining a posture that combines being relaxed and alert at the same time is an excellent way for a listener to attend to a speaker. The listener should adopt a posture that indicates a balance between feeling comfortable with the speaker and the purpose of paying very careful attention to what is being said. A very effective listening stance can be achieved by blending these two important body messages. Elements of a good listening posture include standing or sitting reasonably erect, facing the speaker, and refraining from fidgeting. Gestures from a listener may be as important as the listener's posture in attending to a speaker. Gestures can be a good nonverbal indication of the reaction of the listener to the message. For example, nodding or shaking the head can convey agreement or disagreement with what is being said. Shrugging the shoulders, combined with facial expressions, can indicate ignorance or indifference. Rubbing the chin or scratching the head can indicate thoughtfulness."

Process: Present information on posture and gestures. Demonstrate positive and negative postures and gestures and encourage participants to model your behaviors.

13. Discussion

Content:
    a.   How does posture contribute to attending to a speaker?
    b.   What two messages should a listener's posture attempt to convey?
    c.   Describe what is included in a good listening posture.
    d.   How would you describe your own listening posture?
    e.   What can you do to improve your listening posture?
    f.   What role do gestures play in attending to a speaker?

Process: Conduct discussion using above questions. Provide opportunity for each person to contribute to the discussion by responding to at least one of the questions.

14. Presentation

Content: "*Body orientation* is closely associated with posture. It refers to the positioning of the listener's body relative to that of the speaker's. The body orientation of a listener can include such elements as slightly leaning toward the speaker, squarely facing the speaker, and maintaining an 'open' stance.

    "When listeners incline their bodies toward a speaker, it communicates more attentiveness than does leaning back or slumping in a chair. When listeners are totally engrossed in what they are hearing, they are often said to be on the edge of their seats. This conjures a picture of listeners that not only are sitting erectly, but also leaning forward. This is not to suggest that listeners adopt an exaggerated posture of tilting toward a speaker, but a slight forward bend would be appropriate.

    "Listeners can also squarely face a speaker without being confrontational. For example, a listener who squares his or her right shoulder with a speaker's left shoulder can communicate a high level of attentiveness and involvement with what is being said.

Listeners who turn their shoulders away from a speaker can be seen as disinterested or rejecting the message. In our culture, people who reject others are said to be giving them a cold shoulder. This expression may illustrate the importance of squarely facing a speaker.

"Body orientation also includes being at approximately the same eye level with a speaker. This is particularly important in one-to-one conversations if there is a distinct difference in the amounts of authority ascribed to the speaker and the listener. If a speaker has to bend his or her head back at a severe angle in order to look a listener in the eye, it is a major barrier to communication.

"Maintaining an open posture is also an important part of body orientation. An open posture means a listener is willing to accept the message being conveyed by the speaker. An open posture generally means the listener does not have crossed arms or legs. A closed posture, where the arms and legs are tightly crossed, usually indicates the listener is unwilling to accept the message being conveyed. Picture the manager of a softball team arguing with an umpire over a call made at first base. In addition to verbal expression, the manager may be very animated and engaging in all types of movements. The umpire generally stands with arms tightly folded across the chest. The posture of the umpire clearly indicates rejection of the manager's message."

Process: Present information on body orientation. Demonstrate examples of positive and negative body orientation. Encourage participants to repeat your behavior. Record key points on an easel or chalkboard.

BODY ORIENTATION

- slightly lean toward speaker
- squarely face speaker
- maintain open stance

15. Discussion

Content:
a. What is meant by the term "body orientation"?
b. What is included in the body orientation of a listener to a speaker?
c. Why is it important for speakers and listeners to be at approximately the same eye level in one-to-one conversations?
d. Can you adopt a body orientation that indicates you are willing to listen to what is being said? Please do so.
e. Can you adopt a body orientation that indicates you are unwilling to listen to what is being said? Please do so.
f. How can you make yourself aware of your body orientation when you are a listener?

Process: Conduct discussion using above questions. Provide opportunity for each person to contribute to the discussion by responding to at least one of the questions.

16. Presentation

Content: "The *physical proximity* of listeners to speakers is another component of nonverbal behavior that influences communication. Too much distance between listener and speaker inhibits communication. On the other hand, when a listener gets too close to a speaker, the result is often anxiety, which also inhibits communication. How can one tell what is an appropriate distance? There is considerable evidence that a distance of three feet is comfortable in our society. Obviously, this distance may vary, depending on the level of intimacy that exists between listener and speaker."

Process: Present information on physical proximity. Demonstrate positive and negative examples of physical proximity. Encourage participants to repeat your behaviors.

17. Discussion

Content:
   a.   How does physical proximity influence communication?
   b.   How can a listener determine an appropriate physical distance from a speaker?
   c.   At what distance do you feel comfortable when listening to a friend?
   d.   Does the distance needed for comfort change when you are listening to someone you just met? How so?

Process: Conduct discussion using above questions. Provide opportunity for each person to contribute to the discussion by responding to at least one of the questions.

18. Learning Activity

Preparation: Obtain paper and pencils.

Content: "We are going to divide into groups of three and make some observations about nonverbal behavior. In each group of three, one person will begin as the sender, one as the receiver, and one as the observer. The sender will speak for approximately three minutes, telling the receiver about a favorite leisure activity. The receiver will respond nonverbally as he or she feels appropriate. The observer will watch the receiver and record any nonverbal behaviors that are being demonstrated. After the end of a three-minute period, the roles in the group will change. The person who was the receiver will become the sender, the observer will become the receiver, and the sender will become the observer. The exercise will be repeated for three minutes and the roles will again rotate. Each person will have the opportunity to fulfill each role. We will then come back together as the full group and share our observations."

Process: Explain activity. Divide into groups of three. Provide paper and pencils for observers to record. Encourage observers to make notes of anything that seems interesting to them. Give signal to change roles after three-minute periods have elapsed.

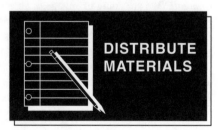

DISTRIBUTE MATERIALS

19. Debriefing

Content:
   a.   What were some of the nonverbal behaviors that were observed?
   b.   Were some of these behaviors common to most of the receivers? If so, which ones?

c. How aware were the senders of the nonverbal behaviors of the receivers? Can you provide examples?
d. What did you obtain from this activity? How will you use it?

Process: Conduct debriefing using above questions. Provide opportunity for each person to respond to at least one of the questions.

20. Conclusion

Content: "Nonverbal behaviors are a very important part of communication. They include eye contact, facial expressions, posture, gestures, body orientation, and physical distance between sender and receiver. The receiver can use nonverbal behavior to tell the sender if the message is being heard and processed. Nonverbal behavior can also tell the sender what the receiver thinks of the message and the sender. It is a powerful tool and one to which all of us should be in tune."

Process: Make concluding statements. Provide participants with an opportunity to ask questions. Attempt to respond to concerns by the participants.

Objective 4.5: Demonstrate verbal behaviors required of an effective speaker.

1. Orientation Activity

Preparation: Prepare several messages prior to the session. Examples of messages could include:

PREPARE FOR SESSION

- Peter Piper picked a pumpkin from the preacher's porch.
- Robin Red Breast is the best dressed robin.
- Little Bo Peep uses her Jeep to shepherd a heap of sheep.
- Little Jack Horner became a mourner when his Turbo Z failed to corner.

Content: "We are going to engage in an activity that is sometimes known as the gossip game. Please form a circle. First introduce yourself to the person on each side of you and find out each person's name. One person will begin by whispering a message to the person on his or her right, who will repeat the message to the person on his or her right, until the message has returned to the point where it started. The object of the activity is to repeat the message accurately so that it arrives back at its start exactly as it began. This activity requires both careful listening and accurate repetition of the message. We will repeat this process several times, choosing a different starting point for each message."

Process: Explain activity. Help form circle. Select various participants to start activity. Emphasize necessity of listening and speaking carefully.

2. Debriefing

Content:
a.   Which of the messages was the most difficult to repeat accurately? Why?
b.   What could you have done to ensure that you were repeating a message accurately?
c.   What does this tell you about the communication process?

Process: Conduct debriefing using above questions. Provide opportunity for each person to respond to at least one of the questions.

3. Introduction

Content: "Just as effective listening is more than the physiological process of receiving sound and sending it to the brain, effective speaking is more than the process of uttering words. There are many things individuals can do to help themselves become effective speakers. Those who make an effort to become more effective speakers are also enhancing their ability to engage in meaningful social interactions."

Process: Introduce topic on verbal behaviors required of an effective speaker.

4. Presentation

Content: "Among the things you can do to become a more effective speaker is to focus on verbal behaviors that enhance your ability to communicate. The verbal behaviors required of an effective speaker include (a) the use of appropriate vocabulary; (b) clear enunciation; (c) avoidance of distracting fillers; (d) the presentation of information in a logical sequence; and (e) the presentation of relevant content. Although there are other verbal behaviors that can influence one's effectiveness as a speaker, mastery of these five behaviors is necessary. Such mastery will have a positive impact on one's ability to communicate.

"The *use of appropriate vocabulary* is fundamental to good communication. Appropriate vocabulary includes the avoidance of slang or offensive terminology. Although slang words are very popular among some people, they are not universally understood or accepted. Slang words are often ambiguous and nebulous, and obscure communication rather than clarifying it. Speakers using slang may have a clear idea of what they wish to say, but if the listeners are unfamiliar with its usage, they will be forced to guess at the meaning and the intent of the speaker. Such a situation does not contribute to the effectiveness of the speaker; in fact, it gets in the way of good communication.

"The use of offensive terminology also detracts from one's effectiveness as a speaker. Offensive terminology includes obscenities and words and phrases that are construed as derogatory comments focused on race, ethnicity, gender, age, religion, disability, or other factors. Speakers who use such words may claim that they do not intend to be offensive but that has little impact on how the words are perceived by listeners. Offensive terminology generally does nothing but erect unnecessary barriers to effective communication.

"*Clear enunciation* is another verbal behavior that contributes to being an effective speaker. Enunciation refers to the clear and full pronouncement and articulation of words. Words that are not pronounced clearly and correctly not only fail to contribute to clarity of meaning; they may contribute to just the opposite—uncertainty and misunderstanding. When listeners are forced to focus intently on deciphering mispronounced words, they may lose sight of the message of the speaker. It is the responsibility of speakers to do more than speak so they can be understood; they must speak so they cannot be misunderstood.

"*Avoiding distracting fillers* is a third verbal behavior that can contribute to being an effective speaker. A filler is a word, phrase, or sound employed by speakers to cover lapses in their trains of thought or to use as a substitute for carefully thinking through what they wish to say. Examples of fillers are sounds such as 'errr' or 'ahhh' and phrases such as 'you know.' Some speakers make such liberal use of fillers that their communication efforts are distorted and difficult to follow. Listeners usually find it very annoying when they have to filter the message of the speaker through an excessive number of fillers. Speakers who use fillers are relying on the listener to dig out the content of the message, rather than making the effort to ensure the message is clear and unable to be misunderstood.

"Another verbal behavior that contributes to being an effective speaker is to *present information in a logical sequence.* Information that has a logical progression from one point to the next is usually easily followed and understood. It provides listeners with opportunities to use appropriate listening skills to monitor the accuracy with which they are receiving messages. Speakers that jump from one point to another, with no apparent pattern or connecting threads between thoughts, are difficult to follow and often appear incoherent. Listeners have to work very hard to receive the messages being sent and there is very little assurance that the messages being received are what the speakers intend.

"A fifth basic verbal behavior that speakers can employ is to *present relevant content.* Information that is not pertinent to a conversation is pointless, even though it may be accurate. Such information is not helpful to communication. It is distracting and can lead both speakers and listeners on a path that moves away from the topics that should be central to the conversation. Adhering to the verbal behavior of presenting relevant content requires speakers to think carefully before they open their mouths. Although this is a process that is widely admired, it is also one that is seldom practiced by those who would benefit most from it. Presenting relevant content is a process that requires constant self-monitoring."

Process: Present information. Use easel or chalkboard to list five major verbal behaviors:

- use appropriate vocabulary
- enunciate clearly
- avoid distracting fillers
- present information in logical sequence
- present relevant content

5. Discussion

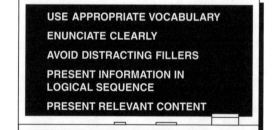

Content:

    a.   Do you feel that you need improvement in any of the verbal behaviors we have identified? If so, which ones?

b. What will you actually do to enhance your performance in those verbal behaviors needing improvement?
c. Can you provide examples of how you have used any of these verbal behaviors to become a more effective speaker? If so, what are they?
d. How will you use this information?

Process: Conduct discussion using above questions. Provide opportunity for each person to contribute to the discussion by responding to at least one of the questions.

6. Learning Activity

Preparation: Prepare a list of messages. Examples of messages could include:

PREPARE FOR SESSION

- Go to your room, put on your hat, coat, and mittens, then return and sit on the sofa.
- Trace each pattern on the paper. Cut out each pattern, then sit with your hands folded and wait for further instructions.
- Yes, you can get to the library from here. Go through the double doors at the end of this hallway. Turn to the right and start down that hallway. The library will be the first door on your left.
- Mary and Keesha were playing basketball. They each jumped for the ball just as Jim walked by. They bumped into each other and fell into Jim. He was knocked down. He was angry, but he was not hurt. It really was accidental.

Content: "This activity is a version of the gossip game. Some of you will be asked to listen to a message and to correctly repeat it to others. Remember, when you are repeating a message, enunciate carefully, confine yourself to relevant information, and do not add extraneous material such as fillers. Four of you will be asked to leave the room and be ready to repeat a message that will be given to you. The rest of you will act as observers. One of the four persons who left the room will be asked to return and listen to a message I will read to him or her. A second person will be asked to return and listen to the message, which will be related from memory by the first person. A third person will be asked to return and will listen to the message from the second person. The fourth person will then enter, listen to the message from the third person, and repeat it to the group. We will then select four more people to leave the room and the process will be repeated with a different message. This process will continue until each person has had the opportunity to be among a group of four that leaves the room."

Process: Explain activity. Select four participants to leave room. Read message to first person asked to return. Participants can be given opportunity to make up messages for the groups of four. Emphasize need for speakers to enunciate clearly, avoid fillers, have a logical progression, and use relevant content.

7. Debriefing

Content:
a. What did you do to help yourself remember the message you were given?
b. What did you do as speaker to help the listener understand the message?

   c.   Did you notice changes in the messages when they were repeated from one person to the next? If so, provide examples.

   d.   Why do you think changes occurred?

   e.   What does this indicate about the process of communication?

Process: Conduct debriefing using above questions. Provide opportunity for each person to respond to at least one of the questions.

8. Learning Activity

Preparation: Obtain paper and pencils.

Content: "We are going to do an activity that will provide each of you with the chance to give verbal directions to the rest of the group for drawing a picture. Each of you will be given paper and pencil. Go someplace in the room and draw a simple picture, but do not show it to anyone. Return to the group, place the picture face down in a pile, and form a circle around the pile of pictures. One person will take a picture from the pile, not allow anyone else to look at it, and give directions to the group that will enable them to duplicate the picture as nearly as possible. The group will listen carefully and try to follow the directions that are given. The directions should be as clear and simple as possible. For example, if the person giving directions is looking at a picture of a house, the directions could begin by saying 'Draw a long line across the bottom of your paper. Draw a parallel line in the middle of the paper. Connect the ends to make a box. Put a door on the middle of the bottom line.' The directions would continue until all parts of the house were described. Each person will be given the chance to look at a picture and give directions to the group."

Process: Explain activity. Provide pencils and sufficient paper. Ensure that only the person giving directions can see the picture being described. Provide opportunity for each participant to be a describer. Emphasize necessity of providing relevant content in a logical sequence.

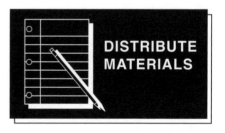

DISTRIBUTE MATERIALS

9. Debriefing

Content:
   a.   What difficulties did you have in giving directions?
   b.   What difficulties did you have in receiving directions?
   c.   Was it more difficult to give or receive directions? Why?
   d.   Other than looking at the picture, how could receiving directions be made easier?

Process: Conduct debriefing using above questions. Provide opportunity for each person to respond to at least one of the questions.

10. Learning Activity

Content: "This activity is similar to a mouse finding its way through a maze. We will use chairs, books, coats, and other objects to make a maze in this room. One person in the group will be blindfolded; another will be selected to give directions to guide the blindfolded person through the maze. The directions must be simple and accurate. After the blindfolded person has been successfully directed through the maze, a new person will be blindfolded and the shape of the maze will be changed. A new person will be selected to give directions. This process will be repeated until each person has had the opportunity to be blindfolded and to give directions. Remember, directions should have a logical sequence, be easily understood, and have no unnecessary content."

Process: Explain activity. Use objects to make maze. Monitor activity to ensure safety of blindfolded person. Emphasize clarity of directions.

11. Debriefing

Content:

    a.   Did the presence of a blindfolded listener make you a more careful speaker? If so, how so?

    b.   Did wearing a blindfold make you a more careful listener? If so, how so?

    c.   Did the inability of the blindfolded listener to see any gestures you wanted to make have an influence on your ability to give effective directions? If so, how so?

    d.   What is your assessment of the importance of presenting relevant information in a logical sequence, without distracting fillers?

Process: Conduct debriefing using above questions. Provide opportunity for each person to respond to at least one of the questions.

12. Conclusion

Content: "The ability of people to engage in meaningful social interaction is often dependent on their communication skills. An integral part of communication is effective speaking. Utilization of basic verbal skills can help one become a more effective speaker. Practicing the use of these skills requires purposeful effort and attention; the result should be improvement in communication and social interaction."

Process: Make concluding statements. Provide participants with an opportunity to ask questions and voice concerns. Attempt to respond to all questions and concerns.

Appendix E
Leisure Education
Specific Program #5

USE RESOURCES FACILITATING LEISURE PARTICIPATION

Purpose, Goal, and Objectives

Purpose: Provide opportunities for participants to learn how to locate and identify sources of information about leisure opportunities; identify specifics to solicit advice from information sources about leisure; and use printed, human, and agency resources that facilitate leisure participation.

GOAL 5: KNOWLEDGE AND UTILIZATION OF RESOURCES FACILITATING LEISURE PARTICIPATION.
Objective 5.1: Identify information to solicit from leisure resources.
Objective 5.2: Use printed resources facilitating leisure participation.
Objective 5.3: Use human resources facilitating leisure participation.
Objective 5.4: Use agency resources facilitating leisure participation.

Goal and Objectives: Performance Measures

GOAL 5: KNOWLEDGE AND UTILIZATION OF RESOURCES FACILITATING LEISURE PARTICIPATION.

Objective 5.1: Identify information to solicit from leisure resources.
Performance Measure: Given a paper and pencil, within five minutes, and identifying six of the seven specifics with associated explanations on two consecutive occasions:
  (a) identify seven specifics to solicit from sources of information about leisure opportunities: (1) activities; (2) facilities and location; (3) schedules; (4) cost; (5) equipment and apparel; (6) people; and (7) transportation; and
  (b) provide a brief explanation of why he or she should obtain this information: (1) activities (e.g., determine what is offered); (2) facilities and location (e.g., determine where it is); (3) schedules (determine when it is offered); (4) cost (determine how much it is); (5) equipment and apparel (determine what needs to be done); (6) people (determine who is available); and (7) transportation (determine how to get there).

Objective 5.2: Use printed resources facilitating leisure participation.
Performance Measure: Given a newspaper, telephone book, directories and pamphlets, and a paper and pencil, within 10 minutes and identifying six of the seven specifics on two consecutive occasions:

(a) choose a leisure service agency; and
(b) determine the following about the agency: (1) activities; (2) facilities and location; (3) schedules; (4) cost; (5) equipment and apparel; (6) people; and (7) transportation.

Objective 5.3: Use human resources facilitating leisure participation.
Performance Measure: Given the opportunity to speak with neighbors, experts associated with a recreation activity, and friends, and a paper and pencil, within 10 minutes, and identifying six of the seven specifics on two consecutive occasions:

(a) choose a leisure service agency, and
(b) determine the following about the agency: (1) activities; (2) facilities and location; (3) schedules; (4) cost; (5) equipment and apparel; (6) people; and (7) transportation.

Objective 5.4: Use agency resources facilitating leisure participation.
Performance Measure: Given the opportunity to speak with personnel at the chamber of commerce, parks and recreation department, or other leisure service agency, and a paper and pencil, within 10 minutes, and identifying six of the seven specifics on two consecutive occasions:

(a) choose a recreation agency, and
(b) determine the following about the agency: (1) activities; (2) facilities and location; (3) schedules; (4) cost; (5) equipment and apparel; (6) people; and (7) transportation.

Goal and Objectives: Content and Process

GOAL 5: KNOWLEDGE AND UTILIZATION OF RESOURCES FACILITATING LEISURE PARTICIPATION.

Objective 5.1: Identify information to solicit from leisure resources.

1. Orientation Activity

Preparation: Obtain paper and pencils.

Content: "Pretend that you have just moved to a home in a new community. Choose a recreation activity. Write this activity at the top of the paper I have given each of you. Next, write one question you would like answered about this activity in order for you to participate in the community. For example: I choose basketball and I would like to know 'Where is the closest court to my home?' After you have completed this step, stand up and begin walking around the room. Find someone who is standing and not talking with anyone. Introduce yourself to the person and find out the person's name. Share your activity and your need for information. Find out the person's activity and the question he or she would like answered. Together, come up with an additional question to which you need the answer and one question helpful for the other person. Record the additional question and write the name of the person who helped you think of the question immediately after the question. Continue meeting with other participants, trying to make your list of questions related to your recreation activity as long as possible."

Process: Distribute paper and pencils to the participants. Encourage them to generate as many questions as possible. If some participants are reluctant to approach others, assist them by walking with them and modeling the desired behavior.

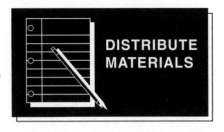

DISTRIBUTE MATERIALS

2. Debriefing

Content:
   a. What are some questions you wanted answered about your activity?
   b. Now that people shared some of their questions, what questions can you add to your list?
   c. Why do you think we did this orientation activity?

Process: Conduct debriefing using above questions. Provide opportunity for each person to respond to at least one of the questions.

3. Introduction

Content: "Knowing sources of information about leisure opportunities is an essential step in becoming independent and accepting the responsibility for taking control of one's life. But knowing sources of information is only a first step. It is not the responsibility of these sources to think of everything potential participants might want to know about a leisure opportunity. Rather, it is the responsibility of the individual to ascertain the information he or she needs to know and to take the steps necessary to acquire that information."

Process: Introduce topic of identifying specifics to solicit information from sources of information about leisure.

4. Presentation

Content: "The types of information that would be of benefit to potential leisure participants may vary from activity to activity and from person to person. For example, the issue of crowding or numbers of participants might be of concern to one person and a matter of indifference to another. One person might wish to know if the hiking trails are heavily used on the weekends and another person may not care whether or not the beaches are crowded on weekends. Thus, one person feels a need to have a specific item of information relative to a leisure opportunity, while another person is not interested in that kind of information regarding the activity in which he or she is interested. In general, however, the types of information that are most useful concerning leisure opportunities include cost, transportation, equipment, skill required, location, hours of operation, and any unique requirements, such as membership or reservations.

"The costs associated with a leisure activity should be among the first things a potential participant investigates. Often, there is a direct cost assessed to participants. Direct costs usually take the form of *admission* or *user fees*. Examples of direct costs would be the the price of admission to a movie theater or a swimming pool, the team entry fee for a volleyball league, the price of lift tickets at a ski area or the entrance fee to a national park.

"Admission or user fees are often not the only cost associated with participation in a leisure activity. Some activities may have additional costs related to *transportation, lodging, meals, equipment, and clothing*. These costs may be greater than the price of direct participation in the activity. When one is attempting to determine the cost of participating in an activity, all of these factors must be carefully considered.

"When considering cost, it is important to keep abreast of the changes that are occurring among many leisure service providers. Public park and recreation agencies, in particular, now have a fee for many activities that used to be free. Efforts must be made to determine if there is a fee and how much it is. Other leisure service providers periodically increase their participation fees in order to keep up with the expenses of operating and to realize a reasonable profit. Determining the costs of participation in an activity must be based on current information."

Process: Present information on cost. Use easel or chalkboard to illustrate examples of costs:

- admission
- user fees
- transportation
- lodging
- meals
- equipment
- clothing

ADMISSION
USER FEES
TRANSPORTATION
LODGING
MEALS
EQUIPMENT
CLOTHING

5. Discussion

Content:
   a. What is a direct cost associated with leisure participation?
   b. Can you give some examples of direct costs? If so, please do.
   c. What other kinds of costs might be associated with leisure participation?
   d. Why is it important to have current information related to cost of participation?
   e. How do you feel about having to pay to participate in an activity provided by the municipal park and recreation department?

Process: Conduct debriefing using above questions. Encourage all participants to contribute by responding to at least one of the questions.

6. Learning Activity

Content: "We are going to do an exercise to start us thinking about costs associated with participation in a leisure activity. Think of an activity in which you have not yet participated, but are eager to try. Identify the types of things which cost money. After you have done this, determine the total amount it would cost you to participate in this activity. When you are finished, be prepared to share your results with the rest of the group."

Process: Explain activity. Emphasize necessity to be thorough. Move to debriefing when finished.

7. Debriefing

Content:
 a. What activity did you choose?
 b. What kinds of expenses are associated with your activity?
 c. Are there any additional expenses? If so, what are they?
 d. What was the total amount of your expenses?
 e. What was the most expensive item?
 f. Were you surprised by the number of things that must be considered when trying to determine costs of participation? If so, how?
 g. Of what value was this exercise to you?

Process: Conduct debriefing using above questions. Encourage all participants to contribute by responding to at least one of the questions.

8. Presentation

Preparation: Develop a handout containing the following questions:

PREPARE FOR SESSION

• Is activity within walking distance?
• Is walking the best transportation?
• If too far to walk, what are other modes?
• Am I able to use all available modes?
• What are advantages and disadvantages of different modes?

Content: "Transportation is another factor about which specific information is needed. Opportunities for participation in many activities depend on the ability of the participants to get to specific locations, but these sites may not be accessible by all modes of transportation. If there are several modes of transportation that could be utilized, which mode is the most feasible? There may be many modes of transportation, but not all of them may be available to some individuals. Determining specifics about transportation is an important task.

"When considering transportation relative to participation in a leisure activity, there are several questions to which one must find the answers. For example:

 a. Is the location of the activity within walking distance?
 b. Is walking the best form of transportation to use?
 c. If it is too far to walk, what other modes of transportation are available?
 d. Am I able to use all the modes that are available?
 e. What are the advantages and disadvantages of the different modes of transportation?

"Answering these questions will provide information that is helpful in making decisions about participating in a specific leisure activity."

Process: Present the material on using transportation to get to a recreation activity.

9. Presentation

Content: "Knowledge of the advantages and disadvantages of common modes of transportation may help individuals identify questions they wish to ask regarding participation in specific leisure activities. In general, the following information appears to be relevant:

"*Walk.* There is no direct cost involved and it is a beneficial exercise. It requires extra time, is sometimes fatiguing, and poses the risk of being caught in inclement weather.

"*Cycle.* A bicycle is more efficient than walking, is fairly speedy, and is also a healthful exercise. Bicycles must be securely locked when not in use and also put the rider at the mercy of the weather.

"*Taxi.* A taxi leaves the responsibility of driving and dealing with the traffic to another person, eliminates a parking problem, and provides door-to-door service. They can be fairly expensive compared to other modes of transportation and sometimes necessitate a lengthy wait until one is available.

"*Automobile.* Your car is convenient, allows independence, and usually is a great time-saver. Operating a car can be expensive and requires a safe, secure parking area.

"*Bus.* Using the public transportation system is usually inexpensive, eliminates parking problems, and removes the responsibility of driving. You must be familiar with the bus schedules and adapt your transportation needs to it. Buses do not necessarily operate all hours of the day or on both days of the weekend. Some neighborhoods are not well-served by buses.

"*Train.* For some people, trains provide a nice alternative to flying. They are not as expensive as flying but are more expensive than many other forms of transportation. Their schedules are often inconvenient and sometimes they have trouble staying on schedule.

"*Airplane.* Flying is a fast, convenient method to travel great distances. It is relatively expensive and often requires the traveler to arrange for other modes of transportation after the destination is reached.

"There may be other, more exotic modes of transportation, but the above are most relevant for traveling in and between communities and recreation areas in our country."

Process: Present information on modes of transportation. List modes on chalkboard; list advantages and disadvantages of each:

- walking
- cycling
- taxi
- private automobile
- bus
- train
- airplane

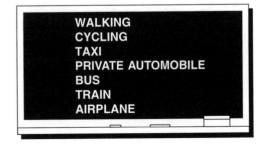

WALKING
CYCLING
TAXI
PRIVATE AUTOMOBILE
BUS
TRAIN
AIRPLANE

10. Discussion

Content:
a. What modes of transportation are available to you within your community?
b. Are they available and accessible to all citizens?
c. Are there recreation areas in your vicinity that are not served by public transportation? If so, what are they?
d. What other modes of transportation can be used to reach these areas?

Process: Conduct discussion using above questions. Encourage all participants to contribute to the discussion by responding to at least one of the questions.

11. Presentation

Content: "The mode of transportation about which the most questions are asked appears to be the bus. What does one need to know in order to use a bus system effectively? Basically, one needs to know the following:

a. What does it cost?
b. Are passes or tokens available for purchase?
c. What is the schedule (i.e., routes; time of arrival and departure)?
d. Where can one obtain schedules?
e. What are the days and hours of operation?
f. Where can one call for information?

"Other helpful information concerning buses includes: (1) in most cases, either the exact fare or a pass or token is required because drivers do not carry or make change; (2) buses are equipped with devices (cords or buttons) that passengers may use to notify the driver that they wish to get off at a certain point; (3) the types of areas that are typically served by buses include shopping malls, athletic facilities, urban parks, and downtown areas; and (4) transfers are available to allow individuals to change buses to get to a desired location."

Process: Present information on buses. Write on the chalkboard the following abbreviated questions:

- Cost?
- Passes or tokens?
- Schedule?
- Where are schedules?
- Bus stops?
- Operation times?
- Call for information?

COST?
PASSES OR TOKENS?
SCHEDULE?
WHERE ARE SCHEDULES?
BUS STOPS?
OPERATION TIMES?
CALL FOR INFORMATION?

12. Discussion

Content:
a. What do you need to know to use the bus?
b. Have you used the bus system? If so, when did you use it and where did you go?

    c. Did you experience any difficulty in using the bus? If so, how?
    d. Would you use the bus again?
    e. Are you familiar with any recreation areas or facilities that are easily accessible by bus? If so, what are they?
    f. Are the buses in this community accessible to all people with disabilities?

Process: Conduct discussion using above questions. Encourage all participants to contribute to the discussion by responding to at least one of the questions.

13. Learning Activity

Preparation: Obtain paper, pencils, and local bus schedules.

Content: "Knowing about the bus system should give one the confidence needed to use it when the occasion arises. This activity will help you gain confidence in using the bus system. Each of you has been given pamphlets describing the services offered by the bus system. These pamphlets provide information concerning fares, schedules, routes, and hours of operation. Select a recreation area or facility as your destination and find the answers to the following questions:

    a. Where do I go to meet the bus?
    b. When do I need to be there?
    c. What is the fare?
    d. Where will I get off the bus?
    e. Where will I go to board the bus to return home?
    f. What time will the bus be there?
    g. What time does the last bus leave?
    h. What is the closest bus stop to my home?
    i. What time will I get home?

    "Write your answers to the questions on the paper that will be provided to you. Be prepared to share your answers with the group. When you do, the group will be asked to judge your responses for accuracy."

Process: Explain activity. Provide pencil, paper, and local bus schedules. Provide individual assistance as necessary. Give each participant opportunity to share answers with group and receive feedback during debriefing.

14. Debriefing

Content:
    a. What was your destination?
    b. Did you find answers to all the questions?
    c. Could you select other destinations and still find the answers?

d.   Did you find several options related to arrival and departure times for your destination?
e.   How will you use this information?

Process: Conduct debriefing using above questions. Encourage all participants to contribute by responding to at least one of the questions.

15.   Presentation

Content: "Equipment is another area for which answers to specific questions must be obtained. Knowing what to ask about equipment is a step toward independence and control. If one is thinking about participating in a recreation activity, questions about equipment should include the following:

a.   What equipment, if any, is required to participate in the activity?
b.   Does the organization that provides the opportunity also provide any equipment?
c.   If participants must supply the equipment, is it available on a rental basis?
d.   If equipment is available, from whom and for how much can it be rented?
e.   If the equipment must be purchased, where can it be bought and at what cost?
f.   Is special clothing required? If so, what kind and from where?"

Process: Present information on equipment. List abbreviated questions on board:

- What equipment?
- Does organization provide equipment?
- What equipment rental?
- Who rents?
- How much is rental?
- Buy where?
- What cost?
- What special clothing?

> WHAT EQUIPMENT?
> DOES ORGANIZATION
>   PROVIDE EQUIPMENT?
> WHAT EQUIPMENT RENTAL?
> WHO RENTS?
> HOW MUCH IS RENTAL?
> BUY WHERE?
> WHAT COST?
> WHAT SPECIAL CLOTHING?

16.   Discussion

Content:
a.   In what activities have you participated that required some type of equipment?
b.   Where and how did you obtain the equipment?
c.   What are additional questions related to equipment, other than the ones presented?

Process: Conduct debriefing using above questions. Encourage all participants to contribute by responding to at least one of the questions.

17.   Presentation

Content: "Skill level is also a factor about which specific information must be obtained. If individuals are in the process of determining the feasibility of participating in a particular activity, their skill level or readiness should be a primary consideration.

Questions to be asked could include the following:

a. What are the prerequisites, if any, for this particular activity?
b. Do I meet those prerequisites?
c. Does the activity require the same level of skill from all participants or are allowances made for people with different levels of skill?
d. Is some type of demonstration or proof of skills required?
e. Is a minimum level of knowledge and basic physical skills required?
f. Is instruction in required skills available from some source?

"Learning the answers to these and similar questions will enable participants to make intelligent decisions regarding leisure participation."

Process: Present information on skill level. Use board to list abbreviated questions:

- What prerequisites?
- Do I meet prerequisites?
- Allowances for different levels?
- Skill demonstration?
- Knowledge and physical skills?
- Is instruction available?

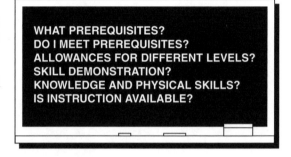

WHAT PREREQUISITES?
DO I MEET PREREQUISITES?
ALLOWANCES FOR DIFFERENT LEVELS?
SKILL DEMONSTRATION?
KNOWLEDGE AND PHYSICAL SKILLS?
IS INSTRUCTION AVAILABLE?

18. Discussion

Content:
a. In what activities have you participated that required more than beginning skills?
b. Where and how did you obtain those skills?
c. Could you have participated without them?
d. Are there other questions regarding skill that should be asked? If so, what are they?

Process: Conduct discussion using above questions. Encourage all participants to contribute to discussion by responding to at least one of the questions.

19. Presentation

Content: "There are other factors about which specific information must be obtained to determine the feasibility of participation in a particular activity. These include the physical location of the areas or facilities where the activity is offered, the hours the activity is available, and whether participation is available to the general public on a first come-first served basis or if there are some kinds of restrictions in place. For example:

a. Is the activity available in more than one place?
b. Where are these places and can I get to them?
c. When I get to them, can I participate freely or must I have a reservation or be a member of a group or the facility?

d. If I need a reservation or a membership, how can I obtain one?
e. What are the days and hours when the activity is available?
f. Can I be there sometime during those days and hours?

"These are the types of questions to which you must have answers. Obtaining the answers removes any uncertainty about the possibility of participating in a leisure activity."

Process: Present information on other factors. Use board to list abbreviated questions:

- Is activity available?
- Where are places?
- Do I need reservation or membership?
- How can I get reservation or membership?
- What is schedule?
- Can I be there then?

20. Discussion

Content:
a. Have there been instances where you have had to find answers to the above questions? If so, for what activity?
b. Why is it necessary to have answers to these questions?
c. Are there other questions that need to be asked? If so, what are they?

Process: Conduct debriefing using above questions. Encourage all participants to contribute by responding to at least one of the questions.

21. Learning Activity

Preparation: Prepare slips of paper with activities in advance of the session. Activities could include:

- take a weekend ski trip
- enroll in oil painting class
- learn to play racquetball
- enroll in basic automobile maintenance class
- take scuba lessons
- learn to bowl
- enroll in glass-blowing class
- learn archery

Content: "You are going to be given an opportunity to apply all that you have learned about identifying the specific kinds of information needed to determine the feasibility of participating in a particular leisure activity. This is an exercise that you can do in groups of three or four. There are several slips of paper in the container in the middle of the table. Each slip of paper has an activity written on it. Each group will draw a slip of paper from the container and identify specific questions that must be answered regarding the activity on it. Questions should be grouped into the following categories:

a. cost;
b. transportation;
c. equipment;
d. skill;
e. location;
f. hours of operation; and
g. other requirements.

"You are not required to find the answers to the questions. The purpose of this exercise is to identify the questions. When you are finished, you may share your questions with the larger group."

Process: Explain activity. Divide into small groups. Provide each small group with the opportunity to share with larger group.

22. Debriefing

Content:
a. Did you generate questions you wanted to ask that we had not identified in class? If so, what were they?
b. What is your opinion regarding the number of questions that need to be answered?
c. Why do you think we did this exercise?
d. What use will you make of what you learned from this?

Process: Conduct debriefing using above questions. Encourage all participants to contribute by responding to at least one of the questions.

23. Conclusion

Content: "No one can know everything necessary for participation in all leisure activities. But knowing what questions to ask about participation is a major step toward independence and being in control of one's own life in leisure. After one knows which questions to ask, time and energy can then be focused on obtaining answers."

Process: Make concluding statements. Provide opportunity for questions.

Objective 5.2: Use printed resources facilitating leisure participation.

1. Orientation Activity

Preparation: In advance, make up three cards per person with the following written on each card:

- pamphlets and brochures
- newspapers
- phone books

Content: "Each of you has been given three cards containing three different types of printed resources that could help you take part in enjoyable recreation activities. The three types of printed sources are (a) pamphlets and brochures, (b) newspapers, and (c) phone books. Fan your three cards out as if you were playing a card game so that only you can see them. Find a person, introduce yourself, and find out the person's name. Then, using the person's name, ask the person to take one of your cards. The other person will then do so. Now the person can call you by name and offer you one of his or her cards. You accept and take a card. Once you have each swapped cards, go to another person and repeat the process. The object is to get three cards that list the same printed sources. Once a person gets three of a kind, he or she will hold up the cards and state the type of printed sources. All participants must then participate in a brief discussion about that source of information. Once we finish talking about that source of information, we will resume the orientation activity until another person gets three of a kind."

Process: Distribute three cards to each participant. Walk around the room and help any participants having trouble. Once a person gets three of a kind, the debriefing questions can be asked.

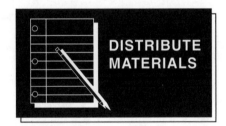

2. Debriefing

Content:
  a.   How can the printed sources help you to participate in leisure?
  b.   What other printed materials could we use to find out about the recreation activity?
  c.   Why do you think we did this orientation activity?

Process: Conduct debriefing using above questions. Provide opportunity for each person to respond to at least one of the questions.

3. Introduction

Content: "There is a lot of information about opportunities for leisure participation in and near most communities. Much of the information is in printed form and is a valuable resource for those who utilize it. The information is available from many sources. Tapping these resources can help you make the most of your leisure."

Process: Introduce topic of using printed resources facilitating leisure participation.

4. Presentation

Content: "To take full advantage of one's leisure it is necessary to be well-informed about several aspects of leisure participation. For example, one needs to know what kinds of opportunities are available, who provides such opportunities, when and where can one participate, how much it costs, and eligibility requirements. Much of this information is available in printed form. Some of it appears in *pamphlets and brochures* that are focused on the offerings of a specific agency, such as a municipal park and recreation department; some of it is in publications that cover a variety of topics, such as *newspapers;* and some of it appears in sources that are harder to find and use, such as the yellow pages of a *telephone book.* Knowing where to look and what to look for will help you benefit from the printed information that is available."

Process: Present the information on the many different types of printed resources available to facilitate leisure participation. List the key points on an easel or chalkboard:

PAMPHLETS AND BROCHURES

NEWSPAPERS

TELEPHONE BOOK

- pamphlets and brochures
- newspapers
- telephone book

5. Presentation

Preparation: Obtain telephone book.

PREPARE FOR SESSION

Content: "A telephone directory is a valuable source of information. If one knows the name of a specific agency, organization, or other leisure service provider, the white pages will provide the telephone number where the service provider can be called and be put in direct contact. If one does not know the name of a specific agency or organization, the yellow pages will provide categories of goods and services providers. Searching through the yellow pages sometimes requires a little effort because they are often organized in a manner that is different from what we expect. But after a person has become familiar with how they are organized, they can assist one in obtaining a considerable amount of information. Many telephone directories also have a section of pages that is colored blue. The blue pages provide information about local government agencies, such as the municipal park and recreation department. One can find the telephone numbers for the recreation centers, swimming pools, special facilities (e.g., the zoo), and the administrative offices of the park and recreation department. The blue pages also provide information about state and federal offices located in the local community."

Process: Present information about telephone directories. Have directory on hand to use as demonstration model.

6. Discussion

Content:
a. How can printed information be of value to you?
b. What examples of printed material did you use to learn about leisure opportunities?
c. How can a telephone directory assist you in learning about leisure opportunities?
d. What are examples of how you have used the yellow pages to help you find information about a particular leisure activity?
e. How have you used the blue pages to learn about a leisure opportunity?

Process: Conduct discussion using above questions. Encourage all participants to contribute to the discussion by responding to at least one of the questions.

7. Learning Activity

Preparation: Obtain telephone books, pencils, and develop list. Prepare a list of recreation activities, which could include the following items:

- recreation centers
- parks
- movie theaters
- swimming pools
- shopping malls
- restaurants
- museums
- health clubs
- bowling alleys
- sight-seeing tours

Content: "We are going to participate in an activity that will help us feel confident about our ability to use effectively the yellow and blue pages. Each of you will be given a telephone directory and a sheet of paper that contains a list of areas, facilities, organizations, or other suppliers of goods and services that have the potential to provide opportunities for leisure participation. Use the directory to locate an example of each item on the list. Record the specific name, address, and telephone number of each example. Also record the page number where you found the information. When you are finished, we will go around the group and ask each of you to give your example for a particular item. When you respond, give the page number in the directory where you found it so that all may turn to it and see it for themselves."

Process: Explain activity. Distribute directories and list of entities. Remind participants to record name, address, telephone number, and relevant directory page number. Provide opportunity for each participant to give an example.

8. Debriefing

Content:
   a. Did you have difficulty finding an example for each item? If so, which ones?
   b. Which of the sections (white, yellow or blue) is easiest to use? Why?
   c. What kinds of information can the directory supply you with?
   d. Do you feel confident in using the telephone directory to help locate information?
   e. What is an example of how you will use this information in the future?

Process: Conduct debriefing using above questions. Encourage all participants to contribute by responding to at least one of the questions.

9. Presentation

Content: "Newspapers are another valuable source of printed information and can be of great help in learning about leisure opportunities. Although they sometimes carry feature stories that give information on particular activities, such stories do not appear on a regular basis. But newspapers contain other features that can be used to one's advantage.

"Newspapers often provide information about registration procedures and deadlines for activities sponsored by the municipal park and recreation department. They also often print a schedule of local sporting events. Daily papers also provide television listings and advertisements for what is playing at the theaters, along with their starting times and price of admission. Sunday newspapers usually have an entertainment section devoted to leisure opportunities in the local community. Many newspapers perform a public service by printing the local park and recreation department's program offerings (e.g., Winter, Spring, Summer, and Fall) and providing it as a special insert in a Sunday paper.

"The information provided by newspapers includes what is happening, where it is located, and what it costs to participate. Newspapers have the advantage of being current, thus one can usually rely on the information obtained from them to be accurate."

Process: Present information on newspapers. Use daily and Sunday papers as demonstration models. List key points:

- registration procedures
- schedule of sporting events
- television listings
- movie advertisements
- entertainment section
- recreation department program listings

> REGISTRATION PROCEDURES
> SCHEDULE OF SPORTING EVENTS
> TELEVISION LISTINGS
> MOVIE ADVERTISEMENTS
> ENTERTAINMENT SECTION
> RECREATION DEPARTMENT
> PROGRAM LISTINGS

10. Discussion

Content:
   a. What can you learn about chances for leisure participation from a local newspaper?

b. What sections of a newspaper are likely to provide you with pertinent information?

c. What is an example of how you used a newspaper to learn about a leisure opportunity?

Process: Conduct debriefing using above questions. Encourage all participants to contribute by responding to at least one of the questions.

11. Learning Activity

Preparation: Obtain Sunday newspaper, paper, and pencils.

Content: "We are going to use pencil and paper to make a list of all the leisure opportunities we can find in a Sunday newspaper. Please get into groups of three or four. Each group will be given a Sunday paper. Look through the paper carefully and make a record of each source of information you find concerning a leisure opportunity. Record the section, page number and, if available, headline or heading. When you are finished, we will compare results."

Process: Examine paper and prepare list of opportunities prior to session. Explain activity. Provide paper, pencil, and Sunday paper. Provide each group with the opportunity to share its list.

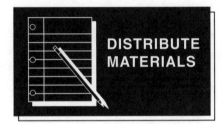

12. Debriefing

Content:
a. In how many different sections did you find information?
b. In which section did you find the most information?
c. Is there some information that is more easily understood than the rest? If so, what is it? Why is it?
d. What is your opinion of the variety of information?
e. What did you learn from this activity?
f. How will you use this information?

Process: Conduct debriefing using above questions. Encourage all participants to contribute by responding to at least one of the questions.

13. Presentation

Content: "Pamphlets and brochures are another source of printed information available to those who want to learn more about leisure opportunities. They are usually organized to provide information that is easy to read and understand. Pamphlets and brochures may be organized around a single topic such as public fishing areas, the range of programs and services offered by the local park and recreation department, the geographic location of specific facilities such as the street addresses of municipal recreation centers, or in some other manner.

"Pamphlets and brochures are usually published by park and recreation departments and agencies such as YMCA, YWCA, Jewish Community Centers, Boys' Clubs, and Girls' Clubs. Private organizations, such as health and fitness clubs, may also describe their programs and services in such publications. In addition, travel agencies use them to illustrate their services.

"Where can one get these publications? They are available, at no cost, from the agency or organization that produces them. Usually all you have to do is make a request by a telephone call, letter, or personal visit and you'll be given what you want. They are available from local chambers of commerce and are often distributed in Welcome Wagon kits provided to newcomers. Church groups will sometimes obtain and distribute such publications to their congregations, particularly those pamphlets and brochures provided by public agencies.

"State and federal agencies also publish pamphlets and brochures describing areas and facilities under their control and the programs and services which they provide to the public. They give such information as where to go, how to get there, what to bring, and what to do after you arrive. They also are available upon request and at no cost."

Process: Present information on pamphlets and brochures. Bring demonstration models to session. Distribute samples to participants.

14. Discussion

Content:
   a.   Have you obtained pamphlets or brochures to learn about leisure
        opportunities? If so, please describe. Did you find them useful?
   b.   Who provides pamphlets and brochures?
   c.   How can you get them?
   d.   What can you learn from such publications?

Process: Conduct debriefing using above questions. Encourage all participants to contribute by responding to at least one of the questions.

15. Learning Activity

Preparation: Obtain paper, pencils, and develop list. Prepare a list of types of information for brochures, which could include:

* What is being offered?
* Who is offering it?
* Where is it offered?
* When is it offered?
* What is the cost?
* Who can participate?
* What is required to participate?
* Is there a telephone number to call for additional information?

Content: "This is a two-part exercise designed to help you use pamphlets and brochures as resources to facilitate your leisure participation. This exercise will be done in groups of three. During the first part each group will generate a list of the kinds of information that should be included in a pamphlet or brochure. When each group is finished making its list, we will combine them to make a master list.

"After the master list is compiled, each group will use it to judge the value or effectiveness of pamphlets and brochures with which it will be supplied. This will be the second part of the exercise. Each group will be given the opportunity to express its judgment of the pamphlets and brochures given it."

Process: Explain activity ahead of the session. Use list to supplement lists from participants, if necessary. Compile master list and distribute. Provide each group with the same five or six pamphlets and brochures. Emphasize task is to judge information provided, not appearance of brochures. When finished, move to debriefing.

DISTRIBUTE MATERIALS

16. Debriefing

Content:
    a.   Which brochure provided the best information? Why?
    b.   Which provided the least information?
    c.   Are you confident you can use brochures to help learn about leisure opportunities?
    d.   How will this exercise be helpful to you?

Process: Conduct debriefing using above questions. Encourage all participants to contribute by responding to at least one of the questions.

17. Conclusion

Content: "Printed information can be a great asset in learning about leisure opportunities and making decisions relative to participating in them. Knowing how to obtain printed information and how to use it after it is acquired enables one to be less dependent on others and more self-reliant. Learning how to utilize such sources is an indication of the acceptance of greater responsibility."

Process: Make concluding statements. Provide opportunity for questions.

Objective 5.3: Use human resources facilitating leisure participation.

1. Orientation Activity

Preparation: Develop card sets for participants (each set contains three cards). Make up three cards per person with one of the following written on each card:

PREPARE FOR SESSION

- use telephone
- write letters
- go and visit

Content: "Each of you has been given three cards containing three different types of *human resources* that could help you participate in enjoyable recreation activities. The three human resources are (a) using a telephone, (b) writing letters, and (c) making visits. Fan your three cards out as if you were playing a card game so that only you can see them. Find a person, introduce yourself, and find out the person's name. Then using the person's name, ask the person if he or she would like to take one of your cards. The other person will then take a card. Now the person will call you by name and offer one of his or her cards. You then accept and take a card. Once you have swapped cards, move on to another person and repeat the process. The object is to get three cards that list the same human sources that could help you participate in a recreation activity. Once a person gets three of a kind, he or she will hold up the cards and state the type of human resource. All participants must then participate in a brief discussion about that source of information. Once we finish talking about that source of information, we will resume the orientation activity until another person gets three of a kind."

Process: Distribute three cards to each participant. Walk around the room and assist any participants encountering difficulty. Once a person gets three of a kind, the debriefing questions can be asked.

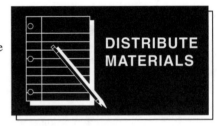

DISTRIBUTE MATERIALS

2. Debriefing

Content:
a. How can the human resources help you participate in leisure?
b. What other materials could we use to find out about the recreation activity?
c. Why do you think we did this orientation activity?

Process: Conduct debriefing using above questions. Provide opportunity for each person to respond to at least one of the questions.

3. Introduction

Content: "People who are attempting to gather as much information as possible in order to make decisions about their leisure participation must learn to use as many sources of information as they can. Printed sources of information are excellent, but may not always be available. Often the quickest and most efficient method of gathering information will be to get it from other people. Developing the ability to get information from leisure service providers is an important task."

Process: Introduce topic of using human resources facilitating leisure participation.

4. Presentation

Content: "In general, there are three methods by which you can get information about opportunities for leisure participation from other people. One common method is by using the *telephone,* another is to request information through written *letters,* and a third method is to *visit* in person and speak directly to individuals from whom one is seeking assistance. People who know how to use human resources to facilitate their leisure participation are skilled at these three ways of obtaining information."

Process: Present information on the different ways participants can access human resources. List key points on an easel or chalkboard:

USE TELEPHONE
WRITE LETTERS
TALK IN PERSON

- use telephone
- write letters
- talk in person

5. Presentation

Content: "Using a telephone is a quick and efficient way to obtain information from a leisure service provider. It is quick in that it usually provides instant answers to questions. It is efficient in that it allows one to speak directly with others without having to be in their presence. This saves travel time and expense. Successive telephone calls enable a person to communicate with several other individuals in several other locations, all in a short time period. This is a major advantage of the telephone.

"To use the telephone successfully and efficiently, one needs to know who to call and precisely what information one is seeking. The following procedure would be appropriate:

a.   Obtain the telephone number of the agency or facility you wish to call.
b.   If possible, know the name of the person to whom you wish to speak.
c.   Know in advance the questions you wish to ask and what information you are seeking. For example, what hours are they open, how much does it cost, where are they located, or what kinds of services do they provide? If it is helpful, write down the questions you wish to ask.
d.   Dial the desired number.
e.   When the phone is answered, greet the person and say you are seeking information.
f.   Ask your questions. If necessary, make written notes of the answers.
g.   When you have all the information you need, thank the person, say 'good-bye,' and hang up the receiver.

"It is important to speak clearly, in a moderate tone and with sufficient volume. Use good telephone manners. Be polite. Do not chew gum, eat, or drink while using the telephone. Turn down the volume of radios or television sets or turn them off if they would create unnecessary interference. Try to call at a time when there will be little or no noise from other people at your end of the line.

"If the person who answers the phone asks you with whom you would like to speak and you don't know a name, tell him or her you want to speak with someone who can answer your questions. If you are asked if you can 'hold,' that means you are being asked to wait before someone will come on the line to speak to you. You decide if you want to 'hold' or if you want to call back at a later time. When you are polite and use good telephone manners, you have the right to expect the same from those with whom you are speaking. If you are unhappy with the way you are being treated on the phone, you have the right to ask for better treatment."

Process: Present information on use of the telephone. Outline procedure on chalkboard:

> OBTAIN TELEPHONE NUMBER
> KNOW NAME OF PERSON
> KNOW QUESTIONS
> DIAL NUMBER
> GREET PERSON
> SAY YOU ARE SEEKING INFORMATION
> ASK YOUR QUESTIONS
> MAKE NOTES OF ANSWERS
> THANK PERSON
> SAY 'GOOD-BYE'

- obtain telephone number
- know name of person
- know questions
- dial number
- greet person
- say you are seeking information
- ask your questions
- make notes of answers
- thank person
- say 'good-bye'

6. Discussion

Content:
a. What advantages does use of the telephone have over writing or visiting in person when one is seeking information?
b. What are possible additions to the telephone procedure outlined on the board?
c. Have you used the telephone to seek information related to leisure participation? If so, please describe.
d. What is included in good telephone manners?

Process: Conduct discussion using above questions. Encourage all participants to contribute to the discussion by responding to at least one of the questions.

7. Learning Activity

Preparation: Obtain paper and pencils.

Content: "Each of you will be given the chance to use the telephone to seek information about an opportunity for leisure participation. Each of you will prepare a leisure-related question for which you want an answer. You will then determine the agency or leisure service provider that is best suited to provide the answer. Outline, in writing, the procedure you will follow to ask the question and receive the answer. When you are finished, you will tell the group about your procedure. The group may make suggestions for change. When you are satisfied with the outline, you will then make the call and obtain the information."

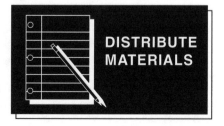

DISTRIBUTE MATERIALS

Process: Explain activity. Provide pencil and paper. Remind participants they may use procedure on board as model for their outline. Provide each participant with opportunity to share outline with large group. After calls are made, move to debriefing.

8. Debriefing

Content:
   a. What question were you trying to answer?
   b. Who did you call for the answer?
   c. Did you have difficulty in reaching the right agency or service provider? If so, please explain.
   d. What answer did you receive?
   e. What was your impression of the agency or person that gave the answer? Why?
   f. How confident are you about using the phone to get information about leisure services?
   g. For what other purposes will you use the telephone?

Process: Conduct debriefing using above questions. Encourage all participants to contribute by responding to at least one of the questions.

9. Presentation

Preparation: Write several sample letters.

Content: "There are times when seeking information by writing is the most feasible method to use. A letter may be used when you do not have access to a telephone, lack transportation to the information source, or do not have time to make a personal visit. It may be that you simply prefer to write. Whatever the reason, acquiring information by writing and asking for it is one more way of being able to use human resources to facilitate leisure participation.

"When writing a letter, you must be very careful in explaining what information is being sought. This means you must think clearly and be sure that the questions being asked are easily understood and you are asking for the right information. Unlike the telephone, where clarification can be sought and received instantly, a letter that is not clear can result in unnecessary delay and additional correspondence.

"There is a format to follow that is helpful in organizing a letter. If a writer uses a format similar to the following, the reader will find it very helpful:

   a. Write the date near the top and at the left margin.
   b. Put your address and telephone number under the date.
   c. Next, put the name and address of the person or agency to whom you are writing.
   d. Write the salutation (Dear _____:).
   e. Write the body of the letter.
   f. Close by thanking the person or agency.
   g. After the body of the letter, write 'Sincerely.'
   h. Sign your name.

"Using this format will help you organize your letter, but remember that to be very clear about what you are asking is the most important feature. The more specific the questions, the more likely they will be answered to your satisfaction."

Process: Present information on writing a letter. Distribute sample letters to demonstrate as models. Put suggested format on chalkboard:

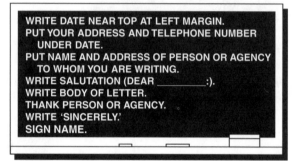

DISTRIBUTE MATERIALS

- Write date near top at left margin.
- Put your address and telephone number under date.
- Put name and address of person or agency to whom you are writing.
- Write salutation (Dear _____:).
- Write body of letter.
- Thank person or agency.
- Write 'Sincerely.'
- Sign name.

WRITE DATE NEAR TOP AT LEFT MARGIN.
PUT YOUR ADDRESS AND TELEPHONE NUMBER UNDER DATE.
PUT NAME AND ADDRESS OF PERSON OR AGENCY TO WHOM YOU ARE WRITING.
WRITE SALUTATION (DEAR _____:).
WRITE BODY OF LETTER.
THANK PERSON OR AGENCY.
WRITE 'SINCERELY.'
SIGN NAME.

10. Discussion

Content:
   a.   Why should we make letters clear and accurate?
   b.   Have you written letters to get information about leisure participation opportunities? If so, please describe.
   c.   Are there questions or suggestions related to the sample format? If so, what are they?

Process: Conduct discussion using above questions. Encourage all participants to contribute by responding to at least one of the questions.

11. Learning Activity

Preparation: Obtain paper and pens (pencils).

Content: "Each of you will be given the chance to practice writing letters to seek leisure-related information. You will select three different agencies or leisure service providers and decide what information you wish to seek from each of them. Write a letter to each of them, asking them what you want. When you finish writing, you will read each of your letters to the group. The group will listen and, if needed, make suggestions for improvement. You will then choose one of your letters and send it. If you wish, you may mail all three."

Process: Explain activity. Provide pen and paper. Ensure each participant has opportunity to read his or her letters to group. Encourage constructive suggestions.

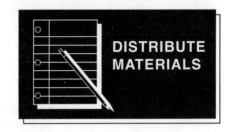

DISTRIBUTE MATERIALS

12. Debriefing

Content:
 a. To whom did you write?
 b. What did you ask?
 c. Was it difficult to express clearly what you were asking for?
 d. How do you feel about your ability to write a clear letter?
 e. How else will you use your letter-writing ability?

Process: Conduct debriefing using above questions. Encourage all participants to contribute by responding to at least one of the questions.

13. Presentation

Content: "The third method that is commonly used to obtain information from other individuals or agencies is to visit with them face-to-face. There may be several reasons why one would prefer to obtain information in this manner. Visiting a leisure service agency or facility enables one to see the place, talk directly with the people who are answering questions, and pick-up any free materials they may have.

"There is a pattern of behavior that is appropriate when visiting a leisure-service provider for the purpose of obtaining information. Usually the first thing you find when entering the agency is a reception desk. Go directly to the desk. If you are looking for a specific person, it is best to have made an appointment with that person. Tell the receptionist you are there to see that person. If you do not have an appointment, the receptionist can help you get the information you need or direct you to people who can help you. Be clear in stating what you are seeking. After you have what you came for, thank those who helped you, and leave."

Process: Present information on visiting in person. Demonstrate behaviors while they are being discussed.

14. Discussion

Content:
 a. Have you visited a leisure agency to ask for information? If so, please describe.
 b. Where are some places you could visit to seek information?
 c. Can you describe the appropriate behavior for visiting a place to ask for information? If so, please do.
 d. Why should one go directly to a receptionist's desk or counter?
 e. Why is it important not to loiter after you have what you came for?

Process: Conduct debriefing using above questions. Encourage all participants to contribute by responding to at least one of the questions.

15. Learning Activity

Content: "This activity is like a homework assignment. Each of you will select a leisure service provider and make plans to visit that person sometime within the next week. Before you visit, decide what it is you want to find out. You may have many questions you want to ask. If you wish, you may write these questions to remind yourself of what they are. Each of you will tell the group what you are asking before making the visit. If appropriate, the group may make suggestions for additions or changes. After your visit, you will share the results with the group."

Process: Explain activity. Provide each participant with opportunity to share questions with group prior to making visit. Emphasize deadline of one week for visit to occur. Debrief after visit.

16. Debriefing

Content:
    a.   Where did you visit?
    b.   What were you trying to learn?
    c.   What did you learn?
    d.   Were you comfortable during the visit?
    e.   Where are some other places you could visit?

Process: Conduct debriefing using above questions. Encourage all participants to contribute by responding to at least one of the questions.

17. Conclusion

Content: "Developing the ability to utilize human resources to facilitate leisure participation is a necessary task. Dealing with others should always be done in a polite and courteous manner. Doing so will enable one to take full advantage of all the resources available to obtain information and make intelligent decisions related to leisure."

Process: Make concluding statements. Provide opportunity for questions.

Objective 5.4: Use agency resources facilitating leisure participation.

1. Introduction

Preparation: Prepare sheets of paper with the following questions, one question per sheet:

PREPARE FOR SESSION

    1.   What are examples of state and national facilities and areas that can be used for recreation purposes?
    2.   What are examples of voluntary or youth-serving agencies that can be used for recreation purposes?

3. What are examples of facilities that are available through the public schools that can be used for recreation purposes?
4. What are examples of commercial or private facilities that can be used for recreation purposes?

Content: "Each of you has been given a colored sheet of paper with a question written on the top of it. Find a person, introduce yourself, and find out the person's name. Ask the person the question written at the top of your paper. If the person is able to answer it, write the response on the paper

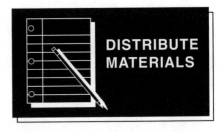

DISTRIBUTE MATERIALS

and record his or her name immediately following the answer. If someone else has already provided that answer, write the new name beside the name of the last person that provided you with that information. If the person is unable to answer the question, read him or her whatever information, if any, is recorded on your paper. Now the person will ask you his or her question. Try to answer it as best you can. The person will respond in the same way you did to him or her. The object is to get as many answers as possible to your question. Once you have both tried to answer each other's questions, thank the person and find another person and begin the process again. Continue until you speak with everyone in the room or I provide the signal to stop."

Process: Walk around the room and assist any participants having difficulty. Once a person gets three of a kind, the debriefing questions can be asked. Establish a signal to stop the activity, such as flickering of the lights.

2. Debriefing

Content:
   a. How can the agency sources help you to utilize your leisure?
   b. What other agencies could we use to find out about the recreation activity?
   c. Why do you think we did this orientation activity?

Process: Conduct debriefing using above questions. Provide opportunity for each person to respond to at least one of the questions.

3. Introduction

Content: "Most communities contain a variety of agencies, organizations, and enterprises that exist for the primary purpose of making leisure opportunities available to the general public, or to certain segments of it. These entities can be a very valuable resource for most of us. The greater your knowledge of such resources, the broader your options for taking part in enjoyable and satisfying activities."

Process: Introduce topic of using agency resources facilitating leisure participation.

4. Presentation

Content: "The leisure service providers that exist in a community cannot always be neatly categorized. They are sometimes quite diverse and what exists in one community may not exist in another. But, in general, the providers can be placed in one of the following categories:

    a.   public;
    b.   voluntary;
    c.   school;
    d.   religious organizations; or
    e.   private/commercial.

"Developing an understanding of each of these categories can help individuals take better advantage of their services."

Process: Present information on public agencies. Use chalkboard or easel to list major points:

- public
- voluntary/youth-serving
- school
- church/religious
- private/commercial

PUBLIC
VOLUNTARY/YOUTH-SERVING
SCHOOL
CHURCH/RELIGIOUS
PRIVATE/COMMERCIAL

5. Presentation

Content: "*Public agencies* are supported by some level of government. They are agencies that are funded primarily by tax dollars. In our country, the city, county, state, and federal governments all have agencies that manage areas and facilities for the purpose of providing leisure opportunities for their citizens. The most common of these public leisure-service agencies is the municipal (city) park and recreation department.

"Municipal park and recreation departments, because they are supported by public taxes, provide programs and services for all segments of the public within their jurisdiction (the city limits). Some of their programs are designed to appeal to specific groups, such as youth, elderly, or people with disabilities. Some are designed to appeal to specific interests, such as athletic competition, arts and crafts, or outdoor recreation. Some of their programs are designed to accommodate large groups of people and some are designed to appeal to small groups and individuals. Some programs are highly structured and require formal leadership. Some are informal and allow for direction to come from the participants. Although it is not possible for municipal departments to provide all things to all people, they do attempt to provide a diversity of offerings that will appeal to a diversity of people. They operate on a year-round basis and provide facilities and services in most geographic areas of the community.

"Although municipal departments are funded primarily with public monies, they often assess a participation fee or admission charge. The fees are usually very reasonable and are collected to defray expenses, rather than to generate a profit. Thus, the fees are generally less than one would pay for a similar program or service in the private sector.

"Because municipal departments are public agencies, they are obligated to provide for the public and are prohibited from discriminating against any groups or individuals. They are the major, and in some instances the only, provider of leisure services for some segments of the population, including the economically disadvantaged and people with disabilities.

"Information about their programs and services is available through a variety of sources. Newspapers often carry their program schedules, along with information related to registering and participating. Radio and television stations sometimes provide coverage. Pamphlets and brochures may be obtained at most recreation centers, special facilities (such as a zoo or observatory), and their administrative offices. Employees of municipal park and recreation departments are public servants. It is their obligation to serve the public by aiding its participation in their programs.

"State and federal government agencies also provide leisure opportunities, although they are less involved than municipal departments in offering direct programs. State and federal agencies are more likely to provide areas and facilities, such as *state and national parks, forests, wildlife refuges,* and other *outdoor recreation areas.* State and federal agencies do provide direct programming in their *hospital, prison,* and *military* facilities."

Process: Present information on public agencies. Use chalkboard or easel to list examples of state and federal facilities and programs that can be used for recreation purposes.

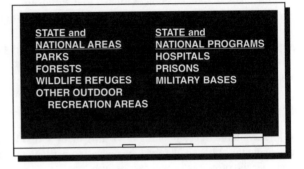

STATE and NATIONAL AREAS	STATE and NATIONAL PROGRAMS
PARKS	HOSPITALS
FORESTS	PRISONS
WILDLIFE REFUGES	MILITARY BASES
OTHER OUTDOOR RECREATION AREAS	

STATE and NATIONAL AREAS

- parks
- forests
- wildlife refuges
- other outdoor recreation areas

STATE and NATIONAL PROGRAMS

- hospitals
- prisons
- military bases

6. Discussion

Content:
a.   Why are municipal departments obligated to serve the public?
b.   In which programs provided by the municipal department have you participated?
c.   Did you have to pay to participate? If so, how much?
d.   How did you learn about their programs?
e.   How else can one learn about their services?
f.   In which programs would you like to take part but have not yet done so?
g.   What has prevented you from participating?

Process: Conduct discussion using above questions. Encourage all participants to contribute to the discussion by responding to at least one of the questions.

7. Presentation

Content: "*Voluntary/youth-serving agencies* make an important contribution to the spectrum of leisure opportunities available in most communities. Voluntary/youth-serving agencies are entities such as the *YWCA, YMCA, Jewish Community Centers, Girl Scouts, Boy Scouts, Girls' Clubs* and *Boys' Clubs.* Because they are not government agencies, they have the option of choosing what kinds of programs to offer and to whom they wish to offer them. These agencies generally focus on a specific segment of the public and direct their programs and services toward it. Some agencies, such as the Ys, serve a broader portion of the public than other agencies, such as the Scouts. The Scouts focus on a limited age group and, often, on one gender. The Ys offer a wider variety of programs to more age groups and usually to both genders.

"Voluntary/youth-serving agencies often offer instructional classes in recreation activities as part of their programs. Most of these classes are designed to accommodate beginners. Learning about these classes and how to participate in them can provide individuals with broader choices related to their leisure.

"These agencies depend on contributions, membership dues, program participation fees, and support from organizations such as the United Way. They do not receive support from tax dollars and are responsible for generating their own funds. The fees assessed for participating in their programs are usually moderate and within the reach of most of us.

"Voluntary/youth-serving agencies are eager to provide leisure opportunities to as many participants as possible. They publicize their programs through the mass media and their own printed pamphlets and brochures. Information concerning their programs is also available by telephoning or visiting them. Individuals who are interested in acquiring the skills and knowledge needed to participate in a variety of activities can consider the offerings of voluntary/youth-serving agencies as part of the total leisure package available in a community."

Process: Present information on voluntary/youth-serving agencies. Use chalkboard or easel to list examples of agencies and major points:

- YWCA
- YMCA
- Jewish Community
  Centers
- Boys' Clubs
- Girls' Clubs
- Boy Scouts
- Girl Scouts

8. Discussion

Content:
   a.   Which voluntary/youth-serving agencies exist in our community?
   b.   How do voluntary/youth-serving agencies differ from municipal park and recreation departments? How are they alike?
   c.   Have you participated in leisure programs provided by a voluntary/youth-serving agency? If so, please describe.
   d.   Have you ever wanted to participate in one of their programs, but were unable? If so, please describe.
   e.   How can one learn about their programs?

Process: Conduct debriefing using above questions. Encourage all participants to contribute by responding to at least one of the questions.

9. Presentation

Content: "In many communities the *public schools* are a major provider of leisure opportunities. In some instances, the public recreation program is offered through the schools; in other instances, the schools cooperate closely with the municipal park and recreation department. A major way in which schools cooperate with municipal agencies is by allowing the use of school facilities. Most schools have facilities such as *outdoor playing fields, playgrounds, gymnasiums, auditoriums, shops,* and *multipurpose rooms* that can support a wide variety of recreation activities.

"Some schools are involved in community education programs that offer a wide range of activities to all segments of the population, not just the school-age population. The program offerings are similar to those that would be found in a municipal park and recreation department or some voluntary/youth-serving agencies. They serve to increase the richness of leisure opportunities in a community."

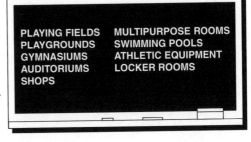

Process: Present information on schools and leisure opportunities. List examples on an easel or chalkboard of possible facilities available through the public schools.

- playing fields
- playgrounds
- gymnasiums
- auditoriums
- shops

- multipurpose rooms
- swimming pools
- athletic equipment
- locker rooms

10. Discussion

Content:
- a. What role can the school play in enhancing leisure opportunities in a community?
- b. Which schools in your community are used by the public for recreation purposes?
- c. Are the school's facilities accessible to people with disabilities?
- d. Are there any school-sponsored leisure programs that are open to the public? If so, what are they?
- e. If you wanted to participate in one of these programs, what steps would you take?
- f. Have you ever participated in any of these programs? If so, which ones?

Process: Conduct discussion using above questions. Encourage all participants to contribute to the discussion by responding to at least one of the questions.

11. Presentation

Content: "*Religious organizations* sometimes sponsor recreation activities. Often, these activities are for members of their own parish or congregation, but sometimes they are open to nonmembers. Such programs usually stress fellowship and social interaction.

"In some communities, religious organizations cooperate with the municipal agency by offering to share facilities, if appropriate, and by attempting to avoid duplication of the municipal program. If an individual is seeking a specific type of leisure activity and cannot find it in other places, there is a possibility it can be found through a program sponsored by a religious organization."

Process: Present information on church and religious organizations.

12. Discussion

Content:

    a.   Are you aware of any leisure programs sponsored by religious organizations? If so, what are they?

    b.   Have you participated in such a program? If so, please describe.

    c.   Are there programs in the community in which you have wanted to participate but were unable? If so, what prevented you?

    d.   How can one learn about leisure programs sponsored by religious organizations?

    e.   If such a program existed and you wanted to participate, what would you do?

Process: Conduct debriefing using above questions. Encourage all participants to contribute by responding to at least one of the questions.

13. Presentation

Content: "*The private/commercial sector* offers a very wide variety of leisure opportunities. The breadth of opportunities is so great that it is sometimes difficult to grasp. The private/commercial sector comprises all enterprises that offer leisure opportunities for the purpose of making a profit. This would include *movie theaters, bowling establishments, restaurants, health and fitness clubs, arcades, resorts, amusement parks,* and a host of other enterprises.

"The private/commercial sector uses many methods to inform the public of its offerings. It advertises extensively through newspapers, radio and television, and signs and billboards. Because they are in business to make a profit from the public, they make a strong effort to keep abreast of current trends and to offer those activities that are popular.

"Becoming aware of all the possibilities available through the private/commercial sector is a task that requires some effort. The effort, however, will result in the reward of having a vast array of possibilities from which to choose. The possibilities of the private/commercial sector further enrich the local leisure opportunities."

Process: Present information on the private/commercial sector. List examples of private or commercial recreation opportunities on an easel or chalkboard:

COMMERCIAL/PRIVATE FACILITIES

- movie theaters
- bowling alleys

- restaurants
- health and fitness clubs
- arcades
- resorts
- amusement parks

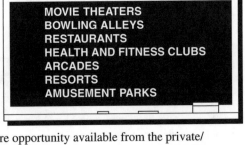

14. Discussion

Content:

a. What is an example of a leisure opportunity available from the private/ commercial sector?
b. What was your last leisure experience through the private/commercial sector?
c. How can you learn what is available through the private/commercial sector?
d. If you could choose any activity available from the private/commercial sector, what would it be?

Process: Conduct discussion using above questions. Encourage all participants to contribute by responding to at least one of the questions.

15. Learning Activity

Preparation: Obtain telephone books, brochures, pamphlets, and newspapers. Create master list of types of information desired. List could include:

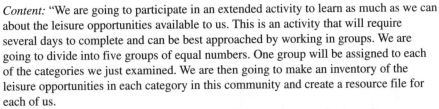

- name, address, and phone number of agency or organization
- programs and activities offered
- transportation available to reach activity sites
- costs of participation, if any
- special equipment required, if any
- membership or eligibility restrictions, if any

Content: "We are going to participate in an extended activity to learn as much as we can about the leisure opportunities available to us. This is an activity that will require several days to complete and can be best approached by working in groups. We are going to divide into five groups of equal numbers. One group will be assigned to each of the categories we just examined. We are then going to make an inventory of the leisure opportunities in each category in this community and create a resource file for each of us.

"We must first agree about what we want to know about entries in each category. Each group will generate a list of the kinds of information that would be helpful to include about all of the agencies, organizations, and enterprises in our resource file. The lists will be compared to see that we have not overlooked anything and a master list will be created. After we have agreed on the content of the master list, each group will use all the means at its disposal to gather the information desired. The information will be duplicated so that each of you will have your own leisure resource file."

Process: Explain activity. Divide into groups. Assign one group to each of the following:

- public
- voluntary/youth-serving
- school
- religious organizations
- private/commercial

Provide telephone directories, brochures, pamphlets, newspapers, and other tools to groups. Obtain information and duplicate, collate, and distribute.

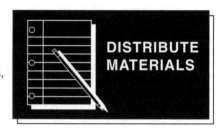

DISTRIBUTE MATERIALS

16. Debriefing

Content:
  a. Did you have difficulty in getting information you desired? If so, how did you cope with the difficulty?
  b. What is your opinion of the variety of resources that have been identified?
  c. Of what value will this resource file be to you?

Process: Conduct debriefing using above questions. Encourage all participants to contribute by responding to at least one of the questions.

17. Conclusion

Content: "Each of the categories of leisure-service providers that we have examined makes a contribution to the total resources available in a community. To effectively utilize those resources, one must know something about them. Knowing differences and similarities that exist among these categories can provide valuable guide posts in arriving at intelligent decisions related to leisure participation."

Process: Make concluding statements. Provide opportunity for questions.

Appendix F
Leisure Education
Specific Program #6

MAKE DECISIONS
ABOUT LEISURE PARTICIPATION

Purpose, Goal, and Objectives

Purpose: Provide opportunities for participants to learn to identify personal leisure participation goals, and activities to achieve these goals, by using a decision-making process.

GOAL 6: DEMONSTRATE ABILITY TO MAKE DECISIONS REGARDING LEISURE PARTICIPATION.

Objective 6.1: Identify leisure goals.
Objective 6.2: Identify activities to achieve leisure goals.
Objective 6.3: Demonstrate knowledge of the advantages and disadvantages of doing identified activities.
Objective 6.4: Demonstrate ability to prioritize advantages and disadvantages of doing identified activities.
Objective 6.5: State a leisure decision.

Goal and Objectives: Performance Measures

GOAL 6: DEMONSTRATE ABILITY TO MAKE DECISIONS REGARDING LEISURE PARTICIPATION.

Objective 6.1: Identify leisure goals.
Performance Measure: Given paper and pencil, within five minutes and with 100% accuracy on two consecutive occasions:
  (a) determine two personal leisure goals (e.g., get to know other people, improve my physical fitness, enhance my skills, do something I like); and
  (b) state one reason for developing each of the two leisure goals (e.g., "I would like to make more friends," "I want to get more exercise to become more physically fit," "I want to take lessons to improve my tennis skills," "I want to do more activities for my own enjoyment").

Objective 6.2: Identify activities to achieve leisure goals.

Performance Measure: Given a list of two personal leisure goals, paper and pencil, within five minutes and with 100% accuracy on two consecutive occasions:

(a) identify three recreation activities to achieve each of the leisure goals (e.g., get to know other people: join a church group, play softball, join a square dance club, volunteer at a hospital; improve the way I feel about myself: learn to swim, take a self-defense course, learn to drive; improve my skills: attend a workshop to learn better communication skills, join and attend a fitness center, read a book, learn basic car maintenance); and

(b) describe why each activity was chosen (e.g., join a church group: "I know people who have met some of their best friends at church groups;" learn to swim: "I often feel helpless around the water and I think learning to swim would help me feel better about myself").

Objective 6.3: Demonstrate knowledge of the advantages and disadvantages of doing identified activities.

Performance Measure: Given a verbal prompt, within two minutes on two consecutive occasions, participant will identify two advantages and two disadvantages each of at least two activities intended to achieve a personal leisure goal.

Objective 6.4: Demonstrate ability to prioritize advantages and disadvantages of doing identified activities.

Performance Measure: Given the list of advantages and disadvantages from previous performance objective, within two minutes, participant will place the advantages in order from most desirable to least desirable and the disadvantages from least desirable to most desirable.

Objective 6.5: State a leisure decision and demonstrate knowledge of the rationale for that leisure decision.

Performance Measure A: Given the prioritized list of advantages and disadvantages from the previous performance measure, within two minutes, participant will state a leisure decision.

Performance Measure B: Given the leisure decision from the previous performance measure, within two minutes, participant will state the reason for making the leisure decision.

Goal and Objectives: Content and Process

GOAL 6: DEMONSTRATE ABILITY TO MAKE DECISIONS REGARDING LEISURE PARTICIPATION.

Objective 6.1: Identify leisure goals.

1. Orientation Activity

Content: "Please arrange yourselves in a circle for an activity that will help you begin to think about identifying personal leisure participation goals. Take a minute to think of a recreation activity in which you are strongly interested, but have not yet done. It should be an activity in which you have a realistic chance to participate. We will go around the circle clockwise and you may take turns introducing yourselves by your first name and telling the group which recreation activity you would like to try. Remember, it should be an activity you are interested in doing."

Process: Explain the activity. Arrange participants in a circle. Allow time for participants to think of an activity. Ensure that each participant has an opportunity to introduce himself or herself and state activity.

2. Introduction

Content: "A personal goal is something you want to accomplish, acquire, or maintain. It is something you are willing to take some action to achieve. To achieve a goal it is helpful to have both the desire to achieve the goal and the willingness to expend the effort required to do so. Identifying personal leisure goals is an important step in growth and development. As we develop skills and knowledge, we are in a better position to have a meaningful and rewarding leisure lifestyle. Developing leisure goals becomes the first step in a decision-making process you can use regarding leisure participation choices. Identifying goals will be used as step number one in a five step decision-making process."

Process: Introduce topic on identifying personal leisure participation goals. Write on an easel the phrase "personal goal" and then add the following words as they are stated "desire and willingness."

3. Presentation

Content: "Identifying personal leisure goals is a process that requires concentration and energy. There are some guidelines available to help in the process. Following these guidelines should make the task of identifying personal leisure goals a rewarding process.

a. *Your goals are your own.* You are more likely to achieve goals you set for yourself than you are to achieve goals set for you by others. Goals are based on your own values. This does not mean that you cannot adopt a goal that has been suggested by someone else. It does mean that if you are adopting the goal, you have thought it through carefully, determined it as something desired, and made a commitment to accomplish it. In general, however, the best goals for you are those you have identified for yourself.

b. *Goals are clear, precise, and written.* Writing goals tends to clarify them and make them more real. When a written goal is not stated clearly, it often means it has not been thought through clearly. Goals are often revised as they are the subject of more thought. Putting them in writing helps the process of revision. Also, when goals are written, we are more likely to feel a commitment to accomplishing them. A written goal serves to remind you of its presence.

c. *Some goals are accomplished in the short term.* A short-term goal is one that can be accomplished in a relatively short time, such as several days or a few weeks. Short-term goals that are easily attainable are very valuable. They can give you the confidence needed to tackle long-term and more challenging goals. Short-term goals are also more easily controlled. There are fewer chances of unforeseen circumstances interfering with the achievement of short-term goals.

d. *Goals are based on values.* Most individuals have a belief system that places a high priority on values. Goals should be identified in accordance with your belief system. An important consideration for you is how you will feel when the goal is accomplished. If the goal is achieved at the expense of your values, the feelings of reward and satisfaction that should come to you will be diminished by feelings of sorrow and guilt.

e. *Goals are realistic.* Identifying goals is a necessary first step to accomplishing them, but if they are not realistic, they belong to the realm of fantasy. A common difficulty for people who are setting goals for the first time is that they set them too high; however, that does not imply that goals must be low—it simply means there must be a reasonable chance to attain your goal. Who is the best judge of what is realistic? You are. If it feels right to you, if it makes sense to you (and perhaps to trusted friends), then it can be regarded as realistic.

f. *Goals are measurable.* Goals must be written in such a manner that individuals will know when they have been successful in attaining them. Goals should, therefore, be clear to you. Others should agree with you if you have attained your goals, if the goals are measurable.

g. *Goals have definite deadlines for achievement.* Assigning target dates for the achievement of goals helps you maintain focus on what you need to accomplish. The achievement of goals by target dates results in feelings of satisfaction. Target dates can be altered if changing circumstances warrant it, but they should remain a part of every written goal.

"To summarize, the process of identifying goals is most effective when the goals are personal, clearly written, at least some are short-term, moral and ethical, realistic, measurable, and include deadlines for achievement."

Process: Present information on identifying goals and areas where personal leisure goals are often focused. List guidelines and areas on easel or chalkboard:

> GOALS ARE YOUR OWN
> GOALS ARE CLEAR, PRECISE, AND WRITTEN
> SOME GOALS ARE ACCOMPLISHED IN THE SHORT TERM
> GOALS ARE BASED ON MORAL AND ETHICAL VALUES
> GOALS ARE REALISTIC
> GOALS ARE MEASURABLE
> GOALS HAVE DEADLINES FOR ACHIEVEMENT

- goals are your own
- goals are clear, precise, and written
- some goals are accomplished in the short term
- goals are based on moral and ethical values
- goals are realistic
- goals are measurable
- goals have deadlines for achievement

4. Discussion

Content:

a. What is the value of determining your own goals?
b. What advantage is there to writing your goals?
c. Have you ever written a personal goal? If so, please describe.
d. What is the value in having some short-term goals?
e. What role do deadlines play in establishing goals?

Process: Conduct discussion using above questions. Encourage all participants to contribute to the discussion by having each person respond to at least one of the questions. If participants are prepared to share some of their goals, you can record these on an easel or chalkboard. Record the areas presented by the participants in response to the last question on the easel or chalkboard.

5. Learning Activity

Preparation: Obtain paper and pencils.

Content: "We are going to identify some leisure goals. Each of you will be given pencil and paper. Take a few minutes to think about some things you would like to accomplish. Do not worry about whether others will be impressed with your goals. The only person who has to approve your personal goals is you. Remember, when you identify personal goals, it is important to be realistic. Try to identify a minimum of five personal leisure goals. Write your goals on your sheet of paper. Do not be concerned at this point with the way your goals are written; just write them on the paper. When you are finished, you will have the chance to share some of your goals with the group. Take your time and have fun."

Process: Explain the activity. Provide participants with pencil and paper. Allow sufficient time for participants to identify their goals. Encourage each participant to share his or her goals with the group.

6. Debriefing

Content:
   a.   In what way was this exercise difficult or easy?
   b.   What contributed to you identifying your goals?
   c.   Of the goals you identified, which two are the most important to you?

Process: Conduct debriefing using above questions. Encourage all participants to contribute by responding to at least one of the questions.

7. Learning Activity

Content: "Now that you have identified some personal leisure goals, take a few more minutes and identify which are long-term and which are short-term. Look at your list of goals and put an 'L' by those goals you think are long-term and an 'S' by those you think are short-term."

Process: Explain the activity. Provide an example if participants appear to be having difficulty. After a few minutes, move to debriefing.

8. Debriefing

Content:
   a. Did you have both long-term and short-term goals on your list?
   b. How did you decide which was a long-term goal and which was a short-term goal?
   c. How can achieving short-term goals lead to the accomplishment of long-term goals?
   d. Which short-term goal do you want to accomplish first?

9. Conclusion

Content: "You have been given some guidelines to follow in the process of identifying personal leisure goals. Applying these guidelines should be helpful. Identifying goals is simply a matter of deciding what you want to do in the short-term or long-term. Identifying goals is the first step to achieving them and the first step in making decisions about leisure participation."

Process: Make concluding statements. Provide opportunities for questions.

Objective 6.2: Identify possible activities to achieve leisure goals.

1. Orientation Activity

Content: "We are going to do an activity that will help us become aware of the variety of recreation activities that exist. Please arrange yourselves in a circle. I will select a person to begin the activity. That person will introduce himself or herself and name a recreation activity that begins with the letter 'A' (e.g., archery). The first person to the left will introduce himself or herself and name an activity that begins with the letter 'B' (baseball). The next person to the left will introduce himself or herself and name an activity that begins with the letter 'C' (e.g., crossword puzzles). Play will continue clockwise around the circle. If a person gets stuck on a letter, the group may help by suggesting activities. If the group gets stuck, go to the next letter. Let's try to get through the alphabet twice. The second time around, the activity named for a letter must be different from that which was named the first time."

Process: Explain the activity. Arrange participants in a circle. If a participant is unable to name an activity after one minute, ask the group to help. If the group cannot help after one minute, proceed to next letter. Create a relaxed atmosphere by encouraging participants to contribute to the activity and supporting those individuals who may be having difficulty identifying an activity.

2. Debriefing

Content:
   a. Were there any activities named which were new to you? If so, which ones?
   b. Which activity mentioned is your favorite?
   c. Did this exercise help you think of any activities you might choose to help you meet a personal leisure goal? How so?

Process: Conduct debriefing using above questions. Encourage all participants to contribute by having each person respond to at least one of the questions.

3. Introduction

Content: "Identifying personal leisure goals is the first step in making decisions regarding leisure participation. When personal leisure goals have been identified, you can examine recreation activities that will help you achieve these goals. Identifying possible activities to achieve your leisure goal is the second step in the decision making process. There are many activities that have the potential to help you achieve your goal. The more aware you are of possible activities, the more choices you will have."

Process: Introduce topic of identifying activities to achieve leisure goals.

4. Presentation

Content: "After you determine the personal leisure goals you would like to achieve, the next step is to consider which activities could assist you in meeting your goals. It is likely that several activities could help you achieve each of your specific leisure goals. You do not need to participate in, or even identify, all of these possible activities. It is helpful, however, to be aware of a variety of activities that will assist you in achieving your goal."

Process: Present information on identifying activities to achieve goals.

5. Discussion

Content:
    a. What is the value of being aware of a variety of recreation activities?
    b. What are some different recreation activities that will help you achieve your goals?
    c. What could you do to increase your knowledge of possible recreation activities?

Process: Conduct discussion using above questions. Encourage all participants to contribute to the discussion by responding to at least one of the questions.

6. Learning Activity

Preparation: Obtain paper, scissors, magazines, and glue. Prepare sheets by dividing a piece of paper into 25 equal squares. Put name of one recreation activity into each square. Activities could include art, bowling, checkers, dining out, exercising, fishing, golfing, and hiking.

PREPARE FOR SESSION

Content: "We are going to play a type of cooperative bingo to help us think about different recreation activities. I will give each of you a sheet that has been divided into 25 equal squares, five across and five down. Each square contains the name of a recreation activity. Each of you will be given a pair of scissors, glue, and several magazines. Look through the magazines for pictures that match the recreation activities in the squares. When you find a picture that matches, cut it out and glue it to the appropriate square. You must fill five squares horizontally, vertically, or diagonally to complete your bingo. When you are finished check with another person to see if that person got bingo. If the person did not get bingo please assist the person until he or she has bingo. Keep assisting each other until all group members are finished. You have 10 minutes to complete cooperative bingo. Try to beat the clock and work together. Please begin."

Process: Explain activity. Distribute sheets. Provide scissors, glue, and magazines. Give signal to begin.

7. Debriefing

Content:

a. Of the pictures you found, how many showed activities in which you participate?
b. Did you find activities you have not tried but that you would like to try? If so, which ones?
c. What did you learn about possible activities available to you?
d. Of all the pictures you found, which is the most interesting to you? Please explain.
e. What are your comments about cooperative bingo?

8. Conclusion

Content: "Identifying activities that can lead to the achievement of personal leisure goals is an important part of making decisions about your leisure participation. The more knowledge you have, the easier it is to identify activities."

Process: Make concluding statements. Provide opportunities for participants to ask questions.

Objective 6.3: Demonstrate knowledge of the advantages and disadvantages of doing identified activities.

1. Orientation Activity

Preparation: Obtain a paper bag. Write advantages and disadvantages of leisure participants on slips of paper. Some examples include:

ADVANTAGES	DISADVANTAGES
• exercise	• tiring
• see others	• expensive
• fun	• time-consuming

Content: "I have a paper bag and in the bag are slips of paper containing often used advantages and disadvantages to participating in activities. An example of an advantage might be 'It is great exercise,' and example of a disadvantage might be: 'It costs too much.' I will come around to each of you. Please select a slip of paper from the bag and read it, indicate if it is an advantage or disadvantage and give a leisure activity you feel is appropriate to the statement. So if you select 'it costs too much' you would say it is a disadvantage and an appropriate activity might be 'golf.'

Process: Explain the activity. Offer participation opportunity to each individual.

2.   Introduction

Content: "Remember that the first step of decision making is the identification of goals. When you have identified several activities that might contribute to the achievement of your personal leisure goals, the second step of the decision-making process has been completed. But, there are several equally important decision-making steps that remain. The third step requires that you consider the advantages and disadvantages of the activities you have identified to accomplish your personal leisure goals. Reviewing the advantages and disadvantages of possible activities is necessary before informed decisions about leisure participation can be made."

Process: Introduce topic on reviewing advantages and disadvantages of possible activities to accomplish personal leisure goals.

3.   Presentation

Content: "Reviewing the advantages and disadvantages of activities will help eliminate those activities that might not help you achieve your leisure goals. Using swimming as an example, advantages are it can be fun, it provides exercise for your body, and swimming can cool you down on a hot summer day. Disadvantages may be that swimming is not always an activity that is accessible to you, there must be a pool, there might be fees involved, you may not have transportation to a pool, and you need to have a certain level of skill before you can swim independently.

"Here is another example. Suppose one of your personal goals is to have a pet to enjoy in your free time. Looking at the advantages of owning a pet, there is companionship and fun involved in owning a pet. The disadvantages might include additional money spent on food, trips to the vet, and finding someone to care for your pet while you are away. It is helpful to think about the advantages and disadvantages of decisions before you make them."

Process: Provide above information. You may want to solicit examples from participants. On an easel or chalkboard write the following:

SWIMMING

ADVANTAGES	DISADVANTAGES
• fun	• not always accessible
• good exercise	• need a pool
• cool down	• fees
	• transportation
	• skill

4. Discussion

Content:

    a. What are some other advantages of swimming not previously mentioned?

    b. What are some other disadvantages of swimming not previously mentioned?

    c. What are some other advantages or disadvantages with having a pet not previously mentioned?

    d. Why should we determine the advantages and disadvantages of activities before we make a leisure decision?

Process: Conduct discussion using above questions.

5. Learning Activity

Preparation: Make approximately ten cards (same number of participants) and have equal numbers of cards with a beach scene and a mountain scene for participants to choose. Add more scenes such as city scenes until groups are relatively equal.

PREPARE FOR SESSION

Content: "We are going to do an activity to look at the advantages and disadvantages of different travel destinations. Each of you must make a choice. Pick one of the following cards: if you picked a beach card you are in group one, if you picked a mountain card you are in group two. In a few moments you will divide into your groups to discuss traveling to Hawaii, Disneyland, New York City, or the Grand Canyon. Suppose that these are trip locations you are anxious to visit. List the advantages and disadvantages of traveling to each location. Make a group decision about which location you would select to visit. Report to the group your choice and why you made that choice. You will have ten minutes to make your group decision."

Process: Provide directions and allow ten minutes for the groups to list advantages and disadvantages of each location on paper and make a selection.

6. Debriefing

Content:

    a. How did you feel about making a group decision?

    b. Was the group choice your personal choice? If not, what is your choice?

    c. What did you learn from this activity?

Process: Conduct debriefing using above questions. Have each group report on what they discussed.

7. Conclusion:

Content: "Discussing the advantages and disadvantages of an activity can help determine the activity or activities that you will choose to achieve your leisure goals. One way to go through the decision-making process is to follow five steps. To this point we have discussed developing personal leisure goals, selecting a range of possible activities to achieve those goals, and reviewing the advantages and disadvantages of activities."

Process: Make concluding statements. Provide participants with the opportunity to ask questions. Write on a chalkboard or easel the following as it is stated:

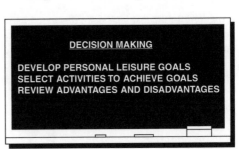

DECISION MAKING

- develop personal leisure goals
- select activities to achieve goals
- review advantages and disadvantages

Objective 6.4: Demonstrate ability to prioritize advantages and disadvantages of doing identified activities.

1. Orientation Activity

Preparation: Obtain paper and pencils.

Content: "I have written a list of six activities on the chalkboard (or easel). I would like you to copy this list onto a piece of paper, but do not place the activities in the order as they appear on the board. Instead, I want you to write down the activity that you think is the best at the top of your page. Below the first activity, list the activity that you think is the second best activity. Continue to list the activities in this way until you have written down all six. After you have finished, we will go around the room and ask several of you to share your list with us."

Process: List six leisure-related activities on the chalkboard or easel. Allow participants several minutes to complete their lists. Once all participants have finished, ask several participants to read their lists aloud.

LEISURE ACTIVITIES

* in-line skating
* tennis
* mountain biking
* painting
* walking
* gardening

2. **Introduction**

Content: "In the last lesson we discussed listing the advantages and disadvantages of identified activities. We learned how listing these advantages and disadvantages is an important step in making leisure decisions and other sorts of decisions too. Today we are going to take things a step further and talk about prioritizing advantages and disadvantages of activities."

Process: Introduce the topic prioritizing goals.

3. **Presentation**

Content: "Determining the advantages and disadvantages of various leisure activities is helpful in making a decision, but it is not enough. Before you can make a leisure decision, it is helpful to first prioritize these advantages and disadvantages. Someone tell us what 'prioritizing' means? Correct, prioritizing means putting things in order such as best to worst or favorite to least favorite. Once advantages and disadvantages are prioritized, we are in a better position to compare advantages to disadvantages. By prioritizing things, we give weight to different advantages and disadvantages so that some are more important in our decision making than others.

"For instance, there are advantages and disadvantages of owning a pet. Advantages might include companionship and stress reduction. Disadvantages might include expense and time commitment. When you look at these advantages and disadvantages, it might seem to you that the advantages of companionship and stress reduction are worth the added expense and time commitment while to another person it might seem that the expense of owning a pet outweighs all other considerations. An important thing to keep in mind about prioritizing is that it is a very personal process and almost everyone will have different priorities."

Process: Present information on prioritizing. If time allows provide additional examples or solicit examples from participants. Write the following on a chalkboard or easel:

OWNING A PET	
ADVANTAGES	**DISADVANTAGES**
COMPANIONSHIP	EXPENSE
STRESS REDUCER	TIME

OWNING A PET

ADVANTAGES   **DISADVANTAGES**

* companionship
* stress reducer

* expense
* time

4.   Discussion

Content:
   a.   How does prioritizing help people make decisions?
   b.   Are all advantages and disadvantages equally important to each person? Please explain.
   c.   What did you learn from this activity?

Process: Conduct discussion using above questions. Encourage all participants to answer at least one question, and allow participants to ask their own questions about prioritizing.

5.   Learning Activity

Preparation: Obtain paper and pencils.

Content: "As we have learned, there are both advantages and disadvantages to almost all activities. We are going to do an activity that will demonstrate how to prioritize advantages of activities. Let's move to the grass outside for this activity. I want you to pretend that it is a beautiful spring Saturday morning and you have the entire day free to do whatever you want. The birds are singing, the air is crisp and clear, and you have the whole day in front of you.

   "Across the top of a piece of paper, I want you to write three activities you might do on a Saturday morning. Then below each activity, I want you to write a list of all of the advantages for doing that activity that you can think of, try to list at least 10. Next, for each item on each list, write down a number between 1 and 10. Assign each advantage a number, attaching smaller numbers to the activities that are the most important to you. It is alright to put the same number down twice, but be sure to choose your numbers carefully."

Process: Explain the activity to participants. Be sure all participants have a piece of paper and a pencil or pen. Allow participants plenty of time to complete their lists.

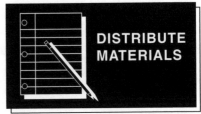

DISTRIBUTE MATERIALS

6.   Debriefing

Content:
   a.   How did you decide which advantages were most important to you?
   b.   Were many of the advantages equally important? Which ones?
   c.   Looking at your lists of advantages, which activity had the most advantages?

Process: Conduct debriefing using above questions. Allow participants to ask their own questions, and encourage all participants to answer at least one of the questions.

7.   Learning Activity

Preparation: Obtain paper and pencils.

Content: "We have just been prioritizing advantages of doing specific recreation activities. Now we will do an activity to concentrate on prioritizing disadvantages. Look at the three activities you listed earlier and, on the same piece of paper, add columns and list the disadvantages of doing those three activities, numbering them as you did before. You will again be prioritizing, this time considering the disadvantages of participating in an activity."

Process: Explain the activity to participants. Be sure all participants have a pencil and paper and adequate time to complete their lists.

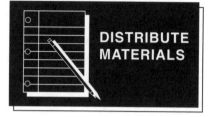

DISTRIBUTE MATERIALS

8. Debriefing

Content:

    a. How did you decide which disadvantages would have more weight?
    b. Were many of the disadvantages equally important? Which ones?
    c. Looking at your list of disadvantages, which activity had the most disadvantages?

Process: Conduct debriefing using above questions. Allow participants to answer at least one question and encourage discussion.

9. Conclusion

Content: "As discussed in this lesson it is important to determine the advantages and disadvantages of identified activities. Prioritizing those advantages and disadvantages becomes the next step in decision making. Making decisions is a personal process, and prioritizing can help you make the best decision possible."

Objective 6.5: State a leisure decision and demonstrate knowledge of the reason for that leisure decision.

1. Orientation Activity

Preparation: Obtain a small bag and create cards (using poster board or cardboard) with different high-risk, unusual activities written on the cards.

PREPARE FOR SESSION

Content: "I am passing around a bag that contains cards with different activities written on them. Each of you take two cards, then decide which activity you prefer. We will then go around the room and you will state a reason why you prefer one activity over the other. These are rather different activities so make your choices and tell us why you made your choices."

Process: Allow each participant to select two cards and state reason for his or her activity choice.

2. Presentation

Content: "Once you have considered the advantages and disadvantages of a leisure choice and prioritized the advantages and disadvantages you can make your leisure decision. After all this careful consideration, you will probably find it easier to make a choice and then to state a reason for your decision. Why did I choose a particular recreation activity? Did some of the advantages outweigh the disadvantages or did the disadvantages outweigh the advantages? Will this activity help me accomplish my leisure goal? We all have to make our own decisions which are based on personal reasons such as personal income, availability of time, resources, transportation, friends and other resources. Discussing the decisions that we make may help us understand the total decision-making process."

Process: Present decision information. Write on a chalkboard or easel: "Make a choice and identify reasons for that choice!"

3. Learning Activity

Preparation: Obtain paper bags, banana, soda bottle filled with water, orange, and a dollar. Prior to the activity, prepare four small brown paper bags numbered 1, 2, 3, 4. Each bag should contain one object: Bag Number 1 contains a banana; Bag Number 2 contains a soda bottle filled with water (the bottle should be resealable); Bag Number 3 contains an orange; and Bag Number 4 contains a dollar. The tops of the bags should be folded shut so no one can see inside. Do not let anyone see the bag preparation. There will be one extra bag (i.e., more bags than participants), so when activity is completed, there will be one unopened bag remaining.

Content: "This activity will help you make a decision and then state a reason for that decision. I need three people for this activity. You must listen and do as instructed. Do not jump ahead or look in any bags, please wait for your instructions.

"First, I want you to choose a bag and stand behind it. Each one of you must choose a different bag. Okay, this is your bag for now.

Why did you pick that bag? Would having more information have helped you make a different decision? Is it easy to make decisions without having much information? Let's move on.

"The second thing I want you to do is lift the bag by the top only. Now you can feel how heavy your bag is. Do you still want to keep your bag? If you do not want your bag anymore, you can trade with someone or trade for the extra bag. Do you think you have enough information to choose a bag, or would more information be helpful?

"The third thing I want you to do, without looking inside, is to feel what is in the bag. This way you can get more information about what might be inside your bag. To do this, hold the bag over your head with one hand and reach inside the bag with your other hand. Now you know even more about what is in the bag. If you want, you can keep the bag. If you do not want the bag, you can trade again with someone or trade for the extra bag but you can not feel any bag but your own bag. Now, I want you to make a decision without knowing for sure what is in the bag you are holding.

"Look inside the bag and pull out what's in there."

Process: Recruit three volunteers and provide directions.

4. Debriefing

Content:
a. Are you happy or disappointed with your choice?
b. Why did you decide to keep that bag?
c. What were your reasons for not keeping the bag or not trading the bag?
d. Thinking about each step associated with decision making, try to explain your decisions as each step progressed.
e. How did you feel about this activity?
f. What did you learn from this activity?

Process: Conduct debriefing using above questions.

5. Learning Activity

Content: "You are going to work with another person to make some decisions. I will provide each group with an example of a leisure goal, then you will determine at least one activity using the remaining five steps of the decision-making process. Please follow the steps as we have discussed them. To help you, I have written the five-step process on the board."

Process: Divide the participants into groups of two. Write the five-step decision-making process on the board or on a large sheet of paper taped to the wall. Provide each group with a leisure goal. You can make up you own leisure goal or use one of the goals listed below. Different groups can use the same goal. Possible leisure goals might include getting in shape, meeting new people, learning to control stress, finding fun ways to spend time with my family, or learning more about music. These are possible goals, and groups are free to develop their own goals.

The five steps in decision making are:

1. Identify leisure goals.
2. Identify activities for those leisure goals.
3. List the advantages and disadvantages of chosen leisure activities.
4. Prioritize the advantages and disadvantages of doing those leisure activities.
5. State a leisure decision and the reason for that leisure decision.

6. Debriefing

Content:
a. How did you determine an appropriate activity for your goal?

    b.   Which of the decision-making steps were most helpful in choosing an activity?

    c.   Which of the decision-making steps were easier to do than others?

    d.   Was it difficult to make an activity choice? Why, or why not?

Process: Conduct debriefing using the above questions. Try to get each participant to answer at least one question.

7. Learning Activity

Preparation: Obtain a set of prepared index cards and an envelope for each participant. Using five index cards, write the words "Step One" on the first, "Step Two" on the second, and continue labeling procedure through the fifth card. In addition, to the "Step Five" card, put the word "Activity" on the left side and the word "Reason" on the right side. Create a set of cards and place in envelope for each participant.

PREPARE FOR SESSION

Content: "To review everything we have learned regarding decision making and to emphasize the final step, this activity will provide you with the opportunity to make a leisure decision and give the rationale for your activity choice. You will receive an envelope with five index cards inside. Those index cards represent the five steps of decision making. Determine a personal leisure goal and indicate this on the card marked 'Step One.' Then choose three activities that might help you accomplish your goal and list them on the card marked 'Step Two.' On the card marked 'Step Three' list three advantages and disadvantages of each possible activity. On card 'Step Four' prioritize the advantages and disadvantages in order of importance by ranking them 1–4, 1 being the most important advantage or disadvantage. On the card marked 'Step Five' by the word *activity:* chose the activity you think would best help you accomplish your leisure goal. Then indicate beside the word *reason:* the reason(s) why you selected that activity over the other two. This will be your decision-making envelope to keep. Use this process as a guide for future decision making."

Process: Explain activity. Distribute envelopes with card sets. Allow adequate time for completion of each step.

DISTRIBUTE MATERIALS

8. Debriefing

Content:

    a.   How can using the five-step decision-making process result in better leisure decisions?

    b.   Why is prioritizing advantages and disadvantages important?

    c.   Why is it important to provide a rationale for your leisure decision?

    d.   How do you feel this five-step process will assist you in making future decisions?

Process: Conduct debriefing using the above questions. Try to get each participant to answer at least one question.

9. Conclusion

Content: "As we have discussed, there are five steps in the process of making almost any decision. Sometimes, we make decisions without thinking about each step of the process, but other times it is helpful to think about the five steps, especially for complicated decisions. Making decisions effectively is important because as you gain the ability to make decisions you can take more control of your life."

Process: Make concluding statements. Provide opportunities for questions.

References

Aguilar, T. E. (1986). Leisure education program development and evaluation. *Journal of Expanding Horizons in Therapeutic Recreation, 1,* 14-20.

Aguilar, T. E. (1987). Effects of a leisure education program on expressed attitudes of delinquent adolescents. *Therapeutic Recreation Journal, 21*(4), 43-51.

Aguilar, T. E., & Asmussen, K. (1989). An exploration of recreational participation patterns in a correctional facility: A case study. *Journal of Offender Counseling, Services & Rehabilitation, 14*(1), 67-78.

Aguilar, T. E., & Munson, W. W. (1992). Leisure education and counseling as intervention components in drug and alcohol treatment for adolescents. *Journal of Alcohol and Drug Education, 37*(3), 23-34.

Ajzen, I., & Driver, B. L. (1991). Prediction of leisure participation from behavioral, normative, and control beliefs: An application of the theory of planned behavior. *Leisure Sciences, 13,* 185-204.

Alberti, R., & Emmons, M. (1995). *Your perfect right: A guide to assertive living.* San Luis Obispo, CA: Impact.

American Psychological Association. (1994). *Publication manual of the American Psychological Association* (4th ed.). Washington, DC: Author.

Anderson, S. C., & Allen, L. R. (1985). Effects of a leisure education program on activity involvement and social interaction of mentally retarded persons. *Adapted Physical Activity Quarterly, 2*(2), 107-116.

Anson, D., & Shepherd, C. (1990). A survey of postacute spinal cord patients: Medical psychological, and social characteristics. *Trends: Research News from Shepherd Spinal Center, Atlanta, GA.*

Argyle, M. (1996). *The social psychology of leisure.* London, UK: Penguin Books.

Ashton-Schaeffer, C., & Kleiber, D. A. (1990). The relationship between recreation participation and functional skill development in young people with mental retardation. *Annual in Therapeutic Recreation, 1,* 75-81.

Askins, J. (1997). Gone fishin'. *Team Rehab Report, 8*(3), 35-37.

Austin, D. R. (1989). Therapeutic recreation education: A call for reform. In D. M. Compton (Ed.), *Issues in therapeutic recreation: A profession in transition* (pp. 145-156). Champaign, IL: Sagamore.

Backman, S. J., & Mannell, R. C. (1986). Removing attitudinal barriers to leisure behavior and satisfaction. *Therapeutic Recreation Journal, 20*, 46-53.

Bandura, A. (1977). *Social learning theory.* Englewood Cliffs, NJ: Prentice Hall.

Barry, V. (1997). *The dog ate my homework: Personal responsibility—How to avoid it and what to do about it.* Kansas City, MO: Andrews and McMeel.

Beard, J. G., & Ragheb, M. G. (1980). Measuring leisure satisfaction. *Journal of Leisure Research, 12*, 20-32.

Beck-Ford, V., & Brown, R. (1984). *Leisure training and rehabilitation.* Springfield, IL: Charles C. Thomas.

Bedini, L. A. (1990). The status of leisure education: Implications for instruction and practice. *Therapeutic Recreation Journal, 24*(1), 40-49.

Bedini, L. A., & Bullock, C. C. (1988). Leisure education in the public schools: A model of cooperation in transition programming for mentally handicapped youth. *Journal of Expanding Horizons in Therapeutic Recreation, 3*, 5-11.

Bedini, L., Bullock, C., & Driscoll, L. (1993). The effects of leisure education on factors contributing to the successful transition of students with mental retardation from school to life. *Therapeutic Recreation Journal, 27*(2), 70-82.

Bem, D. J. (1972). Self-perception theory. In L. Berkowitz (Ed.), *Advances in experimental social psychology, 6,* (pp. 1-62). New York, NY: Academic Press.

Berger, A. A. (1995). *Cultural criticism: A primer of key concepts.* Thousand Oaks, CA: Sage.

Berger, B., & Owen, D. (1992). Mood alteration with yoga and swimming: Aerobic exercise may not be necessary. *Perceptual and Motor Skills, 75*, 1331-1343.

Berk, L., Tan, S., Nehlsen-Cannarella, S., Napier, B., Lee, J., Lewis, J., Hubbard, R., & Eby, W. (1988). Humor associated laughter decreases cortisol and increases spontaneous lymphocyte blastogenesis. *Clinical Research, 36*, 435.

Berryman, D. (1988). Dance movement: Effects on elderly self-concepts. *Journal of Physical Education, Recreation and Dance, 59*, 42-46.

Bete, C. L. (1994). *About understanding diversity.* South Deerfield, MA: Chaning L. Bete.

Bouffard, M. (1990). Movement problem solutions by educable mentally handicapped individuals. *Adapted Physical Activity Quarterly, 7*, 183-197.

Boyd, R., & James, A. (1990). An emerging challenge: Serving older adults with mental retardation. *Annual in Therapeutic Recreation, 1*, 56-66.

Brackenreg, M., Luckner, J., & Pinch, K. (1994). Essential skills for processing adventure experiences. *Journal of Experiential Education, 17,* 45-47.

Bregha, F. J. (1985). Leisure and freedom re-examined. In T. A. Goodale and P. A. Witt (Eds.), *Recreation and leisure: Issues in an era of change* (2nd ed., pp. 35-43). State College, PA: Venture Publishing, Inc.

Brehm, J. W. (1977). *A theory of psychological reactance.* New York, NY: Academic Press.

Brightbill, C. K., & Mobely, T. A. (1977). *Educating for leisure-centered living* (2nd ed.). New York, NY: John Wiley.

Brotherson, M. J., Cook, C., Cunconan-Lahr, R., & Wehmeyer, M. L. (1995). Policy supporting choice and self-determination in the environments of persons with severe disabilities across the life span. *Education and Training in Mental Retardation and Developmental Disabilities, 30,* 3-14.

Bucher, C. A., Shivers, J. S., & Bucher, R. D. (1984). Leisure education and counseling. *Recreation for today's society* (2nd ed., pp. 290-303). Englewood Cliffs, NJ: Prentice-Hall.

Bullock, C. C., & Howe, C. Z. (1991). A model therapeutic recreation program for the reintegration of persons with disabilities into the community. *Therapeutic Recreation Journal, 25*(1), 7-17.

Bullock, C. C., & Mahon, M. J. (1997). *Introduction to recreation services for people with disabilities: A person-centered approach.* Champaign, IL: Sagamore.

Bullock, C. C., Morris, L. H., & Garrett, B. S. (1991). *The community reintegration program.* Chapel Hill, NC: Center for Recreation and Disabilities Studies, Curriculum in Leisure Studies and Recreation Administration. University of North Carolina at Chapel Hill.

Bullock, C. C., Morris, L., Mahon, M. J., & Jones, B. (1992). *School-community leisure link: Leisure education program curriculum guide.* Chapel Hill, NC: The Center for Recreation and Disability Studies, Curriculum in Leisure Studies and Recreation Administration, University of North Carolina at Chapel Hill.

Buriel, R. (1987). Ethnic labeling and identity among Mexican Americans. In J. S. Phinney & M. J. Rotheram (Eds.), *Children's ethnic socialization: Pluralism and development* (pp. 134-152). Beverly Hills, CA: Sage.

Burr, J. A., & Mutchler, J. E. (1993). Nativity, acculturation, and economic status: Explanations of Asian American living arrangements in later life. *Journal of Gerontology: Social Sciences, 48*(2), S55-S63.

Burton, S. (1992). Families and the aged: Issues of complexity and diversity. *Generations, 17*(3), 8-9.

Busser, J. A. (1990). *Programming for employee services and recreation.* Champaign, IL: Sagamore.

Caldwell, L. L., Adolph, S., & Gilbert, A. (1989). Caution! Leisure counselors at work: Long-term effects of leisure counseling. *Therapeutic Recreation Journal, 23*(3), 4-7.

Caldwell, L. L., Smith, E. A., & Weissinger, E. (1992). The relationship of leisure activities and perceived health of college students. *Society and Leisure, 15,* 545-556.

Capitman, J. A., Hernandez-Gallegos, W., & Yee, D. L. (1991). "Diversity assessments" in aging services. *Generations, 15*(4), 73-76.

Cappel, M. L. (1990). Cross-cultural barriers to effective delivery of therapeutic recreation services. *Research Into Action, 7,* 41-49.

Chadsey-Rusch, J. (1990). Social interactions of secondary-aged students with severe handicaps: Implications for facilitating the transition from school to work. *The Journal of the Association for Persons with Severe Handicaps, 15*(2), 69-78.

Chadsey-Rusch, J. (1992). Toward defining and measuring social skills in employment settings. *American Journal on Mental Retardation, 96,* 405-416.

Chinn, K. A., & Joswiak, K. F. (1981). Leisure education and leisure counseling. *Therapeutic Recreation Journal, 15*(4), 4-7.

Coleman, D. (1993). Leisure based social support, leisure dispositions and health. *Journal of Leisure Research, 25*(2), 350-361.

Coleman, D., & Iso-Ahola, S. (1993). Leisure and health: The role of social support and self-determination. *Journal of Leisure Research, 25*(2), 111-128.

Collard, K. M. (1981). Leisure education in the schools: Why, who, and the need for advocacy. *Therapeutic Recreation Journal, 15*(3), 8-18.

Collins, B. C., Hall, M., & Branson, T. A. (1997). Teaching leisure skills to adolescents with moderate disabilities. *Exceptional Children, 63*(4), 499-512.

Colozzi, G., & Pollow, R. (1984). Teaching independent walking to mentally retarded children in a public school. *Education and Training of the Mentally Retarded, 19*(2), 97-101.

Compton, D. M., & Goldstein, J. E. (Eds.). (1977). *Perspectives of leisure counseling.* Alexandria, VA: National Recreation and Parks Association.

Connolly, M. L. (1977). Leisure counseling: A values clarification and assertive training approach. In A. Epperson, P. A. Witt, & G. Hitzhusen (Eds.), *Leisure counseling: An aspect of leisure education* (pp. 198-207). Springfield, IL: Charles C. Thomas.

Coontz, S. (1996). Where are the good old days? *Modern Maturity, 39*(3), 36-43.

Cooper, W. E. (1989). The metaphysics of leisure. *Philosophy in Context,* *19,* 59-73.

Crandall, R., & Slivken, K. (1980). Leisure attitudes and their measurement. In S. E. Iso-Ahola (Ed.), *Social psychological perspectives on leisure and recreation* (pp. 261-284). Springfield, IL: Thomas.

Crawford, D. W., & Godbey, G. (1987). Reconceptualizing barriers to family leisure. *Leisure Sciences, 9,* 119-127.

Crawford, D. W., Jackson, E. L., & Godbey, G. (1991). A hierarchial model of leisure constraints. *Leisure Sciences, 13,* 309-320.

Csikszentmihalyi, M. (1975). *Beyond boredom and anxiety.* San Francisco, CA: Jossey-Bass.

Csikszentmihalyi, M. (1990). *Flow: The psychology of optimal experience.* New York, NY: Harper Collins.

Csikszentmihalyi, M. (1992). A theoretical model for enjoyment. In M. Allison (Ed.), *Play, leisure and quality of life: Social scientific perspectives* (pp. 11-23). Dubuque, IA: Kendall Hunt.

Csikszentmihalyi, M. (1993). *The evolving self.* New York, NY: Harper Collins.

Csikszentmihalyi, M. (1997). *Finding flow: The psychology of engagement with everyday life.* New York, NY: Harper Collins.

Csikszentmihalyi, M., & Csikszentmihalyi, I. S. (Eds.). (1988). *Optimal experience: Psychological studies of flow in consciousness.* New York, NY: Cambridge University Press.

Csikszentmihalyi, M., Rathunde, K., & Whalen, S. (1997). *Talented teenagers: The roots of success and failure.* New York, NY: Cambridge University Press.

Cunconan-Lahr, R., & Brotherson, M. J. (1996). Advocacy in disability policy: Parents and consumers as advocates. *Mental Retardation, 34,* 352-358.

Dattilo, J. (1994). *Inclusive leisure services: Responding to the rights of people with disabilities.* State College, PA: Venture Publishing, Inc.

Dattilo, J. (1995). Instruction for preference and generalization. In S. Schleien, L. Meyer, L. Heyne, & B. Brandt (Eds.), *Lifelong leisure skills and lifestyles for persons with developmental disabilities* (pp. 133-145). Baltimore, MD: Paul H. Brookes.

Dattilo, J. (in press). *Leisure Education: Specific Programs.* State College, PA: Venture Publishing, Inc.

Dattilo, J., & Barnett, L. A. (1985). Therapeutic recreation for persons with severe handicaps: An analysis of the relationship between choice and pleasure. *Therapeutic Recreation Journal, 21*(3), 79-91.

Dattilo, J., & Bemisderfer, K. (1996). *Project TRAIL leisure education curriculum.* Athens, GA: University of Georgia.

Dattilo, J., & Hoge, G. (1999). Effects of a leisure education program on youth with mental retardation. *Education and Training in Mental Retardation and Developmental Disabilities, 34*(1), 20-34.

Dattilo, J., & Kleiber, D. A. (1993). Psychological perspectives for therapeutic recreation research: The psychology of enjoyment. In M. J. Malkin & C. Z. Howe (Eds.), *Research in therapeutic recreation: Concepts and methods* (pp. 57-76). State College, PA: Venture Publishing, Inc.

Dattilo, J., & Light, J. (1993). Setting the stage for leisure: Encouraging reciprocal communication for people using augmentative and alternative communication systems through facilitator instruction. *Therapeutic Recreation Journal, 27*(3), 156-171.

Dattilo, J., & Murphy, W. D. (1987). The challenge of adventure recreation for individuals with disabilities. *Therapeutic Recreation Journal, 21*(3), 14-21.

Dattilo, J., & Murphy, W. D. (1991). *Leisure education program planning: A systematic approach.* State College, PA: Venture Publishing, Inc.

Dattilo, J., & O'Keefe, B. M. (1992). Setting the stage for leisure: Encouraging adults with mental retardation who use augmentative and alternative communication systems to share conversations. *Therapeutic Recreation Journal, 26*(1), 27-37.

Dattilo, J., & Smith, R. (1990). Communicating positive attitudes toward people with disabilities through sensitive terminology. *Therapeutic Recreation Journal, 24*(1), 9-17.

Dattilo, J., & Sneegas, J. (1987). Leadership strategies for therapeutic recreation specialists. *Programming Trends in Therapeutic Recreation, 8*(3), 5-8.

Dattilo, J., & St. Peter, S. (1991). A model for including leisure education in transition services for young adults with mental retardation. *Education and Training in Mental Retardation, 26,* 420-432.

Davis, L. N. (1974). *Planning, conducting, and evaluating workshops.* Austin, TX: Learning Concepts.

Deci, E. L. (1975). *Intrinsic motivation.* New York, NY: Plenum.

Deci, E. L. (1980). *The psychology of self-determination.* Lexington, MA: Lexington Books.

Deci, E. L., Eghrari, H., Patrick, B. C., & Leone, D. R. (1994). Facilitating internalization: The self-determination theory perspective. *Journal of Personality, 62*(1), 119-142.

Deci, E. L., & Ryan, R. M. (1985). *Intrinsic motivation and self-determination in human behavior.* New York, NY: Plenum.

Deci, E. L., & Ryan, R. M. (1991). A motivational approach to self: Integration in personality. In R. Dientsbier (Ed.), *Nebraska Symposium on Motivation: Vol 38. Perspectives on Motivation* (pp 237-288). Lincoln, NE: University of Nebraska Press.

Dehn, D. (1995). *Leisure step up.* Ravensdale, WA: Idyll Arbor.

Demchak, M. (1990). Response prompting and fading methods: A review. *American Journal on Mental Retardation, 94,* 603-615.

DeVellis, R. F. (1977). Learned helplessness in institutions. *Mental Retardation, 15*(5), 10-13.

Devine, M., Malley, S., Sheldon, K., Dattilo, J., & Gast, D. (1997). Promoting self-initiated community leisure participation for adults with mental retardation. *Education and Training in Mental Retardation and Developmental Disabilities, 32*(3), 241-254.

Dishman, R. K. (Ed.). (1994). *Advances in exercise adherence.* Champaign, IL: Human Kinetics.

Dishman, R. K. (1995). Physical activity and public health: Mental health. *Quest: The Academy of Kinesiology and Physical Education Papers, 47,* 1-10.

Dowd, E. T. (Ed.). (1984). *Leisure counseling: Concepts and applications.* Springfield, IL: Charles C. Thomas.

Dunn, J. K. (1981). Leisure education: Meeting the challenge of increasing leisure independence of residents in psychiatric facilities. *Therapeutic Recreation Journal, 15*(3), 17-23.

Dunn, J. K. (1984). Assessment. In C. A. Peterson & S. L. Gunn, *Therapeutic recreation program and design: Principles and procedures* (2nd ed., pp. 267-320). Englewood Cliffs, NJ: Prentice-Hall.

Dunn, N. J., & Wilhite, B. (1997). The effects of a leisure education program on leisure participation and psychosocial well-being of two older women who are home-centered. *Therapeutic Recreation Journal, 31*(1), 53-71.

Ellis, G. D. (1989). The role of science in therapeutic recreation. In D. M. Compton (Ed.), *Issues in therapeutic recreation: A profession in transition* (pp. 109-124). Champaign, IL: Sagamore.

Ellis, G. D., & Witt, P. A. (1986). The leisure diagnostic battery: Past, present, and future. *Therapeutic Recreation Journal, 20*(4), 31-47.

Epperson, A., Witt, P. A., & Hitzhusen, G. (1977). *Leisure counseling: An aspect of leisure education.* Springfield, IL: Charles C. Thomas.

Evans, C. A., & Cunningham, B. A. (1996). Caring for the ethnic elder. *Geriatric Nursing, 17*(3), 105-110.

Ewert, A., & Hollenhorst, S. (1989). Testing the adventure model: Empirical support for a model of risk recreation participation. *Journal of Leisure Research, 21*(2), 124-139.

Fache, W. (1995). Leisure education in community systems. In H. Ruskin & A. Sivan (Eds.), *Leisure education: Towards the 21st century* (pp. 52-79). Provo, UT: Department of Recreation Management and Youth Leadership, Brigham Young University.

Fache, W. (1997). Developing leisure education in the primary schools. *World Leisure and Recreation, 39*(2), 34-38.

Falvey, M. A. (1986). *Community based curriculum: Instructional strategies for students with severe handicaps.* Baltimore, MD: Paul H. Brookes.

Faw, G. D., Davis, P. K., & Peck, C. (1996). Increasing self-determination: Teaching people with mental retardation to evaluate residential options. *Journal of Applied Behavior Analysis, 29*(2), 173-188.

Festinger, L. (1957). *A theory of cognitive dissonance.* Stanford, CA: Stanford University.

Ford, A., Brown, L., Pumpian, I., Baumgart, D., Nisbet, J., Schroeder, J., & Loomis, R. (1984). Strategies for developing individual recreation/ leisure plans for adolescent and young adult severely handicapped students. In N. Certo, N. Haring, and R. York (Eds.), *Public school integration of severely handicapped students: Rational issues and progressive alternatives* (pp. 245-275). Baltimore, MD: Paul H. Brookes.

Foxx, R. M., Faw, G. D., Taylor, S., Davis, P. K., & Fulia, R. (1993). "Would I be able to . . . ?": Teaching clients to assess the availability of their community living life style preferences. *American Journal on Mental Retardation, 98*(2), 235-248.

The G. Allan Roecher Institute. (1990). *Making friends: Developing relationships between people with disabilities and other members of the community.* Downsview, Ontario, Canada.

The G. Allan Roecher Institute. (1991). *Leisure connections: Enabling people with a disability to lead richer lives in the community.* Downsview, Ontario, Canada.

Garner, R. (1990). When children and adults do not use learning strategies: Toward a theory of settings. *Review of Educational Research, 60,* 517-529.

Gass, M. A. (1993). The evolution of processing adventure therapy experiences. In M. A. Gass (Ed.), *Adventure therapy: Therapeutic applications of adventure programming* (pp. 219-229). Dubuque, IA: Kendall/Hunt.

Geertz, C. (1983). Thick description: Toward an interpretive theory of culture. In R. M. Emerson (Ed.), *Contemporary field research: A collection of readings* (pp. 37-59). Prospect Heights, IL: Waveland.

Godbey, G. (1985). *Leisure in your life: An exploration* (2nd ed.). State College, PA: Venture Publishing, Inc.

Godbey, G. (1991). Planning for leisure in a pluralistic society. In T. L. Goodale & P. A. Witt (Eds.), *Recreation and leisure: Issues in an era of change* (3rd ed., pp. 137-148). State College, PA: Venture Publishing, Inc.

Goffman, E. (1959). *The presentation of self in everyday life.* New York, NY: Doubleday.

Goffman, E. (1963). *Stigma: Notes on the management of spoiled identity.* New York, NY: Touchstone.

Goodale, T. L. (1991). Is there enough time? In T. L. Goodale & P. A. Witt (Eds.), *Recreation and leisure: Issues in an era of change* (3rd ed., pp. 33-46). State College, PA: Venture Publishing, Inc.

Green, F. P., Schleien, S. J., Mactavish, J., & Benepe, S. (1995). Non-disabled adults = perceptions of relationships in the early stages of arranged partnerships with peers with mental retardation. *Education and Training in Mental Retardation and Developmental Disabilities, 30*(2), 91-108.

Greenwood, C. M., Dzewattowski, D. A., & French, R. (1990). Self-efficacy and psychological well-being of wheelchair tennis participants and wheelchair nontennis participants. *Adapted Physical Activity Quarterly, 7,* 12-21.

Guralnick, M. J., Conner, R. T., & Hammond, M. (1995). Parent perspectives of peer relationships and friendships in integrated and specialized programs. *American Journal on Mental Retardation, 99*(5), 457-476.

Gushiken, T. T., Treftz, J. L., Porter, G. H., & Snowberg, R. L. (1986). The development of a leisure education program for cardiac patients. *Journal of Expanding Horizons in Therapeutic Recreation, 1,* 67-72.

Halberg, K. J. (1989). Issues in community-based recreation services. In D. M. Compton (Ed.), *Issues in therapeutic recreation: A profession in transition* (pp. 305-324). Champaign, IL: Sagamore.

Hamilton, J. (1981). Attention, personality, and the self-regulation of mood: Absorbing interest and boredom. *Progress in Experimental Personality Research, 10,* 281-315.

Harackiewicz, J., & Sansone, C. (1991). Goals and intrinsic motivation: You can get there from here. *Advances in Motivation and Achievement, 7,* 21-49.

Harry, B. (1997). Multicultural perspectives. *TASH Newsletter, 23*(1), 9-11.

Hayes, G. A. (1977a). Professional preparation and leisure counseling. *Journal of Physical Education and Recreation, 48*(4), 36-38.

Hayes, G. A. (1977b). Leisure education and recreation counseling. In A. Epperson, P. A. Witt, & G. Hitzhusen (Eds.), *Leisure counseling: An aspect of leisure education* (pp. 208-218). Springfield, IL: Charles C. Thomas.

Haywood, L., Kew, F., & Braham, P. (1989). *Understanding leisure.* London, UK: Century Hutchinson.

Henderson, K. A. (1995). Leisure in a diverse society: Designing a course. *Schole, 10,* 1-15.

Henderson, K. A. (1997). Diversity, differences and leisure services. *Parks and Recreation, 32*(11), 24-35.

Hetzroni, O. E., & Harris, O. L. (1996). Cultural aspects in the development of AAC users. *Augmentative and Alternative Communication, 12,* 52-58.

Heyne, L. (1997). Friendship. In S. Schleien, M. Ray, & F. Green (Eds.), *Community recreation and people with disabilities: Strategies for inclusion* (2nd ed., pp. 129-150). Baltimore, MD: Paul H. Brookes.

Heyne, L. A., & Schleien, S. J. (1994). Leisure and recreation programming to enhance quality of life. In E. C. Cipani & F. Spooner (Eds.), *Curricular and instructional approaches for persons with severe disabilities* (pp. 213-240). Boston, MA: Allyn and Bacon.

Heyne, L. A., & Schleien, S. J. (1996). Leisure education in the schools: A call to action. *Leisurability, 23*(3), 3-14.

Heyne, L. A., Schleien, S., & McAvoy, L. (1993). *Making friends: Using recreation activities to promote friendship between children with and without disabilities.* Minneapolis, MN: Institute on Community Integration.

Hill, A. B., & Perkins, R. E. (1985). Towards a model of boredom. *British Journal of Psychology, 76,* 235-240.

Hoge, G., & Dattilo, J. (1995). Recreation participation patterns of adults with and without mental retardation. *Education and Training in Mental Retardation, 30*(4), 283-298.

Hoge, G., Dattilo, J., Schneider, S., & Bemisderfer, K. (1997). Transition through recreation and integration for life. In S. Schleien, M. Ray, & F. Green (Eds.), *Community recreation and people with disabilities: Strategies for inclusion* (pp. 180-185). Baltimore, MD: Paul H. Brookes.

Hoge, G., Dattilo, J., & Williams, R. (in press). Effects of a leisure education program on the perceived freedom of youth with mental retardation. *Therapeutic Recreation Journal.*

Holland, J. (1997). Enhancing multicultural sensitivity through teaching multiculturally in recreation. *Parks and Recreation, 32*(5), 42-50.

Hoover, J., Wheeler, L., & Reetz, L. (1992). Development of a leisure satisfaction scale for use with adolescents and adults with developmental disabilities: Initial findings. *Education and Training in Mental Retardation, 27,* 153-160.

Hopper, C., & Wambold, C. (1978). Improving the independent play of severely, mentally retarded children. *Education and Training of the Mentally Retarded, 13,* 42-46.

Howe, C. Z. (1989). Assessment instruments in therapeutic recreation: To what extent do they work? In D. M. Compton (Ed.), *Issues in therapeutic recreation: A profession in transition* (pp. 205-222). Champaign, IL: Sagamore.

Howe-Murphy, R., & Charboneau, B. G. (1987). *Therapeutic recreation intervention: An ecological perspective.* Englewood Cliffs, NJ: Prentice-Hall.

Hughes, S., & Keller, M. J. (1992). Leisure education: A coping strategy for family caregivers. *Journal of Gerontological Social Work, 19*(1), 115-123.

Hultsman, E. Z. (1993). The influence of others as a barrier to recreation participation among early adolescents. *Journal of Leisure Research, 25*(2), 150-164.

Hultsman, J. T., Black, D. R., Seehafer, R. W., & Hovell, M. F. (1987). The Purdue stepped approach model: Application to leisure counseling service delivery. *Therapeutic Recreation Journal, 21*(4), 9-22.

Hultsman, W. (1995). Recognizing patterns of leisure constraints: An extension of the exploration of dimensionality. *Journal of Leisure Research, 27*(3), 228-244.

Hunnicutt, B. K. (1988). *Work without end: Abandoning shorter hours for the right to work.* Philadelphia, PA: Temple University Press.

Iso-Ahola, S. E. (1980). *The social psychology of leisure and recreation.* Dubuque, IA: Wm. C. Brown.

Iso-Ahola, S. E. (1983). Social psychological foundations of leisure and resultant implications for leisure counseling. In T. E. Dowd (Ed.), *Leisure counseling: Concepts and applications* (pp. 97-125). Springfield, IL: Charles C. Thomas.

Iso-Ahola, S. E. (1986). A theory of substitutability of leisure behavior. *Leisure Sciences, 8*(4), 367-389.

Iso-Ahola, S. E. (1994). Leisure lifestyle and health. In D. M. Compton & S. E. Iso-Ahola (Eds.), *Leisure and Mental Health* (pp. 42-60). Park City, UT: Family Development Resources.

Iso-Ahola, S. E., MacNeil, R. D., & Szymanski, D. J. (1980). Social psychological foundations of therapeutic recreation: An attributional analysis. In S. Iso-Ahola (Ed.), *Social psychological perspectives on leisure and recreation.* Springfield, IL: Charles C. Thomas.

Iso-Ahola, S. E., & Park, C. J. (1996). Leisure-related social support and self-determination as buffers of stress-illness relationship. *Journal of Leisure Research, 28*(3), 169-187.

Iso-Ahola, S. E., & Weissinger, E. (1987). Leisure and boredom. *Journal of Social and Clinical Psychology, 5*(3), 356-364.

Iso-Ahola, S. E., & Weissinger, E. (1990). Perceptions of boredom in leisure: Conceptualization, reliability, and validity of the leisure boredom scale. *Journal of Leisure Research, 22,* 1-17.

Ivey, A. E. (1987). Cultural intentionality: The core of effective helping. *Counselor Education and Supervision, 26*(3), 168-172.

Jackson, E., Crawford, D., & Godbey, G. (1993). Negotiation of leisure constraints. *Leisure Sciences, 15,* 1-11.

Jackson, J. (1992). The fabric of a nation. *Modern Maturity* (June-July): 23.

Janney, R. E., Snell, M. E., Beers, G. K., & Raynes, M. (1995). Integrating students with moderate and severe disabilities: Classroom teachers= beliefs and attitudes about implementing an educational change. *Education Administration Quarterly, 31*(1), 86-114.

Jekubovich, N., Dattilo, J., Williams, R., & McKenney, A. (in press). The effects of a leisure education program on adults with chemical dependencies. *Therapeutic Recreation Journal.*

Jendrek, M. P. (1995). Grandparents who parent their grandchildren: Circumstances and decisions. *The Gerontologist, 34,* 206-216.

Johnson, D. E., Bullock, C. C., & Ashton-Shaeffer, C. (1997). Families and leisure: A context for learning. *Teaching Exceptional Children,* Nov./Dec., 30-34.

Johnson, L. P., & Zoerink, D. A. (1977). The development and implementation of a leisure counseling program with female psychiatric patients based on value clarification techniques. In A. Epperson, P. A. Witt, & G. Hitzhusen (Eds.), *Leisure counseling: An aspect of leisure education* (pp. 171-197). Springfield, IL: Charles C. Thomas.

Johnson, R. T., & Johnson, D. W. (1994). An overview of cooperative learning. In J. S. Thousand, R. A. Villa, & A. I. Nevin (Eds.), *Creativity and collaborative learning: A practical guide to empowering students and teachers* (pp. 31-44). Baltimore, MD: Paul H. Brookes.

Joswiak, K. F. (1979). *Leisure counseling program materials for the developmentally disabled.* Washington, DC: Hawkins and Associates.

Kaplan, R. M., & Saccuzzo, D. P. (1993). *Psychological testing: Principles, applications, and issues* (3rd ed.). Pacific Grove, CA: Brooks/Cole.

Kay, T., & Jackson, G. (1991). Leisure despite constraint: The impact of leisure constraints on leisure participation. *Journal of Leisure Research, 23,* 301-313.

Kelland, J. (Ed.). (1995). *Protocols for recreation therapy programs.* State College, PA: Venture Publishing, Inc.

Keller, M. J., & Hughes, S. (1991). The role of leisure education with family caregivers of persons with alzheimer's disease and related disorders. *Annual in Therapeutic Recreation, 2,* 1-7.

Keller, M. J., McCombs, J., Pilgrim, V. V., & Booth, S. A. (1987). *Helping older adults develop active leisure lifestyles.* Atlanta, GA: Georgia Department of Human Resources.

Kelly, J. R. (1983). *Leisure identities and interactions* (2nd ed.). Boston, MA: Allen and Unwin.

Kelly, J. R. (1987). *Freedom to be: A new sociology of leisure.* New York, NY: Macmillan.

Kelly, J. R. (1990). Leisure and aging: A second agenda. *Loisir et Société/ Society and Leisure, 13,* 145-168.

Kelly, J. R. (1996). *Leisure.* Boston, MA: Allyn and Bacon.

Kimmel, D. C. (1992). The families of older gay men and lesbians. *Generations, 17*(3), 37-38.

Kimeldorf, M. (1989). *Pathways to leisure: A workbook for finding leisure opportunities.* Bloomington, IL: Meridian Education Corporation.

Kleiber, D. A. (1981). Leisure-based education. *Leisure Information, 4*(7), 3-4.

Knapp, C. (1990). Processing the adventure experience. In J. Miles & S. Priest (Eds.), *Adventure education* (pp. 189-197). State College, PA: Venture Publishing, Inc.

Kraus, J., & Crewe, M. (1987). Prediction of long-term survival of persons with spinal cord injury. *Rehabilitation Psychology, 13,* 205-213.

Kraus, R. (1994). *Leisure in a changing America: Multicultural perspectives.* New York, NY: Macmillan.

Kunstler, R. (1991). There but for fortune: A therapeutic recreation perspective on the homeless in America. *Therapeutic Recreation Journal, 25*(2), 31-40.

Lanagan, D., & Dattilo, J. (1989). The effects of a leisure education program on individuals with mental retardation. *Therapeutic Recreation Journal, 23*(4), 62-72.

Lee, L. L., & Mobily, K. E. (1988). The NTRS philosophical position statement and a concept of three freedoms. *Journal of Expanding Horizons in Therapeutic Recreation, 3*(3), 41-46.

Lee, Y., & Skalko, T. K. (1996). Multicultural sensitivity: An innovative mind-set in therapeutic recreation practice. *Parks & Recreation, 31*(5), 50-53.

Legon, J. (1995, February 5). Is it "Hispanic" or "Latino"? Groups clash over terms. *The Athens Daily News/Athens Banner-Herald,* p. D5.

Leitner, M. J., Leitner, S. F., & Associates. (1996). *Leisure enhancement.* New York, NY: The Hawthorn Press.

Lepper, M. R., Green, D., & Nisbett, R. E. (1973). Undermining children's intrinsic interest with extrinsic rewards: A test of "overjustification" hypothesis. *Journal of Personality and Social Psychology, 28,* 129-137.

Levy, J. (1997). Leisure education: From an age of dominionism to an age of sustainable living. *World Leisure and Recreation, 39*(2), 7-11.

Lippmann, W. (1930). Free time and extra money. *Woman's Home Companion 57,* 31-32.

Long, M. (1984). Aerobic conditioning and stress inoculation: A comparison of stress-management interventions. *Cognitive Therapy Research, 8*(5), 517-542.

Lord, M. A. (1997). Leisure's role in enhancing social competencies of individuals with developmental disabilities. *Parks & Recreation, 32*(4), 35-39.

Lovell, T., Dattilo, J., & Jekubovich, N. (1996). Effects of leisure education on individuals aging with disabilities. *Activities, Adaptations and Aging, 21*(2), 37-58.

Luckner, J. L., & Nadler, R. S. (1995). Processing adventure experiences: It's the story that counts. *Therapeutic Recreation Journal, 29*(3), 175-183.

Mactavish, J. B. (1997). Building bridges between families and providers of community leisure services. In S. J. Schleien, M. T. Ray, & F. P. Green (Eds.), *Community recreation and people with disabilities: Strategies for inclusion* (2nd ed., pp. 71-84). Baltimore, MD: Brookes.

Mager, R. F. (1997). *Preparing instructional objectives* (3rd ed.). Atlanta, GA: The Center for Effective Performance, Inc.

Mahon, M. J. (1994). The use of self-control techniques to facilitate self-determination skills during leisure in adolescents and young adults with mild and moderate mental retardation. *Therapeutic Recreation Journal, 28*(2), 58-72.

Mahon, M. J., & Bullock, C. C. (1992). Teaching adolescents with mild mental retardation to make decisions in leisure through the use of self-control techniques. *Therapeutic Recreation Journal, 26*(1), 9-26.

Mahon, M. J., & Bullock, C. C. (1993). An investigation of the social validity of a comprehensive leisure education program. *Annual in Therapeutic Recreation, 4,* 82-95.

Mahon, M. J., Bullock, C. C., Luken, K., & Martens, C. (1996). Leisure education for persons with severe and persistent mental illness: Is it a socially valid process? *Therapeutic Recreation Journal, 30*(3), 197-212.

Mahon, M. J., & Martens, C. (1996). Planning for the future: The impact of leisure education on adults with developmental disabilities in supported employment settings. *Journal of Applied Recreation Research, 21*(4), 283-312.

Malaney, G. D., & Shively, M. (1995). Academic and social expectations and experiences of first-year students of color. *NASPA Journal, 33*(1), 3-18.

Malik, P. (1990). Leisure interests and perceptions of group home residents. *Annual in Therapeutic Recreation, 1,* 67-74.

Malkin, M. J., Phillips, R., & Chumbler, J. (1991). The family lab: An interdisciplinary family leisure education program. *Annual in Therapeutic Recreation, 2,* 25-36.

Malkin, M. J., Voss, M. C., Teaff, J. D., & Benshoff, J. J. (1994). Activity and recreational therapy services in substance abuse treatment programs. *Annual in Therapeutic Recreation, 4,* 40-50.

Mannell, R. C., & Kleiber, D. A. (1997). *A social psychology of leisure.* State College, PA: Venture Publishing, Inc.

Mannell, R. C., Zuzanek, J., & Larson, R. W. (1988). Leisure states and "flow" experiences: Testing perceived freedom and intrinsic motivation hypotheses. *Journal of Leisure Research, 20,* 289-304.

Massimini, F., Csikszentmihalyi, M., & Delle Fave, A. (1988). Flow and biocultural evolution. In M. Csikszentmihalyi & I. Csikszentmihalyi (Eds.), *Optimal experience: Psychological studies of flow in consciousness* (pp. 60-81). Melbourne, Australia: Cambridge University Press.

McCormick, B., & Dattilo, J. (1992). Examining the social world of Alcoholics Anonymous: Implications to leisure education. *Annual in Therapeutic Recreation, 3,* 33-43.

McDonald, R. G., & Howe, C. Z. (1989). Challenge/initiative recreation programs as a treatment for low self-concept children. *Journal of Leisure Research, 21*(3), 242-253.

McDowell, C. F. (1976). *Leisure counseling: Selected lifestyle processes.* Eugene, OR: Center for Leisure Studies.

McDowell, C. F. (1983). *Leisure counseling: Concepts on helping strategies.* Eugene, OR: Sun Moon Press.

McFall, R. M. (1982). A review and reformulation of the concept of social skills. *Behavioral Assessment, 4,* 1-33.

McGill, J. (1996). *Developing leisure identities.* Brampton, Ontario, Canada: Brampton Caledon Community Living.

McGuire, F., & O'Leary, J. (1992). The implications of leisure constraint research for the delivery of leisure services. *Journal of Park and Recreation Administration, 10,* 31-40.

McKeachie, W. J. (1986). *Teaching tips: A guide for the beginning college teacher* (8th ed.). Lexington, MA: D. C. Health and Company.

Meichenbaum, D. H. (1995). Cognitive-behavioral therapy in historical perspective. In B. Bongar & L. E. Beutler (Eds.), *Comprehensive textbook of psychotherapy* (pp. 140-158). New York, NY: Oxford University Press.

Meyer, L. H., Cole, D. A., McQuarter, R., & Reichle, J. (1990). Validation of the assessment of social competence for children and young adults with developmental disabilities. *The Journal of the Association for Persons with Severe Handicaps, 15*(2), 57-68.

Minke, K. M., Bear, G. G., Deemer, S. A., & Griffin, S. M. (1996). Teachers' experiences with inclusive classrooms: Implications for special education reform. *The Journal of Special Education, 30*(2), 152-186.

Mobily, K. (1984). Leisure and retirement: The need for leisure counseling. *The Physical Educator, 41*(1), 6-15.

Mobily, K., Lemke, J., Ostiguy, L., Woodward, R., Griffee, T., & Pickens, C. (1993). Leisure repertoire in a sample of Midwestern elderly: The case for exercise. *Therapeutic Recreation Journal, 25,* 84-99.

Mundy, J. (1976, March). A systems approach to leisure education. *Leisure Today, Journal of Physical Education and Recreation,* 18-19.

Mundy, J. (1997). Developing anger and aggression control in youth in recreation and park systems. *Parks & Recreation, 32*(3), 62-69.

Mundy, J., Ibrahim, H., Robertson, B., Beningfield, W., & Carpenter, G. (1992). Quincentennial leisure awareness: The 500 year journey. *The Journal of Physical Education, Recreation and Dance, 10,* 50-54.

Mundy, J., & Odum, L. (1979). *Leisure education: Theory and practice.* New York, NY: John Wiley & Sons.

Munson, W. W. (1988). Effects of leisure education versus physical activity or informal discussion on behaviorally disordered youth offenders. *Adapted Physical Activity Quarterly, 5*(4), 305-317.

Munson, W. W., Baker, S. B., & Lundegren, H. M. (1985). Strength training and leisure counseling as treatments for institutionalized juvenile delinquents. *Adapted Physical Activity Quarterly, 2*(1), 65-75.

Murphy, J. F. (1975). *Recreation and leisure service: A humanistic perspective.* Dubuque, IA: W.C. Brown.

Neulinger, J. (1974). *The psychology of leisure.* Springfield, IL: Charles C. Thomas.

Neulinger, J. (1981a). *The psychology of leisure* (2nd Ed.). Springfield, IL: Charles C. Thomas.

Neulinger, J. (1981b). *To leisure: An introduction.* Boston, MA: Allyn and Bacon.

Nietupski, J., & Svoboda, R. (1982). Teaching a cooperative leisure skill to severely handicapped adults. *Education and Training of the Mentally Retarded, 17,* 38-43.

O'Dell, I., & Taylor, G. A. (1996). The role of leisure education in parks and recreation. *Parks & Recreation, 31*(5), 14-20.

Osgood, N. J., Meyers, B. S., & Orchowsky, S. (1990). The impact of creative dance and movement training on the life satisfaction of older adults. *Journal of Applied Gerontology, 9,* 255-265.

Owen, P., & Gannon, T. A. (1994). *Choice-making: recreation and leisure.* Cincinnati, OH: University Affiliated Center for Developmental Disorders.

Park, H. S., & Gaylord-Ross, R. (1989). A problem-solving approach to social skills training in employment settings with mentally retarded youth. *Journal of Applied Behavior Analysis, 22,* 373-380.

Patrick, G. W. (1982). Clinical treatment of boredom. *Therapeutic Recreation Journal, 16,* 7-12.

Pawelko, K. A., & Magafas, A. H. (1997). Leisure well-being among adolescent groups: Time, choices and self-determination. *Parks and Recreation, 32*(7), 26-39.

Peregoy, J. J., Schliebner, C. T., & Dieser, R. B. (1997). Diversity issues in therapeutic recreation. In D. M. Compton (Ed.), *Issues in therapeutic recreation: Toward the new millennium* (2nd ed., pp. 275-298). Champaign, IL: Sagamore.

Peterson, C. A. (1989). The dilemma of philosophy. In D. M. Compton (Ed.), *Issues in therapeutic recreation: A profession in transition* (pp. 21-34). Champaign, IL: Sagamore.

Peterson, C. A., & Gunn, S. L. (1984). *Therapeutic recreation program and design: Principles and procedures* (2nd ed.). Englewood Cliffs, NJ: Prentice-Hall.

Peterson, C. A., Maier, S. F., & Seligman, E. P. (1993). *Learned helplessness: A theory for the age of personal control.* New York, NY: Oxford University Press.

Petty, R. E. (1995). Attitude change. In A. Tesser (Ed.), *Advanced social psychology* (pp. 195-255). New York, NY: McGraw-Hill.

Pieper, J. (1963). *Leisure the basis of culture.* New York, NY: Random House.

Popkin, R. H., & Stroll, A. (1993). *Philosophy made simple.* New York, NY: Doubleday.

Prager, D. (1998). *Happiness is a serious problem: A human nature repair manual.* New York, NY: HarperCollins.

Putnam, J. W., Werder, J. K., & Schleien, S. J. (1985). Leisure and recreation services for handicapped persons. In K. C. Lakin & R. H. Bruininks (Eds.), *Strategies for achieving community integration of developmentally disabled citizens* (pp. 253-274). Baltimore, MD: Paul H. Brookes.

Rancourt, A. (1991). Older adults with developmental disabilities/mental retardation: A research agenda for an emerging sub-population. *Annual in Therapeutic Recreation, 1,* 48-55.

Realon, R. E., Favell, J. E., & Lowerre, A. (1990). The effects of making choices on engagement levels with persons who are profoundly multiply handicapped. *Education and Training in Mental Retardation, 25*(3), 299-305.

Rehabilitation Research and Training Center in Mental Illness. (1987). *Social and independent living skills: Recreation and leisure module.* Los Angeles, CA: Robert Paul Liberman, M. D.

Reid, D. H. (1975). *An analysis of variables affecting leisure activity behavior of multi-handicapped retarded persons.* Unpublished doctoral dissertation. Florida State University, Tallahassee, FL.

Riches, V. (1996). *Everyday social interaction.* Baltimore, MD: Paul H. Brookes.

Richler, D. (1984). Access to community resources: The invisible barriers to integration. *Journal of Leisurability, 11*(2), 4-11.

Riddick, C. (1985). Life satisfaction determinants of older males and females. *Leisure Sciences, 7,* 47-63.

Risisky, D., Caldwell, L. L., & Fors, S.W. (1997). The prevention of HIV among adolescents: A leisure education intervention. *Journal of Health Education, 28*(6), 350-356.

Robertson, I. (1977). *Sociology.* New York, NY: Worth.

Romer, L. T., White, J., & Haring, N. G. (1996). The effect of peer mediated social competency training on the type and frequency of social contacts with students with deaf-blindness. *Education and Training in Mental Retardation and Developmental Disabilities, 31,* 324-338.

Root, M. P. P. (1990). Resolving "other" status: Identity development of biracial individuals. In L. S. Brovin & M. P. P. Root (Eds.), *Diversity and complexity in feminist therapy* (pp. 185-205). Binghampton, NY: Haworth Press.

Ruskin, H., & Sivan, A. (1995). *Leisure education: Towards the 21st Century.* Provo, UT: Department of Research Management and Young Leadership, Brigham Young University.

Russell, R. V. (1996). *Pastimes: The context of contemporary leisure.* Dubuque, IA: Brown & Benchmark.

Rybezynski, W. (1991). *Waiting for the weekend.* London, UK: Penguin Books.

Sable, J., & Gravink, J. (1995). Partners: Promoting accessible recreation. *Parks & Recreation, 30*(5), 34-40.

Sachs, M. L. (1984). Psychological well-being and vigorous physical activity. In J. M. Silva & R. S. Weinberg (Eds.), *Psychological Foundations of Sport* (pp. 435-444). New York, NY: Human Kinetics.

Salisbury, C. L., Evans, I. M., & Palombaro, M. M. (1997). Collaborative problem-solving to promote the inclusion of young children with significant disabilities in primary grades. *Exceptional Children, 63*(2), 195-209.

Salisbury, C. L., Gallucci, C., Palombaro, M. M., & Peck, C. A. (1995). Strategies that promote social relations among elementary students with and without severe disabilities in inclusive schools. *Exceptional Children, 62*(2), 125-135.

Salisbury, C. L., Palombaro, M. M., & Evans, I. M. (1993). *Collaborative problem solving: Instructor's manual.* Pittsburgh, PA: Allegheny Singer Research Institute, Child and Family Studies Program.

Samdahl, D. M. (1986). *The self and social freedom: A paradigm of leisure.* Unpublished doctoral dissertation. University of Illinois, Champaign, IL.

Sands, D. J., & Doll, B. (1996). Fostering self-determination is a developmental task. *Journal of Special Education, 30*(1), 58-76.

Saville-Troike, M. (1989). *The ethnography of communication: An introduction* (2nd ed.). Boston, MA: Basil Blackwell.

Scheltens, K. S. (1990). Personality characteristics of adolescents who misuse alcohol. *Research Into Action, 15,* 40-45.

Schleien, S. J., & Larson, A. (1986). Adult leisure education for the independent use of a community recreation center. *JASH, 11*(1), 39-44.

Schleien, S. J., Meyer, L., Heyne, L., & Brandt, B. (1995). *Lifelong leisure skills and lifestyles for persons with developmental disabilities.* Baltimore, MD: Paul H. Brookes.

Schleien, S. J., & Ray, M. T. (1988). *Community recreation and persons with disabilities: Strategies for integration.* Baltimore, MD: Paul H. Brookes.

Schleien, S. J., Ray, M., & Green, F. (1997). *Community recreation and people with disabilities. Strategies for inclusion* (2nd ed.). Baltimore, MD: Paul H. Brookes.

Schleien, S. J., Tuckner, B., & Heyne, L. (1985). Leisure education programs for the severely disabled student. *Parks and Recreation, 20,* 74-78.

Schor, J. B. (1992). *The overworked American: The unexpected decline of leisure.* New York, NY: HarperCollins.

Searle, M., & Mahon, M. (1991). Leisure education in a day hospital: The effects on selected social-psychological variables among older adults. *Canadian Journal of Community Mental Health, 10*(2), 95-109.

Searle, M., & Mahon, M. (1993). The effects of a leisure education program on selected social-psychological variables: A three month follow-up investigation. *Therapeutic Recreation Journal, 27*(1), 9-21.

Searle, M., Mahon, M., Iso-Ahola, S., Sdrolias, H., & Van Dyck, J. (1995). Enhancing a sense of independence and psychological well-being among the elderly: A field experiment. *Journal of Leisure Research, 27*(2), 107-124.

Seligman, M. E. P. (1975). *Helplessness: On development, depression, and death.* New York, NY: W. H. Freeman and Company.

Seligman, M. E. P. (1990). *Learned optimism.* New York, NY: Pocket Books.

Shaw, S. (1992). Family leisure and leisure services. *Parks & Recreation, 27*(12), 13-16, 66.

Shaw, S. (1994). Gender, leisure and constraint: Towards a framework for the analysis of women's leisure. *Journal of Leisure Research, 26*(1), 8-22.

Sheffield, E. A., Waigandt, A. C., & Miller, D. A. (1986). Post assault leisure counseling for sexual assault victims. *Journal of Expanding Horizons in Therapeutic Recreation, 1,* 56-63.

Sheldon, K., & Dattilo, J. (1997). Multi-culturalism in therapeutic recreation: Terminology clarification and practical suggestions. *Therapeutic Recreation Journal, 31*(3), 148-158.

Shephard, R. J. (1994). Determinants of exercise in people aged 65 years and older. In R. K. Dishman (Ed.), *Advances in exercise adherence* (pp. 343-360). Champaign, IL: Human Kinetics.

Shiver, J. S. (1981). *Leisure and recreation concepts: A critical analysis.* Boston, MA: Allyn and Bacon.

Shoultz, B., & McBride, M. (1996). Serving the whole person: The journey to embracing diversity. *Impact, 9*(3), 1-27.

Sivan, A. (1997). Research development in leisure education research and implementation. *World Leisure and Recreation, 39*(2), 41-44.

Sivan, A., & Ruskin, H. (1997a). Editor's Note. *World Leisure and Recreation, 39*(2), 3.

Sivan, A., & Ruskin, H. (1997b). Successful models for leisure education in Israel. *World Leisure and Recreation, 39*(2), 39-40.

Skalko, T. K. (1990). Discretionary time use and the chronically mentally ill. *Annual in Therapeutic Recreation, 1,* 9-14.

Smith, N., Kielhofer, G., & Watts, J. (1986). The relationship between volition, activity pattern, and life satisfaction in the elderly. *Journal of Occupational Therapy, 40,* 278-283.

Smith, E. R., & Mackie, D. M. (1995). *Social psychology.* New York, NY: Worth.

Snell, M. (1992). *Systematic instruction of persons with severe handicaps* (4th ed.). New York, NY: Macmillan.

Sobel, D. S. (1995). Rethinking medicine: Improving health outcomes with cost effective psychosocial interventions. *Psychosomatic Medicine, 57,* 234-244.

Sontag, J. C. (1996). Toward a comprehensive theoretical framework for disability research: Bronfenbrenner revisited. *The Journal of Special Education, 30*(3), 319-344.

Soukhanov, A. H., et al. (Eds.). (1992). *The American heritage dictionary of the English language* (3rd ed.). Boston, MA: Houghton Mifflin.

Sparrow, W. A., Shinkfield, A. J., & Karnilowicz, W. (1993). Constraints on the participation of individuals with mental retardation in mainstream recreation. *Mental Retardation, 31*(6), 403-411.

Strachan, K. (1995). Leisure education: Independent living resource center (Winnipeg). *Leisurability, 22*(4), 19-21.

Stumbo, N. J. (1992). *Leisure education II: More activities and resources.* State College, PA: Venture Publishing, Inc.

Stumbo, N. J. (1995). Social skills instruction through commercially available resources. *Therapeutic Recreation Journal, 29,* 30-55.

Stumbo, N. J., & Thompson, S. R. (1986). *Leisure education: A manual of activities and resources.* State College, PA: Venture Publishing, Inc.

Sylvester, C. D. (1985). Freedom, leisure, and therapeutic recreation. A philosophical view. *Therapeutic Recreation Journal, 19*(1), 6-13.

Tauber, R. (1994). *Acting lessons for teachers: Using performance skills in the classroom.* Westport, CT: Praeger.

Teeters, C. (1991). Permission to learn: Leisure and the American school. *Journal of Physical Education, Recreation, & Dance, 10,* 28-31.

Terman, D. L., Larner, M. B., Stevenson, C. S., & Behrman, R. E. (1996). Special education for students with disabilities: Analysis and recommendations. *The Future of Children, 6*(1), 4-24.

Tinsley, H. E. A., & Tinsley, D. J. (1984). Leisure counseling models. In E. T. Dowd (Ed.), *Leisure counseling concepts and applications* (pp. 80-96). Springfield, IL: Charles C. Thomas.

Tripp, A., & Sherrill, C. (1991). Attitude theories of relevance to adapted physical education. *Adapted Physical Activity Quarterly, 8,* 12-27.

Trower, P. (1984). A radical critique and reformulation: From organism to agent. In P. Trower (Ed.), *Radical approaches to social skills training* (pp. 47-88). New York, NY: Croom Helm Ltd.

Turiel, E. (1987). Potential relations between the development of social reasoning and childhood aggression. In D. Corwell, I. M. Evans, & C. R. O'Donnell (Eds.), *Childhood aggression and violence: Sources of influence, prevention, and control* (pp. 124-135). New York, NY: Plenum Press.

Valdés, L. F., Barón, A., Jr., & Ponce, F. Q. (1987). Counseling Hispanic men. In M. Scher, M. Stevens, G. Good, & G. Eichenfield (Eds.), *Handbook of counseling and psychotherapy with men* (pp. 203-217). Newbury Park, CA: Sage.

Voeltz, L. M., Wuerch, B. B., & Wilcox, B. (1982). Leisure and recreation: Preparation for independence, integration and self-fulfillment. In B. Wilcox & G. T. Bellamy (Eds.), *Design of high-school programs for severely handicapped students* (pp. 175-209). Baltimore, MD: Paul H. Brookes.

Wade, M. G., & Hoover, J. H. (1985). Mental retardation as a constraint on leisure. In M. G. Wade (Ed.), *Constraints on leisure* (pp. 83-110). Springfield, IL: Charles C. Thomas.

Wake leisure education program: An integral part of special education. (1991). Chapel Hill, NC: The Center for Recreation and Disability Studies.

Wall, M. E., & Dattilo, J. (1995). Creating option-rich learning environments: Facilitating self-determination. *Journal of Special Education, 29*(3), 276-294.

Wall, M. E., & Gast, D. (1997). Caregivers as teachers: Using constant time delay to teach adults how to use constant time delay. *Educational Training in Mental Retardation and Developmental Disabilities, 32*(3), 213-228.

Wankel, L. M. (1993). The importance of enjoyment to adherence aid psychological benefits from physical activity. *International Journal of Sport Psychology, 25,* 151-169.

Wassman, K. B., & Iso-Ahola, S. E. (1985). The relationship between recreation participation and depression in psychiatric patients. *Therapeutic Recreation Journal, 19,* 63-70.

Wehman, P., & Moon, M. S. (1985). Designing and implementing leisure programs for individuals with severe handicaps. In M. P. Brady & P. L. Gunter (Eds.), *Integrating moderately and severely handicapped learners: Strategies that work* (pp. 214-237). Springfield, IL: Charles C. Thomas.

Wehmeyer, M. L. (1996). Self-determination as an educational outcome: Why is it important to children, youth and adults with disabilities? In D. J. Sands & M. L. Wehmeyer (Eds.), *Self-determination across the life span: Independence and choice for people with disabilities* (pp. 15-34). Baltimore, MD: Paul H. Brookes.

Wehmeyer, M. L., & Schwartz, M. (1997). Self-determination and positive adult outcomes: A follow-up study of youth with mental retardation or learning disabilities. *Exceptional Children, 63*(2), 245-255.

Weis, C., & Jamison, N. (1988). Hidden disabilities: A new enterprise for therapeutic recreation. *Therapeutic Recreation Journal, 22,* 9-17.

Weissinger, E., & Caldwell, L. (1990). Antecedents of leisure boredom in three college samples. In *Abstracts from the 1990 Symposium on Leisure Research* (p. 41). Arlington, VA: National Association for Recreation and Parks.

Weissinger, E., Caldwell, L., & Bandalos, D. (1992). Relation between intrinsic motivation and boredom in leisure time. *Leisure Sciences, 14,* 317-325.

Welton, G. (1979). Leisure in the formative years. In H. Ibrahim & J. Shivers (Eds.), *Leisure emergence and expansion* (pp. 111-155). Los Alamitos, CA: Hwong.

Wenz-Gross, M., & Siperstein, G. N. (1996). The social world of preadolescents with mental retardation: Social support, family environment and adjustment. *Education and Training in Mental Retardation and Developmental Disabilities, 31*(3), 177-187.

Westling, D. L. (1996). What do parents of children with moderate and severe mental disabilities want? *Education and Training in Mental Retardation and Developmental Disabilities, 31*(2), 86-114.

White, J. E. (1997). I'm just who I am. *Time,* 32-36.

Williams, R., & Dattilo, J. (1997). Effects of a leisure education on self-determination, social interaction, and positive affect of young adults with mental retardation. *Therapeutic Recreation Journal, 31,* 244-258.

Williams, W., Brown, L., & Certo, N. (1975). Components of instructional programs for severely handicapped students. In L. Brown, T. Crowner, W. Williams, & R. York (Eds.), *Madison's alternative for zero exclusion: A book of readings* (Vol. 5, pp. 8-28). Madison, WI: Madison Public Schools.

Witt, P. A., & Ellis, G. D. (1987). *The leisure diagnostic battery: Users manual.* State College, PA: Venture Publishing, Inc.

Witt, P. A., Ellis, G., & Niles, S. H. (1984). Leisure counseling with special populations. In T. E. Dowd (Ed.), *Leisure counseling: Concepts and applications.* Springfield, IL: Charles C. Thomas.

Wittman, J., Kurtz, J., & Nichols, S. (1987). *Reflection, recognition, reaffirmation: A frame of reference for leisure education including activities, techniques, and resources.* Plaistow, NH: Sterling Press.

Wlodkowski, R. J., & Jaynes, J. H. (1991). *Eager to learn: Helping children become motivated and love learning.* San Francisco, CA: Josey-Bass.

Wolery, M., Ault, M., & Doyle, P. (1992). *Teaching students with moderate to severe disabilities.* White Plains, NY: Longman.

Wolery, M., Bailey, D., & Sugai, G. (1988). *Effective teaching: principles and procedures of applied behavior analysis with exceptional students.* Boston, MA: Allyn & Bacon.

Wolfe, R. A., & Riddick, C. L. (1984). Effects of leisure counseling on adult psychiatric outpatients. *Therapeutic Recreation Journal, 28*(3), 30-37.

WRLA International Charter for Leisure Education. (1993). In A. Sivan, Recent developments in leisure education research and implementation. *World Leisure and Recreation, 39*(2), 43.

Wuerch, B. B., & Voeltz, L. M. (1982). *Longitudinal leisure skills for severely handicapped learners: The Ho'onanea curriculum component.* Baltimore, MD: Paul H. Brooks.

Zhang, J., Gast, D., Horvat, M., & Dattilo, J. (1995). The effectiveness of a constant time delay procedure on teaching lifetime sport skills to adolescents with severe to profound intellectual disabilities. *Education and Training in Mental Retardation and Developmental Disabilities, 30,* 51-64.

Zoerink, D. A. (1988). Effects of a short-term leisure education program upon the leisure functioning of young people with spina bifida. *Therapeutic Recreation Journal, 22*(3), 44-52.

Zoerink, D. A., & Lauener, K. (1991). Effects of a leisure education program on adults with traumatic brain injury. *Therapeutic Recreation Journal, 25*(3), 19-28.

Subject Index

F

facilities 89
failure 80, 87, 88, 90, 94
family 103, 104
fears 93
feasibility 128
feedback 37, 38
fitness 45
flexible 78
flow 36, 37, 38, 41, 46
formation 109
free time 2, 3
freedom 3, 4, 5, 13
friends 51, 52, 55, 57, 58
friendship(s) 40, 44, 55, 56, 57, 58, 61, 85, 87

G

goals 1, 3, 9, 12
Golden Age 7
Gospel of Consumption 8
graduated guidance 116, 119, 120
grouping 111

H

happiness 20
helpless 27, 28, 29, 31

I

idleness 3, 7
illness 10, 11
implement 106, 112, 117
incarcerated 63, 70, 74
independence 127
individual differences 148, 154, 155
individuality 44
Industrial Revolution 8
initiative 66
instructional strategies 131, 136, 139, 140
integration 49, 51, 52, 59
interact socially 76, 84
interpersonal constraints 25, 26
intimacy 45
intrapersonal constraints 25
intrinsic motivation 4, 21, 22, 23, 24, 28, 30, 31
introduction 95, 99, 100, 104, 105, 106, 110, 111

Author Index

Other Books From Venture Publishing

File o' Fun: A Recreation Planner for Games & Activities—Third Edition
    by Jane Harris Ericson and Diane Ruth Albright
The Game Finder—A Leader's Guide to Great Activities
    by Annette C. Moore
Getting People Involved in Life and Activities: Effective Motivating Techniques
    by Jeanne Adams
Great Special Events and Activities
    by Annie Morton, Angie Prosser and Sue Spangler
Inclusive Leisure Services: Responding to the Rights of People With Disabilities
    by John Dattilo
Internships in Recreation and Leisure Services: A Practical Guide for Students
    (Second Edition)
    by Edward E. Seagle, Jr., Ralph W. Smith and Lola M. Dalton
Interpretation of Cultural and Natural Resources
    by Douglas M. Knudson, Ted T. Cable and Larry Beck
Introduction to Leisure Services—7th Edition
    by H. Douglas Sessoms and Karla A. Henderson
Leadership and Administration of Outdoor Pursuits, Second Edition
    by Phyllis Ford and James Blanchard
Leadership in Leisure Services: Making a Difference
    by Debra J. Jordan
Leisure and Leisure Services in the 21st Century
    by Geoffrey Godbey
The Leisure Diagnostic Battery: Users Manual and Sample Forms
    by Peter A. Witt and Gary Ellis
Leisure Education: A Manual of Activities and Resources
    by Norma J. Stumbo and Steven R. Thompson
Leisure Education II: More Activities and Resources
    by Norma J. Stumbo
Leisure Education III: More Goal-Oriented Activities
    by Norma J. Stumbo
Leisure Education IV: Activities for Individuals With Substance Addictions
    by Norma J. Stumbo
Leisure in Your Life: An Exploration—Fourth Edition
    by Geoffrey Godbey
Leisure Services in Canada: An Introduction
    by Mark S. Searle and Russell E. Brayley
Leisure Studies: Prospects for the Twenty-First Century
    edited by Edgar L. Jackson and Thomas L. Burton
The Lifestory Re-Play Circle: A Manual of Activities and Techniques
    by Rosilyn Wilder
Marketing for Parks, Recreation, and Leisure
    by Ellen L. O'Sullivan
Models of Change in Municipal Parks and Recreation: A Book of Innovative Case
    Studies
    edited by Mark E. Havitz

More Than a Game: A New Focus on Senior Activity Services
    by Brenda Corbett
Nature and the Human Spirit: Toward an Expanded Land Management Ethic
    edited by B. L. Driver, Daniel Dustin, Tony Baltic, Gary Elsner, and George
    Peterson
Outdoor Recreation Management: Theory and Application, Third Edition
    by Alan Jubenville and Ben Twight
Planning Parks for People, Second Edition
    by John Hultsman, Richard L. Cottrell and Wendy Z. Hultsman
The Process of Recreation Programming Theory and Technique, Third Edition
    by Patricia Farrell and Herberta M. Lundegren
Programming for Parks, Recreation, and Leisure Services: A Servant Leadership
    Approach
    By Donald G. DeGraaf, Debra J. Jordan and Kathy H. DeGraaf
Protocols for Recreation Therapy Programs
    edited by Jill Kelland, along with the Recreation Therapy Staff at Alberta
    Hospital Edmonton
Quality Management: Applications for Therapeutic Recreation
    edited by Bob Riley
A Recovery Workbook: The Road Back From Substance Abuse
    by April K. Neal and Michael J. Taleff
Recreation and Leisure: Issues in an Era of Change, Third Edition
    edited by Thomas Goodale and Peter A. Witt
Recreation Economic Decisions: Comparing Benefits and Costs (Second Edition)
    by John B. Loomis and Richard G. Walsh
Recreation Programming and Activities for Older Adults
    by Jerold E. Elliott and Judith A. Sorg-Elliott
Recreation Programs That Work for At-Risk Youth: The Challenge of Shaping the
    Future
    by Peter A. Witt and John L. Crompton
Reference Manual for Writing Rehabilitation Therapy Treatment Plans
    by Penny Hogberg and Mary Johnson
Research in Therapeutic Recreation: Concepts and Methods
    edited by Marjorie J. Malkin and Christine Z. Howe
Simple Expressions: Creative and Therapeutic Arts for the Elderly in Long-Term
    Care Facilities
    by Vicki Parsons
A Social History of Leisure Since 1600
    by Gary Cross
A Social Psychology of Leisure
    by Roger C. Mannell and Douglas A. Kleiber
The Sociology of Leisure
    by John R. Kelly and Geoffrey Godbey
Steps to Successful Programming: A Student Handbook to Accompany Program-
    ming for Parks, Recreation, and Leisure Services
    by Donald G. DeGraaf, Debra J. Jordan and Kathy H. DeGraaf

Therapeutic Activity Intervention With the Elderly: Foundations & Practices
    by Barbara A. Hawkins, Marti E. May and Nancy Brattain Rogers
Therapeutic Recreation: Cases and Exercises
    by Barbara C. Wilhite and M. Jean Keller
Therapeutic Recreation in the Nursing Home
    by Linda Buettner and Shelley L. Martin
Therapeutic Recreation Protocol for Treatment of Substance Addictions
    by Rozanne W. Faulkner
Time for Life: The Surprising Ways Americans Use Their Time
    by John P. Robinson and Geoffrey Godbey
A Training Manual for Americans With Disabilities Act Compliance in Parks and
    Recreation Settings
    by Carol Stensrud

Venture Publishing, Inc.
1999 Cato Avenue
State College, PA 16801

Phone: (814) 234-4561; Fax: (814) 234-1651